For Miguel,
With thanks,
admiration,
and a fig hug.

Emmanuel

To V.

The Collegial Phenomenon

The Social Mechanisms of Cooperation among Peers in a Corporate Law Partnership

EMMANUEL LAZEGA

OXFORD

UNIVERSITY PRESS

OXFORD
UNIVERSITY PRESS

Great Clarendon Street, Oxford OX2 6DP

Oxford University Press is a department of the University of Oxford.
It furthers the University's objective of excellence in research, scholarship,
and education by publishing worldwide in

Oxford New York

Athens Auckland Bangkok Bogotá Buenos Aires Cape Town
Chennai Dar es Salaam Delhi Florence Hong Kong Istanbul Karachi
Kolkata Kuala Lumpur Madrid Melbourne Mexico City Mumbai Nairobi
Paris São Paulo Shanghai Singapore Taipei Tokyo Toronto Warsaw
with associated companies in Berlin Ibadan

Oxford is a registered trade mark of Oxford University Press
in the UK and in certain other countries

Published in the United States
by Oxford University Press Inc., New York

© E. Lazega 2001

The moral rights of the author have been asserted
Database right Oxford University Press (maker)

First published 2001

British Library Cataloguing in Publication Data
Data available

Library of Congress Cataloging in Publication Data
Data available

ISBN 0-19-924272-0

1 3 5 7 9 10 8 6 4 2

Typeset by Newgen Imaging Systems (P) Ltd., Chennai, India
Printed in Great Britain
on acid-free paper by
T. J. International Ltd., Padstow, Cornwall

Acknowledgements

I am grateful to the current and former members of Spencer, Grace & Robbins (a pseudonym), a north-eastern US corporate law partnership, for taking the time to answer my questions, and particularly to the managing partner at the time of the study for his advice and trust. SG&R requested anonymity; any name used in the book is an alias.

This study was funded mainly by the Swiss National Foundation for Scientific Research. I am grateful to Jean Kellerhals and Christian Lalive d'Epinay, at the Department of Sociology, University of Geneva, for their early and continued support for this project. Fieldwork was also conducted with support from the Department of Sociology, Yale University, and from Yale Law School. I am particularly grateful to Geoffrey Hazard, as well as to Miguel Centeno, Deborah Davis, Kenneth Mann, Albert Reiss, and Stanton Wheeler for help and advice at this stage.

Papers from which this book has been put together were also written and published with support from Lasmas-Cnrs in Paris and Clersé-Cnrs, at the University of Lille I, for which I am particularly grateful to Alain Degenne, Roxane Silberman, Michèle Amiot, and Alexis Ferrand.

Network analyses were sometimes carried out with help from several specialists using complex and experimental statistical techniques. I am indebted to co-authors on various papers, including Marijtje Van Duijn, David Krackhardt, Marie-Odile Lebeaux, Philippa Pattison, and Stéphane Vari.

Invitations to the Interdisciplinary Centre for the Social Sciences in the Netherlands, and to the Lazarsfeld Center, Columbia University, provided opportunities to discuss many issues presented in this book with highly stimulating colleagues. I am particularly grateful for these opportunities to Henk Flap, Sigi Lindenberg, Tom Snijders, and Harrison White.

Helpful suggestions were provided by many colleagues on papers published during the last ten years. I would like to thank those who took the trouble to comment on the July 1999 draft of this book: Benoit Bastard, Susan Bianconi, Miguel Centeno, Alain Chenu, Deborah Davis, Robert Dingwall, Bill Felstiner, Henk Flap, David Lazega, Lise Mounier, Charles Perrow, Tom Snijders, Harrison White, and the Oxford University Press reviewers and editors.

Contents

List of Figures

List of Tables

Introduction

Collective action among peers—that is, cooperation among individuals who are, or tend to be, formally equal in power—is an important problem in social and economic life. For example, an increasingly large number of organizations find themselves involved in knowledge-intensive production. This means that they must permanently try to adjust to technological changes, to encourage higher quality, innovation, and participation. These changes and adaptations are often associated with an apparent decline of Taylorian rationalization of work. In this old model, competence, and regulatory and decision-making authority are concentrated at the top; objectivation and routinization of tasks are for the bottom. As a consequence of this decline, organizations involved in knowledge-intensive work try to reduce the number of hierarchical levels in their formal structures. They try to involve many more members and stakeholders in regulatory activity. In turn, organization theorists—after a century of critique of Weberian bureaucracy as a basic principle—focus on such contemporary flattening and decentralizing organizations.

In spite of this attention, collective action among peers remains a puzzle for the social sciences. Contemporary sociology does have a tradition of thought about egalitarian relationships in organizations and society. This tradition debates the possibility of organization without hierarchy. In particular, since Robert Michels's *Political Parties* (1911), many sociologists have pointed to the fact that flat organizations are also highly structured, a theme underlying discussions of the 'iron law of oligarchy' (for a review, see Rothschild and Whitt 1986). However, there is little empirically grounded work researching how organizations without permanent bosses and followers, in which all members ultimately have a formally equal say in running operations or exercising control, are able to operate.

In the history of sociology, two reasons at least may explain a relative lack of progress in the study of specific social mechanisms that underlie cooperation among peers. First, the debate between Max Weber and Michels was framed by Weber so as to focus on the 'illusion' of pure democracy and on a general bureaucratization process (Scaff 1981). Since then, the idea of a relatively general collegial model—to use Weber's own vocabulary—with its own characteristics and influence within the bureaucratic model, or as an alternative to this model, has attracted little attention—although there are clear indications in classics such as *Union Democracy* by Lipset, Trow, and Coleman (1956) that it resurfaces periodically.

Secondly, Weber himself mainly discusses collegiality as a means for hierarchy to control experts or as a way to restrain autocratic control. This has led to a reduction of the issue of cooperation among peers to one of a conflict between two forms of status—that is, between professional expertise and hierarchical coordination.[1] In this perspective, professional settings have been of particular interest to the study of this form of collective action. These include corporate law firms, engineering and technology firms, architecture firms, advertising agencies, medical wards, consulting firms, investment banks, scientific laboratories, religious congregations, and many other organizations bringing together recognized experts.[2]

More generally, however, complexity, concern for quality and innovation, and high variability of tasks usually lead to the right to participate in decision making and share economic returns (Woodward 1965; but see also Burns and Stalker 1966; Parsons 1968; Stinchcombe 1959), even in non-professional settings. Work on 'plural' forms of organizations (see e.g. Bradach and Eccles 1989) shows that the issue of cooperation among peers is also relevant in countless collegial pockets that can be found in larger bureaucratic organizations. In matrix (Davis and Lawrence 1977) or project-based structures, for example, individual members have to function with frequently changing task assignments and group attachments, to report to more than one superior, and to rely on expertise of colleagues from other work units. Whenever members deal together with complex decisions that cannot be routinized, this issue reappears.

THE COLLEGIAL ORGANIZATION AND
ITS GENERIC SOCIAL MECHANISMS

In order to understand cooperation among peers as an issue of interest to organizations in general, saying that activities are governed by objectives and results—no longer by Taylorian standard procedures and pyramids—is not enough. A first step consists in defining the characteristics of an idealtypical collegial organization, as distinguished from bureaucracy. A second, theory-guided step consists in identifying and analysing generic social mechanisms that characterize this organizational form and help it govern itself.

At the intersection of the sociological literatures on organizations and on the professions, increased interest for a general principle of 'collegiality' has recently produced original neo-Weberian theories that have proposed a set of formal characteristics differentiating 'collegial' or 'polycratic' organizations from bureaucratic or monocratic ones. Waters's work (1989, 1993) on the collegial or 'polycratic' model, for example, offers a fresh look at this old issue, and the present book builds on his contribution. He defines collegial organizations as 'those in which there is dominant orientation to a consensus achieved between the members of a body of experts who are theoretically equals in their levels of expertise but who are specialized by area of expertise' (1989: 956).

Here I argue that this neo-Weberian description of a collegial form is useful but not sufficient by itself to explain collective action among peers, because it is based almost exclusively on the idea of voluntary contracts, formal structure, and formal consensus.[3] This approach is limited because there are many tensions in the collegium, and there are obvious conflicts between the individual and the collective interest, for which it does not account. What is missing in this approach is a deeper understanding of the social processes that help collegial organizations solve typical problems of collective action and cooperation. In my view, a combined neo-Weberian and structural approach is needed for that purpose. This approach provides a deeper view of how such collegial organizations operate, a more realistic picture of the 'collegial phenomenon'—an expression echoing Michel Crozier's *Bureaucratic Phenomenon* (1963). It often questions pervasive discourse on idealized collegiality among peers. As in model approaches such as Crozier's or Peter Blau's (1964), our approach to this phenomenon is based primarily on understanding power in such collective actors. Power is defined as the ability of individuals or groups in the organization to impose their will on others as a result of resource dependencies. In the case of collective action among peers, however, such dependencies are often less permanent and more complex than in bureaucracies. Power is shared, then aggregated upwards to be exercised simultaneously by several positions in a 'polycratic' system. There are also norms concerning this exercise, especially for legitimization of inequality and justification of acceptance of inequality.

In effect, what does a 'structural' approach mean? The term structural refers to regularities observed in multiple and informal relationships between members— for example, strongly personalized co-workers' ties, or advice ties, or even friendship ties. Such ties provide access to key production-related resources such as co-workers' goodwill or advice, or to resources that are not directly connected with the production process, such as friendship. In an organization, stable and durable relationships represent multilateral resource interdependencies. They aggregate and combine into an informal pattern of ties that is called 'structure' because it captures many kinds of opportunities and constraints for members in their attempts to manage such resources. It is important to note that, in the Weberian tradition, these social and informal relationships have long been considered by the bureaucratic model as particularistic obstacles to efficient collective action (Perrow 1986). In the collegial model, however, some of these durable relationships become the basis of a social discipline that helps members cooperate and exchange, monitor, pressure, and sanction each other, and negotiate precarious values. Without such an approach of resource interdependencies and social relationships, it is difficult to understand generic social mechanisms (Hedström and Swedberg 1998*a*) that characterize any form of collective action, particularly among rival partners (Bourricaud 1961).

For any sociological theory of collective action, such generic social mechanisms necessarily include, first, an exchange system of multiple social resources; secondly, a control regime; and, thirdly, a process of (re)negotiation of rules and underlying precarious values. They are part of what Crozier and Friedberg (1977) would call the 'concrete action system' of any type of organization.[4] As shown by Granovetter (1985), specifying such mechanisms goes beyond statements of 'embeddedness' seeking to prove the economic efficiency of social ties. The specific mechanisms that help flat or collegial organizations operate are not necessarily comparable to that of more bureaucratic and pyramidal organizations, because they are based on the specificity of resource interdependencies that characterize complex relationships between formally equal partners. Sketching this system for collegial organizations (or for collegial pockets in bureaucratic organizations) will, therefore, require specific methods that are able to look into complex resource interdependencies. Methods such as network analysis both strengthen sociologists in their theories and allow them to look at economic activity from this original perspective.

Thanks to such generic social mechanisms, flat organizations can achieve results that many economic theories did not think they could: for example, help members participate in collective action when they are expected to free-ride; coordinate the activities of interdependent entrepreneurs when they are expected to ignore each other as competitors; monitor and sanction deviant peers back to good conduct; stabilize policy making or change the rules of the game when promises from the past are difficult or impossible to keep. Specifically, analyses will show that they are highly functional in addressing—among others—such problems as enhancing economic performance and quality control (Chapter 4); cultivating and mitigating status competition (Chapter 5); and integrating the firm by preventing easy defection by teams (Chapter 6). It is by focusing on such mechanisms of social organization (sometimes called self-organization) and by approaching the issue of collective action among peers from a structural perspective that this book adds value in research on collective action among peers.

A BROADLY CONCEIVED STRUCTURAL APPROACH

What does the expression 'combined neo-Weberian and structural approach to cooperation among peers' mean? How exactly does it help in reasoning about collegial organizations? This approach is broadly conceived as having the five following characteristics.

The first is that it combines an understanding of the interests of actors themselves with that of their organization as a whole, thus bridging the levels of individual and collective action. It does so both by looking at the organization as a small political community and by using information on relationships between members as information on their resource interdependencies and derived power relationships. In effect, in organized settings, participation in collective action—for example, team production, regulatory activity, or enforcement of previous agreements—requires cooperation with others. This cooperation is expressed through routine interactions that allow transfers or exchanges of various kinds of resources. Examples for such resources include information, co-workers' goodwill, advice, sometimes moral or emotional support, and many other means that serve individual and collective ends. Particularly in collegial organizations, all members have some resources that are important to others; therefore, they all have, although to various degrees, some power. These interdependencies are the product of a formal division of work and of informal exchanges and circulation of all sorts of production-related resources through social ties. Together with formal dimensions of structure, they aggregate to form an opportunity structure that constrains members' choices in access to resources. In that respect, structural analysis is compatible with what Crozier (1963; Crozier and Friedberg 1977) calls 'strategic' analysis. Indeed, the former presupposes the latter and offers sophisticated measurements of resource interdependencies, status, and power. This means that, along with the analysis of structural determinants of action, one must draw on a perspective that allows for some individual freedom of choice and provide behavioural assumptions that include some kind of strategic rationality.

The second characteristic of this broadly conceived structural approach, one that separates it from earlier and narrower forms of structuralism, is its capacity to look jointly at economic and symbolic activities. Saying that actors use their resource interdependencies as a source of power presupposes a form of rationality that includes cost–benefit calculations, but also symbolic activity such as appropriateness judgements (based on previous investments in relationships, recognition of identities, identifications in reference groups, and the use of various forms of authority arguments) allowing individuals to politicize their exchanges and controls. For example, volatile, intangible, or immaterial resources, such as knowledge, cannot be accumulated, bartered, and shared outside such identity politics and boundary management (Blau 1964; Lazega 1992a, 1999b).[5] Opportunity structures do not explain behaviour mechanically: actors do not always perceive a course of action as an opportunity. They often make choices of courses of action based on symbolic or normative criteria, to meet others' expectations. They politicize exchanges not only to reduce costs, but to maintain shared principles that they think will help them.

Note that, in this perspective, power is not purely formal and unidimensional. It is not reduced to a phone call from the White House. If actors politicize their exchanges and controls, they must be assumed to have a trained capacity to perceive relationships among others (and underlying resource interdependencies) and to manipulate these relationships. Social relations and the resources that they concentrate do matter for power among peers. This also means that collegial is not a synonym for congenial and nice. Partners can manage their interdependencies in informal but truly Machiavellian ways. Status competition among peers can be all the more ferocious, as it is heavily personalized. Collegial committees can be as brutal as autocrats when they vote like lynch mobs.

Actors' politicization has two combined but potentially conflicting dimensions: niche seeking and status competition, both based on selections of or investments in relationships. A member's social niche can be defined as a relational context, or subset of other members in the organization, with whom this member commits him/herself to exchange many different types of resources at a relatively lower cost, an advantage that can be called bounded solidarity[6] (for the complete definition, see Chapter 1). As seen above, in spite of professional ideologies picturing them as independent entrepreneurs ('their own men/women'), individual professionals are strategic and *inter*-dependent entrepreneurs who need access to production-related resources. Politicization is manifest in the selection of these exchange partners. It is rational because members try to build or join such multifunctional production contexts as if they were stable quasi-groups in which these resources are more easily available to them than outside these quasi-groups.

Politicization of exchanges means that selection of partners is based on particularistic identification to others (intuitions about how one's long-term interests are compatible with that of others within a group identified by specific characteristics and similarities, and therefore by a form of bounded solidarity). Niche building or seeking is strategic, but, once built, niches have the advantage of allowing partial suspension of calculating behaviour. Indeed, they are built for that purpose, and thus allow multiplex barters of resources without general equivalent (Blau 1964). The word 'multiplex' qualifies a rich relationship between two persons. It refers to the fact that the two persons have a relationship in which they can transfer and exchange multiple types of resources (Wasserman and Faust 1994). For example, two partners have a multiplex relationship because they are co-workers on many cases, because they also seek each other for advice in difficult professional situations, and finally because they also have social activities outside work together. Analytically, this means that specific local substructures compounding several types of social ties must crystallize for members to be able to cooperate on an ongoing basis in the context of wider collective actors such as organizations.

This solidarity is bounded by identity politics (We-versus-Them reasoning) playing strategically with multiple memberships and hierarchies of allegiances. In short, members must, therefore, be characterized by a *strategic and symbolic rationality*, by a long-term view enabling them both to value the ideology of autonomous action (Freidson 1975, 1999; Sciulli 1986; Waters 1989) and to create various forms of bounded solidarity with potential competitors (thus conditionally suspending their strategic behaviour). This politicization, however, can also lead to any forms of social discrimination that come attached to barter.

As strategic and interdependent entrepreneurs, these individuals also compete for *status*—that is, they try to concentrate resources in their own individual hands so as to benefit from a position of strength when negotiating terms of exchange (that is, bartering) within and outside their quasi-groups (Blau 1964). In sociological theory, status summarizes members' contributions to the collective, their recognition, and a specific form of authority derived from this recognition. However, formally and informally, there are many forms of status, because there are many ways of contributing to the collective. The official member, the most competent, the most popular, the most committed—all these have some sort of status, and participate in the coordination of collective action. One important aspect of status is that members back it by concentrating resources accumulated within niches and beyond niches, in the wider context of the organization. Without this concentration, status remains purely formal; it does not mean a true power to influence either decisions made in the collegium, or terms of exchange with others.

These assumptions about members' strategic rationality lead to a third characteristic of a broadly conceived structural approach. As mentioned above, it bridges the individual and collective levels of action by thinking in terms of multilevel social mechanisms. Examples of such mechanisms provided in this book include generalized exchange (a form of bounded solidarity based on the existence of cycles of indirect reciprocity among selected colleagues), lateral control (a form of early monitoring and sanctioning of deviant conduct that both spreads and concentrates the costs of control), and regulatory change (a form of 'constitutional' redefinition of the rules of the game that is driven by members with multiple forms of status). Multilevel theories—for example, a combination of rational choice and structural analysis (e.g. Blau 1964; Boudon 1981; Burt 1982; Coleman 1990; Crozier and Friedberg 1977; Hechter 1987; Hedström and Swedberg 1998b; Lindenberg 1995; Wippler and Lindenberg 1987), have been available for a long time. For example, purposeful individual action produces unexpected effects at the structural level. However, this combination is rarely focused on explaining stable collective action, or participation in cooperation, and actual empirical work bridging the levels of analysis is scarce. Improving on early approaches, a broadly conceived structural approach identifies the social mechanisms that are derived from, and fuelled by, members' strategic and symbolic rationality (that is, from relational investments, niche building/seeking and status competition).

In effect, niche seeking and status competition represent two rational dimensions of individual politicized behaviour that create some compatibility between the interests of the individual and that of the firm as a whole, micro through macro. For the individual partner, a social niche provides access to multiple resources at a lower relative cost; status provides an advantage in the negotiations of terms of exchange for these resources. As will be shown below, social niches are useful to the organization—for example, because they make a form of solidarity possible for individualistic entrepreneurs; once this solidarity has been introduced, social niches constrain their members into increased performance and contribution; they allow knowledge sharing and thus an unobtrusive form of quality control; they also lower the costs of pressuring deviant partners back to good order. Status competition is also useful for the firm as a whole. It drives and controls brainstorming in the search for innovative solutions to complex problems; it produces different forms of power that can be divided among different partners so as to reach a form of balance of powers; it creates an oligarchy that can be helpful in maintaining a form of normative order, preventing endless discussions of precarious values.

Niche seeking and status competition, however, also represent risks for the firm. Niches can be perceived as factions. They represent an increased risk of the defection of entire subgroups to other firms. This study shows that, nevertheless, the balance of powers reached by status competition can contribute to the prevention of such 'teaming up and out', and thus to the integration of the organization in spite of many centrifugal forces. Status competition also can get out of control and create a problem of 'too many chefs'. In turn, niches help reduce this risk by providing incentives for mitigation of conflicts and methods for exercising restraint. Niche seeking thus helps solve problems raised by status competition, and the other way around.

The fourth characteristic of a broadly conceived structural approach is its use of network analysis as a method for looking at these social mechanisms, at their consequences, at the ways in which niche seeking and status competition are combined. As suggested by the above definition of multiplexity, power among peers and durable collegial cooperation are not understandable without complex social relationships as components of such processes. Network analysis is particularly well suited here, because it analyses systematically the ways in which members politicize their exchanges and controls—that is, the ways in which members select their partners when they transfer and exchange many types of production-related resources, and resulting interdependencies.

In particular, an accent on multiplexity of relationships between members guarantees a more precise understanding of interdependencies and power among economic actors participating in collective action, and therefore of the related social mechanisms themselves. Analytically, this is equivalent to saying that specific, recurrent, local (uniplex and multiplex) substructures of social ties must be identified to understand how members can cooperate and exchange on an ongoing basis in the context of wider and politicized collective actors such as organizations. As will be shown in the case study, such substructural patterns of uniplex or multiplex ties are the building blocks of social mechanisms solving problems of individual action (for instance, by reducing individual transaction costs, thus improving chances of getting ahead) and coordination (for example, by simultaneously cultivating and mitigating status competition, thus solving a 'too-many-chefs' problem).

In addition, the methods of network analysis are particularly well suited to account for the existence of social niches and various forms of status at the level of the organization. Niches are defined as dense subsets of members that combine both cohesion and profile similarity (that is, approximated structural equivalence) *vis-à-vis* the other members of the organization. Various forms of centrality in different networks can be used as indicators of status and power. Combined with specific centrality and constraint measures, profile similarity sometimes helps to detect much more competitive—if not opportunistic—behaviour. For example, members of the firm who are not part of one's niche are considered to be colleagues that can be played off against each other and exploited in the oligarchic status competition process (Burt 1982, 1992).[7]

Finally, the fifth characteristic of a broadly conceived structural theory is its account of collective actors' built-in dependence on cultural—that is, normative—processes. Saying that status provides a position of strength to define terms of exchanges is equivalent to saying that it helps define the values, norms, and rules from which such terms are derived. In early structural sociology, the conceptual relationship between relational structures, on the one hand, and norms and values, on the other hand, has been elusive. In narrow structural approaches, resource interdependencies, more than norms, are considered the only principle of social order (Brint 1992; DiMaggio 1992). My approach, however, aligns itself with a more institutional perspective.[8] In particular, to explain social change or stability, it emphasizes the interpenetration of the interactional and normative realms. For example, contracts and politicized social mechanisms sustaining their enforcement are not sufficient to maintain cohesion and solidarity in a social group, especially when structural constraints are multiple and sometimes contradictory. Members need to learn and interiorize, or at least to commit themselves to, a system of rules and underlying norms and values that contribute to make these contracts meaningful and enforceable. Even if constraints, opportunities, and resource dependencies are viewed as having a more pronounced effect on human behaviour than do cultural norms, the latter do not disappear as a necessary ingredient of collective action. This is particularly the case in collegial organizations, where all partners have regulatory interests and rights, and are confronted with issues that require principled and long-term choices between policy options.

Institutional theories of action have long stressed organizational values, norms, and rules as restraints on grabbing economic behaviour and brutal exercise of power. Such values are debated, contested, and permanently redefined by members. Organizations change in part because they can redefine their formal and informal rules (Reynaud 1989). This institutional level of organization was explicitly formulated by many sociologists (Merton 1957; Parsons 1956a) and by studies of political or micro-political efforts to change the rules by competing interests. Such efforts may or may not be successful, and social arrangements are often stable enough to hide such underlying contests. Structural analysis can help to identify them.

Here, two notions combine a structural and an institutional perspective: Selznick's idea (1957) of precarious values and the notion of 'multi-status oligarchs'. In his institutional conception of the regulatory process, Selznick illustrates the entanglement of structure and culture with the concept of precarious value. A value is precarious because it is always in danger of losing its flag carriers and representatives—that is, the active support by organized interest groups and elites that help preserve it as a candidate for top priority on the list of all competing values. This connection between structure and culture is useful, because any regulatory process is a form of change that involves broken promises in the redistribution of resources (Reynaud and Reynaud 1996). When the rules of the game are changed, some parties come out as losing resources and others as winning resources compared to the previous distribution. This is why, in organizations, regulatory changes need the support of members with both power and legitimacy to push for changes. Specific members, those with multiple and loosely connected forms of status, are the key in such changes, because they can use such dependencies and legitimacy in the regulatory process.

Such an approach is also not incompatible with our earlier rational choice assumptions. In effect, just as they build or join social niches, members manage exchanges of resources using formal and informal rules. Classical institutional approaches to coordination in production have also insisted on the close links between instrumentally rational actions and normatively (or 'axiologically') rational actions (Boudon 1998; Frey 1997). Values count for economic actors, not simply through moral virtue but through politicized negotiation of the terms of exchanges. In our view, culture and structure are therefore related in two ways at least. First, norms help create relationships that are necessary for generic social mechanisms. Others are often chosen as exchange partners, bystanders, or third parties so as to conform to the rules. For example, convergent social expectations create lateral control intervention at the triadic level; they also create the role of multi-target lever (MTL) (see Chapter 7). Members may select exchange partners precisely among others whom they perceive as respecting the same rules of the game, as sharing the same values. Secondly, a relational structure matters in the changes of rules; since any such change means broken promises, it positions members whom I will call *multi-status oligarchs* in a favourable way to redefine priorities between precarious values and derived policy options. Indeed, regulatory changes need the support of members with several forms of status. These oligarchs must have the capacity to promote regulatory changes and deal with the negative effects of broken promises. When differences in power are not huge among members, this capacity often rests on sacrifice of resources by such multi-status oligarchs. As will be shown in Chapter 8, those who can afford to sacrifice resources while not losing power are people who have several *inconsistent* forms of status. Thanks to this inconsistency, or loose coupling, losing one form of status does not entail losing another.

Neither does this approach conflict with symbolic rationality. Beneath every kind of rule, there is a representation of the collective (a convention[9]), or strong reference group for which this rule makes sense (Strong and Dingwall 1985). The latter thus reaches a certain stability that helps economic actors coordinate production and distribution. This definition has strong normative extensions: it helps identify what to expect legitimately in terms of commitments and solidarity in exchanges of resources. Conventions thus include rules to which members refer to select partners for production-related exchanges.

This broadly conceived structural approach is necessary to understand durable cooperation among autonomous professionals, or collective action among peers. It should also make this enterprise of value to more general sociological theory.

OUTLINE OF THE BOOK

Chapter 1 offers the theoretical framework that combines the neo-Weberian and the broadly conceived structural approaches to provide a better understanding of this kind of rational actor and of social mechanisms driven by such behaviour. This framework expands on the view of peers presented above—that is, niche-seeking entrepreneurs carving out a place for themselves in the larger group by selecting relationships and by getting involved in various forms of status competition.

Partnerships are a good example of such collegial organizations, especially those in which social relationships and underlying resource interdependencies tend to be durable. In this book, I present this theory and describe these mechanisms, using as an example a network study of a specific collegial organization, a corporate law partnership in which partners—rational and calculating actors if ever there were any—locked themselves in a cooperative and long-term situation without much hierarchy and formal power differences to enforce their agreement. In such a context, peers are 'interdependent entrepreneurs'. For centuries, partnership agreements as legal contracts have embodied various types of solidarity and mutual obligations among potentially rival business partners. However, very little has been written about cooperation in such organizations and their typical problems of collective action among peers. Partnerships in particular, and collegial, knowledge-intensive organizations in general, are complex social systems that need to find solutions to these typical problems.

This professional services firm is used as a site for testing propositions about how niche seeking and status competition combine to offer an original view of social mechanisms maintaining and using collective responsibility. This makes their firm interesting for someone asking fundamental questions raised by traditional sociology and using a broadly conceived structural approach. How do such durable relationships help maintain individual performance and quality output, deal with opportunistic free-riding, balance the powers of rainmakers and schedulers, and integrate a multi-city firm in spite of many centrifugal forces? This firm is examined using combined methods such as network analysis, ethnography of task forces performing legal work, and organizational analysis of internal politics in the firm.

The collegial form does not necessarily take the form of a partnership contract. Yet the processes going on in this firm, and therefore the whole case examined here, are paradigmatic for what happens in any collegial and knowledge-intensive environment bringing together interdependent entrepreneurs. In Chapter 2, I present the empirical research conducted to ground and test this approach to collegial organizations, using both quantitative and qualitative methods. I present the firm, called Spencer, Grace & Robbins (or SG&R, an alias) and a standard organizational analysis of its operations.[10] Like many experts, lawyers create, apply, or preserve knowledge (Flood 1987; Mann 1985; Nelson 1988; Starbuck 1992). As for any type of collective-action system, this firm is examined from the perspective of resource interdependencies connected to the production process (Crozier and Friedberg 1977). In particular, partners have adopted a compensation system (an equal sharing default rule) that helps (or forces) them to take a long-term view with regard to cooperation and solidarity. For example, they can only expel one of their own if there is near unanimity against him or her. These characteristics may be connected to the fact that they belong to a profession that is usually favoured with monopoly returns,[11] thus loosening the relationship between efficiency, performance, and survival in the market.

Chapter 3 uses the network data to present SG&R as an exchange system for various forms of resources, and members as (broadly conceived rational) status competitors managing and accumulating those resources needed to work and survive in this environment. The analysis of the ways in which these resources are bartered leads to the identification of social niches, informal entities that are shaped by individuals selecting exchange partners under the formal structure of the firm. The effects of differences in members' choices of exchange partners—such as level of hierarchical status (partner/associate), speciality (litigation/corporate), office membership, gender, and law school (Ivy League/non-Ivy League)—is examined to confirm the emergence of these niches. The existence of these entities is then used in the following chapters to provide insights into how collegial organizations find structural solutions to additional key problems: for example, motivating tenured partners, quality control, opportunism in the form of free-riding, and firm integration.

The existence of such niches is then confirmed statistically as is the existence of a *generalized exchange system* and bounded solidarity in the niches. Just as strong interpersonal relations are the key to the functioning of combat units (Shils and Janowitz 1948), so they are also the key to allowing task forces of peers to make decisions (Festinger *et al.* 1950). A realistic view of how a collegial organization operates is then derived from this structural analysis: the relational architecture of the firm (its exchange system) is described to show how SG&R's labour contracts are embedded in a multilevel social system without which the partnership agreement would not be enforceable.

Chapter 4 explains members' economic performance by combining the analysis of the co-workers' network and that of the firm's economic performance data to look at what sustains partners' productivity in a system with such enormous incentives to free-ride (that is, let others work). Using Burt's measurement (1992) of network constraint, I show that members' economic performance is positively correlated with the amount of pressure that their main co-workers (usually members of their social niche) put on them to work longer hours.

Chapter 4 also accounts for members' professional performance. With regard to quality control, I look at the problem of accumulation of knowledge and experience in the firm. Since members try to work in niches, they combine status competition (hierarchy) and knowledge management in various ways, depending on their experience of exchanges with specific co-workers. The consequence of the exchange system for the distribution of knowledge can be seen in the structure of the advice network. The firm's main resource—its expertise and creativity with regard to solving complex legal problems for corporations—is located not only in its mainframe computer, but in the structure of this network (in specific niches) and in specific members sought out for advice by many others. Main advisers—who have acquired a form of status that brings great deference within the firm—are identified. Rules related to the circulation of advice within the firm are extracted from the analysis, among which the most important is the seniority rule: one does not seek advice from people 'below'. The niche system thus solves problems of quality control in an unobtrusive way, while at the same time creating inequalities and favouritism. The circulation of advice favours a few selected associates in their race towards partnership: through short cuts in the network, it provides them with access to very senior advisers. Overall, however, the social exchange system is again shown to be a productive form of corporate social capital: it helps members manage knowledge. But it is also shown to be a selection device because it allocates immaterial or intangible resources in an unequal way.

The solidarity that is provided to members through the generalized exchange system in social niches is fragile, and status competition is a threat to the existence of such a positive social mechanism. Chapter 5 addresses the coexistence of niche seeking and status competition. It shows how multiplex social ties (co-work, advice, and friendship) within niches are used in such a context both to cultivate *and* to mitigate status competition among professional colleagues. As mentioned before, status competition can get out of hand; but social ties interlock to mitigate it in a process involving specific substructures of advice and friendship ties.

Beyond economic performance, quality control, and mitigation of status competition, the exchange system is also useful in maintaining a balance of powers and, consequently, firm integration—particularly in dealing with many centrifugal forces threatening the organization (for example, disputes about sharing profits, secession of rainmakers and their more or less permanent team to another firm, status competition in the work process, and disputes between subgroups representing different offices or specialities). Chapter 6 shows that members of this collegial organization have an interest in maintaining a stable oligarchy—that is, a subset of members with various forms of status. Oligarchs are often under pressure not to fight. They are all the more appreciated because they do not raise controversies, keep a low profile, and present their agreements as renegotiable. Multidimensionality of status is bound to come with processes that help the collegial organization maintain a *balance of powers* between these oligarchs. This is the case at SG&R, where economic and administrative powers are separate, informally but in a strong structural way. This allows two forms of solidarity and integration to coexist, one based on a 'welfare system' of bureaucratic distribution of work, the other based on an informal and 'clientelistic' distribution. Each form of solidarity (welfare, clientelistic) is made possible by members with different forms of status in the organizations ('minders', partners who mind the shop, and 'finders', partners who find new and lucrative clients) who are kept dependent upon each other. In many ways a collegial organization replaces an autocrat with a set of oligarchs who prevent each other from accumulating enough resources to be independent. Collegiality (thus called polycracy) presupposes the interdependency of oligarchs. Cohesion in the oligarchy is reached by a balance of powers and integration *à la Montesquieu.* Maintaining heterogeneity and interdependence of forms of status is often the condition under which rivalry among oligarchs leads to equilibrium.

In Chapter 7, I look at SG&R as a control system (against opportunistic behaviour such as shirking) in which issues of cost of control are as central, if not more so, as in any form of collective action. A structural perspective also helps focus on the relationship between interdependencies and control of enforcement of decisions made by the collegium, as well as between status and control. This issue is of particular importance in formally egalitarian bodies in which practitioners are all nominal equals and interdependent. Free-rider problems quickly arise in such settings, because even a member who did not contribute effectively to the firm's revenues imposes a cost on the organization as a whole by reaping the benefits of membership (Olson 1965). As a consequence, monitoring and policing, especially early graduated sanctions, are considered to be particularly important for ensuring that members' individual commitment to contribute remains credible.

A second-order free-rider problem arises as well—the problem of who will bear the costs of monitoring and enforcing previous agreements and collective responsibility among the formally equal members (Heckathorn 1989; Oliver 1980; Yamagishi 1986).

In such contexts—hierarchical control being relatively weak—there is reluctance, at an early stage, to use formal procedures against colleagues to overcome free-riding and maintain solidarity. Direct command or use of administrative hierarchy is not considered an appropriate means for exercising control, because professionals have many ways of neutralizing formal authority (Bosk 1979; Freidson 1975, 1986; Gouldner 1954.) In fact, early monitoring and sanctioning in collegial organizations also rely on specific forms of interdependencies in the exchanges of resources to protect overall prosperity against individual opportunism or parochial interests. An understanding of such relational constraints explains how members try to keep early monitoring costs low, and themselves motivated to carry on monitoring and sanctioning each other.

These constraints take the form of a *lateral control regime* that helps peers find an early solution to this second-order free-rider problem in formally egalitarian interdependent groups. I use the word 'lateral' to express two facts: first, that this way of exercising informal control is based on the use of third parties as sanctioners—that is, members acting as envoys of the firm in charge of pressuring deviant partners back to good conduct; and, secondly, that these third parties are not hierarchical superiors, but formally equal peers. Consideration of costs narrows the choices of sanctioners appointed by partners exercising early monitoring and sanctioning unobtrusively. In this regime, control costs are reduced for most members, because they play on each others' resource interdependencies. In effect, interdependencies between two partners produce, in the rest of the partnership, expectations that one of the two will intervene on behalf of the firm to curb potentially opportunistic behaviour displayed by the other partner in this dyad. These expectations are built and learned over time. They are also shown to converge and thus to create a constraining pattern of expectations with structural effects. The structure coming out of this convergence of expectations is thus both cultural and structural.

In this structure, however, fear of collusion between the sanctioners and the infractors are then shown to have an additional effect: they shift control costs to uncontroversial partners with a specific form of status—that of 'protectors of the common good'. This status helps them carry more weight with infractors and deal with the danger of preferential treatment reserved to partners too close to punish. Thanks to this social mechanism, individuals find it advantageous, credible, and safe to pursue contingent commitment to rule compliance and mutual control.

Finally, this structural approach also helps to clarify the regulatory process—that is, the redefinition of the rules of the game in such collective actors—by looking at their *members' negotiation of precarious values* underlying policy options. Chapter 8 looks at the last social mechanism, one that helps members to control this regulatory process in the firm. A broadly conceived structural approach to cooperation provides insights into the relationship between interests and values, thus improving our understanding of the combined importance of relational structure and norms in collective action, particularly among peers. A precarious value (Selznick 1957) is one that is essential to the viability of the collectivity but in which most members may have no direct stake. Examples of precarious values include, in collegial organizations, hierarchical authority and professional ethical principles. Subunits fight for the particular values entrusted to them and may continually redefine them to assert their priority over potentially competing values. Client satisfaction, internal coordination, innovation and quality of professional knowledge, societal needs, and employee interests would not be defended or promoted if not represented by powerful subunits or members to which the values in question are paramount, and the organization as a whole would be the poorer (Simpson 1971).

This social mechanism helps collegial organizations solve the problem of endless deliberation about norms and values, and thus about firm management policies regarding issues such as work intake and assignment, compensation, marketing, and peer review. It makes use of the multidimensionality of status ahead of the deliberations themselves. Since members participate in regulatory activities as status competitors, the process is based on renegotiation of rules among multi-status members, or oligarchs. Oligarchs driving the regulatory process are shown to have several inconsistent forms of status. This helps them defend precarious values in ways that seem compatible with the common good, but also prevent certain legitimate values from being later defended forcefully by other members.

In effect, regulatory decisions are also made from within the organizational exchange system. The definition of rules is based on a selection of bi- or multi-status oligarchs who play a leadership role by defining priorities. Their selection brings into the deliberation only oligarchs who, because they have several inconsistent forms of status, are thus able to give priority to one of these forms without disqualifying the others. The negotiation of precarious values, or the emergence of a priority value, requires a cohesive core of multi-status oligarchs clearly identified with such values and in a position to defend their rank with their peers, if not to prescribe them to each other. In short, the debate about precarious values uses in a constraining way the heterogeneity of sources of status observed by the classics. Structure mediates between interests and values because oligarchs can promote some norms while downplaying the importance of others.

To sum up, flat organizations rely not only on an oligarchy but also on specific social mechanisms that produce certain forms of public good (public within the organization). Members' formal positions and property rights are not enough to guarantee the functioning of such organizations. Among these goods, I include a form of solidarity that comes across as a generalized exchange system, a lateral control regime, and a system stabilizing the renegotiation of rules. These are consistent with individual interests and management of resource interdependencies, but they are also the result of a form of social discipline. Individual returns are guaranteed in this system if returns are conceived of as of many types. Incentives exist to undertake socially desirable activities. Members are compelled to bear their share of risk, their part of the costs of transactions within the organization, because of the necessity to manage several resources at the same time, and the impossibility of accumulating some of them forever. In effect, one can say that they are based on these individual interests, provided that the latter are broadly conceived with regard to many long-term goals and with different types of resources. This assumption about how members behave is not unrealistic in the institutional context of collegial organizations in which such mechanisms operate. The latter characterize an organization that is embedded in an institutional environment, without being reduced to it. They operate under specific institutional arrangements but they are not identified with them. The organization works because both an institutional arrangement and social mechanisms based on resource dependencies make it worthwhile for members to undertake socially productive activities.

BEYOND EMBEDDEDNESS STUDIES OF KNOWLEDGE-INTENSIVE FIRMS

One can also hypothesize that, on a day-to-day basis, local offices of even large professional services firms operate thanks to social and informal 'governance' mechanisms such as that listed and combined above. At the global level, power variance in such organizations is presumably too large to allow for these collegial mechanisms to operate, but even that remains to be checked. The informal processes that go on in such organizations—mainly those that combine niche seeking and status competition—must be taken into account when designing flatter structures. They are based on social relationships among members. As acknowledged by Maister (1993), managing firms in which social relationships and resource interdependencies are so complex is not easy and requires much more understanding of the social constraints under which such management is carried out. In my view, additional insights into such constraints require the kind of analysis carried out in this book.

Contemporary management theories of knowledge-intensive organizations and professional services organizations address some of the issues with which this book deals. They sometimes draw on economic literature on services and innovation (see e.g. Baumol and Wolff 1983; Gadrey 1994, 1996; Gadrey and De Bandt 1994; Gallouj 2000) to focus on the variety of forms taken by such organizations. They are concerned with the collegial form, even though that term is not used, and the pressures under which it has to operate. A structural approach differs from such theories precisely thanks to its systematic identification of multilevel and often informal social mechanisms.

Many of the ingredients of a structural approach can be found in the literature on knowledge management and organizational design (Myers 1996). For example, Moss Kanter (1988) or Baker (1994) stresses the importance of power, coalitions, network density, autonomy for innovation, and 'idea realization'. But these ingredients, in my view, are not combined so as to account for elements of informal self-governance. Another example is Starbuck's idea (1992, 1993) of a law firm as a knowledge-intensive firm. Along with authors such as Brock *et al.* (1999), Greenwood *et al.* (1990), or Hinings *et al.* (1991), Starbuck provides a broad definition of this type of organization. In this account, much of the importance of social relations has often been captured as a characteristic of their cultural embeddedness—for example in organizational and/or professional culture.[12] Although such cultures are important, focusing on them often tends to stress that partners must learn social skills when dealing with each other, so as to protect a good ambiance. This often ignores that management of social relationships is equivalent to management of interdependencies and power relationships, not simply a good ambience. It sets aside the fact that, as a consequence, social ties can be the very stuff of coordination, of social mechanisms without which a collegial organization cannot operate and survive in the long run.

These views are limited, because they promote a purely managerial understanding of how knowledge-intensive organizations operate. For example, in this approach, the micro-political processes by which information is elaborated into appropriate knowledge—that is, knowledge that can be used as a premiss for complex decisions—are not taken into account. In Starbuck's view (1993), knowledge-intensive firms learn almost mechanically, by hiring, training, and dismissing personnel. In the view offered here, a firm learns mostly thanks to its collective capacity to stabilize its production of authoritative knowledge. This capacity depends, among other patterns, on the existence of an informally hierarchical advice network. A social process of elaboration and distribution of knowledge can thus help members filter and sift out authoritative answers to specific problems. Knowledge and learning cannot be jointly produced without the existence of authorities that allow generalization and represent experience. Such authorities are often quickly identified in the advice network within the organizations. The authority arguments on which their status games are based are at the heart of such organizations, whether professional or not (Lazega 1992*a*).

This book is, therefore, different from the mainstream theorizing of the knowledge-intensive and professional firms by its emphasis on the pervasive influence of multilevel social mechanisms in these organizations, regardless of their size. The fact that the case study is carried out on data collected in a relatively traditional corporate law firm does not mean, in my view, that such mechanisms are necessarily waning in more bureaucratized professional services firms. At the global level, larger multi-city and multi-country professional services firms operating as a one-stop shop for multinational companies are often managed in different, more bureaucratic ways (Aharoni 1997; Brock *et al.* 1999). However, it would be highly questionable for observers (and foolish for such firms) to ignore the gap between global and local governance and politics. It makes sense to hypothesize that, at the local level, even in large and more bureaucratized partnerships (or perhaps in incorporated firms), such mechanisms also operate as a form of corporate social capital. In effect, they characterize collective action among rival peers, and such local offices are comprised of at least large pockets of such partners. This hypothesis, however, remains to be tested empirically.

   Failing to take into account social mechanisms when making comparisons between global and local levels of collective action leads to technocratic management that believes in easy manipulation of collective efforts among peers. It is not my objective here to derive managerial know-how from this book's understanding of knowledge-intensive organizations. The book's main contribution is to develop an approach to social mechanisms that shows, in particular, how members' niche seeking and status competition are needed to sustain this form of collective action, and can be used to balance each other's negative effects in various social processes.

A broadly conceived structural approach is important for an understanding of the collegial phenomenon or cooperation between interdependent entrepreneurs. In the Conclusion, I raise the issue of the generalization of these results—in particular the question of the existence of these mechanisms in all collegial organizations. I describe some of the implications of this approach for more general theories of collective action, but also for the identification of specific social problems that arise in contemporary organizations and professions. In the work needed to address such issues more generally and more systematically, much remains to be done.

1

A Structural Theory of Collective Action among Peers

Neo-Weberian theories (see especially Waters 1989) have proposed a set of formal characteristics that differentiate collegial organizations from bureaucratic or monocratic ones. In this chapter I argue that these theories are not sufficient by themselves to explain collective action among peers. A combined neo-Weberian and broadly conceived structural approach is needed, one that looks at the individual and organizational levels at the same time. Such an approach assumes that individuals have a strategic rationality. It looks at members as niche seeking entrepreneurs selecting exchange partners, carving out a place for themselves in the group and getting involved in various forms of status competition. From this conception of actors, it derives the existence of generic social mechanisms that are needed to sustain this form of collective action, in particular that of exchange, control, and negotiation of precarious values. It is rooted, first, in the analysis of the production process and task-related resource dependencies; and, secondly, in the analysis of derived governance mechanisms. Looking at such mechanisms helps in understanding how a collegial organization provides structural solutions to problems of collective action among peers: how it cultivates and mitigates status competition; how it maintains performance, quality, and controls; and, finally, how it maintains a form of status differentiation that helps with organizational integration and with the negotiation of precarious professional values.

A CONTRACTUAL BASIS: THE EXAMPLE OF PARTNERSHIPS AS AN INSTITUTIONAL FORM

Professional *partnerships* are good examples to begin with. True partnerships are special types of collective (or 'corporate') actors. Historically, they go back to the earliest times. Their distinctive feature is the sharing of profits and losses in a common business undertaking, and they are held to be a complex entity (Rowley and Rowley 1960).[1] From a collective action perspective, a partnership is an institutional form based on a nexus of contracts between members (practitioners and apprentices). As a legal form, it often assumes formal equality among partners, as well as individual and collective liability. In such collegial organizations, pressure towards consensus is strong. They bring together voluntarily members who want to satisfy their economic, social, and cultural common aspirations through an enterprise that is collectively owned and in which power is exercised as democratically as possible. It is thus a type of organization in which economic and social life are intertwined in a particularly visible way.

This contractual and voluntary basis is crystallized in a partnership agreement, a document in which partners put in writing the terms by which they govern their business affairs and organization. It provides rules for the conduct of the firm and guidelines for individual behaviour. It seeks to promote efficiency in many ways, and is therefore a powerful organizational device. These general principles are then more or less applied to specific firm situations. Partnership agreements apply to the various aspects of a firm's life, the prevailing firm philosophy regarding its practice, and how it should be undertaken. In doing so, they represent an attempt to bring an element of predictability to firm operations and to minimize the room for disputes regarding issues such as the work process, firm management, compensation decisions, and withdrawal terms (for the case of law partnerships, see Eickemeyer 1988). The agreement accomplishes this by setting ground rules as to each partner's rights and responsibilities in connection with these issues, and for the operation of the firm itself. In many ways, it is fundamental, because such rules and procedures help members constrain each other and reach consensus without resorting to coercion. Usually, the agreement also tries to enhance the image of the partnership as a closed professional community in which all partners have rights to participate, especially when they may not sell or transfer their partnership interest.

Agreements are usually comprehensive and difficult to modify. Three main issues (and consequently sources of controversy) are of particular interest to members: firm governance, compensation determination, and conflict management, including sanctions against members who do not abide by the rules. First, the agreement usually imposes a regulatory structure in which the partnership, the 'committee of the whole', is the ultimate authority. It establishes the committees that govern the partnership and a structure to run it on a day-to-day basis, thus delegating limited authority with more or less specificity. The partners establish policy and manage the affairs of the partnership through the partnership meeting. The meeting can, for example, vest an executive committee or a managing partner with the responsibility and authority for overseeing the firm's day-to-day operations. Secondly, a compensation committee is usually in charge of establishing each year a schedule for the distribution of cash and additions or adjustments to individual partners' capital accounts. This committee has to adhere to the agreed-upon principles in establishing partners' shares. An agreement can provide a formula or any other method by which each partner's compensation is determined, and, in setting out this method, it makes clear what weight the firm places on various factors (for example, seniority and loyalty to the firm, finding new clients, billed hours, apprentice training, and community activities that enhance the firm's prestige). Thirdly, conflict resolution mechanisms, including arbitration and mediation, are defined to handle partners' disputes. Formal procedures are used against members who violate the rules, but often as a last resort, especially since monitoring and sanctioning are undertaken not by external authorities but by the participants themselves. In such a case, infractors are likely to be allocated graduated sanctions (depending on the seriousness and context of the offence) by other members, by officials accountable to these members, or by both. If an individual breaks the rules more systematically, sanctions can escalate until members punish the offender (and sometimes themselves) by breaking previous agreements.

Beyond the embodiment of the firm's approach to governance, compensation, and conflict resolution—which are the thorniest issues in most partnerships—the scope of such agreements is much wider. They also regulate admission to the partnership and attempt to anticipate, and provide for, inevitable events such as partner retirement, disability, withdrawal, and death, as well as issues such as the dissolution of the partnership. Indeed, one of the distinctive features of a partnership is the fact that exit is mutually controlled. Even where it results from death, the other partners are usually able to control the repayment of capital to a partner's estate or may have treated this as an insurable event. Even a partner who resigns cannot take his capital out precipitately but must reach an accommodation with the others. Production and collective action among partners are thus formally structured. In theory, firm's members know about such arrangements and order their professional lives accordingly. If the constraint of rules disappears, so does the collective interest and the capacity to work productively together. This legal contract is a set of constraints to which partners voluntarily subscribe. The rules formulated to produce quality work and to monitor this production are jointly defined.

However, in reality partnership agreements are limited: alone, they cannot structure collective action. They cannot function without the *commitment* of the members of the firm. Commitment to this contract requires more than a purely utilitarian and individualistic explanation. In effect, collective action rests upon the existence of a *collective interest*, which includes an individual interest in collective action. In itself, this collective interest is not sufficient to create collective action; it needs to be defended by members who are willing to enforce these rules in concrete situations. Sociological theory has traditionally argued that, in order to make contracts meaningful and enforceable, members have to use constraints by managing their interdependencies and internalize informal social norms. As Durkheim once pointed out, economic contracts are fragile and always destabilized by competition (see also Blau 1964; Macaulay 1963). One indication is that such organizations often seem to resist strong pressures towards incorporation brought about by market pressures and liability issues. Thus, we are entitled to assume that partnerships are characterized by economic but also social features ensuring the maintenance and development of collective action.

The type of collective action specific to partnerships helps members work together and stick to their commitments. Economic cooperation and returns, while serving individual interest, are not entirely motivated by it. Social processes of exchange, recognition, control, and socialization are also involved. What exists is thus a collective interest that is supported by a collegial discipline constructed by these members. As stressed by Reynaud (1989), economic calculation, which is the basis of commitment, incorporates a 'project', a reflection that motivates members, or at least a large majority, to cooperate, even if they have to reduce their benefits or anticipate an uncertain future gain to give up certain present gains. Waters's approach to collegial organizations takes up such a view; it is a renewed synthetic contribution—in the tradition of Weber and Parsons—to the description of collective action among peers.

BEYOND CONTRACTS: THE NEO-WEBERIAN APPROACH TO COLLEGIAL ORGANIZATIONS

Waters's papers (1989, 1993) deal with issues relevant to partnerships by comparing 'collegial' (or 'collegiate') organizations with monocratic and bureaucratic organizations.[2] This comparison is constructed around two dimensions. First, there is the way the distribution of power is arranged: in collegial organizations, power is dispersed or divided among a number of persons ideally conceived to be equals. For instance, colleagues can be both leaders and officials. Power is not vested in a single individual and delegated therefrom, but vested in a collectivity as a whole, distributed on a formally egalitarian basis, and aggregated upwards. Secondly, there are the bases for legitimate claims to share in this distribution of power: for both bureaucracy and collegiality, the central organizing principle is specialized expertise.

Within the bureaucratic administrative staff, differences in specialized performance become the basis for hierarchy. Theoretically superiors have greater knowledge than do subordinates. In collegial organizations, knowledge is conceived of as so individually specialized that individual practitioners cannot be ranked (except in their relationships with apprentices). Thus specialized experts are understood to have the right to equal standing in a distribution of power. (Waters 1993: 65)

Both rational-legal bureaucracy and collegiality are supposed to be organized around specialized performances evaluated on the basis of universalistic criteria. But, unlike in bureaucracies, the 'owner' of the knowledge is not the manager or the client, but the profession and its representatives.

As mentioned earlier to describe more systematically the formal structure of collegial organizations, Waters (1989: 956) defines collegial structures as 'those in which there is dominant orientation to a consensus achieved between the members of a body of experts who are theoretically equals in their levels of expertise but who are specialized by area of expertise'. The main organizational characteristics implied by this statement of the principle of collegiality are as follows.

1. *Theoretical knowledge*: collegiate organization is arranged in terms of the use and application of theoretical knowledge.
2. *Professional career*: members of collegiate organizations are considered as professionals; careers are differentiated in at least two stages (apprentice and practitioner), and provide security of tenure.
3. *Formal egalitarianism*: collegiate organizations are performance-oriented systems, but because professionals are specialists it is difficult to compare

performances; for this reason, collegiate organizations are formally equal systems.

4. *Formal autonomy*: collegiate organizations are self-controlling and self-policing.
5. *Scrutiny of product*: the products of the work done by colleagues must be available for peer review (consultation, second opinion, public dissemination of written opinion).
6. *Collective decision making*: collegiate organization implies the constitution of collective forums in which decisions are made; the committee is the proto-typical collegial decision-making body (general committee, specialist commit-tee, delegative committee); collegiate organizations have complex, frequently hierarchical, committee systems.

These idealtypical characteristics differentiate collegial organizations from bureau-cratic organizations, even though, in most circumstances, collegiality is not the sole decision-making structure but coexists with bureaucracy. A collegial organization is more or less bureaucratic depending on how it is managed.

Based on this approach, Waters (1993) constructs an analytic typology of collegial organizations around two dimensions: 'personnel processes' (selection for official positions, career, leadership claims, closure patterns) and 'decision processes' (ratification, normative arrangements, compliance relationships, control pattern). In the collegial form of interest here, selection for official positions is on the basis of election among professional practitioners. Positions are not filled by appointment. Once a person is selected, his or her career is supposed to be based on tenure and autonomous work practice free of supervision. 'The career advances under the subjective judgment of peers in relation to a set of substantive theoretical standards rather than in terms of a proven capacity to follow rules and commands' (Waters 1993: 73). Leadership claims are more diffuse and tenuous than in bureaucratic organizations. They are supposed to be based on greater expertise. But, 'given that the basis of the claim is evaluated by peers, and that expertise is specialized, this leaves a great deal of space for shifting patterns of leadership'. Closure patterns (that is, how members exclude non-members, how officials exclude simple members, or how leaders exclude ordinary officials) are not supposed to be based on seniority (as in bureaucracies), but on credentialism: 'Closure is maintained by having a certified and/or demonstrably higher level of attainment than others in relation to professional theoretical knowledge' (Waters 1993: 73).

Ratification has to be performed by constituencies of members in order to be authoritative. 'In collegial organizations this ratification takes place on the basis of a consensus between professional peers established in relation to knowledge' (Waters 1993: 75). Normative arrangements influencing decisions are based on a set of abstract procedural norms (Sciulli 1986) 'established to protect the rights of col-leagues to autonomous action, and not merely the rights of vulnerable clients to equality of treatment' (Waters 1993: 75). The compliance relationship is essentially based on status: 'Colleagues comply with collegial decisions because they would otherwise lose status in the professional pecking order, and clients comply because officials have expert status' (Waters 1993: 76).[3] Control pattern is based on peer evaluation of colleagues' expertise: 'Colleagues have a conventional or legal monopoly of expertise in their areas of practice. Their mode of control is therefore one of self-regulation based on peer judgment exercised within the boundaries of a precise set of procedural norms' (Waters 1993: 76). Clearly, only specialized expertise (that is, theoretical knowledge) is ultimately a basis for a legitimate claim to one's share of status, power, and leadership in Waters's framework.

Although extremely stimulating, Waters's synthesis remains very formal. In his approach, for example, production-related resource dependencies, as well as several forms of status, remain untheorized—or rather, attributed to other forms of collective action, not to the collegial one. Formal structure, as described by his reformulation of Weber's and Parsons's ideas, is unlikely to guarantee by itself collective action. If peers are 'theoretically equals' but have to deal with 'tenuous and diffuse' leadership claims and 'shifting patterns of leadership', how does such a system actually work? If ratification 'takes place on the basis of consensus', how is consensus reached? And if there are different forms of status, why would colleagues ever comply with decisions made by someone with a different form of status? If one partner is responsible for a speciality and another for an office, it is often formally unclear whose responsibility decisions are on a given matter; how are these decisions made? To answer such questions, I argue that the broadly conceived structural approach sketched in the introduction is needed, an approach that is able to describe social mechanisms characterizing such an organization. This view assumes a conception of actors' rationality that takes into account their contextualization of their own behaviour: their calculations, but also their politicization of their exchanges and controls through the use of identifications, status, and norms.

BEHAVIOURAL ASSUMPTIONS AND RESULTING SOCIAL MECHANISMS

This means that understanding durable cooperation among autonomous professionals is of value to more general sociological theory because it shows that mechanisms such as those defined by Hedström and Swedberg (1998a), and Stinchcombe (1991) can be explained only when broadly conceived structural and rational choice approaches are combined. Weber knew that neither individual nor common interests create collective action on their own. Rather, social processes support individual commitment to previous agreements, thus helping members deal with each other and develop ties of cooperation. Such processes and the ways in which they bridge levels of analysis need to be further explored. In the sociological rational choice traditions, theories for such a micro through macro combination were provided by many authors (Blossfeld and Prein 1998; Esser 1998; Lindenberg 1995). For example, individual action produces (intentional or unexpected) effects at the structural level that are important to group solidarity because they help members maintain integration processes based on their interdependencies.

To combine these approaches, individuals in organizations must first be seen as interdependent members who need to get access to production-related resources (Blau 1964).[4] A broadly conceived structural theory can make the following behavioural assumptions about members of collegial organizations and their strategies to get access to production-related resources. Actors' rationality is assumed to be 'strategic' (Crozier and Friedberg 1977)—that is, to include a politicized view of action. As such, it includes calculations, but also symbolic activity such as selection of, or investments in, relationships guided by appropriateness judgements (based on recognition of identities in the selection of partners) and value judgements (negotiation of precarious values and norms) that allow individuals to handle their exchanges and controls in ways that seem advantageous to them and to their own collective. In this theory, niche seeking and status competition are components of actors' strategic rationality. Individuals can thus be represented as strategic and interdependent entrepreneurs who politicize their behaviour by using boundary management to seek relatively closed contexts (Feld 1981) in which they can find and exchange these resources at a low cost. Once in such contexts, they seek various forms of concentration of these resources so as to be in a position to define the terms of their exchanges. A multilevel dimension is built into this theory thanks to the notions of niche and multidimensional status. Their importance comes from the fact that they are both structurally combined and assumed to be indispensable for individual peers' commitment to a partnership agreement. Together they are basic components of both members' strategic rationality and of a series of generic mechanisms that characterize and drive collegial organizations. In the following sections I propose a definition of these notions and mechanisms.

Actors seeking bounded solidarity in social niches

Interdependent members of organizations must have access to various production-related resources (for example, clients, co-workers' goodwill, advice). To get access to such resources, members do not entirely rely on formal organization and rules. They are selective in their relational choices and manage their interdependence in their own ways. The social niche of an actor can be broadly defined as a subset of members of the organization selected by this actor, and with whom he or she establishes especially durable exchange relations, whether directly or indirectly, in order to get such an access.[5] Niche building is a form of investment in relationships (Blau 1964; Homans 1961). Actors contextualizing their behaviour in organizations are able and trained to detect the existence of niches based on the criterion of a certain social homogeneity: they use similarities (for example, in terms of office membership, or speciality, or hierarchical status; but also in terms of gender or class—that is, more exogenous attributes) between exchange partners to identify the boundaries of the niche in which they assume that dense exchanges do or will take place. Since a social niche is a pool of colleagues with whom exchanges are characterized by a certain density and multiplexity, sociologists can also check the realism of such a behavioural assumption by detecting a niche through a strong relational cohesion among subsets of actors with similar attributes.

In theory, a social niche is not necessarily a group, because it is not necessarily recognized as a group by its members, even if withdrawal of investments in it could be very costly, and because it does not necessarily have the legitimacy that would be granted to an independent entity by an outside authority. The organization can recognize the importance of social niches for efficient circulation of resources, but it does not favour the emergence of detachable subunits ready for easy defection. Just as a social niche can be either a shelter or a hell for an individual member, it can be an advantage or a threat for the organization that encompasses it. Rather, a social niche can be considered to be a stable quasi-group.

Members operate within microstructures such as niches, which are themselves part of the wider organization. It is rational for members to be niche seeking, because it is rational for them to look for multifunctional contexts that provide them with the resources needed to work productively, and with relative protection from rivalry and competition for these resources. The multifunctional character of niches means that several resources can be exchanged by members, who can thus decrease the costs of interaction as well as those of the resources themselves. Indeed, such niches are also built for that very purpose—that is, to allow multiplex barters[6] of resources without 'general equivalent'. Niche building is strategic, but, once built, niches have the advantage of allowing *partial suspension of purely calculating behaviour* (Boorman and Levitt 1980; Bowles and Gintis 1998; Ekeh 1976). They help members identify partners with similar long-term interests and combine, through identity criteria, these long-term interests and the management of multiple resources. Niches and identities come together because they introduce long-term stability in members' choices and definitions of interests,[7] thus bending fairness judgements (Homans 1961; Kellerhals *et al.* 1988).

This stability is based on the intuition that common characteristics make long-term common interests more likely, and therefore the existence of indirect reciprocity that is necessary for collective action. There is no barter without identities and a very important symbolic dimension.[8] An important individual-level concept accounting for this stability and this process is that of *identification*. Identity is usually a relatively stable and multidimensional set of attributes that members use to make judgements of appropriateness, define themselves, and get recognition as sources of their actions (for credit and accountability) on an ongoing basis. In a politicized world, an actor is always 'loyal' to some allegiance (represented by an attribute) while 'betraying' another (represented by another attribute). Symbolic interactionist thought has theorized the difficulty of compartmentalizing social life so as not to be caught on the 'wrong' side. Identity is what introduces time in action by defining long-term individual and collective interests, whether material or ideal. Politicizing exchanges means using such identifications as bearings for selection of exchange partners. To some extent, members use identity criteria to choose exchange partners who will presumably share values leading to some degree of solidarity. The idea here is that identity is introduced in transfers and exchanges of resources to avoid measuring the value of the heterogeneous resources in multiplex exchanges. The use of identities in multiplex exchanges creates a form of bounded solidarity.

This bounded solidarity can be connected to a form of limited rationality, but in the sense that members do not always use the same criteria to evaluate the fairness of their multiplex barters. Since they establish an exchange system in which multiple resources are often incommensurable, they do not always use the same criteria to evaluate what is a fair multiplex exchange. Analytically, bounded solidarity can be measured in several ways: for example, by the stability of members' choices of exchange partners, a stability that can limit individual autonomy (Blau 1964; Ekeh 1976); or by the existence of generalized exchange cycles—that is, of indirect reciprocity—among them; or by the presence of informal rules imposing multiplexity or preventing members from grabbing all the credit for successful actions.

To get access to such resources, members do not entirely rely on formal organization and rules. They are selective in their relational choices, and this selectivity— together with institutional constraints—produces patterns that make it possible to understand exchanges in the organization. Members manage their interdependence in their own ways, which are both economic, social, and politicized. As seen above, to get access to such resources, they enter exchanges that are multilateral and multiplex.[9] The strategic rationality that is at work in such exchanges plays with attributes and ties.[10] It intervenes in the process of resource allocation by using formal attributes in 'politicized' ways or by introducing other particularistic attributes and preoccupations (for example, gender or law school attended). The latter are more informal and *ad hoc*; they are not necessarily officially recognized by the firm as characteristics that should be used to promote cooperation and allocate resources.

In sum, a social niche offers its members resources at a low cost, a sense of identity and of common long-term interests, and the stimulation that is needed to work productively together. Its multiplex exchange system sustains cohesive and durable work relationships in contexts often dominated by flexibility and short-term calculations. It constitutes a bounded solidarity bloc. A collegial organization can be decomposed into small, flexible, homogeneous, and temporary task forces that must be able to cooperate quickly and efficiently, to react to complex non-standardizable problems. These work groups are nested within more stable niches, where members can barter for the resources they need. Such resources can also be found outside niches, but the likelihood of members reaching outside their immediate context for access to such resources is weak when the resources are available without this effort. Recall, however, that social niches can also become a difficult and very constraining environment, especially when peers lose control of the status competition process.

Analytically, detection of niches requires combining attributes and ties as in the empirical evidence (for the realism of this assumption) that is provided in Chapter 3. Attributes that become identity criteria (in multiplex exchange of production-related resources) can be formal and endogenous—that is, defined and recognized from within the organization as influencing the work process: this is the case for office membership, status (for example, partner or associate), and speciality (for example, corporate or litigation). Through such influences on choices of exchange partners, formal structures constrain actors' abilities to form exchange relationships, and therefore define the extent to which members can choose partners so as to 'optimize' their individual returns (Burt 1992; Flap and de Graaf 1989; Lin and Dumin 1986). Other attributes are informal, or more particularistic and exogenous: for instance, gender and school attended[11] may be used selectively by specific members to get access to resources, and consequently have an effect, at the collective level, on the circulation of such resources. This does not mean that members are necessarily moved to kinship by the simple knowledge of shared characteristics. Nevertheless, the stability that a niche offers in terms of access and exchange of resources comes from introducing time—that is, a long-term perspective—into the exchanges.

Finally, a useful distinction here is between the reason for the existence of social mechanisms and the triggers for such mechanisms. At every stage of collective action, the reason for their existence is the provision of solutions to organizational problems. But their triggers are investment in and of social relationships, establishing them or enriching them, or cutting them or making them poorer. As will be shown in this study, for generalized exchange, the trigger is the selection of exchange partners who contribute to niche building. For social control, it is the use of exchange partners for exercising one's share of individual and collective responsibility. For regulation, it is again the 'sacrifice' of some of one's ties in order to maintain a status quo or to promote regulatory change in the rules.

Relational investments and commitments are often made under specific conditions characterizing social exchange. They appear to be dyadic in nature (that is, to be 'gifts'), but they actually presuppose the existence of collectives in which dyads are embedded. Commitments and management of relationships have multilevel and politicized dimensions. They are made to individuals (exchange partners) in social niches because actors often try to shape as much as possible their opportunity structure. In effect, as shown by social scientists from Mauss (1923), Blau (1964), and Homans (1961) to Flap (1999), social investments—that is, investments of resources that are specific to particular relationship—require follow-up efforts by members of a society. They must try to prevent such investments from becoming sunk costs, from being lost to opportunistic behaviour. Reliability is often assumed to come from investing in relationships that are themselves embedded in a social niche in which multiplex relationship lower the prices of resources.

Actors as status competitors: Power among peers

As well as building niches, members need to manage exchanges that take place in them. The notion of *multidimensionality of status* helps to clarify how such management is carried out. Exchanges are always politicized, because members try to define the terms of those exchanges that are most favourable to them.[12] One way of influencing, and benefiting from, intra- and inter-niche exchanges is to accumulate a resource needed to work productively and thus achieve a form of status. This form of status is equivalent to a source of power among peers, because a member who controls access to large amounts of resources needed by others can also use such resource dependencies to impose favourable terms of exchange.

Among peers, brutal and public demonstrations of raw clout are rare. This is precisely what makes knowledge-intensive collegial organizations interesting from our perspective. By definition, power variance is usually lower than in more stand-ard bureaucratic organizations. This is not to say that inequalities do not exist. Even among equals, some are more equal than others. But collegial organizations need various types of resources to operate, including expertise, and distribution of such diverse resources is rarely as unequal among peers as it is between superiors and subordinates in hierarchies. Weaker peers often vote; they are rarely easy to fire or exclude. Therefore they have views that cannot be ignored altogether in deliber-ations about policies. Rather, peers learn to be more cautiously mild-mannered and Machiavellian, as will become more obvious in subsequent chapters.[13] Power is thus exercised through resource dependencies, coalition building, and various forms of status. A unidimensional definition of hierarchical power does not capture the different ways in which peers can be powerful and represent a form of authority, and the kind of coordination that they can achieve informally (Chazel 1983; Weber 1920). I therefore assume that the notion of status, because it is multidimensional, is central to the study of power among peers from a structural perspective.

This understanding of power among peers echoes the literature on the dynamics of personalization and depersonalization of power (Bourricaud 1964). Among peers, power has an element of 'now you see it, now you don't'; for example, responsibilities in a committee are diluted. Reaching decisions depends on proced-ural rules governing committee meetings, such as partnership meetings, and then enforced by individual members in their practice. This view, however, is too 'legalistic', or too 'formal'. After being depersonalized, power is repersonalized.[14] In effect, players usually want to understand the game played by others, and espe-cially by their representatives in decision-making committees. This repersonaliza-tion of power strengthens accountability of leaders, who are personally held responsible for their acts and asked to live up to their status. It also simplifies a complex situation in which 'important people' are identified as representatives of various interests (Berelson *et al.* 1954). Once 'important people' come to personalize it, power becomes more easily symbolized and localized. In partnerships, and more generally in collegial organizations, power is even personalized twice. In effect, partners' personal liability and damage potential are wider than in incorporated companies. Partners are personally accountable for the consequences of their acts before the whole partnership, because each partner is liable for the rest of his or her partners before the outside world. Individual partners' own actions and plans necessarily interfere with those of their colleagues, upon whom they have little power themselves.

Members can seek many forms of individual status, within and outside such niches, by accumulating different types of resources exchanged for working productively. This role of multidimensional status in mechanisms sustaining collegial organizations is complex. Before moving on to describing these mechanisms, it is useful to summarize in a focused way the sociological perspective on status understood from a structural perspective as the existence of various concentrations of resources helping members solve individual and collective problems.

In general sociological theory, status refers to a member's relative position in the group, both in the formal hierarchy and in the networks of exchanges in the group (Blau 1964; Homans 1961; Hughes 1945; Lenski 1954; Linton 1958; Merton 1957; Parson 1951). Members' status can be understood as a translation of their present and past contributions to the cooperative system of the group into a right to actively participate, and sometimes to lead. Members with status are members whose contributions to the life of the group more than balance their returns, even when the calculus of this balance is difficult. Sociological classics have long stressed the importance and the many dimensions of social status and social approval. Max Weber used to distinguish economic (based on revenue), social (honour, prestige, not only from birth, but from human capital (education)), and political dimensions, which can overlap in stable economic conditions. From a more endogenous perspective, status can be achieved in many ways—for example, based on strong competence, administrative responsibilities, popularity, or even endorsement by other members with status. As stressed by Parsons, then by Bourricaud, the functions of leadership are always exercised by several persons: 'the multiplicity of leaders and the collegial character of their power come from the role differentiation [in groups] and from the difficulty of combining under one head the plurality of roles' (Bourricaud 1961: 109). In Parsons's words, the role of the leader is 'diffuse', not specialized. Therefore, assessing who has status and power, or identifying a hierarchy of statuses in a group, is not an easy task.

In organizations, and particularly among professionals, status means that the individual is considered worthy of being granted an extensive mandate, regarding both personal responsibility and corporate responsibility to regulate community, professional, or internal firm affairs (Bosk 1979). This mandate is derived from—and made measurable by—the concentration of production-related resources, or by the privileges that are granted to members who control such resources. These may include financial compensation, decision-making priorities, more collegial and respectful treatment by peers, and symbolic and moral licensing, as well as escaping pressure for accountability, tests of commitment, and blame for many errors. In addition to making an individual less vulnerable to criticism from colleagues, and insulating him or her from cross-pressures, status has functional prerogatives, including more freedom to select interesting matters and cases on which to work, or the authority to decide how such cases will be handled and dividing the work among others. It is not surprising, therefore, that members of a group compete for status.

Members with status, as individuals, concentrate one or several types of resources; they are also granted a licence (Hughes 1958) to participate in the specific form of leadership that characterizes collegial organizations. Status becomes the capacity to gain favourable reactions from others for one's initiatives and decisions or to have access to an authority argument in deliberations. This licence can become a constraining mandate to participate actively in coordinating collective action: members with status also become the focus of other members' convergent expectations with regard to providing solutions to problems of such collective action. Members with status are under pressure to live up to their status, or they may lose some of it.[15] Such expectations play an important role in the structuring of collective action among peers. They have a strong normative dimension in dense networks from which, more generally, investments cannot be easily withdrawn. Collegial organizations tend to have less stable elites than bureaucracies. Although authority relationships among peers can be clear at times, it is difficult to locate power in them more permanently.

Analytically, each specific form of status can be measured by a corresponding form of centrality in a specific network of ties. As mentioned in the Introduction, in structural explanations in sociology, individuals are portrayed as being subject to particular sets of constraints and opportunities defined by their social context, such as specific social networks through which many resources can circulate (Nadel 1957; White *et al.* 1976). Centrality measures the concentration of a specific type of resource accumulated within niches and beyond niches, in the wider context of the organization. It can thus be used as a measure of status as 'expendable capital' (Blau 1964). Beyond a general understanding of status and status competition, this helps theorize collegial organizations from a broadly conceived structural perspective, using the notion of multidimensionality of status.

Multidimensionality of status, polycracy, and oligarchy

An illustration of multidimensionality of status in partnerships can be found in Nelson's study of corporate law partnerships (1988), which shows that, in spite of a set of rules that tries to smooth the hierarchical nature of their business, law partnerships are very much stratified organizations. Their authority system is based on a distinction between *finders*, *minders*, and *grinders*, a distinction that will be recurrent in this book. With a few exceptions, the finders, or 'rainmakers', are partners who find new and lucrative clients, and bear the greatest responsibility for them. They pass on clients and work for others to handle. Their governing authority is not as formal as that of their corporate analogues. Directives are reached by a form of gentleman's agreement. The minders are partners with managerial roles and responsibility for long-established clients. They typically sit on administrative committees, while still trying to stay professionally credible and billable.[16] The managerial role in medium-sized and large firms arises from the necessity of coordinating diverse practice areas, promoting an efficient organization of work, discussing strategies, and decentralizing control over a large professional staff, especially associates, working on highly specialized matters. In Maister's words (1993), they not only manage the practice, influencing the cost of the work, its quality, and the timeliness of its delivery; they also play a motivational role—for example, by providing clear goals, giving prompt feedback, involving others in decision making, seeking members' opinion, tolerating impatience, and keeping others aware of upcoming and challenging roles. The grinders are hard-working back-room lawyers, either partners who function as little more than salaried staff, or associates who are subject to the demands of partners and perform the actual legal work. Status comes from many sources: contributions to the firm, history of achievements (successful cases), establishing competence, credentials (Bosk 1979; Bourricaud 1961; Bucher 1970; Freidson 1975; Freidson and Rhea 1963).

Since all forms of status are theoretically open to many members of collegial organizations, it is often difficult, as already mentioned, to locate power clearly in them. For example, status derived from knowledge and experience is fragile; it may quickly become obsolete, so members need to keep up with ongoing changes in their discipline; failure to do so means loss of professional status to challengers. But, on the other hand, organizations such as partnerships, like any group based on strong consensus, are interested in the stability and cohesion of a coalition of leaders. An oligarchy is identifiable across the various types of status—including hierarchical status—of its members. The reason for this interest in a stable oligarchy is that going from division to unity with confused unstable coalitions is difficult, especially reaching a tacit solidarity combining diverging interests. An influential 'elite' of members with status is 'respected'[17] (as opposed to 'feared') if it does not fight, and even more if it plays down its status, or presents its agreements as renegotiable soon. For example, when a hierarchical superior is not the most competent and competes with the most competent for influence on the direction to be taken by collective action, they are both, as members of an influential 'elite', under strong pressure not to fight in a way that paralyses collective action.

Finally, since competition for resources and for leadership among peers takes many forms, since status has many dimensions, status in one dimension may be tightly or loosely connected with status in another. This raises issues of status consistency that will be shown to be important in collegial organizations, particularly in the regulatory, or 'constitutional' process. In government by committee, where norms and rules are being promulgated for regulation of exchanges, much of the deliberation combines different forms of status, different constituencies, and different values (such as excellence or loyalty). Analytically, in specific social settings, distribution of members across dimensions of status shows the extent to which, even in a democratic group, an oligarchy of members with consistent forms of status comes out of the requirements of collective action.

In sum, reaching and enforcing decisions, including a formal partnership agreement, are processes that depend heavily on several leaders and multidimensionality of status. Complex status games need to be disentangled in order to understand collegial organizations. But, looking directly at the functioning of coalitions of leaders may not always provide a clear picture of the ways in which collegial organizations operate. A broad structural approach to collegial organizations needs to take social niches and multidimensionality of status into account. In order to understand the role of niche seeking and status competition in such organizations, it is more useful to look first at how they matter in more task-oriented decision-making processes, in the enforcement of decisions made, and in the definition of values orienting decision making. This is why, in the rest of this chapter, I specify the social mechanisms that drive such collegial organizations, especially mechanisms involving exchanges of resources, control of commitment, and defence of precarious values.

The mechanisms providing solutions to problems of collective action among peers do presuppose an institutional context such as that described by Waters, but also processes of management of multiple resources, niche seeking/building, and status competition grounded in the production process itself as much as in open contests for firm leadership. Such processes matter for the cultivation and mitigation of status competition in knowledge-intensive task forces, the extraction of economic performance through relational constraints, quality control, the enforcement of previous agreements, firm integration through status differentiation and the establishment of a balance of powers, and finally the definition of professionalism.

COLLEGIAL ORGANIZATIONS AS PRODUCTION AND EXCHANGE SYSTEMS

Empirical evidence for the existence of social niches tests for the realism of such behavioural assumptions. But niche seeking is also conceived here as a component of a generic social mechanism that produces partial suspension of purely calculating behaviour—that is, bounded solidarity. A test for this efficiency of niches is the detection of the presence of such a solidarity among niche members—for example, through generalized exchange. Generalized exchange involves indirect reciprocity—which, in network analytical terms, can be identified through cycles of transfers of resources between at least three actors. Such cycles indicate the existence of this form of social discipline between niche members, which lowers the cost of access to resources and fosters the development of a 'rudimentary group structure' (Blau 1964). Chapter 3 also provides such a test by detecting a form of generalized exchange among strong co-workers in the case study. Members accept the need to cooperate with others without expecting immediate and direct reciprocity; they count on the fact that it will eventually come back to them indirectly. This establishes a minimal form of task-related solidarity that can be expected by a structural theory of collegial organizations.

However, bounded solidarity among interdependent entrepreneurs is fragile by definition, particularly because its positive effects must be protected from the negative effects of status competition. A structural approach, unlike that of Waters, can expect the organization's exchange system to provide this protection of bounded solidarity. To understand this positive effect of a generic social mechanism, it is useful to focus on the fact that collegial organizations are also deliberative bodies in their production processes. As already mentioned, they can be broken down into small, flexible, multifunctional, and sometimes multidisciplinary work groups (Eccles and Crane 1988) that react to complex non-standardized problems to produce quality knowledge-intensive service. In these flexible and multifunctional partner–associate task forces that process complex problems submitted by clients, work is very intense and interdependence among the members is strong for as long as the case is not closed. Then the task force is dissolved, and the members form different task forces with other colleagues to work on other cases.[18] Partners have to divide the work among the members of their task force and lead this work group through to the client's satisfaction. Activity is thus conducted in temporary work groups in which colleagues can—and often are expected to—share knowledge. In effect, partner–associate task forces constitute the core of temporary task forces that operate through brainstorming and 'status auctions' (Sutton and Hargadon 1996). Professional status competition is thus clearly encouraged among members, across rank differences (practitioner–apprentice, partner–associate), and within ranks.

Cultivating and mitigating status competition among peers

To account for the protection or reinforcement of bounded solidarity, it is useful to look at multiplexity in this exchange system. Since niches are multifunctional, a broadly conceived structural approach can expect multiplexity of ties in the exchange system to help prevent a breakdown of bounded solidarity when status competition gets out of hand. Multiplexity allows for a form of mitigation of status competition among colleagues, thus solving a 'too-many-chefs' problem.[19] The organization can be seen as a 'locally multiplex' or niche-level exchange system— that is, a pattern of ties among members that helps them exchange various resources directly and indirectly, and that allows circulation of production-related resources while mitigating status competition. In order to understand this multiplex exchange system as simply as possible in the context of this book, Chapter 5 illustrates this process by reducing it to the idealtypical interplay of three types of resources that members tend to find in their niche. The first type of resource is commitment to work, or goodwill related to cooperation. The second type of resource is advice.[20] The third type of resource is 'friendship', or role distance, a form of out-of-office socialization and personal support not related to the tasks themselves.

Based on this approach to the functioning of work groups in collegial organizations, the role of interdependence of relationships in the mitigation of status competition can be precisely identified. The logic of the blending of relationships in a multiplex exchange system can be illustrated by an idealtypical process. When deliberating about a case, practitioners and apprentices temporarily play a collegial and egalitarian game in which all arguments have equal weight. Brainstorming based on 'status auctions' puts participants under strong pressure to reach a consensus about a solution to the problem at hand. It is considered useful for finding creative solutions to complex professional problems, but it also creates difficulties that are specific to collegial organizations. In effect, at some point, there is a need for someone, usually the partner in charge, to step in and stop the deliberation.

Practitioners' status—based on greater experience, greater skill and judgement, higher seniority, or responsibility to the client—becomes a ground to justify stopping the exchanges of ideas, and making a decision about how the case will be handled and efforts allocated.

Knowledge-intensive work is thus inextricably mixed with status 'games'. Such status games are easily accepted as long as the group succeeds in finding a consensus on collectively designed solutions. However, stopping the deliberation *without* consensus, as is also often the case, is tricky. Members may withdraw and not be willing to participate fully again. The form of task-related commitment and solidarity established above may quickly disappear. Professional status competition can be stimulating, but can also lead to destructive gridlock.[21] Status conflicts (dissenting partners puffing themselves up) can in turn have negative effects on learning and the circulation of knowledge and experience. Of course, there are moral exhortations to create consensus or defer to the partner in charge, but these can remain artificial and rhetorical. Competition can easily get in the way of cooperation, and professionals know that they can lose control of this process. Status competition is thus a double-edged sword. It is encouraged, but it needs to be contained.

Understanding this process of mitigation is made possible by highlighting a specific form of multiplexity among peers—that is, the structural relationship between choices of three important sources of resources in a collegial organization. Two steps characterize (analytically speaking) the mitigation process. A first step witnesses members who work together turning for advice to someone usually within their niche. Configurations in which a co-worker tie and an advice tie appear together (called 'Blau ties' below) should be frequent: such configurations represent status competition and the first step of its mitigation by seeking advice from higher status partners. The system of interdependence of ties confirms the existence of a first step in the dynamics of mitigation of status competition.

A second step consists in ensuring that the status competition is not simply transferred higher up, thus creating a domino effect if members of the task force turn to several third parties for advice. The solution is either to bring in only one adviser or to turn to advisers who are themselves strongly connected and able to reach consensus or defer to each other more easily than the brainstorming work group itself. Configurations in which an advice tie and a friendship tie appear together should also be frequent: they represent the use of friendship ties to prevent status competition from continuing among advisers. Note that, in this idealtypical process, work and friendship ties are not combined directly. A specific kind of multiplexity should thus help partners control status competition by facilitating the combined circulation of blended resources. Just as power is depersonalized and then repersonalized in collegial organizations (Bourricaud 1964), local exchanges of resources in task forces play a role in mitigating status competition because they are personalized in a very selective way.

Chapter 5 looks at how resources are blended and bartered in the case study to confirm the existence of this idealtypical process of protection of bounded solidarity from the potentially negative effects of status competition. This is done by stressing the positive effect of specific multiplex exchanges (an analysis of the interlocking of the three production-related relationships) for solving the 'too-many-chefs' problem arising especially from brainstorming. This shows the value of looking at any collegial organization as a multiplex exchange system among interdependent members. Resources transferred and/or exchanged concern the production activity, both directly and indirectly although what brings the members together goes beyond just functional interdependence (Lindenberg 1997).

For a broadly conceived structural theory of collective action, it is important to pursue the demonstration of the benefits of this exchange system to the firm as a whole, particularly to its economic performance and its quality control. After they make a form of solidarity possible for individualistic entrepreneurs, social niches are useful to the organization by constraining members into increased performance and contribution; they also allow knowledge sharing and thus unobtrusive quality improvements that are often difficult to track in knowledge-intensive work. In many ways, such a system provides structural solutions to structural problems.

Relational constraint and economic performance

Indeed, collegial organizations also rely on niches to pressure members into being productive. A multilevel and multiplex exchange system, inside and outside niches, should be important to various forms of performance.[22] In effect, depending on rules for pooling and distributing resources, it is usually in partners' collective economic interest to produce as much as possible (thus pursuing their individual self-interest indirectly), but it can also be in their individual interest to let others do the work. For quasi-tenured partners, for example, there are often enormous incentives to free-ride. Getting associates to work well is also a problem: although they may be well paid, there is little chance for them to become partners. If partners can free-ride and associates threaten the quality of work, members' commitment to their labour contract (the partnership agreement for partners and the employment contract for associates) is difficult to sustain on a purely economic and legalistic basis.[23] Because, as Durkheim (1893) pointed out, a contract is always incomplete, members need the expectation that it will be fulfilled. In other words, the contract must be combined with social ties, such as strong collaboration, advice, and friendship, both at the dyadic level and at the structural level. To show that, in such a situation, an exchange system has an effect on his or her commitment, each member's combination of ties (with all the other members) and position in the firm's relational structure must be examined and related to his or her economic performance.

Niche-level relational pressure is one process by which this opportunistic behaviour is also mitigated. In effect, as already seen, niches provide members with work-related resources, a sense of identity and of their long-term interest, but there is also an element of self-entrapment in them. This brings us back to a classical idea that organizational efficiency depends on the quality and configuration of interpersonal relationships between members (see e.g. Lewin 1952). It is not only that people who have more relationships are more assimilated into the organization that makes them perform more on an economic basis. It is also that the structure of these relationships constrains them to do so. At the work-group level, pressure corresponds to high density and cohesion in strong work relationships. As already seen, the generalized exchange system supports cohesive work ties and maintains a specific form of solidarity. Chapter 4 shows that this system also constrains some of its members—those with specific relational patterns and work-group membership—into reaching higher economic performance. Analytically, this is measured using Burt's constraint scores (1992),[24] which are particularly sensitive to the fact that colleagues do not discipline each other equally strongly.

Status and quality control in knowledge-intensive organizations

Through status competition and its mitigation, the multiplex exchange system fulfils an additional function in collegial organizations—that of quality control. In such organizations, problems to be solved are often too complex for one person, and decisions to make too uncertain (Waters 1989). Usually, complexity has its source in the necessity of a division of work (Durkheim 1893). But collegial organizations have added problems of complexity to solve in order to satisfy their clients. What is highly interesting in these organizations is the institutional production of certainty and simplicity. This is why these organizations are particularly common in professional work, where the core task of the worker is to achieve this certainty in a practical way (Dingwall 1976; Dingwall and Fenn 1987). There are many reasons—in any knowledge-intensive organization handling complex and non-routine problems, relying on innovation, and operating in a competitive environment—to try to enhance the quality of work. Knowledge-based services are evaluated by their level of quality, which is also difficult to measure. Maintaining such a level is thus a problem for such firms. There is something about certainty-work that makes it difficult to pin down into an organization, although it may depend upon organizational resources for its accomplishment.[25] Formal ex-post methods, such as official peer-review committees, are considered costly, difficult to implement, often inefficient, and too strongly politicized. A structural approach argues that the firm relies on its exchange system to provide an informal, structural, and preventive solution to this problem of quality control.

Collegial organizations count on a more proactive form of quality control—for example, the fact that its members seek each other's second opinions and share their experiences before they make decisions or send opinions out to clients. In the status competition process, members observe and evaluate (mostly informally) each other's production: they praise big successes, and indirectly sanction (that is, criticize and gossip about) blunders and mistakes (Bosk 1979; Wittek and Wielers 1998). When they seek third parties for advice during the mitigation process, they do so first within their own niche. Thus, collegial organizations also rely on social niches to facilitate quality control when formal peer-review systems fail to produce results. Knowledge construction depends on these social relationships. Reasoning exclusively in terms of human capital, as economists and management theories have done for a long time, presupposes that, once in business, members freely share their knowledge and experience with one another. Rather, a structural theory views quality control as depending on status auctions and competition. It is in members' collective economic interest to share information and experience as much as possible, but it is also in their individual interest—given the status competition process—to do so while increasing as much as possible their individual credit by stressing the value of their own knowledge and experience. Therefore, the niche is certainly where status competition and knowledge management happen at the same time. But members also compete by expanding out of the local task force and niche boundaries to reach and use sources of advice with firm-wide status. This leads to the hypothesis of a very centralized and hierarchical pattern in advice networks, in which a few members are the key to quality control because they accumulate and distribute knowledge and experience in the firm.

These members are sought out for advice by their peers regardless of niche boundaries because they have professional status. The issue here is not so much who knows what, but who has the authority to know, and how is this authority negotiated, constructed, and maintained. In effect, advisers often do not have more technical information to solve a problem; rather they are in a position to take responsibility for decisions regarding quality. Attention to one aspect of a case rather than to another may be the object of a debate. Authority to know helps members impose a certain focus of attention during and after a deliberation. In the selection of relevant and appropriate information, actors need the authority to make an issue salient: peers with status can impose that. Knowledge cannot be shared without authority arguments allowing selected members to assert their authority to know.

Since members tend to work together in temporary task forces nested in more stable niches, it is likely that they will find advisers with this authority to know within this niche. But it is also likely that they will find them outside the niche, thus using resources provided by the firm as a whole (firm-wide status of specific partners) to manage local problems raised by the work process. It allows such members to impose their standards and criteria of quality[26] and to perform much of the firm's proactive quality control. Indeed, Chapter 4 provides evidence for the existence of this solution in the case study by showing that one of the informal rules related to the circulation of advice within the firm is the seniority rule: one does not seek advice from people 'below'. This concentration of the authority to know may be paradoxical in an organization where members are jealous of their formal professional discretion and individual authority to know. But this social process of capitalization and sharing of knowledge works only because it is informal.

A Montesquieu structure for firm integration

However, from the organization's perspective, the exchange system does not have only virtuous effects. One obvious problem facing collegial organizations that rely on such a system of niches is to ensure that the organization remains integrated in spite of many centrifugal forces. Niches are efficient at creating cohesion at the local level, just as interpersonal relations are the key to the functioning of combat units (Shils and Janowitz 1948). But, when multiplex exchanges and bounded solidarity come to be based on a sense of identity, niches may become firms within the firm. Well-knitted teams—that is, subsets of members who recurrently belong to the same task forces—become a threat to the organization because they can defect and take away with them valued members and clients. A structural theory of collective action among peers can use its assumption about status competition and the fact of multidimensionality of status to offer a theory of firm integration that keeps in check the damage that niches could do to overall firm integration.

Specifically, collegial organizations solve this problem by making it difficult for niche members to defect together. This can be achieved by allowing some niche members to reach firm-wide status through accumulation of one type of resource, and the establishment of a *balance of power* between these members with different forms of firm-wide status. The structural solution consists in systematizing the division of leadership work—that is, status inconsistency. Partners are encouraged to accumulate one type of resource, while prevented from accumulating resources providing other forms of status, particularly through a process of destabilization of task forces and circulation of associates (a resource particularly useful to potential defectors). In effect, encouraging specialization of status makes sense from the point of view of the collegial organization, particularly when it tries to undermine the dangerous ability of such niches to secede.

Following Kuty (1998), this balance of powers can be called a *Montesquieu equilibrium*. In this case, the formal structure of the firm actively establishes this informal balance. This contributes to creation or reproduction of invisible inequalities (an informal 'oligarchy') within the firm, while still maintaining integration by making one form of status dependent on the other. In effect, systematizing the division of leadership work, especially by shaping access to important sources of resources such as workforce or client relationships, establishes a relational structure that *counters patronage with 'welfare' solidarity*. This creates a form of informal political power sharing. Collegial organizations try to prevent some partners from becoming too important, particularly by destabilizing 'their' teams and circulating 'their' associates.

Chapter 6 deals with an example of such a Montesquieu structure in the case study. To survive in collegial organizations, interdependent members of a firm need access to resources such as work for clients, and goodwill from cooperative co-workers. In this context, solidary behaviour means that a member is prepared to help out another member, particularly within his or her social niche, who finds him or herself in a difficult situation with regard to such needs (Lindenberg 1997). For example, this includes changing one's priorities for a while because Alter faces an urgent deadline for a client. Or systematically selecting Alter (as opposed to others) as a co-worker on an interesting and visible case brought into the firm. Or exercising restraint by not trying to grab all the credit in a successful case conducted in conjunction with Alter.

The organization helps members get access to such resources and solidary behaviour. It conducts its affairs based on formal rules, which express choices among policy options, and allocate, directly and indirectly, these resources to members (Rowley and Rowley 1960). Authority to handle new files or clients (intake) or to allocate this new work among colleagues (assignment) is distributed more or less formally. For many members (partners and associates), access to work opportunities depends on these intake and assignment policies. A basic 'welfare system' is established—that is, a committee that allocates such resources across professional members of the firm and helps organize cooperation. In spite of their boring aspect, procedures of intake (mainly, whether or not to take in a case) and assignment (mainly, who will do the work) are thus good indicators of solidary behaviour.

In theory, members of a firm know about such formal arrangements and order their professional lives accordingly. But in reality many often behave differently. For reasons that will be described, they do not necessarily trust or count on the official welfare system to get cooperation from one another and to provide solidarity. They can have strong interests in not doing so. For instance, partners have strong incentives to keep control of the files for clients that they bring into the firm, and to use the best possible peers and associates to do the work. Associates are required to bill a minimum number of hours in the year, and have personal incentives to work with influential partners who will carry weight on the day of the decision about their promotion to partnership. Thus, files are not all allocated by the formal channels; members cooperate through other channels. Clientelistic ties and more selective solidarities can be established between, on the one hand, patrons with control of access to the market and, on the other hand, more dependent colleagues. The welfare system is thus intertwined with an informal patronage system. Members thus have a choice between getting access to cooperation through welfare or through patronage. Each can respond to his or her interests and solve his or her problems differently, although the clientelistic match-making process is not formally allowed.

Each type of solidarity is organized by partners with a different form of status. The first is organized by 'minders', the second by 'finders' or 'rainmakers' who establish clientelistic ties with 'grinders' (junior partners, sometimes called 'baby partners', or associates). A social process helps minders maintain firm integration when facing threats of defection by finders. In effect, this situation creates a threat to a firm's integration, because patronage tends to build up teams of specialized members that are in a position to defect. In such professional partnerships, the existence of patronage often represents a danger of disintegration for the firm. Clientelistic solidarity among partners or between partners and associates can create stable work groups that may leave, taking lucrative clients away with them. Thus, in such a situation, members' choice of either welfare or patronage to get cooperation raises a typical problem of collective action.

Actors' niche seeking logic in their choices of co-workers is then shown to have an effect on the coexistence of the two solidarity systems (welfare and patronage), because it creates a structure in which minders occupy a position that helps them prevent finders from mustering the specialized workforce necessary for easy defection. Niche seeking structures the organization in a way that is likely to help minders in their efforts to control finders and their threat of opportunistic behaviour. This structure is called a 'Montesquieu structure', precisely because it reflects the existence of a partial political order. Retrospectively, one of the goals of intake and assignments procedures appears to be to prevent the creation of 'ready-for-easy-defection' work groups within such niches. Thus, status competition at the individual level can have positive effects at the collective levels, particularly when it prevents firm disintegration by imposing a balance of power between two forms of status (or two kinds of oligarchs).

COLLEGIAL ORGANIZATIONS AS LATERAL CONTROL REGIMES

As already seen with the example of the constraining structure of a members' co-workers' network, one of the central problems of collegial organizations is dealing with behaviour perceived to be opportunistic. The issue of conformity is of particular importance in formally egalitarian bodies in which free-rider problems quickly arise. As mentioned in the Introduction, direct command or the use of administrative hierarchy are not considered appropriate means for exercising control, because professionals have many ways of neutralizing formal authority (Freidson 1975, 1986; Gouldner 1954). Therefore, a second-order free-rider problem arises as well—the problem of who will bear the costs of monitoring and enforcement among the formally equal members (Cartwright 1965; Hechter 1984; Heckathorn 1989, 1990; Kandel and Lazear 1992; Oliver 1980; Yamagishi 1986). Collegial organizations, even when they do not shy away from monitoring collective economic efficiency, need ways of controlling and pressuring members or task forces other than hierarchy. Unable to pull rank on peers, members of collegial organizations need decentralized controls. How do such controls operate and deal with the costs of control?

Here the existence of multiplex and personalized ties in social niches, as well as status competition, are again essential to providing an answer. Theories of collective action have already shown that conformity of members to the rules governing the management of common resources requires social control and informal conflict resolution mechanisms (Black 1984; Coleman 1990; Ellickson 1991; Fortado 1994; Hechter 1984, 1987; Heckathorn 1990; Lazega 1995b, 2000a; Lindenberg 1993; Morrill 1995; Ostrom 1990; Reynaud 1989; Taylor 1987; Wittek 1999). Compliance to the rules is contingent on the compliance by others, and therefore members spend time and energy monitoring each other. Infractors are likely to be allocated *graduated sanctions* by other members, by officials accountable to these members, or by both.[27] Such sanctions range from economic losses to social marginalization, then finally to expulsion.

However, beyond general understanding of early monitoring and sanctioning, the way in which a formally egalitarian organization gains 'quasi-voluntary compliance' (Levi 1988) with its rules and agreements must be explained by looking at how costly the graduated and unobtrusive ways (through which such pressures are exercised) are considered to be. Enforcement through negative sanctions can be costly for the sanctioner, particularly when control is mobilized for the protection of the common good in a formally egalitarian body. Attempting to put pressure on other members on behalf of the firm can be costly in relational terms: infractors may accumulate resentment, partners may blame the sanctioner—especially if he or she has personal ties to the deviant party—for failing to achieve results. The issue thus becomes: how then does the organization keep costs of enforcement low? As noted by Bourricaud (1961: 385), Reynaud (1989), and Ostrom (1990), sanctions are not usually automatic. They are not independent of the person who applies them, of the person to whom they are applied, and of the characteristics and relationships of both. Any process of early monitoring and sanctioning must therefore help select sanctioners and build access to infractors. In Chapter 7, I argue that informal processes contribute to maintaining low costs, in particular the politicized use of social resources or relationships between members, as well as a specific form of status called 'protector of the common good'. Practitioners are reluctant to invest systematically their own personal ties for the protection of the common good when the target is not part of their own social niche and relational capital. They also do not have enough such personal ties to cover the entire partnership. They are thus forced to make choices outside their niche and personal network—hence the pressure exercised on some members to become such protectors.

In effect, a structural approach asserts that, the more I need to control others whose job is important to me so that I can do my own job, and the more important are the relationships with these others, the more likely it is that I will have an informal and personalized way of monitoring and sanctioning them that signals that I am interested in these relationships. As part of what Freidson calls 'the rule of the collegium', members tend to avoid open face-to-face conflicts, as well as direct and coercive exercises of power. Therefore, graduated sanctions start with convergent expressions of normative expectations, unobtrusive and unsolicited advice and the spread of gossip. In Freidson and Rhea's words (1963), colleagues informally 'talk to' infractors in order to curb behaviour perceived to be unprofessional or opportunistic. In effect, social ties provide access to infractors and focus their attention, because they represent the existence of underlying resource dependencies. In Mintzberg's words (1979), there is 'mutual adjustment' among peers working in 'adhocracies'. Others refer to this process as gaining 'quasi-voluntary compliance' (Levi 1988), or as achieving autonomous regulation (Reynaud 1989), concertive control (Barker 1993), or compliant control (Heckathorn 1990). Colleagues show infractors that lack of conformity has been detected, must be discussed, and may involve external social costs, such as marginalization or stopping exchanges at various levels. Because interdependent partners need social resources to perform effectively, they are also more exposed to pressures from partners who control these resources. These processes do not necessarily guarantee by themselves that peers will be able to maintain an enduring institution, but a structural theory asserts that any complex system of rules needs them to survive over time.

Little is known about the selection of early sanctioners and monitors among peers—among whom applying rules is never unambiguous because monitors, infractors, and sanctioners are all formally equals. Many views of influence assume that it is based on solidary relations, such as friendship (Breiger 1990; Friedkin 1998; Granovetter 1985; Marsden and Friedkin 1993). It can be argued that such relations provide channels through which disputes can be mediated before they escalate (Lazega and Vari 1992; Morrill 1995).[28] In Chapter 7, I attempt to enhance understanding of quasi-voluntary compliance by highlighting the relationship between cost of control and choices of suitable sanctioners in the collegial organization. According to the structural approach, this selection and underlying expectations should be influenced by factors such as formal dimensions of structure, and by relative status of the protagonists of the control drama (interdependence and control over resources). It should be driven by the convergence of colleagues' expectations, which together exercise a constraint on levers to intervene.

Analytically, three-way data on the selection of sanctioners for a given infractor by each respondent are used to provide evidence, in the case study, of the existence of a social mechanism called 'lateral control regime', which uses members' interdependencies and ties to each other within such niches to put pressure on deviant partners. As mentioned in the Introduction, I use the word 'lateral' to express two facts: first, that this way of exercising informal control is based on the use of third parties as sanctioners—that is, envoys of the firm in charge of pressuring 'deviant' partners back to good conduct;[29] and, secondly, that these third parties are not hierarchical superiors, but peers who are all formally equals. Structural constraints have the effect of narrowing the choices made by partners when they exercise early monitoring and sanctioning more or less unobtrusively by selecting who is going to do the 'talking to'. Again, this mechanism also involves a small number of members with a specific form of firm-wide status, who are expected by their peers to exercise more lateral control than others, regardless of niche boundaries. The informal delegation of responsibility to a few 'multi-target levers', which is at the core of this lateral control regime among equals, tends to make sense from the perspective of individual partners' management of social resources. This control mechanism is thus both horizontally and vertically informal.

In effect, sanctioning costs are lowered when sanctioners are chosen because they are structurally close to the infractor. I define this structural closeness, or proximity, in terms of geography (same office and market), in terms of knowledge background (common speciality), and in terms of social relationships (the existence of a tie between them or membership in the same cohesive subgroups). This proximity reduces the costs of control by spreading them among members of the same niche with easy access to each other. However, it also raises problems with regard to the effectiveness of such controls. If social ties are needed between the sanctioner and the infractor so that the former can access effectively the latter, the organization may not trust the sanctioner if he or she is *too* close to the infractor. Strong ties between the two could induce the sanctioners to reserve special treatment for close infractors, to cover up some of the infractors' behaviour, and to side with them against the collective interest of the firm (Katz 1977). I have argued that this problem is solved by shifting some of the costs to members with a specific form of good-citizen status within the firm. Such protectors of the common good are particularly trusted for these enforcement tasks because they have specific characteristics. These characteristics include, in particular, seniority and a formal responsibility in the firm (which increases their capacity to monitor the infractor but also helps them speak on behalf of the common good without raising additional controversies), and a form of business performance that is not threatening to the infractor—that is, that does not open confrontations that could be related (by the infractor) to individual interests of the sanctioner. These results are consistent with previous work on control processes.[30]

I also use the word regime to stress that selection of sanctioners (and the whole social mechanism) is politicized in a normative way. The type of relational influence examined here among peers is based on two dimensions of collective action: on the one hand, common interests and resource dependencies; on the other hand, normative prescriptions regarding, for example, avoidance of conflict escalation. In a collegial context, important sanctioners should also be less controversial than others: they should be able to speak on behalf of the firm without raising controversies, and without triggering additional conflicts, or being suspected of representing specific coalitions, or individually benefiting from exercising pressure. Influence stems from members' utilitarian logic—from their considerations of potential losses in social resources or costs incurred when exercising (or being subject to) early monitoring and sanctioning—but also from an informal consensus[31] that emerges from a trained capacity of all partners to choose lateral sanctioners. Members do use their relationships, or 'spend' their own relational capital for the purpose of enforcing collective decisions. However, they use it to protect their own relational capital. In order to make lateral control function beyond their social niche, they also build up collective and convergent expectations that designate, for the same purpose, a limited number of members with a protector-of-the-common-good status to enforce their previous agreements.

Such a social construction of the status of protectors is inseparable from normative considerations. Chapter 7 also describes the role and characteristics of these main sanctioners, the social 'territory' in which each of them is perceived to exercise control, and how they are expected to control each other and solve the issue of 'who will guard the guardians'. Especially in heterogeneous or polarized systems, part of their authority and capacity to inspire deference may be due to their assumed ability to use the good connections that they have on both sides. But they draw much of their authority from a normative consensus on their capacity to represent in a credible and uncontroversial way the interests of the firm as a whole. Again, this authority, or the right to speak on behalf of the common good, is supported either by their willingness to serve in administrative positions, or by their importance to firm revenues (but in an unthreatening way—that is, they are not locked in any constituency). They are prepared to act as universal sanctioners, not only because partners on whom they depend for all sorts of resources expect them to intervene—because there is a strong pressure on them to comply—but also because it is one possible way to compete for status. Living up to this specific form of status may not always be pleasant, but it has its own rewards including easy access to, or identification with, other oligarchs. Their firm-specific status is the cornerstone of a wider pattern, the lateral control regime, which helps maintain a cooperative institution.

In sum, when the total cost of control can constitute a severe constraint on any group's ability to attain solidarity and reproduce itself, knowledge of this lateral control regime helps to understand how members keep monitoring costs low, and therefore keep themselves motivated to carry on monitoring each other. The structural approach contributes to a theory of collective action among peers, particularly by identifying a pattern that is both structural and normative in peers' mutual monitoring of conformity to a set of their own rules.

COLLEGIAL ORGANIZATIONS AND THE REGULATORY MECHANISM

As emphasized above, solidarity and compliance require social norms. The status of protector has a built-in normative dimension. This points to the third generic mechanism for which a broadly conceived structural perspective needs to account: the redefinition of the rules of the game by the members. In addition to building niches as appropriate contexts for part of their exchanges, members compete for status and the power to define the terms of these exchanges. Here, my approach emphasizes the interpenetration of the interactional and cultural realms, of interdependencies and values, and contends that contracts and resource dependencies are not sufficient by themselves to maintain cohesion and solidarity in a social group. Members need to commit themselves to priorities in a system of norms and values that contribute to make these contracts meaningful and enforceable. This is particularly the case in organizations where members have regulatory interests and rights, and are confronted with issues that require principled and long-term choices between policy options.

More specifically, this relationship between interdependencies and values can be approached by questions such as how the resource dependencies among members of an organization—as an indication of power relationships among them—eventually affect the capacity of their social group to change its own rules, including important rules such as that related to the distribution of resources among themselves. The Parsonian approach (Parsons 1951) to culture is useful here to look at some aspects of the interplay between structure and norms, if only at the regulatory stage of this interplay. In effect, rules are expressed in policy options and they also represent underlying values. They can thus be considered to be cultural characteristics of the organization. This is consistent with traditional sociological thinking: a system of interpersonal relations and exchanges driving a system of production, on the one hand, and a system of norms, values, or symbols, on the other hand, are inseparable. Through the latter, individuals orient themselves reciprocally in a stable and consistent frame of anticipation (Bourricaud 1961: 77). Members try to promote their own personal interests in their exchanges. But they have to do this by defending values that help them redefine the terms of these exchanges. In turn, however, this assertion and defence of values is itself a structurally constrained process that maintains a form of regulatory stability in the organization.[32] Consequently, it often favours the status quo.

The negotiation of precarious values

Building on Weber's and on Merton's work (1957), Selznick (1957) combines structure and norms by using the notion of precarious values. As mentioned in the Introduction, a precarious value is one that is essential to the viability of the collectivity but in which most members may have no direct stake. It is always in danger of losing its flag carriers and representatives—that is, active support from organized interest groups and elites (at the societal level) that helps preserve it as a candidate for top priority on the list of all competing values. Values are preserved, within organizations, by subunits entrusted with that preservation. Client satisfaction, internal coordination, innovation and quality of professional knowledge, societal needs, and employee interests would not be defended if not represented by powerful subunits or members for which the values in question are paramount (Simpson 1971).[33]

Like any organization, collegial ones have many goals, and hence a chronic lack of normative integration. Members of an organization, especially a collegial one, do not have rigid overarching 'common values' (Crozier and Friedberg 1977). Normative integration, sociologists have long argued, is achieved by an ongoing debate over rules, norms, and values fuelled by incompatibility between different interests and different forms of status (Kellerhals *et al.* 1988). As shown by many authors (Dingwall 1999; Freidson 1999; Hazard 1980; Hughes 1958), professional rules and values, in addition to the law, are the key to the structuring of collective action among professional colleagues. Actors, if they want to win, sometimes have to redefine their priorities in terms of values (Friedberg 1993). For example, partners feel free to develop and change their own conception of professionalism. They calculate their interests, but they also 'negotiate' their values (Kuty 1998). They fuel debates concerning professionalism, especially when members with superior economic power (for example, controlling access to large and lucrative clients) try to impose their own hierarchy of values, their own rules of the game, and their own terms for multiplex exchanges. For example, in decisions of recruitment through co-optation, peers often reach a conflict between loyalty (typically clientelistic criterion) and excellence (ideally bureaucratic and professional criterion).

In particular, a debate about norms is restarted when policies have to be adjusted. Managerial, professional, and entrepreneurial ideologies can conflict in the definition of organizational policies. The 'regulatory' debate among members focuses on the rules that they define for their collective action, the 'rules of the game' (Reynaud 1989). Negotiating precarious values is the ultimate way for members to politicize their exchanges and indirectly seek favourable terms for them. The context of this debate, the conditions under which it is pre-structured, is a basic micro-political issue that raises the question of participation in change.[34]

This points to a process of upstream pre-structuring of the negotiation of precarious values that is central to collective action among peers. In collegial organizations, a variety of subunits and constituencies try to exercise power and defend precarious values through conflicts with other subunits that support other values. Members with status who interpret the partnership agreement and 'read' its underlying norms belong to such subgroups representing a precarious value. Their status is a temporary claim to interpret or redefine a norm in an attempt to convince oneself and others to comply 'voluntarily' to the current rules of the game. They influence policy making and debates about professional behaviour more than other members. For example, administrators—or minders—can step in to arbitrate when conflicts threaten to get out of hand. But their hierarchical status can be challenged, especially on behalf of various conceptions of professionalism.

Note that, up to now, characteristics of the collegial organization were derived from the work process itself. It could be argued that the process of task-related mitigation of status competition works also for reaching regulatory decisions—that is, choices concerned with organizational policy making. But regulatory decisions involve formally all peers, and therefore it is important here to come back to the more commonly accepted context of government by committee (Waters 1989; Wheare 1955) in order to look at the main mechanism used by collegial organizations to manage potential tensions between different values and norms underlying policy options. Contrary to Waters's assessment, however, there are several essential features of debates on professionalism that differ from simple orientation to the best specialized knowledge. In particular, no member can have the last word, once and for all, in such formal discussions. Moreover, a single member can dramatize lack of consensus on various issues and prevent consensus building. A *modus vivendi* is, therefore, usually established among peers. In formal committees and deliberations, such as partnership meetings, debates would be endless if not structured by a mechanism that selects members who will carry more weight than others in regulatory work. A structural approach can help understand, in part, this *modus vivendi* and its construction. The latter is in fact an oligarchic process even in a one-person-one-vote organization (Dahl 1985). In effect, peers' participation in the regulatory debate is informally restricted. I argue that only multi-status members are in a position to help their peers in reaching a temporary form of consensus about priorities in such values.

Multi-status oligarchs and broken promises

Multidimensionality of status in the collegial organization is an important characteristic of the regulatory mechanism. In effect, it allows members with different forms of status to be part of the oligarchy. A first oligarchic process was identified above with the Montesquieu structure. It is a mechanism that requires a balance of powers between minders and finders. In such a mechanism, since no part of these elites can eliminate all its counterparts or opponents, rivalry leads to equilibrium and firm integration. The regulatory mechanism is different in nature: it requires not only a coexistence between members with status (oligarchs), but at least temporary consensus among them and a capacity to convince their peers to accept this consensus. Surprisingly though, studies of committee decision-making processes focusing on the role of multidimensionality of status are not very well developed. A broadly conceived structural approach provides specific insights into this social mechanism. It shows that members with different forms of status define the terms under which exchanges take place. They defend norms from which rules governing the organization are derived. However, this regulatory role of oligarchs can be real only if a social process helps them convince their peers, at least temporarily, about their selection of values to be considered a priority. This raises the question of the nature of this social mechanism.

As already noticed, in collegial organizations, problems to be solved are often too complex for one person, and decisions to be made too uncertain. Indeed certainty-work is a defining characteristic of knowledge-intensive organizations. This is why (even in bureaucracies) leaders can depend upon colleagues and subordinates with valuable expertise. However, complexity is also due to the fact that decision-makers are often 'representatives of representatives' (Bourricaud 1961: 414). As Crozier, and many others, have established, a decision is never simply reduced to a problem-solving technique. It is also a strategy involving various constituencies and compromises. In our politicized situation, organizational constituencies with different interests may conflict, and the reality of these conflicts leads to an enlargement of the circle of responsible leaders into a heterogeneous committee. Interests are defended through a discussion of precarious values by multi-status members—that is, members of an oligarchy of peers.

Therefore, constitutional deliberations take place under the following structural constraints. First, they require that members get involved in status competition and try to reach a form of personalized status that will allow them to speak legitimately on behalf of the firm before all its members. Indeed claims to leadership are based on both capitalized status and assertion of specific policy options (and derived exchange criteria). Without status, one is not much listened to by one's peers.[35] Without policy orientations, status as a concentration of resources is not a sufficient ground to claim leadership among peers: members making such claim need to get involved in consensus building. Secondly, they require members with status to discuss policy orientations and precarious values in a way that has its own logic. Efficient promotion of policy options depends on the shape of this oligarchy—that is, the type of heterogeneity of sources of status existing within the organization. This is where insights from a broadly conceived structural approach and an institutional (that is, normative) perspective need to be combined. They make it possible to understand the negotiation of precarious values and the redefinition of rules in this context.

This negotiation is a social mechanism that helps collegial organizations solve the problem of endless formal deliberation about values by using the multi-dimensionality of status ahead of the deliberations themselves. It consists in authorizing only members with multiple and inconsistent forms of status to intervene so as to prevent legitimate and competing values from being defended later in a forceful way by other members. This selection brings into the deliberation only those oligarchs who have accumulated several forms of status and who represent several precarious values, and are thus able to give priority to one of the latter without disqualifying the others. In other words, values that are not repre-sented by an oligarch accumulating at least two inconsistent forms of status still have the right to exist but are unlikely to become a priority. This selection pre-qualifies for regulatory deliberations only representatives of values ensuring an equilibrium of powers among oligarchs. Control of negotiation of values thus happens before the deliberations themselves. This social mechanism is thus based on a selection of bi- or multi-status oligarchs who play a leadership role by defining priorities.[36]

This is a very useful connection between structure and culture. In effect, any regulatory process is a form of change that involves broken promises and a redis-tribution of resources. In any changes of the rules of the game, some parties will come out as losing resources and others as winning resources compared to the distribution of these resources before the changes—that is, under previous rules (Reynaud and Reynaud 1996). This is why regulatory changes need the support of members with several forms of status—*multi-status oligarchs*. These oligarchs must have the capacity to promote regulatory changes and deal with the negative effects of broken promises. When differences in power are not huge among members, this capacity often rests on sacrifice of resources by such multi-status oligarchs, a form of investment at some risk that yields more power (Blau 1964). Rising above their own individual interests when favouring one policy option and siding with the 'losing' form of status is not a pure sacrifice that in itself would carry the day. As a matter of fact, in the long run, it is no sacrifice at all. But it can be perceived to be one in the short term, which helps multi-status oligarchs legitimize the changes and reach a position where they can ask for similar sacrifices from others as well. Those who can afford to sacrifice resources for consensus and for the common good while not losing power are partners who have several *inconsistent* forms of status. Thanks to this inconsistency, or loose coupling, losing one form of status does not entail losing another. The ongoing debate over values is both fuelled and made manageable by incompatibility between different forms of status. This high road, however, may not be efficient in itself, which is why multi-status oligarchs are also in a position to force these changes on their peers by using their control of resource dependencies. Both power and legitimacy go hand in hand in the management of social change.

Looking jointly at multi-status oligarchy and at forms of status inconsistency in the organization is a helpful way of extending our knowledge about the relationship between culture and structure. The relationships between the various dimensions of status are a key determinant of the ways in which regulatory debates take place, and consequently of the ways in which specific rules and underlying values become priorities for a given collective actor.[37] Chapter 8 provides exploratory analysis of inconsistent forms of status and their influence in the regulatory process in the case study. In this partnership, uni-status members (for example, a highly productive partner who champions one single value—that is, 'merit' in the distribution of compensation) are not much listened to by their peers in debates about policy. Bi- or multi-status members, who are central in several networks *and* highly productive, attract much more attention. They are in a position to arbitrate in the negotiation of precarious values, because they stand to lose something in any compromise reached by the collegium. Almost only oligarchs who are senior, productive, have a good reputation, and are in management can hope to muster enough credibility to impress their colleagues in the deliberation about precarious values. They can decrease the salience of a value that cannot create consensus without ignoring it entirely, thus defining what conformity to the rules and orthodoxy will be. Peers will converge towards positions defended by such oligarchs, whether or not the latter are conformists or anti-conformists relative to one of their forms of status.

The social mechanism authorizing specific forms of status inconsistency between multi-status oligarchs thus allows for a control of negotiation of values that happens before the deliberations themselves. In summary, the negotiation of precarious values, or the emergence of a priority value, requires a cohesive core of pluri-status oligarchs in a position to defend their rank with their peers, if not to prescribe these values to each other.[38] But one of the difficulties is that these multi-status oligarchs are not always clearly identified with such values. The debate about precarious values uses in a constraining way the heterogeneity of sources of status observed by the classics. Structure mediates between interests and values, because oligarchs can promote some norms while downplaying the importance of others. Thus, identifying this mechanism does not bring us back to narrow structuro-functionalism and its search for the universal key to the integration of eternally transcendent values. On the contrary, the relationship between the heterogeneity of sources of status (which guarantees a form of balance of powers) and the consistency of multiple forms of status (allowing for the creation, by oligarchs, of a hierarchy of values) remains a variable one. It depends on the kind of social discipline that exists among oligarchs. Thus a structural approach also helps in describing a social mechanism through which an oligarchy of members is able to define and maintain the rules of the game in collegial organizations. This structural mechanism keeps in check the discussion of values among peers by allowing some, and not others, to participate in a credible way in the debate on the appropriate policy choices of the moment.

The relationships between interests, values, and policies are not direct and straightforward. A social mechanism characterizing the regulatory deliberation among peers introduces complex status games that weigh on policy decisions. As a social mechanism, this form of regulatory deliberation invoking precarious values has a structural basis. It is particularly important in an organization with many goals and not much normative integration. In spite of strong pressure towards consensus in many types of collegial organizations, this political process maintains an underlying turbulence of critical debates. Recall that such debates are important to prevent standardization and bureaucratization of any firm.

A broadly conceived structural approach provides a theory of collective action among peers. This theory takes into account three generic social mechanisms that help to solve the most important problems facing collegial organizations. It uses behavioural assumptions about members' strategic rationality (their niche seeking and their involvement in competition for status) as driving forces for exchanges, controls, and regulation. These mechanisms have a strong informal dimension but nevertheless contribute to the governance of the organization. They provide structural solutions to problems familiar to interdependent entrepreneurs, such as how to cultivate and mitigate status competition; how to maintain performance, quality, and controls; and finally how to maintain organizational integration and help with the negotiation of precarious professional values. In sum, this theory explains the ways in which legally constraining economic contracts and informal social mechanisms are combined to sustain cooperation among rival partners.

The next chapters in this book present a case study, that of a traditional law partnership. This firm is of particular interest because it is built on durable relationships among partners, which make it easier to observe or reconstitute these paradigmatic mechanisms. The case both illustrates this theory and tests analytical approaches that are needed to replicate this work in other settings—whether in small partnerships, multinational professional services firms, or collegial pockets in flattening bureaucracies.

2

Spencer, Grace & Robbins

In this chapter, I present the firm that is used as a case study, a north-eastern US corporate law partnership, in which fieldwork, as presented in Appendix A, was conducted to examine the generic social mechanisms that help coordinate activities of interdependent entrepreneurs. In this firm, formal organizational structure such as the partnership agreement (according to which partners are personally liable for the actions of the others) and the committee system are not sufficient by themselves to account for collective action. Therefore the firm, a successful one in spite of economic difficulties in the north-east at the time of the research, offers a good setting for this examination.

CORPORATE LAW FIRMS: AN INSTITUTIONAL FORM

Much is known about the organizational form of US corporate law firms, their history, and the changes made during the twentieth century (see e.g. Flood 1987; Galanter and Palay 1991; Heinz and Laumann 1982; Laumann and Heinz 1977; Mann 1985; Nelson 1988; Smigel 1969; Starbuck 1992; Tolbert 1988; and many others). These firms provide minimal efficiency gains from sharing common production facilities. As indicated above by Waters's definition, their formal structure is based first on a distinction between administrative staff and professionals, and, secondly, on a distinction among the professionals, between the partners (the owners of the firm) and the associates (salaried and usually younger attorneys who are expected to bill around 1,800 to 2,000 hours of work per year). Partners are at the top of the hierarchy; the partnership as a whole makes most of the important decisions. They manage the firm through a management structure and a system of committees (which do not meet very often). This organizational form is perceived to create difficulties in mobilization and decision making. This is why firms have developed more centralized structures, both formally and informally, run by partners who are either elected officials or more central partners (such as rainmakers who control access to the largest clients). The hierarchical relationship between partners and associates is consistently very clear. Associates must work hard for partners but also exhibit some deference towards them, especially in public or in front of clients.

These firms justify high fees by presenting themselves as the elite of the legal profession, capable of quickly mobilizing large task forces of imaginative attorneys and of handling complex cases requiring sophisticated and constantly updated legal knowledge. To recruit the best possible associates (that is, those coming out of the most prestigious law schools), these firms must be able to give them a hope of becoming partners after six to ten years as associates. If after that period the associate is not co-opted as a partner, he or she must leave the firm. This is the *up-or-out* rule. The most important resource of a law firm is its human, relational, and social capital (experience, level of sophistication, reputation, good relations with clients and among partners, and existence of social mechanisms facilitating collective action). The traditional structure of these firms makes it possible to accumulate and share this capital (Gilson and Mnookin 1985). Law firms are organized around promotion to partnership as a means of protecting these forms of capital and as a means of controlling associates. In so far as their business depends on an unpredictable economy, and thus their growth on a mechanism with inherent risks, these firms cannot have a simple growth policy, if any.

Until the end of the 1980s, this up-or-out rule—along with a favourable economic and political context—pushed the firms towards a growth that maintained their short-term integration. It was easy to recruit associates and promise fast access to partnership. But this growth was also a threat for their long-term integration. In the 1990s most of these firms had to find new ways of controlling their growth and protecting their expertise. Integration through promotion to partnership was threatened by the limitations of the market, the size of these firms, and the competition among them. In reaction to this danger, they restructured and bureaucratized themselves much more. More rules were adopted, the number of committees decreased, firms departmentalized, and important administrative and commercial responsibilities were shared by a smaller number of partners. Criteria for sharing profits tended to diversify. Firms in which seniority had been the only criterion gave more weight to performance and pragmatic ways of measuring it (for example, number of hours billed, number of clients brought in, number of hours spent on administrative responsibilities). This bureaucratization also consisted in standardizing and routinizing as much as possible a maximum of tasks (for example, examining entire boxes of memos to determine whether or not the other side should have access to them, summarizing depositions, registering documents, and so on) and assigning them to paralegal employees.[1] It increased the administrative side of the firm and transferred more authority to professional managers. Many firms introduced formal peer and quality review processes for partners, in addition to accounting controls. In some firms, partners were forced to switch specialities and move into new and more lucrative areas of law. The creation of two-tiered partnerships with 'salaried partners' and 'permanent associates' was widely accepted. Lateral recruitments (buying out specialists from another firm) were considered profitable (that is, they meant less investment in associate training), but they also changed the relational fabric of the firm. Competition among partners and among associates became tougher and cooperation took new forms.

Such changes, often presented as reducing the costs of collective decision making, met with resistance, even though they were perceived to be a matter of survival. Bureaucratization has its limits. The changes nevertheless represented a threat to the way in which the legal profession conducted its business. With the relaxation of the up-or-out rule, human and social capital was also threatened. Fear of behaviour perceived to be 'opportunistic' (rejection of commingling clients, failure to share competencies, partners leaving the firm with important clients, and so on) and discourse on solidarity and loyalty were increasing. The problem of integration was thus well known to members and managed in a way that represented a threat to the organizational form. Even bureaucratized, such formal structures could not alone guarantee the integration of the firm. Owing to changes both internal and external, large law firms were looking for new organizational forms that were more attuned to their environment and that allowed them to control growth more easily. As many observers of the legal profession have shown, old world generalist partners were trying to become lawyers as businessmen and entrepreneurs.

WHAT DO CORPORATE LAWYERS DO?

Descriptions of interesting, sophisticated, and challenging work are a staple of corporate law firms' glossy recruiting devices. But detailed descriptions of knowledge-intensive tasks performed by corporate lawyers, provided by Nelson, Flood, Mann, and others, are very helpful for understanding how interdependent attorneys are in this production context. Lawyering is an industry of information management (Mann 1985). Lawyers' 'knowledge-intensive' work entails much interaction and talk about legal problems. 'The businessman may know to some degree what his problem is, but he will often lack the knowledge and expertise to solve it within a legal context' (Mann 1985: 388). Changes in contexts require redefinition of the problems in which the lawyer holds the balance of power and could strongly influence the client. Corporate attorneys are portrayed as 'highly sophisticated technicians who construct complex transactions so that every contingency is accounted for. It may be drafting a series of interlocking documents . . . or manipulating procedural matters so as to confound the opposition . . . (Mann 1985: 28) They have to 'receive constant flows of information in order to make judgments. This dependency on information streams forces the lawyer–client relationship out of the ideal-typical mold of lawyer controlling client into a relationship where routine matters have to be shared' (Mann 1985: 378–9). Even when they are not involved in 'frontier-type' projects (Maister 1993), lawyers deal with uncertainty and 'construct certainties' for clients (Abbott 1988; Dingwall and Lewis 1983). Flood (1987) has analysed how lawyers make decisions in that context and how these decisions are influenced by their interactions with one another in the firm as much as by their interactions with the clients and the opposition. 'Problem solving for lawyers is a constantly shifting activity, reactive more than proactive, subject to the unknown' (Flood 1987: 42). He refers to Schon's idea (1983) of 'knowing-in-action' instead of technical rationality, a kind of knowing that does not stem from prior intellectual operations, rules, or plans that we would entertain in the mind prior to action.

Lawyers essentially make forays in the dark; the application of legal knowledge (knowledge-in-books) is virtually ineffective in such situations. Only knowledge-in-action works to guide lawyers through the unknown territory of problems and contingency. It is the contingent nature of lawyers' work that is striking; a series of ad hoc steps in response to whatever action has been taken by the other side. (Flood 1987: 396)

Associates are sometimes more versed in the law than partners because they have to do the legal research, but they do not make the decisions concerning the clients. 'The practice of law is essentially based on experience as gained through a master-apprentice craft system where knowledge-in-books is only of peripheral use' (Flood 1987: 397).

Flood compiled an index of practical tasks from lawyers' diaries or time records where they record work schedules for billing purposes. Examples include compiling (documents), conference and teleconference (with lawyers, or other persons), drafting (agreements), meetings (depositions), office administration (billing), preparation (negotiations), research (cases), reviewing (draft contracts), revising (closing documents), sending out (plans, opinions), writing complex contracts, often in international business, large-scale negotiations or litigation (running large lawsuits over a period of years), and recruiting (interviewing).[2] These activities are carried out by talking both on the phone and face to face with lawyers and persons from outside the firm, and by writing. Partners' prerogative is the relationship with the clients (for instance, lunches); associates do more research and actual legal work.

Tasks carried out for clients are broken down into two broad categories: litigation and corporate (or transaction) work.

Corporate lawyers have a large range of tasks: putting together transactions, arranging loan agreements with banks, engaging in international business, incorporating companies, floating securities issues, negotiating the purchase of real estate, and so on. All these tasks can be boiled down to two: office lawyers, especially associates, essentially draft documents (for example, a letter of guarantee) and negotiate them.[3] Sometimes they advise their clients about issues outside their field (and sometimes competence), such as investment programmes (which is a broker's job) and may have to hide errors and gaps of knowledge. The collective memory of the firm is thus important in the process of document creation. For this type of work, lawyers engage in complex processes of practical reasoning (Garfinkel 1967: 11). 'The process of formulating a document recognizably acceptable to all the actors is an unfolding and contingent process' (Flood 1987: 271). Discussions are often about who will have the authority to make a decision on such issues. It is often a matter more of business than of law: lawyers as transaction costs engineers. Not much legal knowledge and expertise are involved in putting these transactions together. Of course, if needed, the lawyers could call upon the background knowledge of the firm, but they actually do not apply many legal principles in their work.

Litigation lawyers are ex-post, more combative fixers. They do manage documents, but their work tends to be less routine and sometimes very intense. Their activity includes discovery or fact investigation, legal research, settlement evaluation and negotiation, and trial presentation if the case does not settle. Theirs is not a smooth, muted, continuous activity, as most office lawyering tends to be. 'Litigation moves in fits and starts: a flurry of activity in writing and filing briefs, say, then nothing for months' (Flood 1987: 316). Litigators are specialists in procedure; form overrides substance. According to Mann (1985), their interesting moment is before the filing of the lawsuit, when they are relatively unconstrained. The pre-legal interplay of power and knowledge allows them to define the terms in which the conflict will play out. In large-scale litigation, work is conducted in task forces of partners and associates supported by an infrastructure that can become quite complex (satellite task forces working full time at the client's offices, and so on). Their task is often to make their client's statements look 'lawyerly'—that is, to exclude extraneous information and to make it more tightly argued. Litigators often consider that litigation is real lawyers' work, that this is where lawyers are really in charge, even with sophisticated clients, because this is where the real challenges and satisfactions come from.[4]

DIVISION OF WORK AND INTERDEPENDENCE

Interdependence among attorneys working together on a file may be strong for a few weeks and then weak for months. Partners' work consists, in addition, of several types of tasks associated, on the one hand, with establishing and maintaining a client base, and, on the other, with monitoring and/or running task forces of at least two attorneys to carry out legal work for the clients.[5] The more senior the lawyer becomes in the hierarchy of the firm, the more that lawyer's time is spent on direct interaction with the clients and less with law books (Mann 1985: 397–8). Especially for partners, 'in the practice of law, one finds very little law. Instead, one sees substantial amounts of face to face interaction or conversing on the telephone, but legal research and writing, as such, constitute a minor portion of lawyers' work' (Flood 1987: 67). In order to develop business, partners have networking strategies, including lunching with clients, meeting prospects or contacts who will provide access to new clients, switching from social talk to business talk, discussing business, asking for business. Established firms with a strong reputation find it easier to attract clients. One ideal situation is to grow with the clients, establish a paternalistic relationship with them ('protecting them'), anticipate their needs, and keep them happy. Partners become 'rainmakers' when they have many active corporate clients providing regular work, and when they can cross-sell services to these clients, which benefits other members of the firm. This brings in not only money, but also power to influence decisions within the firm, whether or not the partners sit on important committees. In order to monitor and/or run a task force to perform the actual work, partners design a strategy, divide the tasks among themselves and associates, manage costs, and motivate the members to get the work out. When associates are young, partners must supervise them to prevent gross and visible mistakes. Finally, partners have to deal with one another: running a client-oriented, knowledge-intensive organization means that partners try to protect the firm's human capital and social resources, such as its network of clients, through policies of commingling partners' assets (clients, experience, innovations) (Gilson and Mnookin 1985) and the maintenance of an ideology of collegiality. In that respect, informal networks of collaboration, advice, and 'friendship' (socializing outside) will be shown to be key to the integration of the firm.

Associates' work also consists of several types of tasks. Under the 'Cravath system', young associates watch their seniors analyse and break a large problem involving complicated facts down into its component parts. The associate is then given one of the small parts and thoroughly and exhaustively does the part assigned to him or her. An associate usually has to do the fact searching, prepare the questions for witnesses, write the brief, and so on. Associates can be more versed in the law than partners, especially because they have to do the research, but they are not the ones who make the decisions concerning the clients. When projects are staffed parsimoniously ('running a lean outfit'), associates are frequently overworked and can have a bad time coping with partners who can 'pull rank'. Competition between firms is so great that the training component (of associates) has fallen away and the extraction of profit has become paramount. Instead of observing how problems are broken down into their components, associates are frequently assigned a piece of a problem with no knowledge of how it fits into the general picture,[6] and required to specialize very quickly. They complain about not getting enough feedback on their work, not receiving sufficient training, being left to flounder, not being given complete instructions, and not having the means to reconstitute the overall scope of a case. Tensions between different departments (litigation, corporate, and so on) affect them profoundly; some are considered exciting, others dull. Departments are greedy for associates, especially in the most profitable fields. There are a few areas of potential task-related conflict between partners and associates, such as typing demands on secretaries (letters for partners, memoranda and briefs for associates writing to deadlines).

Given that lawyering has become an industry of information management (Mann 1985: 40), support staff's work is also of great importance. The practice of corporate law has become heavily routinized:

Documents are drafted from standard forms ever-present on the word processor. Although changes are made to fit the specific situation, no document is drafted from point zero. Much of the discovery process . . . entails examining boxes of intra-company memoranda to determine whether they should be seen by the other side, which requires no legal skills. Much of this kind of work is now performed by paralegals who are considerably cheaper than associates. (Flood 1987: 37–8)

The paralegals carry out routine matters, filing forms, checking court dockets, summarizing depositions, filing documents with various clerks in the city and county office. Support staff generally includes secretaries, paralegals, messengers, librarians, accountants, data processors, mailroom clerks, and telecommunications people. An office manager is in charge of these personnel. No real career opportunity and often high turnover can make a paralegal job a frustrating one; it is also easy to fob a paralegal off with an excuse. Particularly in this aspect of their work, lawyers emphasize efficiency, marketing, and profits.

SPENCER, GRACE & ROBBINS

SG&R is a north-eastern US firm that belongs to this context and has the characteristics of corporate law firms described by these organizational studies. In the 1960s and 1970s, the firm was a wealthy one.

> The firm was very well known among Wall Street law firms. If you needed a local counsel in our state for some particular reason—in those days there was a hell of a lot of antitrust litigation—we would probably be the firm that was hired first; they'd find us before they'd find the competition.... Some people, especially among the senior people, were, and still are, independently wealthy. Their parents owned manufacturing companies and we handled their business. Money was rather irrelevant to them. Their families had been important members of the community since the colonial days. That meant that they would urge associates to do as much public-interest community-oriented, charitable work as possible, the opposite of what other partners thought should be done.... I come from a family of lawyers. But even as a junior partner my wife and I couldn't believe the amount of money that we were making, even with the lockstep compensation system. And I was at the bottom of the ladder, god knows how much money the other guys were making.... At the time, to bill our services and decide what the dollar amount should be, there was a conference at the end of the case with all the lawyers who worked on it. Did we do a good job? Up. Did we do a poor job? Down. Can the client really afford to pay? Up. They cannot afford to pay? Down. Was it really hard work, a lot of weekends? Up. Not? Down. etc. This grand attitude towards work changed as a result of our recruiting practices. We hired people who came not from upper-middle-class families, but from working-class families. They were the brightest at law school. And so they come, and for a couple of years they work hard, and they see that they are doing well, and six years later they are made partners. They look around and they see that there are all the other guys with large houses in the country, horses, summer places in Maine, flying off to do salmon fishing in Iceland, or spending three weeks a year in the South of France. All that stuff. And they want it too. But they start off from a baseline of zero. They have nothing. This is why things changed and status competition became an issue much more. People began to pay attention to business and productivity, and became more competitive. (Former Partner No. 1)

Fieldwork was conducted between 1988 and 1991, a period ending in an economic downturn, later to be recognized as a recession. Although its market was not limited to this geographical area, SG&R was in strong competition with other law firms for the same clients, mainly large and medium-sized companies in the region. Practising law had become even more competitive when clients started routinely spreading their legal work among several firms. The region had an ageing industrial base, and demand for legal services was not increasing. Some specialities (bankruptcy, environment, corporate litigation) were growing fast, others (real estate, corporate) were declining. The large law firms of the 1980s are notorious for having taken advantage of the spread of mergers and acquisitions in the world of business. At the time of the study, SG&R was not seriously involved in this world of takeover wars and proxy fights.

At the time of the network study, in 1991, SG&R comprised seventy-one lawyers (thirty-six partners and thirty-five associates), in three offices (which will be identified as Office I (the largest), II, and III (the smallest)). It had doubled its size eight years earlier through the merger of Spencer Grace with Robbins. It was formally structured, based on the Cravath model, halfway between what Nelson (1988) describes as the 'traditional'—without formally defined departments—and the 'bureaucratic' types.[7] All the lawyers in the firm were interviewed.

SG&R was a general practice firm, a less than 20-million-dollar operation competing with many other firms, its size and larger, in the region. By 1991 northeastern standards, SG&R was no longer among the very richest law firms and its members were not the greediest in the profession. In this respect, it is interesting to listen to former partners who left the firm and to the reasons they provide. One example is provided by former Partner No. 1:

> My problem was I didn't care about the client. I mean I didn't care. I could have been just as well on the other side and gotten just as much out of it. I defended a lot of malpractice cases for hospitals and doctors and what I really believed was that the other side was right. We didn't do a lot of labour litigation, but when we did do that, I was in charge. So here I was, a leftie, and I am negotiating labour contracts on the management side. I was very uncomfortable. You put so much of yourself in it, and you care about it from a craft perspective. So I felt sometimes that I was on the wrong side, working for corporate America.... Plus my experience on the corporate side was disappointing. For the most part, what I did was represent start-up electronics companies. I cared about this, because the clients were my age, we used to party together, make trips together, get drunk together, and chase women together, that kind of thing. That was very exciting. But on the technical side, it was not very exciting. I didn't really understand the electronics business, so all the difficult decisions they would make. All I was doing was converting their decisions into standard contracts. That was boring. For those two reasons, I left. (See also the story of former Partner No. 2 in Chapter 7).

Nevertheless the firm put associates and partners under strong pressure to perform. Although not departmentalized, the firm broke down into the two general areas of practice described above: the litigation area (half the lawyers of the firm) and the corporate area (anything other than litigation, including tax, real estate, probate, and so on). SG&R partners and associates were graduates from both Ivy League and non-Ivy League law schools. Partner billing rates were pushed up to meet what the market would bear. Partners were proud of the fact that no partner had ever left to practise with another law firm. As in the other firms of the same size, first-year associates started with large salaries (compared to other entry-level professionals). There was a minimum of 1,800 billed hours a year required from associates. Time to partnership was increasing to an average of eight years, with the tendency being to extend this. It took longer and longer for associates and young partners to become independent profit centres. Like all the firms in its region, SG&R was still on the up-or-out system. The firm was all white. It included three women among the thirty-six partners, and fifteen women among the thirty-five associates.

The means by which economic prestige was derived in this firm, as in most firms, changed as careers moved on. In the early years, billable hours were prestige (since associates do not control the rate). The extent to which the fees were collected was an indicator that associate and junior partners were given good work. As attorneys grew in stature, they became more involved in non-chargeable marketing; their rates increased as their time sheets grew in non-billable hours (that is, their work was chargeable to a client code, but not billed to that client): senior partners gained economic prestige from bringing in clients and from organizing work without interference from anyone.

Although long-standing relationships with clients were increasingly a thing of the past, the roster of clients in 1991 included regional banks and branches of worldwide financial institutions and insurance companies, media and publishers, hospitals, utilities, transit authorities, local and state authorities, universities, telecommunications, firms in the paper and automobile industry, as well as multinational engineering, food, and distribution companies. Many of these companies had their own legal staff or departments, doing routine work that used to be farmed out to outside law firms. Therefore, SG&R thought of itself as doing non-routine sophisticated legal work. Like its competitors, the firm tried to capitalize on opportunities, but not with New York City aggressiveness. It was still learning to go after clients with new marketing tools, and new attitudes towards competition.[8] One practice could feed another with business. But seeking new specialities or recasting a practice area could create a very difficult problem. In this context, companies broke exclusive ties that they had with their law firm and shopped for lawyers on an *ad hoc* basis, while law firms competed for one-time jobs and still tried to retain their clients. Like many other firms, SG&R took retainers from corporate clients in exchange for being on call to represent them in case of legal trouble.

The firm was considered by its partners as 'democratic'. It was a relatively decentralized organization, which grew out of a merger, but without formal and acknowledged distinctions between profit centres. Sharing work and cross-selling among partners was done mostly on an informal basis. As will be detailed later, given the classical stratification of such firms, work was supposed to be channelled to associates through specific partners, but this rule was only partly respected. Partners' compensation was based exclusively on a seniority lockstep system, where the only variable was how long an individual had been a partner, without any direct link between contribution and returns. Partners could argue informally about what contribution might 'fairly' match benefits, but the seniority system mechanically distributed the benefits to each once a year.

The firm went to great lengths, when selecting associates to become partners, to take as few risks as possible to ensure that they would, in terms of business, 'pull their weight'. Great managerial resources were devoted to measurement of each partner's performance (time sheets, billing, collecting, expenses, and so on), and this information was available to the whole partnership. A weak performance could not be hidden for long, triggering concerns about relative standing. However, such firms usually made considerable profits, which helped partners overlook the fact that some voluntary contributions to shared benefits were not always consistent with the successful pursuit of collective interest. In extreme cases, partners had the power to 'punish' each other seriously by preventing a partner from reaching the next seniority level in the compensation system. As already mentioned, a partner could be expelled only if there was near unanimity against him or her. Buying out a partner was very difficult and costly. Therefore, despite the existence of direct financial controls, the firm did not have many formal ways of dealing with free-loading. The harm that a single partner could inflict on others might become very substantial in the long run. Conversely, partners could try to insulate one of their own informally by, at the very least, not referring clients, not 'lending' associates, and not providing information and advice.

Given the informality of the organization, a weak administration (run by a certified public accountant) provided information, but did not have many formal rules to enforce. The firm had an executive committee consisting of a managing partner and two deputy managing partners, who were elected each year, renewable once, among partners prepared to perform administrative tasks and temporarily transfer some of their clients to other partners. This structure was adopted during the 1980s for more efficient day-to-day management and decision making. The managing partner at the time of fieldwork was not a 'rainmaker' and did not concentrate strong powers in his hands. He was a day-to-day manager who made recommendations to functional standing and *ad hoc* committees (executive, finance, associate, marketing, recruitment, ethics, paralegals, and so on) and to the partnership.

On the one hand, this managing partner had a reputation for caution, for deferring decisions to consult with his partners, for trying to get to know all his partners and build consensus. Partners were formally equals; they did not take orders. On the other hand, some partners were more equal than others, and more influential in partnership meetings. If you wanted to secure a partnership for an associate, you made sure that these partners were on your side, although you never knew ahead of time how the partnership would vote. There were no real shot callers in this firm: ambiguity about firm leadership is constitutive of this type of organization.

This case is consistent with Nelson's observations (1988) of traditional law firms. In this context, power, whether formal or informal, has to take into account this dimension of equality and cannot assert itself systematically without relying on an ideology of collegiality. Partners who attract large clients or manage the firm wield more influence when important decisions are made. But formal egalitarianism among partners is maintained as a feature of their 'professionalism' (Waters 1989), and power retains a quality of 'now you see it, now you don't' (Nelson 1988).

SG&R IN ITS CONTEXT: THE MARKET FOR LEGAL SERVICES IN THE REGION

SG&R's market was not exclusively limited to the region, but it was not large enough to become truly multinational (to open branch offices abroad, for instance), although it got business from foreign and multinational companies. It had its established client base, but the situation was perceived as very competitive, especially since clients had started to spread work around systematically. Threat of market exit was strong enough (with less than ten similarly sized corporate law firms competing in the state), however, to strengthen the social mechanisms described in this book. Since the 1970s, market forces and built-in pressures had encouraged a very rapid growth. Although it did not have unlimited possibilities for diversification, the firm had followed the two traditional paths to growth: general service growth and growth by special representation, attempting to expand in a specialized field and then to consolidate the remainder of the client's legal business; but also capitalizing on specialities developed for regular clients by offering services in those specialities to other clients on a case-by-case basis. A shift to this second form of growth seemed to be dominant at the time of the study, with attempts to develop and promote interdisciplinary task forces that were expected to make the first form of growth possible again, bringing back a general service relationship with newly established clients. Such a strategy, however, was often limited by potential conflicts of interest with existing clients.

The nature of the work had also slowly changed. Legal professionals in the early 1990s were required to do a type of work that they were not doing in the 1980s. Especially in a period of recession, internal counsel had taken over more and more of the routine aspect of corporate legal work, and a growing proportion of corporate practice now involved either litigation, which often makes unpredictable and intensive time demands, or rapidly changing and complex technical areas, which require constant monitoring of new developments. Like all generalist law firms, SG&R was thus moving away from predictable, more readily scheduled work towards the more uncertain and unpredictable areas of practice.

The trend towards speciality representation was a general phenomenon that had transformed the client base of even the most established general service firms. The shift to special representation had profoundly affected the market for large law firm services. The amount and complexity of legal regulation and litigation maintained a generally high level of demand for legal services. However, economically, a rising aggregate demand for such services did not guarantee the economic success of individual firms. The shift in growth pattern to speciality firms and away from general service firms, and the attendant rise in competition between large firms and between internal counsel and firms had increased the level of economic uncertainty. Law firms found it increasingly more difficult than before to maintain traditional sources of work (big-ticket items). In-house counsels had become more aggressive shoppers for legal services, were more price sensitive (information about the cost of services was now been more actively monitored), and took their work to a greater number of firms.

Even if the business volume grows, growth rates do not necessarily increase.[9] SG&R and its competitors were not adding lawyers at the same rate as they had done in the 1980s. They did not readily disclose business setbacks, but neither did they expect to grow as quickly in the 1990s as they had done in the 1980s. As already mentioned, some areas of the market had been slowing down at the end of the 1980s (corporate, real estate), and other areas were busier (environmental, bankruptcy). Growing demand in those areas were at the partner level, which meant more lateral hires. The firms that I observed between 1988 and 1991 had not yet faced the acid test of seeing one area of practice dry up to the point that people were sitting in their offices with nothing to do. Like its competitors, SG&R cut back on new associate hiring, and had even fired a small group of associates six months before the study.

The shift towards special representation and the rise of internal counsel had led to the commercialization of the relationships between corporate clients and the large law firms, which stimulated firms' entrepreneurial behaviour. But the frame of mind remained different from that found among lawyers interviewed in New York City. The idea was that, for the time being, some specialities made more money than others, but nobody knew where the economy would go, so they remained general practice firms. 'We have lots of people doing lots of different things, we stick together as long as people do their hours and get their hourly rates' (the managing partner at the time of the study). Also, despite the fact that legal services were often consumed in conjunction with other services, SG&R had not adopted strategies of hiring non-lawyer professionals (in investment advice, accounting, consulting on business matters, and so on).

Some of the efficiency of the social mechanisms described in this study may be explained by the perception of a risk of bankruptcy. The processes described may have been significantly influenced by this economically pressured environment. They may have taken on some urgency and necessity—even limited—because the alternative was collective economic failure. This is partly where the energy comes from to kick these processes into action and to sustain them. SG&R was thus particularly well suited for observation of social mechanisms characterizing the collegial organizational form. In effect, among other characteristics, it was a private partnership, it allowed each partner one vote in important decisions, an equal share of firm profits (weighted by seniority) regardless of contribution, and it had expulsion rules that provided quasi-tenure to its partners, thus strongly emphasizing the necessity of trying to reach consensus among them. Partners thus locked themselves in a cooperative situation which helps identify basic mechanisms of this type of cooperation.

SG&R's PARTNERSHIP AGREEMENT

Production and collective action among attorneys were formally structured by a partnership agreement. As seen above, this agreement represents an attempt to bring an element of predictability to firm operations and to minimize room for disputes regarding issues such as firm management, compensation decisions, and withdrawal terms (Eickemeyer 1988). In the context described here, the processes of growth and specialization had only recently—that is, in the 1970s—introduced pressures for firms such as SG&R to put in writing the terms by which they governed their business affairs and organization.

The agreement defined each partner's rights and responsibilities in connection with these issues, and for the operation of the firm itself. It also tried to enhance the image of the partnership as a closed[10] professional community in which all partners have rights to participation. After describing SG&R's philosophy, I will come back to the limitations of such agreements. They establish collective responsibility but, alone, they cannot structure collective action. Members need to apply these rules in concrete situations. To make such a partnership agreement meaningful and enforceable, members also have to manage their interdependencies, commit themselves, and internalize social norms.

As the partnership agreement put it, each partner 'confirms, ratifies, and assumes all prior business, assets and liabilities' existing since SG&R was established, without limitation. All partners had equal access to the books, documents, and records of the partnership. Each partner had one vote on all matters submitted to the partnership meeting. Each of the partners of the partnership was bound to devote his full time and attention to, and use his best efforts in the furtherance of, the affairs and business of the partnership. Each partner had to obtain the prior approval of the managing partner before he undertook any activity that might conflict with his full-time commitment to his partnership duties, whether or not such activity involved payment or remuneration. Examples of such activity included service on a board of directors, service on municipal, state, or federal boards, committees, or associations, and teaching positions.

Agreements are usually comprehensive and difficult to modify.[11] They attempt to anticipate, and provide for, inevitable events such as partner retirement, disability, withdrawal, and death, as well as issues such as dissolution. Three main issues or sources of controversy are of particular interest here: the formal governance structure, the compensation system, and the admission to and expulsion from the partnership.

Formal governance structure

The agreement imposed a regulatory structure. The partnership, the committee of the whole, was the ultimate authority. It vested a managing partner with the responsibility and authority for overseeing the firm's day-to-day operations. SG&R grew by merger. A first change came with the merger, as it produced a large executive committee, whose members had ill-defined roles and authority, and whose governance was loose. A second change created a managing partner elected every year, renewable once, which in 1991 seemed to most partners to be a more workable governing structure in control of the everyday management of the firm. The managing partner could act as a policy-maker by making recommendations to the partnership, but the firm was not structured in a way that concentrated much power in his or her hands. There were committees for different functions and areas. As already mentioned, an administrator helped the managing partner manage the firm on a day-to-day basis. The bounds of authority of the managing partner were not very clearly defined.

The partners established policy and managed the affairs of the partnership through the vehicle of the partnership meeting. Unless the partnership agreement expressly required a specific percentage of the vote on a question, the decision of a majority of the partners in attendance at such a meeting at which a quorum was present was binding. A majority of all the partners constituted a quorum. Each partner had one vote. The partnership meeting could delegate responsibility for its duties to the various partners or groups of partners or to employees of the partnership. The partnership could also revoke the delegation of any responsibilities it had previously delegated.

The affairs of the firm were thus managed by a managing partner and the partnership meeting. Specific authority was reserved to the partnership meeting and all residual authority was vested in the managing partner. Those matters specifically reserved to the partnership meeting included the following.

1. The setting of numerical and geographical guidelines for associate hiring, the setting of associate salaries, and associate evaluations and terminations.
2. Choosing new members of the partnership.
3. Consideration and determination of major financial questions, including capital expenditures exceeding $100,000.
4. Non-economic policy questions regarding the production of quality legal work.
5. Any material change in the location and size of the firm's offices, in the number of lawyers assigned thereto, and in the business conducted by the firm.
6. Election and removal of a managing partner and assistants to the managing partner. The managing partner and the assistants were elected by secret ballot to one-year terms. They could not succeed themselves after serving two consecutive one-year terms. A vote of 75 per cent of the entire partnership could remove a managing partner or assistant from office before the end of his term.

Monthly partnership meetings conducted the business of the firm. The partnership meeting elected a managing partner from among the partners. Except for the matters mentioned above, all of the residual authority to manage the firm was granted to the managing partner, who also initiated action in areas reserved to the partnership meeting. Among the responsibilities of the managing partner was determination of which questions facing the firm came under the jurisdiction of the partnership meeting. The partnership meeting also elected two assistants to the managing partner from among the partners. The assistants were to be available to serve as contact persons with the other partners and employees and to act for the managing partner as directed by him in his absence.

A compensation committee, consisting of two partners—the most senior partner in each of the two largest offices—established each year a schedule for the distribution of cash and additions or adjustments to capital accounts. This committee had to adhere to the following principles in establishing shares of partners in cash distributions and capital accounts.

1. Each partner who had completed fourteen years of service as a partner of the partnership received a share of cash distributions equal to that of each such partner.
2. The capital account of each partner who had completed fourteen years of service as a partner was equal to the capital account of each active partner who had credited service of fourteen years or more as a partner.
3. From the first through to the fourteenth year, partners who had equal years of service as partners were assigned equal shares in cash distributions and the capital of the partnership.
4. During the first through to the fourteenth years of partnership, partners proceeded in equitable annual increments from the shares of a newly admitted partner to the shares of a fourteen-year partner. Partners with longer years of service as partners had larger shares of the cash and capital of the partnership than partners with lesser years of service as partners.

A recruiting committee appointed by the managing partner had as members at least one resident member from each of the firm's offices. The committee was responsible for hiring the firm's associate lawyers. It had authority, as assigned to it from time to time by the partnership meeting, to make decisions about, for example, the numbers and salaries of potential associate lawyers, and the nature and amount of legal experience desired of the potential associate lawyers to be hired. An ethics and conflicts of interest committee, appointed by the managing partner, ruled on such questions and reported its findings to the managing partner.

The managing partner might from time to time establish and appoint members to other committees of the partnership, such as a committee to evaluate and assign new matters, a committee to supervise associate workloads and training, a committee to supervise paralegal hiring, workloads, and training, a committee to evaluate and recommend various insurance coverages for the partnership, a committee to review needs for office space, a committee to supervise the operations of corporate and business matters, a committee to supervise litigation matters, and a committee to supervise probate, trust, and estate matters. These committees were supposed to report their doings to the managing partner.

> We have a governing structure with one managing partner and two assistant managing partners. The roles of the two assistant managing partners are not terribly well defined, and tend to be more whatever the managing partner wants to give them to do. In the role of managing partner, basically it's a question of what it is that they don't have authority to do as opposed to spelling out what they can do. There are some gray areas where I get to decide whether an issue falls in my jurisdiction or goes to the partnership. The primary things that clearly aren't my decisions are making partners, certainly terminating partners, termination of associates; actually associates' salaries, studying partnership compensation, these are things that aren't mine, although certainly in some of these areas, maybe almost all of them I have a fair amount of role to play. For

example, we have a compensation committee, composed of the two most senior partners in each office who have reached 65 [years old], Partners 1 and 5. This compensation committee has an extremely limited function, as we are on a pure lockstep system. They would meet to set the percentage of a new partner, or prevent—we call it 'whack down'—that of a partner who does not pull his weight from reaching the next level of compensation, which is an exceptional situation. Another example is associates' salaries, which really I can't set myself. I make recommendations and I think since I have been doing it there hasn't been any particular discussion about what I recommended. I have limited the spending to $100,000 for any one thing. If one spends more than that, one has to come to the firm for that. I can't close or open new offices. That's the range of the things that are not in my role specifically. But other than that I can do most things, which generally means the day-to-day operations, ultimately being responsible for the non-lawyer staff, hirings and firings and salaries, budgetary work, financial planning. We have a firm administrator who is actually a certified public accountant who has been with the firm for longer than I have. He is the chief non-lawyer administrator; he does a lot of financial work, but I ultimately work with him and set the budgets. In fact, partnership compensation is pretty much worked out with him, subject to approval by a compensation committee, and again a lot of the work that we do on that is the bulk of what is ultimately decided.... We have relatively little, if anything, in writing about committee duties. We have a number of committees that function in very specific areas, but they do not meet very often. I would guess every partner in the firm is at least on one of these committees, and they play an extremely important role. I guess I am ex officio a member of all these committees; I work with them, I understand what they are doing. But generally what these committees are would be the hiring committee responsible for hiring associates and the associate coordinating teams. There are two of those, one in the litigation area, one in the corporate area; that's one of our general breakdowns here. Those three partners play a role in associates' work assignments, associate reviews, and associate training; those are very important committees. We have an ethics and conflicts of interest committee, which never meets. It is more like two partners I draw upon when we have ethical issues, conflicts which are a little more confusing. We have two lawyers on the library committee, which works with the librarian for acquisitions the library should make. There is a space committee which tends to be an *ad hoc* committee depending upon space needs; we are adding some space in a couple of our offices, so several of those are relatively active. We have an insurance committee, which deals with the whole range of insurance, from malpractice to health insurance. We have a client development, new business committee, which has been relatively active since last year; in fact we are doing a fair amount in that area right now. Other than that we really have very little in the way of a committee structure. In particular, we have no executive committee. The assistant managing partners simply have whatever duties the managing partner wishes to assign to them. (The managing partner at the time of the study)

Thus, power was not spun out to a tight web of powerful committees with the managing partner in the middle. Apart from long-term decisions, what a managing partner might or might not do without going back to his or her partners was not very explicitly defined. This vague approach was considered to be more in tune with the style and preferences of SG&R partners. It had been adopted because it was expected to be the path of least resistance. The managing partner was prevented from concentrating too much power (which made informal social mechanisms even more indispensable). It was also sometimes disappointing to some, who would have liked to see a strong leader at the helm, speeding things up. In spite of its small size, the firm was too large to adapt its structure to the people who were available for fulfilling certain jobs. It therefore limited the number of management jobs. In some firms, the partnership does not create certain specific functions without knowing whether it entails light or heavy duties, and who commits him or herself to be in charge of it. But, at SG&R, discussion about the structure was separate from the question of whether or not there would be candidates for the job. The structure looked good on paper, but the turnover rule helped make it work.

The compensation system

Compensation determination was one of the most sensitive issues in this firm as in any other. As indicated above, the compensation system followed by SG&R's compensation committee established a system based exclusively on seniority, a lockstep system of plateaux, where partners reached the share of full partner after approximately fourteen years. A majority of partners wanted to hold onto this traditional system as long as possible, as it was associated with 'no bad feelings, no mean grasping behaviour, no political problems' (Partner 1), although it did not design ways of 'dealing with people who are clearly unproductive' (Partner 13). This compensation system did not reward successful business generation and rainmaking, billed hours, client servicing, firm administration, or unusual expertise brought to deals. There were no merit raises nor bonuses of any type.

For most partners, a seniority-based compensation enhanced cooperation and protected a cooperative environment. Introducing merit criteria or a bonus system meant creating incentives for grabbing clients or associates (compensation-bred competition among lawyers). Despite the fact that clients were unequivocally clients of the firm, practically speaking the partners knew that the major clients were used to dealing with certain people (their 'primary lawyers'). Some acknowledged that their minds could change about this system of compensation if a senior partner left the firm for another firm, taking away a major client (to the extent that it was actually feasible).

Partner 1 summarized the firm philosophy with regard to compensation:

> Our compensation system is something that we want to preserve because it eliminates a lot of back-stabbing. It makes it a much more relaxed, pleasant, uncompetitive place. People aren't looking over their shoulders or trying to justify their existence every day. The rather mean, personally grasping characteristics that you can get in a system that rewards individuals for how many clients they bring in or how much work they control or how many associates they keep busy, those are all things that can be unpleasant because it discourages people from sharing work easily with others. With our system, there is no hoarding of cases or associates. It takes out of that equation the selfish thing. It promotes cooperation. But you have got to be successful to be able to afford it. If you

are not successful, then people start looking around and saying, 'Hey, he is taking out more than I am and I'm working harder'.... Again, one of the factors is that our cooperation system is keyed towards everyone doing what he can for the firm as a whole, and shared equally. That is significant. Contributions are going to vary. Most of us are essentially self-driven, for me the stimulation coming from being in competition with the other side. I want to win. There is mutual respect for other people's ability to perform at the partnership level. Firm practice changes all the time, and you need people with sufficient flexibility and skills to move into new areas. That creates mutual respect. By and large, one major criterion for partnership is to be able to deal with diverse problems, and capacity to shift.

In this system, an age-graded pyramid easily shows that it was mostly the older lawyers who got a larger share of the profits. The client base changes only gradually, so more senior lawyers were still likely to have greater client responsibility (and therefore compensation) than younger lawyers. Each member's expectations were clear, although the system was periodically challenged. As will be shown in Chapter 8, a fault line existed between the values of the firm's older partners and those of the younger ones.

Partners had a capital account managed by the firm. A partner's capital account was defined to include his or her share of undistributed income left in the partnership over the period of time he or she was a partner; plus his or her share of unbilled time and accounts receivable, and of other assets and liabilities, as determined under the accrual method of accounting in conformity with generally accepted accounting principles. The amounts did not reach very high levels compared to other businesses, since a law firm is generally not a capital-intensive firm. Each year, the capital accounts for each partner were adjusted according to the partner's share of additions to the capital of the firm for that year. Newly admitted partners were not required to make a capital contribution at the time of admission. A partner who died, retired, withdrew, or was expelled was entitled to the amount that was in his capital account at the date of his death, retirement, withdrawal, or expulsion.

The amount in a partner's capital account represented his entire interest in the equity of the firm, and no additional payments were made to him based on the good will of the partnership or the value of any tangible or intangible asset or property interest of the firm, whether or not such asset or property interest was, under generally accepted accounting principles, contained on a balance sheet of the firm. In the event that additional capital was required, each partner made a contribution to the capital of the partnership in proportion to his or her share of the total capital of the firm.

This compensation system tended to be exceptional. In effect, many firms that, at the time of the study, were 'suffering' from decreasing growth rates made efforts to divest unproductive partners of their partnership interests, reinforcing distinctions between the strata of lawyers in the firm, with some partners forming an entrepreneurial elite controlling the greatest share of power and profits, and other partners assuming *de facto* status as salaried employees (Nelson 1988). This compensation system made defection an issue for very productive partners, such as Partner 15:

> With very little effort, I could transform Office III into a different law firm. It would be easy and in the short term financially advantageous. But I am not motivated to do that. (1) I come from Spencer Grace in Office I, I am rooted there, in terms of friendship, and it is against my nature to be disloyal. (2) The size of the overall entity, three cities, gives me access to clients and the type of work that I want, high profile. In the long range, it would be a mistake. Financially, status on the short term would be enhanced. . . . In the long range, I want to make this office bigger. Loyalty and business are equally important. I am asked to do important and interesting things because I am in a large firm. Fun and loyalty and interesting work are more important to me than more money. When I get referrals for national clients it is because I am in a prestigious firm capable of throwing ten litigators in a suit, and a general practice firm capable of representing large clients.[12]

For a sociologist, it makes sense to suppose that, in many ways, SG&R's system relies on specific forms of generalized exchange to protect overall prosperity against individual opportunism or parochial interests. I will look at this hypothesis, and at the extent to which it characterizes collegial organizations, in the next chapter. Saying that does not mean that partners were naive, or that they had affection for each other. They counted on forms of indirect and postponed reciprocity, but they also monitored the situation closely; they watched each other as much as their practice allowed it. There was something Rawlsian[13] in partners' rationale for equality, not only in that it controlled status competition, but also in that it was assumed to correspond to the facts in the long run (average contribution).

Admission to and expulsion from the partnership

As seen in Chapter 1, status differences between partners and associates are a characteristic of collegial organizations. The up-or-out rule is a mechanism central to many law firms and their efforts to protect their human and social capital. Valued associates must perceive a reasonable chance for advancement. In this firm, an affirmative vote of 80 per cent of all partners was required for this decision, with abstention considered to be a vote in favour of admission. A newly admitted partner participated in the profits and losses of the partnership, and assumed the liabilities of the firm jointly with the other partners. Young partners needed to prove themselves—that is, bring business to the firm and show that they could keep associates busy—sometimes by doing some of more senior partners' 'dirty work'.

In the presentation of the firm to prospective law students, and in partners' discourse about their firm, it was stressed that members cared about their personal and family life. This signalled that it was supposed to be accepted, in this firm, that members did not consider their relative status within the firm to be the most important thing in the world. This also signalled that they were prepared to moderate their competition for resources because their status comparisons were not exclusively local and limited to the firm. They had other reference groups in life. Partners' discourse was often moral about the fact that people's self-esteem should not depend very strongly on how large their incomes were in relation to those of other partners. Indeed, the partnership tried to make sure that such problems did not emerge (particularly with its informal rules presented below). But this discourse was also ambiguous: hard work was encouraged, and moral sanctions against concerns about relative position were legitimate only when protecting the compensation system, the relative equalization of income.

Along with admission to partnership, it is useful to mention issues of withdrawal, disability, termination, expulsion, and dissolution. There were procedural rules regulating the way in which partners were allowed to withdraw. Retirement was mandatory at age 70, and the partner was entitled to his or her share of the cash distributions and to the amount of his or her capital account. At 65, partners were supposed to start reducing their efforts, 'phasing themselves out', and their share in the partnership's cash distributions was reduced. The partnership could also look at these partners' past performance and reduce their share by up to 25 per cent of their prior year's share if it thought it was justified. Payments upon death, expulsion, retirement, and withdrawal were expensive for the firm. The partnership spread them over several years and, for example, restricted the annual amounts of such payments to a percentage of the firm's net distributable cash income. Withdrawing partners who left the firm to practise law elsewhere were forbidden from soliciting or attempting to establish an attorney–client relationship with any client of the firm during three months. Violation was sanctioned by a reduction in the amounts given back to the departing partner as part of reimbursement of his capital account.

A 'permissible period of disability' allowed a partner to receive his or her share of the partnership profits during twelve months. A partner was considered 'disabled' when he or she had failed or was failing or was unable to devote his or her ordinary and expected time to the partnership affairs because of a physical or mental condition. Whether or not a partner was to be considered 'disabled' was determined by an 80 per cent vote of all of the partners. Beyond twelve months, an 80 per cent vote could reduce such a disabled partner's share in the partnership's cash distribution or eliminate such shares entirely. A disabled partner could be forced to retire or withdraw from the partnership upon an 80 per cent vote of all of the partners.

A partner could be expelled only upon a vote of 90 per cent or more of all the partners. An abstention was recorded as a vote against expulsion. The partnership could be dissolved and terminated upon the affirmative vote of 80 per cent of the partners.

The rule is 90 per cent affirmative votes of all partners to expel a partner. Abstention counts against expulsion. We have expelled only two partners in twenty years. Both extremely serious situations. For one of them, there was a unanimous vote: this person went way around the bend with a number of things. The second guy didn't want to be part of us. A petition was circulated, saying 'I would vote to expel him.' He was presented with that and resigned. But expulsion is extremely hard to exercise. Three persons can block it. At least two of our partners are good examples of that. One of them is a decent guy on a personal level. He says that under pressure he does things; but he is a corporate lawyer, and there is no pressure on him usually, so he just doesn't do it. The other partner is in a different situation. He was at the low end [of the performance scale] for a long time. Partner 5 went to talk with him. He claims that there isn't anything to do. He says: 'I am a corporate lawyer, my kind of work has dried up, I am out there in the bushes, hustling, doing everything I can.' That is difficult to check. But there is also the fact that some of the people he has worked with do not want to do so again, because they think his competence is in doubt. Partner 17 is extremely good in his field. He once volunteered to go and see this partner to share some work with him. He went to see him, but he says this partner did a horrendously poor job. So with our 90 per cent rule, we don't cover for that. Apart from these examples, all the other partners do carry their weight. Of course, 'You're hot this year, you'll be down next year.' But there is no need for a compensation committee that would just do what it wants to do, with all the subjectivity involved. (The managing partner at the time of the study)

INFORMAL RULES

The above list of characteristics of formal structure (partnership rules) and core issues has to be extended with a set of informal rules adopted by the firm. These rules were not included in writing in the partnership agreement and were mainly designed to prevent conflicts among partners. These rules reflect the fact that, as in many other firms, partners at SG&R viewed their firm as an elite institution, with its 'uniqueness stories' and specific culture.

Partner 19 summarized these informal rules as follows:

1. We don't take an ownership interest in any client. If we are offered stock, we don't take it. Cash for services.
2. We don't invest in a building together. Purposely, the firm does not own the floors it occupies in the three cities. Owning your building complicates your life. It adds a level of complexity, and an element of greed: we make money in this building, let's buy another one. Lawyers often mix in other businesses because they have access to investment information. But we are not so superdriven by money. If you come to the firm and say: 'I don't want to represent this company because they are unethical, shady, someone who would complain about the bill all the time, become litigious,' the firm would agree.
3. Anti-nepotism rule: we don't hire anyone who is related to a partner. A son who is a lawyer doesn't work here. That's very important. Otherwise you get into very important problems. The same is true with a partner's wife [when she is an associate]. Can you imagine voting for partner when the person [coming up for partnership] is a partner's wife?
4. Everybody is expected to the best of his or her ability to be considerate and decent to anybody lower (associate or staff). You get yourself kicked out if you disobey. We had a partner kicked out for threatening associates with bad reviews if he didn't like their answers. That's a fast way to be fired as a partner.

5. No moonlight work. Most have high standards of integrity, they won't try to compensate themselves outside the firm. In other firms, people make side deals, mix roles, because they are both the lawyer and a colleague investor.
6. We don't borrow to pay partners. If there is no money at the end of the month, the partners don't get paid. Zero. It is healthy: you don't build up a huge debt.
7. You don't tolerate sexual advances to a secretary or a younger lawyer. That would be a major breach of propriety. You would be fired right away. Most partners have stable lives, happily married, very straight in that way, very moral.

Investing in a client, side deals, sexual advances, children in the firm, those are all forbidden, very explosive issues. Most firms don't forbid that. I know an accounting firm where they invest in real estate together, get paid in kind (a suit at the clothing firm), not in cash. They accumulated debt to pay partners. That firm blew apart. It is tempting to get stock from a client, to help them sometimes. But we don't. All these rules are useful to keep cohesiveness. There are one or two people who don't fit in that category. You can tolerate a few, not many. We are not very greedy. Not driven by maximizing income. If a firm is driven by profit to the point that it would start bending the rules, you start losing cohesiveness. Money is perceived as a measurement of your value. If somebody tinkers with the money formula, it is much more than the money itself. It is symbolic.

Together with the formal rules about firm operations, such as compensation and governance, this set of rules was a consistent system. It certainly defined restraints to several types of behaviour and exchanges between members. And yet, as often noted by specialists of professional services firms (Maister 1993) in many members' perception the firm was not very organized, and the informality of some of these rules expressed a form of resistance to bureaucratization that could be explained as an expression of traditional ideals of professional autonomy and participation:

I would define our culture as a 'passion for anarchy', that's one way of putting it. It is not organized, nothing is organized. I think the hallmark of the firm is non-organization. Not disorganization, but non-organization. Completely informal. There is an antipathy to organizing anything, to doing anything in an organized way. We will have to seriously organize ourselves eventually, but the fact that we have a managing partner, that's as far as we got so far in recognizing that.   (Partner 6)

Here, non-managers manage lawyers, the hierarchical system is not as important as most people think. It is tough to get someone's attention. What keeps the firm together is the managing partner and partnership meetings. Very little time is spent on managing. Nobody has been to a management, leadership, or group dynamics course. This is management by trial and error. Planning, training, personnel management, marketing: people don't spend time on this.   (Partner 3, a former CEO of a large company)

Apart from the fact that the partnership kept ultimate control over the most important decisions, the extent to which the firm should structure itself more formally was debated at the time of fieldwork. It could have reduced even further the number of standing committees performing or supervising essential functions. It could have departmentalized (what some partners called a form of 'regimentation') to detract from former informality, or have established a very clear and tight accountability structure, with powerful department chairs, stricter client intake and assignment procedures, and more controls over financial and human resources. The strength of the administrative side of the firm could have been enhanced too: the firm could have gone from a weak and specialized administrator to strong business managers reporting exclusively to a managing partner who would have delegated to them a great deal of authority and responsibilities. Chapter 8 derives value commitments by partners from policy choices on the agenda of the firm. It uses such choices to look at the regulatory mechanism from a structural perspective, one that goes beyond the simple description of the culture of the firm.

In the next sections of this chapter, I present additional and important organizational characteristics of SG&R. Their description provides the background of the social mechanisms identified in subsequent chapters.

THE EXAMPLE OF DEPARTMENTALIZATION

Among changes in governance structure, the *departmentalization* of the firm, for example, was seen by many partners as a critical step on this path to reorganization. It would introduce significant changes in the actual organization of work and it was debated in the firm. Creating formal departments and shifting several important functions to them focus members' accountability: someone is in charge and responsible for the productivity of every individual. Departments then become increasingly influential, even though they may not always make the biggest difference in terms of revenue; they play an important role in associate training, in partnership decisions, in improving profitability through control of intake and assignments (making better use of human capital), and supporting partners' marketing activities.

But in 1991, many other partners at SG&R already felt that the firm was too bureaucratized, burdened with too many rules and procedures. In addition, some areas of practice (such as the corporate practice) were more difficult to departmentalize; they needed more than the creation of an administrative umbrella. Since corporate practice comprises different areas supporting corporate clients (general corporate law, banking, securities, labour, and so on), it has required more distinctions between practice groups, and very flexible systems of collaboration and coordination. Others felt that departmentalization would be a positive step if department heads could restrict themselves to diffusing information, improving the efficient performance of routine tasks such as keeping controls in place or making sure that everyone filled in the forms for the associates' evaluation. Many worried about department heads losing sight of the interests of the firm as a whole, especially when trying to promote their own associates to partnership. A few voices argued that growth creates the need for more firm-wide conscious integration and coordination efforts between formal departments throughout the firm: there should be departments looked at as profit centres even if that created interdepartmental tensions; everyone's performance should be monitored and appraised more tightly; department heads should be able to force partners to bill on time and to speed up collection:

> What changes with the departments is accountability. You can't run a law firm like a club anymore. Or a nice place to hang your hat and to be convivial and collegial. We hope we are still collegial. We are. We hope we can continue that and still be businesslike. But it's a different world out there. There was a time when people came to SG&R because it was SG&R. Period. That's where you went to get good-quality legal work done and there wasn't a hell of a lot of competition. It's not true anymore. There are lots of terrific smaller firms, some bigger ones out there. If you don't pay attention to business . . . you have to be out there hustling and marketing—it's becoming more of a business, to the regret of a lot of people, but a lot of other people say it's about time, you know. It's a service business. (Partner 26)

But SG&R was not departmentalized at the time of the study. The firm met with resistance either when it considered dropping areas of practice for marketing purposes, or when it pushed some of its lawyers towards different practice areas.[14] Collective action thus was very loosely coordinated in terms of leadership and procedures to follow.

RELATIONS BETWEEN OFFICES IN A MULTI-CITY FIRM

There are at least two major differences between a single-office firm and a multi-city firm. First, it is more complex to hold together a firm with multiple locations. Secondly, the cost structure is much less efficient in a multi-office firm than in a single location firm, because of the need to duplicate many functions and positions in several offices (law library, rent, support staff). Growing to become multi-city creates a management challenge in itself (the duplication of everything, for instance), owing to the question of centralization: how far is it possible to centralize such a firm without controlling the market itself?

In some firms each office operates very independently. Offices basically have their policy-making and management structure; they simply refer work to each other, and share a central overhead such as the accounting system in one location, or computer services for the whole firm. Otherwise, they are really a group of independent offices. Other firms have a strong centralized management, and each office follows the rules coming from the main office. Offices are really branch offices: decision making is central and local offices implement it.

Like other firms, SG&R developed self-conscious strategies for growth in new specialities and through merger and branching, in order to diversify into new fields and new geographic markets. A good indicator of the rise in entrepreneurial activity has been the attempts to establish a presence in different markets, through opening branch offices in other large cities and mergers with smaller firms (Nelson 1988). This had serious consequences for the internal organization of both previous firms, forcing the firm to develop an efficient and flexible structure. SG&R grew through a merger between what was called Office I and Office II, and the firm as a whole was still one profit centre. Office III used to be a branch of Office I before the merger. Formally the firm was not highly centralized. Its partners liked to think of it as a firm without one single centre. But, informally, the situation was different. On the one hand, Office I was still twice as large as Office II. In addition, there was no speciality in Office II that was not replicated in Office I; but there were several disciplines in Office I that were not replicated in Office II. Therefore, Office I was much more central. On the other hand, some of the firm's biggest clients were in Office II; thus it did not make much sense to consider Office I as a real centre controlling the firm's business.

Especially after the merger, the relationships between offices were dominated by the feeling of one office versus the other.

In the beginning there was clearly an Office I mentality and an Office II mentality. They weren't different profit centres, but they would look, the figures were there, how much money did you make, what percentage of our total did you contribute, what percentage of your total did we contribute, and there was a sort of looking down upon one office as those people who are not as sophisticated, not as well trained, they are a smaller office. I don't sense that as much now as I did then because six years have passed and an increasing number of partners and associates have never known anything but this single firm, and because the small office is growing.　(Partner 6)

In this firm, one problem with being multi-city was that partners did not always get to know associates from other offices, which could count when partnership decisions were made. The fact that all the specialities were not represented in one single office created interdependence between offices. A partner from one office could use a senior associate from another office, because the senior associate might be the only person in the firm to know bankruptcy law well enough to work on a particular case. Nevertheless, partners from one office could have superficial opinions about the associates from another office if they had not used them for their own work. Another risk with being multi-city was the risk of polarization of the firm. There were always issues that could create tensions between offices, although for every issue of firm management there could be people on both sides of the issue in all three locations. Management issues might be determined geographically, and not by members' interests. Here is an example:

One issue which may polarize the firm could be whether we should stop our insurance defence work or not; it would have infinitely less effect on Office II lawyers, who do almost none of it, than it will on Office I lawyers, where a number of partners really don't have the confidence to go on to other things, or they haven't grown intellectually to go on to more complicated litigation, but who do this thing very well. It would have much greater effect upon Office I lawyers than Office II lawyers; but even there I don't think that the decision of whether to do more or not will be a Office II vs. Office I issue because there are a number of lawyers in Office I who feel that we shouldn't continue.　(Partner 6)

Efforts to interact on a more personal level with people from other offices were perceived to be effective by some, not by others (for lack of time or for any other reason).

Office II has a culture different from ours. People who work in our office have more sense of humour than in the other office [laughs]. We're more fun. There were economic advantages to the merger, but also drawbacks, although not dramatic: it is now a more impersonal firm. People don't know each other as well. There are newer people in the other office I am less comfortable with. Firm culture is not as well defined now as it was before the merger. But this is a small drawback to other advantages. It's work. Most people have too much to do until they do it. The impression is that this is one of the best places to work in. It's work, but once you accept that, it is hard for me to imagine a nicer place to work. We are all frustrated sometimes, but it is a cooperative place compared to what goes on elsewhere.   (Partner 22)

SG&R claimed that there was a balance between decentralization (independence) and centralization, and that loyalties were not divided between the firm and the geographical market of each office. The extent to which policy issues could really polarize the firm, transform offices into solid and opposed blocks, was difficult for members to measure. The firm did not acknowledge such difficulties. On the one hand, management issues could be considered as determined by interests, not by the site; an issue like 'what effect will certain pension plans have on younger partners who want to make money now, as opposed to older partners who would like to save it for their retirement', did not polarize the firm in terms of offices, because there were older partners and younger partners in both places.

The risks with being multi-city that were perceived and expressed in the interviews were of different types. First, when offices were of very different sizes, it introduced the risk that they be considered as satellites of the largest, not as parts of a whole. Secondly, financial controls were broken down by office: comparisons could be made, which might create tensions. In some firms, partners accept not having access to such data and leaving it to the discretion of the managing partner to decide when a situation becomes problematic or unprofitable to the point that it has to be brought to the attention of the partnership. Third, despite the fact that sophisticated communication systems made coordination easier, people who were not in the main or largest office could feel that they did not always know enough of what was going on at the centre. Management was sensitive to this and tried to organize institutional events to 'bring them in'. Assignments and practice groups helped in this, as did firm functions and partners' meetings. Most committees had representation from at least two of the offices. Fourthly, the evaluation of associates could be more problematic and had to be organized. Fifthly, the way members used one another could be linked to their specialities, but patterns of relationships and cooperation could develop between lawyers in the same place, thus creating social niches (see Chapter 3). Offices developed their own idiosyncratic rules, which threatened the integration of the firm. Here again, informal social mechanisms will be shown to help deal with this issue.

WORKFLOW: INTAKE AND ASSIGNMENTS

SG&R formal structure attempted to coordinate the work process. In its effort to organize its practice, the firm formally regulated intake (mainly, who decides whether or not to take in a case, based on what criteria) and assignment (mainly, who will do the work). There were many reasons for implementing an intake policy. The firm wanted to be sure that it was not using its resources on work that was either less interesting or less profitable than other work that it might be able to get. ('We are trying to bring in the most productive work possible and get rid of the work which is less profitable without penalizing the lawyers who happen to be doing it at the time' (Partner 22)). It was also preoccupied with situations that were not technical conflicts of interest, but were nevertheless undesirable in business terms (a 'political' conflict of interests). There were various reasons to implement assignment policies, such as increase the productivity of a firm by using people and human capital more efficiently, or establishing some fairness in the distribution of the workload. The latter was often expressed by members of the Assignment and Training Committee (ATC), called the 'schedulers' by some associates:

> I have to make sure that people are busy doing the right things, taking on the right case. When a matter comes in, that issue of who is going to be assigned the case is a very important issue for most law firms and certainly has been for us, and we've had an increasingly sophisticated process for doing that. Fifteen years ago it was absolutely accepted by every lawyer in the firm that, if a client called you up and said would you handle this case, you could handle it. It was yours. Nobody would ever challenge that. That is no longer true. Now, no matter who you are in the firm, if somebody calls you up and says will you handle this case, that lawyer does not have the authority to take the case on his own. He should run it through an intake procedure, which may be me, and I, along with the other section, or along with our managing partner, we may talk about whether or not the lawyer who originated that case ought to get to handle it. And in fact some of the biggest and really the only fights we ever really had have involved that issue where a very large case with a lot of publicity came into the office to a particular lawyer and we concluded that he shouldn't handle it. That he was not the best lawyer for the case. And we said it's going to another lawyer. And that lawyer didn't like it and he took it to the managing partner, and to the partnership meeting, and we had a lot of dis-cussion about it. And the decision we made stood. And we established a fairly important precedent that our intake system was going to decide who's going to get the case and who's going to do the work. Most of time it's not a problem. Most of the time the lawyer who originates the business is perfectly appropriate to do it. Sometimes also a lawyer will originate business, he'll get a call from someone, and he won't want to do it. Then in the process of intaking it through me he'll say to me can you find someone to do this? That's also something that I will do. I'll assign it to somebody.... My job is not so much a job of making sure that everybody's busy. It is really making sure that some people aren't too busy. And the problem is not finding enough work for people. The problem is making sure that some people don't have too much. And we often try to take work away from people. Say 'look, you got too much, take these files, give them to

so and so who doesn't have as much as you have to do right now.' We try and keep a fairly even workload, but it's very hard to do, frankly, because some people enjoy working 2,500 hours a year, other people don't like to work more than 1,800 hours a year.   (Partner 13)

In such firms, intake and assignment procedures are always somehow flexible (Maister 1993). Flexibility, at least in the implementation of one of the two steps, seems to be imperative, because workflow depends on the nature of the practice and on variable client relationships. In some areas, clients usually come directly to the lawyer. In others, lawyers may work on files because they were given these files when they were associates and they stayed on these files. SG&R was well established and corporate clients were passed down from partner to partner over the years. Clients came to partners through referrals from other lawyers in the community or through cross-selling by partners from another area of practice.

SG&R had an intake procedure. Its lawyers, like most lawyers working in large firms, thought of themselves as the ultimate professionals because they had to handle the most complex legal cases, as opposed, for instance, to inside counsels who dealt with more routine matters. This meant that it was selective in terms of choice of clients and, consequently, recruitment of new lawyers. I was not able to reconstitute a homogeneous representation of the 'good client', but three criteria were often mentioned: large and solvent corporations, absence of conflicts of interests with the largest corporate clients already represented, and the possibility of repeat business. In any case, new clients had to be cleared with the managing partner. But this requirement was not systematically respected. I even met a partner who did not know about it. Others acknowledged that they had problems saying 'no' to people. Clients whose work had been turned away might not call again. Partners just took in the work, knowing that some colleagues were cooperative and would help with the workload. Unless there was an obvious reason to think about a political conflict (a conflict of interest with another partner or a client represented by another partner), they just went ahead. Partners at SG&R had been talking for years about moving towards being more disciplined.

> On the corporate side of the practice each lawyer develops an expertise in two or three areas, and work is funnelled to them on an *ad hoc* basis; there is no formal channel or organized way of making these decisions. It is done very informally amongst partners: somebody would walk into my office and say 'Sam, are you busy?' and I would say yes or no. Work comes from partners in the same speciality or from other areas of practice. When you do corporate and commercial litigation, you service clients of the firm when corporate partners ask you to. That is not true for people who do insurance defence work (serious product liability cases, professional malpractice cases), where the lawyer is the contact person with the insurance company. The strength and the growth of the firm have been more heavily than in the past in the litigation side. There are good reasons for this. First, intake also depends on the sources of work, which vary a lot. Second, assignments also depend on clients' requirements, which also vary a lot.   (Partner 16)

Assignments were more formally organized for associates, through an associate committee (the ATC). This procedure was based on the traditional view about professional training: associates should be trained mostly on the job, informally, or by a 'mentor'.

> Associates get it by osmosis. For instance, they see how I deal with my clients because they sit in conferences with me, and I think they pick up from that the way I picked up when I was an associate, how you do it. A lot of it is judgement, a lot of it is instinct. Everything is really client specific, situation specific, facts specific. There are times when I want the associates to speak up because an associate may have a knowledge of an area of fact or an area of law that if he does not speak up the client would be misled in the course of the conversation. There are other times when the associate may legitimately feel that I am doing something that doesn't seem to make any sense. But I know why I do it this way. I know why I am holding back or coming forth with something. It is based upon my knowledge of the client and my knowledge of when to say things and when not to say things. The associate in that situation may very well be tempted to say something and he shouldn't say anything. Because he ought to sense, and I hope he does sense, that I am deliberately not saying what he thinks I should say, what I think I should say at this time, because the situation isn't ripe, and the ultimate goal would be better achieved if that came later, or came in a different setting, over dinner, in a one-on-one conversation. If for instance I am telling the client, an important person, that he's made a fool of himself, that he's made a stupid decision, that is not the sort of thing I would say in front of another person. I would say it tactfully, and I would say it in a such a way that no one else would hear me saying what might be embarrassing to him.   (Partner 6)

Following this philosophy of apprenticeship in the legal profession, partners analyse and break down a complex problem into several parts, and assign to each associate working with them and observing this exercise a small part of the tasks that they perform.

But often, assignment is actually done by the partners who brought in the client. In this multi-city firm, in particular, some partners were so used to assigning work themselves (without resorting to the ATC) that they often complained about the problems of identifying associates with the right expertise, and of putting together the right task force. Sources and types of assignments seemed to vary and to be differently distributed. Lawyers differed in the extent to which they spent time on assignments received directly from clients, on those received through a formal assignment system, and on 'spot assignments' (no continuing involvement in the matter). It varied with the field, with the amounts of work received through referrals in the community, or through cross-selling. More systematic research would have been necessary to establish how work was initiated, divided, performed, and reviewed. Access to that information, however, was not provided.

In sum, at SG&R, management had to be flexible with assignment as much as with intake. With regard to intake, new clients had to be cleared with the managing partner, but this requirement was not systematically respected. As for assignment, the staffing of cases was often done by the partners who brought in the client. But assignments were more formally organized for associates, through an associate committee. This was not surprising in a firm that was not departmentalized and where compensation was based on a strict lockstep seniority system. The firm counted on the cooperative spirit of its partners to smooth difficulties related to workflow.

ASSOCIATE TRAINING, WORKFLOW, AND CAREER

As Nelson (1988) summarizes it, at the base of the law firm's professional pyramid are the young partners and associates, or 'grinders'. They play an important economic role, and their recruitment and organization are a critical function in every large firm. In the long run, they are obviously indispensable for the reproduction of the organization. In the particular conditions of the economy at the beginning of the 1991, firms were anxious to hire the 'right people' who would adapt to the firm. Associates' income went up in the 1980s. Such financial incentives can be explained partly by competition between firms, but also by the heavy workload coupled to uncertainty as to whether associates would be made partners and offered an opportunity to pursue their career in the firm where they grew up as lawyers.

In the short term, attempts of SG&R to manage growth were immediately translated into decisions about associate recruitment. For instance, lateral hires made it even more difficult for associates who had come up through the ranks. Every associate was reviewed twice a year by the partnership for work performance and 'collegiality'. There was competition between associates, but, given the fact that the process was very long, they were not often visibly competing with each other; the partners played down the fact that the firm was a competitive environment. The firm denied having reached the point where making it to partnership did not depend exclusively on the quality of the work and the associate's relation to partners, but on economics. However, the criteria could vary with economic pressure experienced by the firm. In addition, apart from market pressures and built-in pressures to grow, leverage ratios (that is, number of associates per partner) depended on the nature of the practice and the area of law. Since anticipating demand has not always been easy, the criteria to decide whether or not an associate was satisfactory could change (loosen or become tougher) over time.

> We try to anticipate demand. We do not grow for the sake of growing and we certainly don't hire associates for the sake of maintaining any kind of arbitrary leverage ratio. We do not do that. That is very stupid to do that. You must grow so that you have enough people to get the work done for your clients. And it's a tricky thing, because you don't want surplus capacity. You don't want lawyers, whether they are young associates or older lawyers, sitting around with nothing to do. That's very expensive. Very, very expensive. On the other hand, you don't want to be in a position where you can't serve the clients properly because you have too few people. So it's always a guessing game. But we try to put ourselves in a position where we have just a bit too few. People wish

they had another couple of people. 'Gee, we've got too much work to do. If we only had another guy.' Don't get that guy. Just keep going that way. You'll be fine.   (Head of the hiring committee at the time of the study)

One criterion for associates who wanted to become partners was that they were expected by partners to prove themselves economically profitable to the firm. Starting associates in corporate law firms such as SG&R were paid large salaries compared to other young professionals coming out of graduate school. Partners routinely complained that the cost of practising law had increased (mainly because of associates' salaries and because new technology had made it a more capital-intensive business), and that the increase in billing rates for starting associates was lagging behind the rise in the salaries they were paid.

Hard work and the extent to which the fees were collected were indicators that an associate was given good work and that it was carried out well. A rule of thumb in the firm was that, after a few years, associates should gross three times what they earned as a salary. A figure that often comes up in the professional literature is that total cost of an associate is on average 1.3 times his or her direct salary. Data were not available to push the analysis much further. Hours worked minus hours billed is equal to non-billable time; it is equivalent to a capped service agreement, or to training time, but it is often read as an inefficiency index. Some partners considered this as a good but wasted hour resource. This difference was expected to be high for young associates and to go down with senior associates. There was no formal penalty for this difference in the firm, but associates knew that, if it did not go down, their chances of becoming partners decreased. Profitability of associates—that is, what they were paid minus what they earned—had to increase with time. Hours billed minus hours collected was also a dreaded index: associates knew that if it was high for someone on a whole year, he or she could be blamed for it.

I was not able to collect 'hard' data about the number of hours worked by each associate for each partner. But, as mentioned above, SG&R's accounting system prevented systematic fudging of associate figures by partners (that is, at the associates' expense—which would not prevent both from doing it jointly).

A look at the Martindale–Hubbell Directory shows that the firm recruited from a broad range of law schools, including the most prestigious. Career patterns were still modelled after the Cravath system, although the up-or-out rule was in fact being called into question. The firm experienced high levels of turnover by associates, and that turnover was increasing between 1988 and 1991.

Nelson's work (1988) shows that the major events in careers within law firms are linked to specialization, to large cases or transactions, to gains in client responsibility, and to phases of subspecialization or management responsibilities. Law schools tend to prepare generalist lawyers. Lawyers in traditional firms have less structured careers than those in more bureaucratic firms. As happened in many other firms, and sometimes without acknowledging its influence, SG&R management guided the distribution of workforce into needed areas. Careers were shaped in various ways to suit the needs of the firm. The organization used indirect pressures (shaping opportunities) instead of requiring lawyers to do what they were told to do. This is shown in Partner 29's presentation of the beginning of his career:

> Let's say you have the average typical associate; they will work for a while with a lot of different people, they will get training in our in-house seminars and little by little they are going to say 'Gee I like tax and securities, I find those areas particularly interesting,' and they will let that be known, and they will probably start getting more and more assignments if they are doing good work in those areas, and they will start building up their own expertise in those areas. As a result of that they will probably somewhat narrow the number of partners they work with, and it isn't unusual for you to get the mentor relationship coming out of that narrowing. I can think for example that there were two or three partners here when I was an associate who I worked a lot with, and one I think was very key in training me in securities law; another one was very key in training me in the utilities law area. It just turned out that I probably worked more with those two because I started doing more and more securities and utility work, I started getting known by those clients more, so I was gaining client acceptance, and you just start that sort of snowball downhill so that they start teaching you more, and relying on you more, because you are gaining that knowledge and experience that they find helpful.

As already mentioned, two firm-wide associate committees, one for litigation, the other for corporate lawyers, were supposed to assign work to associates, decide about priorities, and control their productivity. However, the span of control was too wide, and the members of the committees sensed that they were losing control over their people; there were too many associates to keep track of. In addition, to the extent that associates could be satisfied with their training and supervision, the firm was conscious that it was not doing as well as it would have liked to with training (it was not formal enough). Each associate had a 'mentor' who was supposed to read his or her work, but this was not always happening; the pressure of business prevented many attorneys from sitting down and chatting or socializing together, or partners from giving associates the whole picture of the case on which they were working together. There was a difficulty communicating with associates, since they were not always upfront in their criticism of the partnership. Associate review was done by the same committee that interviewed all the partners. In a multi-city firm, this could be problematic, and most partners had to rely on the report of this committee. There was a growing fear of back-stabbing when the firm got so big that associates had to be judged not only on the quality of their work, but also compared to other associates competing for a limited number of partnership slots.

Most associates were never certain that their loyalty would eventually be rewarded by partnership. For example, friends and contacts that young associates needed to nurture to show that they could bring in new business were often still in a position of being unable to afford the firm (present billing rates were too high for them). In the meantime, they worked long hours and were well paid. Judging by their strategic evaluation and attempts to work with important partners, they tried to create a good reputation for themselves while learning as much as they could from the partners they considered the best professionals (in terms of solving legal problems—that is, the content of the tasks—and in terms of the management of client relationships). In the absence of a career prospect within the firm, associates were told that they would receive the training and develop the skills and competencies that would help them manage their own career elsewhere. However, recall that training was often judged insufficient by both partners and associates. It depended on the pedagogical capacity of partners, but also on relationships with partners, which were not always direct. From a business perspective, after a few years, they could become potential competitors for partners, although usually not very threatening ones.

BUILT-IN PRESSURES TO GROW AND STRATEGIC PLANNING

The problem of growth is one of the main problems for medium-sized law firms (by 1991 standards). It is the question of controlling uncertainty and facing change in a market that may not carry a larger firm. The issue of how to deal with growth forces the lawyers to build an overall view of their business. Minders and practice leaders usually act as such 'guardians of the long-term' (Maister 1993). Attempts to control growth can take several forms. First, firms train and employ a growing core paralegal workforce, which is not on a partnership track, but whose work often does not differ much from that of an associate. Secondly, they try to predict, through strategic planning, the nature of demand in legal services. To the extent that demand is predictable, a firm will try to reshape the nature of the practice and, instead of hiring, request more flexibility from attorneys, sometimes forcing them to switch to more lucrative specialities. Assimilating laterals is often considered to be a profitable operation facilitating growth, an asset for generating new business. But some lawyers also consider lateral partners' loyalty to be mixed. Thirdly, some firms think of dropping hourly rates as a system of evaluation of work, to replace it with a different form of evaluation, identifying the value of what is done by the firm and charging for it regardless of how much time it takes to do it. Fourthly, another method is to impose more selective constraints on client intake, looking only for the most interesting and profitable business (in spite of the fact that lawyers do not like to turn work away). Finally, leverage is no longer the only key to success: firms usually want to concentrate on hiring and keeping 'really good people', including a growing proportion of lateral attorneys.

Firms also reach different degrees of sophistication in their strategic planning and self-restructuring, which often means more bureaucracy. To most lawyers, strategic planning means thinking about the future, essentially defining the size that the firm wants to be, and that the community will support. The traditional way of dealing with the risk of growth getting out of hand was always to be a little too small (to run a 'lean' operation) rather than too big. Additional elements such as associate turnover (lateral movement) also make it more difficult to make projections about growth. For SG&R in 1991, strategic planning was first a question of reshaping the nature of the practice—for instance, by designing new intake policies, or by dropping or developing some areas of law. The most urgent problem was to identify the practice areas that were solid and worth investing in for the future, the areas where the firm was strong for one reason or another.

No we don't have a policy concerning growth. Some of our partners have begun to say wait a minute, why are we just automatically hiring x new people next year, have we really analysed what we are doing, whether we need those people, whether we are doing things in an uneconomic or inefficient way that we require all these new people, whether there are areas of the law that we are practising that themselves are uneconomical. (Partner 6)

The answer to the question 'Do we know where we want to be?', I would say the answer is no, there is a great deal of discussion and debate about that right now, which came up in the last couple of weeks in the context of how many new associates are we looking for next fall, and that opens the question, some people say hey we are too big, we are bigger than we ever wanted to be when we joined the firm, others say you can't just stop growth, so I would say that at this point we don't know what we want to be, but that's one of the things we focus on right now I think, and I would guess next year we'll come to a better understanding and agreement. (Partner 20)

The firm did not have a growth policy *per se*, provided that such an expression has a realistic meaning. Members projected their needs for the next year and hired accordingly. Strategic planning was not used as a measure of performance and the firm did not have a sophisticated master plan over five years. Compared to the beginning of the 1980s, the percentage of lawyers hired had fallen in 1989 and 1990. The average time to partnership was eight years, and it was becoming longer. The up-or-out rule was still the general one, although some at the firm were considering the creation of different types of partnership (or permanent salaried positions). There was already one permanent associate.

But the choices that planners faced were ultimately choices that could be contested within the firm, and therefore they were in a way 'political', not purely technical. SG&R partners seemed divided between, on the one hand, a certain resistance to the pressure to grow, and, on the other hand, a more managerial approach to the control of growth and to reorganization.

Some thought that they did not particularly want the firm to get bigger; they felt that its size was very nice because it was big enough to do most things they wanted to, from the most complex litigation to the most complex corporate transaction (they could staff it). These lawyers favoured the traditional technique:

What you see happening now is each year the hiring committee will come to the partnership with projections of what they would recommend as the number of associates we would hire for our summer programme and as full time associates in the Fall. And those numbers are derived based upon the partnership's projections of future business, you are looking ahead a number of months so you can be right on target, you can be a little off on the high side or the low side, and you won't know that until you are there. And I think that we tend to take the long view on that. My own feeling is that in most instances in the past we probably underhired, in terms of finding yourself midway through the year and thinking 'Gee everybody is really very busy, you can't get the help you wish you could'. (Partner 29)

There was a kind of growth that they wanted to avoid:

Whether our growth will be because we reach a momentum where we keep growing whether we have to or not, it is hard to tell; in a sense work may very well expand to give work to the people who are there, it may be that a law firm will do things for a particular client that it needs not do in order to give that client quality service, just because it has the people there and has to keep them occupied. It may take ten depositions when only one would be necessary. Until ultimately there is the economic point where the client says 'Why are we doing this?' And of course you cannot say 'because we have a lot of people and we have to keep them working'. That's what you are trying to avoid. (Partner 6)

From the traditional attitude towards growth, the risk of stopping growth was also to face a change in relationships among professionals, particularly among associates.

So far we haven't had the bad fighting, the back-stabbing, the competition between associates for partnership. We never said 'OK we have five associates, only one of you is going to be a partner,' we have never done that. We argue about this in partners' meetings, we right now are going through the growing pains as to who we want to be. I think we are big right now, but do we want to continue to get bigger, do we want to hold the line, are we too big, is the client base enough to support where we are growing, is the community we are in big enough to support where we are at? I don't know, I came here in 1965, and I honestly say that we went from x lawyers to whatever we are today, without giving any serious thought to that growth, it just happened, and the work has been there. We have always said that the work would be there if you hire good people and if you do good work. (Partner 13)

A more entrepreneurial attitude was expressed by Partner 5:

The law firm industry is very crowded and very undifferentiated in the sense that everybody's got the same problems, and everybody's dealing with the same issues, and you come up against something and you think 'This is such a terrible problem' and then you realize that everybody's got exactly the same problem. Some people may not have dealt with it yet, some people may have already dealt with it, but everybody's going to deal with it sooner or later and nobody's got terribly innovative answers. I mean it's not like an industry where somebody is going to invent the electric light bulb or the new microchip or some other thing that's going to completely turn everything upside down and make one player in the industry the clear leader. Just you've got a lot of dogs chewing on the same bone or trying to chew on the same bone. And growth is one of those issues. The common wisdom used to be grow, grow, grow, you had to grow really fast, and leverage is the key to success, and the more associates per partner you had, that's the way you really run a profitable business. There has now been a backlash against that in the literature, I mean in the consultant literature and things like the *American Lawyer* and those rags that comment on the practice of law in large firms.

They are saying that it's crazy to have this kind of perpetual motion machine of growth completely divorced from demand and that if you run a factory, you don't say 'I've got a certain number of people on the assembly line and I've got to promote them this year, so I'm going to promote them and pay them more money even if the business isn't there.' You make adjustments depending upon what the demand for your product is. And law firms traditionally have not done that. If you had said two years ago 'What's your plan of growth?', we would have said 'We have no specific plan, but we really have to grow and more growth is better.' I think that we are starting to realize that that is not necessarily so, particularly when there has been this huge explosion of the number of lawyers and the size of law firms, and it is increasingly difficult to hire and keep good people. So we want to have a more flexible approach to all of those things. But will we be bigger? Yes. I think that we have to grow, but I also think that we are better off always being a little bit too small rather than being too big. And we think that we are not going to grow as quickly in the next ten years as we did in the last ten years. I'd much rather be in a position of saying 'Jesus, we just don't have enough people to get the work done' than 'Holy Christ, what are we going to do with all these mouths to feed?' It can really undermine your ethics if you have a lot of idle capacity, because it really puts you potentially at odds with the client. On some level, you always have a little voice saying to you, 'Well you know, you could justify doing this work for the client, and wouldn't it be nice because old Rob down the hall doesn't seem to be that busy right now.' (Partner 5)

ELUSIVE COMMITTEES AND SELECTED MEMBERS WITH STATUS

One of the consequences of the managerial changes in north-eastern law partnerships in the 1980s and 1990s was that they left many partners with the feeling of being shut out of the decision-making process, and with the feeling that relationships among themselves were changing too. This was particularly true when the reorganization of the firms included the creation of new and different partnership statuses. As Nelson (1988) and Maister (1993) summarize it, one pervasive phenomenon occurring in law firms is increasing stratification among lawyers. Whether recognized formally by changes in the partnership agreement or not, many firms consist of a dual partnership in which lawyers with substantial client responsibilities run the firm and take home a major portion of the profits while other lawyers function as little more than salaried staff.

At SG&R, which operated under a one-partner-one-vote rule, most partners did not feel left out of the decision-making process, even though the formal committee system was not very active. In effect, the partnership meeting, the committee of the whole, was well attended, remained sovereign, and ran the firm without much subcommittee work. Partners often felt too busy to carry out much of that kind of task. As in many professional services firms, they were timekeepers, and much of the time spent on subcommittee deliberation was often considered a waste, the typical 'postponable activity' (Maister 1993), a topic for jokes. Informal social mechanisms obviously supplemented this weak form of formal coordination.

It is nevertheless useful to identify the partners who were official members of these committees, while at the same time representing various forms of status in this collegial organization. In this section, I anticipate some of the later chapters by identifying such key partners, or oligarchs, who could be considered important to collective action in specific ways. This identification is based on ethnographic material, performance data, and the network study of the firm (which will be presented in the following chapters). I have narrowed the choice down to ten persons.

Partner 1 was an Office I litigator, the most senior partner in the firm, a member—with Partner 5, the most senior partner in Office II—of the compensation committee. He was considered to be a very strong personality, an authority figure, extremely focused on his professional work, and hard working. He was considered very important to the firm. 'All litigation people look up to Partner 1, who taught us everything we know' (Partner 13). Of Partner 26, people said that he was 'brought up in Partner 1's world'. One partner called him 'Partner 1 the Monarch', another 'Straight model citizen type, a model of rectitude'.[15] He ranked fourth on the performance scale in terms of dollars brought in in 1990.[16] He belonged to a category of partners who had high scores in all the key networks examined in the later chapters.

Partner 2 was an Office I corporate lawyer, a man from an 'established and intellectual family', as one of his partners called him. He was next in seniority to Partner 1. Considered 'a man of breadth, judgement, and compassion', with 'very decent, humane, sensitive instincts', he ranked first on the performance scale in terms of dollars brought in for 1990. When comparing him to Partner 1, Partner 26 said: 'If they both had a problem at the same time, I'd open the window and jump out of it!' Partner 2 was Partner 17's mentor. Given the stature of Partner 17, he was directly and indirectly one of the most respected partners in the firm, in the three offices. He was very much listened to at partnership meetings for policy orientation, and had a very high centrality score in the advice network, but not in the co-workers' or friendship networks.

Partner 4 was a corporate lawyer in Office I.[17] Some called him, when comparing him to Partner 1, the 'Secretary of State'. He was part of a closely knit group of corporate partners. Others referred to them as 'bright but groupy: they drink hard, they play hard, they work hard'. He was active on the marketing committee and ranked fourth in the seniority ladder and second on the performance scale (in terms of dollars brought in). He was very much listened to at partnership meetings for policy orientation, and had a very high centrality score in the co-workers' network, but not in the advice or friendship networks.

Partner 5 was the most senior litigator in Office II, a typical minder, a man with 'stature', an assistant to the managing partner and a member—with Partner 1— of the compensation committee. 'He is easy going and concerned about his co-workers. Most of us feel comfortable with him. He is very responsive' (Partner 18). He ranked seventh on the performance scale in terms of dollars brought in. He was listened to at partnership meetings for policy orientation, but did not have very high starlike centrality scores in the other networks, perhaps because there fewer members in Office II than in Office I.

Partner 6 was a widely recognized specialist in his domain, who sat on American Bar Association committees. He had the reputation of being a formal and outspoken partner who 'does not suffer fools lightly', 'a prima donna' who 'tends to be on his own more than the rest of us'. In spite of his professional status, some thought that he viewed Partner 1 'somewhat jealously professionally'. He had an average ranking on the performance scale in terms of dollars brought in. He was not much listened to at partnership meetings for policy orientation. He had a high centrality score in the advice network (coming mainly from associates), but not in the co-workers,' or friendship networks.

Partner 13 was a senior litigator in Office I. He was the typical minder who sat on the ATC. One of his partners said about him that he was 'a family man, a sensitive, insightful, compassionate, helping kind of person. He is the real Mr Nice Guy, a kind of a kinder gentler partner, he is notable for that.' 'He is a big cheerleader around here.' Associates considered him one of the easiest partners to talk to, but others saw him as the main 'scheduler' on the litigation side. In spite of record high centrality scores in the three key networks (co-workers', advice, and friendship), he was not much listened to at partnership meetings for policy orientation. He ranked fourteenth on the performance scale in terms of dollars brought in in 1990.

Partner 17 was a medium-seniority corporate partner in Office I. He was also a member of the ATC on the corporate side. He had an average ranking on the performance scale in terms of dollars brought in, but he was one of the most central persons of the firm, with an Ivy League background and a unique structural profile (see Chapters 3 and 8). Some compared him to Partner 1 without the seniority. Partner 2 had been his mentor when he was an associate. He was very much listened to at partnership meetings for policy orientation, and had a very high centrality score in the three key networks.

Partner 18 was a medium-seniority litigator in Office II, a typical finder who ranked third on the performance scale in terms of dollars brought in in 1990 (and first the next year). He was a former protégé of Partner 5, with an entrepreneurial outlook on the firm. He did not have high centrality scores in the firm's networks.

Partner 20 was the managing partner of the firm at the time of fieldwork, a medium-seniority litigator in Office I. He was the ultimate minder, considered to be a true consensus builder, who consults before he decides: 'He knows everybody, what everyone's problems are. He talks on a confidential basis with more people than anybody around.' He is 'a very good role model for the future managing partners'. He had high centrality scores in the advice network and was very much listened to at partnership meetings for policy orientation; but he did not have very high scores in the co-workers' and friendship networks.

Partner 26 was an assistant to the managing partner who also sat on the hiring committee. He had high centrality scores in the three key networks and was very much listened to at partnership meetings for policy orientation. His relational profile will be shown to be exceptionally complex and diversified. He ranked tenth on the performance scale in terms of dollars brought in.

This list is closed only artificially. Many partners were important in ways that are not accounted for here. For example, Partner 15 was a typical entrepreneur; he had left Office I to establish Office III with three associates in a different city. Partner 30, a young lateral partner from a large New York City firm, supported Partner 26 in his attempt to change the rules of the partnership. More can be found on several others in next chapter's section on niches and power. Each partner was a character in his or her own way. For the purpose of this book, however, it is not necessary to account for all this diversity.

SG&R's organizational form between bureaucracy and collegiality implemented the partnership contract. In this form, members ideally adopt rules consensually to coordinate their actions without coercion. Rules for conducting the firm's affairs are of course meant to enable members of the firm to devote most of their productive energy to practising law. The formal organization clearly has an effect on how members work. It attempts to allocate key resources such as cases and workforce according to rules specified above (intake and assignment). But committee work is often inefficient and endless, and rules still have to be contextualized, interpreted, applied, or enforced. In spite of the consensus needed for this type of organization to thrive, committees and rules are not efficient by themselves, in the sense that there is nothing automatic in their efficiency. Then what explains why members bow and comply? Organizational sociology has long shown that it is the concrete action system (Crozier and Friedberg 1977; Reynaud 1989; Sainsaulieu 1977), which does not correspond exactly with the formal structure designed by management rules, that makes collective action possible. No firm agreement can function without this system, the social mechanisms that characterize it, and the commitment of the members of the firm. A firm such as SG&R thus faced standard problems of collective action in the enforcement of its partnership agreement.

In this action system, bureaucratic rationalization is limited. Relationships and various forms of authority (status) are important to the efficiency of rules. As already stated, my goal is to show that three generic social mechanisms construct this commitment to living by this agreement and provide structural solutions to SG&R's problems of collective action among peers. The next chapter identifies the niches built by the members of the firm, the bounded solidarity that these niches represent, and the relationship between niches and forms of status in the firm.

3

Niches and Status in the Firm:
A Specific Exchange System

In this chapter, I am concerned with identifying the social niches and the forms of status that could be found in the firm; then with testing for the existence of the first mechanism that helped members manage their social resources in order to fulfil their commitment to a broadly understood labour contract—that is, generalized exchange within these niches and in the firm as a whole. I first identify the resources exchanged; I then use various statistical analyses to confirm the existence of niches, identify their characteristics, and check for the presence of cycles of indirect reciprocity characterizing generalized exchange among members, particularly in the network of exchanges of the first basic resource—that is, co-workers' goodwill.

LOOKING AT THE PRODUCTION STRUCTURE
AS A COMPLEX EXCHANGE SYSTEM

Following the description of this institutional form in the previous chapter (the Cravath system), it is also useful to summarize what we know about how SG&R actually operated on a day-to-day basis. The partnership agreement defined the partnership as a whole as the ultimate authority, but a managing partner operated without much committee work, and the boundary between what he decided and what went to the partnership as a whole was kept somewhat fuzzy. Regulatory participation of all partners made it difficult sometimes to reach consensus. Much of members' work was complex, non-standardized, and difficult to control by formal peer review committees. Client intake and work assignments were formally organized, but actual workflow often bent the rules. Compensation was based on a rigid lockstep seniority system, but some instability was created by actual (two partners out of thirty-four) and potential free-loading. Division of work was as sophisticated as in any other corporate law firm, but SG&R was not departmentalized. The firm was considered a single profit centre by its accounting system, but there was a risk of polarization between its two main offices about policy issues stressing some diverging interests. Associates' work was lucrative and important to the firm, but their career was still highly uncertain. In a competitive and downturn market, strategic planning did not help much with ensuring economic growth and in dealing with built-in pressures to grow in size.

The formal structure of this organization was therefore clearly unable to ensure, by itself, ongoing collective action among peers. It clearly relied on informal mechanisms for its operations and its reproduction. In order to explain the observed stability of the firm at the time, we need to uncover these mechanisms. I have argued that a structural approach helps in this task. In effect, in organized settings, partici-pation in collective action—that is, task-force production, regulatory activity, or enforcement of previous agreements—requires cooperation with others. This cooperation can be looked upon as routine transfers or exchanges by members of various kinds of resources (Bearman 1997; Bienenstock and Bonacich 1993, 1997; Blau 1964; Bonacich and Bienenstock 1997; Breiger and Ennis 1997; Cook 1987, 1990; Crozier and Friedberg 1977; Ekeh 1976; Flap *et al.* 1998; Galaskiewicz and Marsden 1978; Gouldner 1960; Han and Breiger 1999; Lévi-Strauss 1949; Lin 1982, 1995; Willer 1999): such resources include information, co-workers' goodwill, advice, friendship, emotional support, and many others. From a structural per-spective, this means that specific local and multiplex[1] substructures of social ties must crystallize for members to get access to such resources and to be able to cooperate on an ongoing basis.

Structural analysis of cooperation and management of various types of social resources enhances understanding of effective participation in collective action by highlighting the relationship between choices of important sources of resources in a specific type of organization. I look at how three important production-related resources (co-workers' goodwill—understood as strong commitment to collab-oration—advice, and friendship—understood as a form of role distance) were exchanged by members. Specifically, I analyse the interlocking of ties among members and define broader sets of expected interdependencies among transfers and exchanges that went beyond any transfer of a single resource. I argue that regularities in these substructures contributed to the creation of typical transfers and exchanges providing structural answers to the problem of members' participation in collective action.

To understand how these resources can be both an individual and a collective asset, it is useful to represent it as a multiplex and generalized exchange system. In effect, when staying at the dyadic level, it is difficult to get a sense of how exchanges use different resources at the same time, and of the overall pattern of exchanges of these resources in the firm. Recognizing this more generally, Lévi-Strauss (1949) distinguished two forms of exchange: direct or restricted exchange (dyadic) and indirect or generalized exchange (structural). Asymmetries in the transfers of resources, along with the dependencies attached to them, can create a generalized exchange system. This form of generalized exchange system can also be said to be 'locally multiplex'. This means that productive members can share several types of resources with task-force members, with or without immediate reciprocity (Blau 1964). Their cooperation involves forms of bounded solidarity and indirect reci-procities that take several resources into account.

In order to share these resources on an ongoing basis, members try to build or join stable quasi-groups, or niches, in which these resources are more easily available to them as individuals in this organization. A social niche is defined as a position in which flows of important resources have been, at least temporarily, secured by members among themselves (that is, by members sharing common attributes and identities). A niche can thus be represented as a position of structurally equivalent members *and* as a dense group of members (a clique) (Borgatti and Everett 1992; Freeman 1992). The important point is that such niches are a necessary intermediate level between individuals and the overall structure. It is often where most transfers and exchanges of resources happen for a given member. It provides the organization with the means of putting pressure on the members (thus increasing their productivity) and of circulating resources in a context where opportunism and strategic rationality are suspended. It provides members with resources needed to produce and survive in this organization, as well as—for the most central ones—with opportunities to exploit or play off non-members against each other. Acknowledging the existence of this level with its advantages and dangers to both the individual members and to the firm makes it possible to understand various social processes within the firm.

THREE PRODUCTION RESOURCES: CO-WORKERS' GOODWILL, ADVICE, AND FRIENDSHIP

The role of these substructures in the exchange mechanism can be grasped by recalling the work process typical of professional members in this organization, as well as the resources needed to carry it out. In this context, *temporary* task forces composed of partners and associates (at least one of each) constituted the core of multifunctional and sometimes multidisciplinary (litigation, corporate) work groups. Recall that, in such partner–associate task forces, partners kept their autonomy in the negotiation of means and ends, and associates could—and were often expected to—share knowledge and expertise. Legal task forces were case driven; they had to be sufficiently large to handle specific tasks. They could also become specialized boutiques within the firm, created by the fact that a general practice firm had to grow and, given the increasing complexity of the law, transform its generalists into specialists narrowing their focus. Under pressure to achieve, members could work simultaneously on several files and participate in several task forces. The firm was thus broken into small, flexible, and heterogeneous work groups (Lazega 1992*b*), which had to be able to cooperate quickly and efficiently, to react to complex non-standardized problems, solve them, and dissolve themselves. The importance of cooperation in these task forces to effective individual participation was evident from the fact that individual economic performance was positively and significantly associated with task-force membership and constraint, as will be shown below.

This picture of case-driven task forces thus illustrates why and how a structural approach to cooperation should examine transfers and exchanges of resources central to the functioning of such organizations. Specifically, it suggests that regularities in the transfer and exchange of resources should enable members to participate effectively in collective action, in an orderly and ongoing basis. In other words, the analysis of a locally multiplex and generalized exchange system is the key to showing, on a case-by-case basis, how members managed their social resources in order to cooperate in the production of quality service. In fact, this approach to collective action in terms of resource dependencies and exchange substructures had the advantage of taking into account multifunctional and instrumental dimensions of collective action.

I consider three types of resources to be central to the functioning of the firm.[2] Such resources were important, because many things could go wrong in the organization when they were too scarce or distributed in a way that gave some members too much damage potential.

The first type of resource is co-workers' goodwill.[3] Given the flexibility needed to accommodate clients' needs, and the size and complexity of some of the files, a good co-worker was a real resource for the individual attorneys in firms such as SG&R. As seen above, formal structure imposed constraints on the work process. In general, a file (a case) was handled by at least two lawyers, one partner and one associate. The partners analysed a complex problem and broke it down into several parts, assigning to each of the associates working with them, and observing this exercise, a small part of the tasks to be performed. In this type of structure, partners and associates need one another. Partners depend on each other for many reasons. They may have the same clients, represent large and complex files. The form of cooperation is thus dictated by the requirements of the market. In addition, one well-known way of keeping a client is to cross-sell services that can be provided by partners of different specialities. Thus, a client who initially needs advice for a specific problem, say buying a shopping mall, will also be offered tax and litigation services by the firm. This increases revenues and helps to establish a relationship with the client.

As mentioned earlier, interdependence among attorneys working together on a file at SG&R could be strong for a few weeks, and then weak for months. Access to work opportunities depended on intake and assignment policies, on which partners relied to try to prevent possible (ethical and business) conflicts among themselves. In its effort to organize its practice, rather than hiring lawyers from outside the firm, the firm could impose undesired co-workers—rival partners, associates unknown to a partner, difficult or unhelpful partners to associates. Associates and partners had to be prepared to work with firm colleagues, and sometimes with other partners and associates who would not be first on the list of preferred co-workers. Forced cooperation was routine for many partners and most associates, but members also gave themselves room to manœuvre and be strategic in their choices of co-workers. Sharing work and cross-selling among partners were done mostly on an informal basis, although less so when including associates. Given the classical stratification of such firms, work was supposed to be channelled to associates through specific partners, but this rule was only partly respected. Members did not rely entirely on the assignment committee to form their task forces. Recall that firm policy was not always enforced exactly as it was formally meant to be. It conflicted mainly with lawyers' own strategic preferences when they put together a task force to work on a file. Formal assignments did compete with individual preferences. This meant that, to some extent, members selected their strong co-workers themselves. To choose co-workers in this collegial context was thus a delicate operation. Associates competed for the attention of partners. Partners competed for the best associates and for prestige within and outside the firm.

Under such constraints, members of the firm had two preoccupations: finding interesting work, and getting cooperation from colleagues to carry it out, especially colleagues interested in a long-term relationship, *and not in taking advantage of them*. The first preoccupation of individual members who were timekeeping was with building strong, secure, and durable work relationships with others: partners with other well-connected partners and with reliable associates; associates with rewarding partners. Members thought that they were more 'assured' of receiving the cooperation that they wanted from strong work ties than from more superficial ones. Strong work ties are thus both a form of perceived interdependence and a sort of insurance policy. They open the horizon beyond short-term security. Most members wanted to share work with reasonable people who pulled their weight and did not grab all the credit for themselves, especially in successful cases.

The second type of resource is advice. Members involved in 'certainty work' rely constantly on advice from others. Advice is an important resource in professional and collegial organizations (Wilensky 1967). Without it, corporate lawyers could not solve in a satisfactory manner the usually complex legal problems that they handle. The nature of knowledge-intensive work requires accumulation, transfers, and exchanges of knowledge and experience. SG&R organized work among experts, who often referred to abstract legal knowledge. In this context, transfers and exchanges of advice among members could be seen as vital, indeed as one of the main reasons for the existence of such knowledge-intensive firms in general. Advice could be seen as a product of goodwill, but it was also different from goodwill in the sense that it could be provided by someone who was not a strong co-worker. In law firms of this type, advice is not billed to the advice-seeker. It does not show in lawyers' time sheets or in firm accounts. Advisers may not claim official credit in successful cases. Lawyers who are not assigned to a case may advise, but if they want to claim their share of the credit they would have to become official co-workers on the case. This is accepted only beyond a certain contribution and negotiated with the lawyers already in charge. It is difficult to predict unilaterally when providing advice may become collaboration. To seek advice in such a context of business, career, and symbolic competition is, therefore, sometimes a delicate operation. In a law firm that structures itself so as to protect and develop its human and relational capital (Gilson and Mnookin 1985; Nelson 1988; Smigel 1969; Wilensky 1967), such a resource is particularly vital to individual members. Members at SG&R saw expertise as accumulated by the firm, and—in their situation of collective responsibility— ended up relying constantly on advice from others. For example, how far-reaching was yesterday's decision by the State Supreme Court on a basic question of corporate law? What about the upcoming partnership decisions? How about Partner X's way of putting this or that deal together? In sum, members sought out for advice could be considered to be members with high status (Blau 1964). Whereas the strong co-workers represented members' perceived reliance and interdependence upon each other for cooperation, advice represented intelligence and experience that were exchanged for status recognition. To illustrate this connection between advice and status, here are some of the statements provided along with the sociometric choices:

> Usually advice involves something of another area of law, one that I am not practising. Among the people who can answer, I choose those with experience and the smartest, those who have proved that they have good ideas. With associates, it is different: I can ask for their reaction, but I have to decide for myself. One thing I have learned is that nobody knows everything. Don't ignore the young people. The most stupid guy can sometimes have a good idea.   (Partner 12)

> On a particular file, I would go to the partner with whom I work on this file. So the list looks a lot like the co-workers' list, although not entirely. There have been times where I got other people's perspective—for instance, when other partners with whom I have already worked on similar files have helped me, or when I need to know the implications for the client in other fields. I am a corporate lawyer, and the people I ask are usually in the litigation department.   (Associate 42)

In this law firm, as in many others, the difference between advisers and co-workers was based on the fact that a partner could seek another partner's advice without including the adviser as a co-worker in the file at hand (and thus share risks and credit).

> I never hesitate to bring other partners in on an advice basis because I can control how much of that time gets billed. Because of our compensation system, I don't fear any personal repercussions from calling other partners. I may or may not write it down, but as the billing partner I have the final say, together with the MP, on what to bill a client. The general rule is: bill straight time for the attorneys on the case. If I feel that I have a justification to bill it up for partner consultation or down for associate inefficiency, I have the responsibility to take that up with the MP to determine the bill. Changes in the compensation system would mean a change in my way of thinking about cases. Advice would get billed, and I am not sure I would consult a partner and bolster his hours on one of my files. Nor would I be likely to introduce him to 'my' clients. That's one of the reasons we stay with this system.   (Partner 25)

The third type of resource will be called friendship, a flexible form of open-ended support that is not related to the tasks themselves. Rather, it is a form of 'backstage resource', to use Goffman's idea (1961) of a place where actors retreat to get the distance that is needed to show that the demands of their roles are beneath their capabilities.[4] I understand the resources provided by this friendship in a non-sentimental way: a willingness to help in difficult situations, socialization, motiva-tion, emotional support, information, exciting approaches to otherwise boring and sparkless work, and a definition of the situation (Maister 1993: 163). A friend is considered as a potential source of many resources—for example, of help in asserting or negotiating one's roles and status, or in carving out a place for oneself in the group. Indeed, at SG&R, mutual friendship ties were extremely valuable because they represented a form of insurance policy against expulsion. Recall that partners could be expelled only when 90 per cent of all partners affirmatively voted for the 'termination' of one of their own. With thirty-six partners, it took abstention by two 'unconditional' partners to deadlock the vote. The importance of this definition of friendship is that it does not assume reciprocity and is not directly connected to the work process itself. However, among business heads, sympathizing hearts also mean interference. Therefore, in the professional context of SG&R, choices of friends and management of friendship ties were not easy. More than interdependence was needed to strengthen them. Lawyers said that, in their firm, such ties tended to be forged among associates of the same class, or between associates who went together to the same law school, and lasted throughout their careers.

Friendship ties have been shown to strengthen participation to collective action, especially in organizations where collective indecision is frequent. They are important to participation, commitment, productivity, and involvement (Krackhardt 1992). The more you think you have friends, the more you participate, and the more you accept the negative outcomes of status comparisons. Status games are sometimes mitigated by friendship (Lazega and Van Duijn 1997), because it helps peers keep their exchanges (giving and taking) vague. Friends can therefore help members buttress and deal with potential threats of opportunism and mitigate the potentially negative effects of interdependence; they help in gaining approval from partners with whom collegial relations are fragile and unstable, subject to stress and centrifugal forces.

Friendship sometimes means providing support and approval, even multilateral solidarity. But, since power and status are systematically personalized and depersonalized in collegial organizations (Bourricaud 1964), it might still be surprising that friendship ties are emphasized here as a third type of resource to be considered systematically in a competitive corporate environment. When speaking about the firm in general, many members perceived that, at SG&R, there were not many bases other than business for building ties with others. This underlied discourse about the firm as 'almost exclusively' an economic unit. Listen for example to Partners 18, 6, and 19:

> Our firm is almost exclusively a joint economic enterprise. If I were to pick up a paper tomorrow morning and learn that a lawyer was hit by a car, I would be concerned. If he is in my firm, I would be more concerned. But that marginal difference would not be that significant. Unless I work with him, know his family and his children. There are lots of lawyers in the community that I care more about than some of my partners. I see a partnership more like an economic unit. There is the economic sense of mutual obligation, of enhanced goodwill and cooperation. We help each other with work. I expect more goodwill from a partner than from a stranger, but that's all. 'I'll be glad to do that.' But my whole life does not revolve around my partners. When people are too close, it creates problems too. And it is not necessary for partnerships to survive. There is a leap of faith that's required that a partner would not seek a circumstance that is harmful to me. That may be naive. Our compensation system is a guarantee for that leap of faith. A change in that would undermine the sense of security that I feel with my partners. (Partner 18)

To the extent to which we deal less and less with human beings and more and more with corporations and corporate personalities, it also has an effect on the perception of the firm as a business rather than a profession. There is a certain hardening of the people in the firm. You are not dealing with the individual, you don't see the tears roll up in the eyes of individual human beings, you are dealing with corporations and businesses who talk about the bottom line all the time. That makes you think of yourself as a business dealing business to business, rather than a profession with whatever mystique that has. And that also hardens you, we are only talking about money here, we are not talking about lives, feelings, compassion, it's all business. One tends to imagine that the first two reactions of any lawyer in one of these offices to the news that a lawyer has dropped dead will be: how will I get his larger office, and how will that affect the increase in my compensation since there is one less slice in the pie? When Kennedy was assassinated, I was in my office with an associate, and someone burst in and said, 'Have you heard Kennedy was assassinated', and the associate said, 'How will that affect the stock market?' That was his natural, instinctive, immediate first reaction.   (Partner 6)

This firm is not a family. You get very little emotional reward or support. Rather lonely in that regard. Some here and there, within friendships, but not overall. Some partners go out drinking. There is an awful lot of heavy drinking here. You have a committee meeting at the end of the day, and many partners would have two or three martinis and a bottle of wine with dinner. That's one of the ways they release stress and become somewhat personal. Traditional bonding. Our lemon parties are cocktails. Firm social get-togethers is more for sharing information and catching up with what people are doing. . . . Very little energy has been devoted to people really becoming friends. There is a certain reluctance to letting down one's guard. In the beginning, you are being evaluated and judged all the time. Now I feel when I go home that I retreat to lick my wounds, but I am not going to show my partners. I was fired by a client a few weeks ago. It is unpleasant, and I felt stunned. But I wouldn't go and tell my partners. I'll go home and tell my wife. There is a good side to it too: you don't have to deal with your partners too.   (Partner 19)

Against this background, *collective* expressions of personal support were rare, and surprising to some members:

When my mother died in January, she was the only person in my life, I was struck by the letters I got from my partners, and by what they said. They were handwritten letters, showing a genuine understanding and compassion, not just pro forma. Which indicates to me that there are reservoirs here that can be tapped, and the firm has to be careful not to dry these reservoirs up. I have seen too many firms dry up all the wells of compassion, money machines filled with dislike: 'I've got what I want and the hell with you.'   (Partner 6)

Indeed friendship ties were not needed to drive the work process itself. Therefore, partners tended to keep associates at arm's length, and friendship ties with most other partners were often uneasy. But, even when general discourse on present-day collegiality often stressed the contrast between a business-oriented firm and an idealized collegial past, members did mix professional and social ties with some *selected* colleagues in the firm. The select few could still help accept negative outcomes of status comparisons, and help deal with potential threats. The partners quoted above spoke more of a general atmosphere, not of the existence of selected friendships and personalized relationships in the firm. This comes across in Partner 13's following observation:

> When the firm was small among other things all partners had a good idea of what other partners were doing. There was a much greater level of social integration, I think, firm-wide. And a tendency to look much more inwardly towards the firm almost as a sort of family away from a family. In our instance probably thirty years ago the partners in the firm tended to represent the most central social circle for themselves. When the firm gets to be this size there is still a tendency to look inwardly toward the firm but it's obviously no longer a closely knit family because there are lots of partners that you won't see for weeks at a time. And so there tends to be if anything a tendency for partners to start to look outward from the firm as opposed to inward to the firm. The closeness tends to be reduced. Now what you have are people whose predominant social circles may include other lawyers within the firm. But probably include many more people outside the firm. That's a healthy development, not an unhealthy development.

Direct interaction between lawyers could be closed, guarded, and sometimes hostile. Much of their time could be spent jockeying for a position, as much as trying to solve a problem. Struggle for status was permanently present within the firm. However, this being said, members did mix professional and social ties with some selected colleagues.

LONG-TERM INDIVIDUAL INTERESTS, IDENTIFICATIONS, AND BOUNDED SOLIDARITY

Considering this organizational analysis of resources associated with production, one might ask where members find such resources. In Chapter 1, I theorized that they are likely to find them in social niches, along with indirect reciprocity and solidarity. For work ties, recall Partner 29's explanation of the informal process by which young associates joined a niche of two or three partners, who would represent their strongest work ties and who would help them specialize and begin their career. Niches exist because exchanges are constrained by many forces, including specialization. Thus, if one looks at the firm as a set of substructures, confirming the existence of an exchange system does not yet indicate under what constraints these exchanges of production-related resources take place. When choosing sources of advice, for example, members may think of their immediate individual interest, of their long-term interest (based on *identities* or similarities in attributes used for mutual identification), or in terms of collective interests (that of the firm). They also think of existing organizational rules of allocation of such resources. Identities—and bounded solidarity rules that come attached to them—are what is needed to deal with long-term conflicts in the distribution of resources. Usually most members can play on similarities and some can pull rank on others; but in collegial organizations pulling rank is costlier in terms of relationships and impossible among partners.

By using their similarities, actors can signal preferential treatment to each other or the fact that they will not take advantage of one another. Therefore, an important step in the analysis will be to check that SG&R's exchange system did contain niches shaped by the formal structure of the firm, by members' homophilous choices of sources of resources, and by their appropriateness judgements.

A first ethnographic illustration is provided by interviews such as that of Partner 11:

> Firm cohesion has changed dramatically as a function of size, and as a result of change in the nature of the profession. The size factor is just a question of time and number of floors. Before, it was impossible not to know what the others were doing. Sharing experiments, knowledge, perceptions of what was important, how the firm should react, was easy. At the end of the 1960s and at the beginning of the 1970s, there was an awful lot of socializing outside the firm, partners and associates alike. At least once a month the entire firm went out together. Now the picture is different. A different atmosphere. We don't have any choice. As you make the decision to grow and to remain a general practice, you have far less contact; in many cases not at all, with many of your partners and associates. I don't have the slightest idea of what many other partners do. You place emphasis on statistical analysis. Profitability. That's my own point of view. I consider myself close to nine or ten partners with whom it isn't different from what it was in the 1970s. But that's all.

To do their work and survive in such a partnership, interdependent members of the firm needed durable relations with at least some colleagues, which provided access to resources such as clients, knowledge, and social support. As seen above, the organization helped members get access to some resources, such as clients and workforce. It conducted its affairs based on a formal structure and formal rules, which expressed choices among policy options, and allocated, directly and indirectly, resources to members. For instance, in order to organize cooperation and help members in getting some cooperation, the firm allocated members themselves to formal positions that were used to enter into exchanges with one another: formal hierarchical status, seniority rank, office membership, speciality. It also allocated resources such as salaries, compensation, and files, based on such positions.

However, the formal organization did not make an unambiguous allocation of all the resources needed to work and survive in this environment. Its rules could conflict. Many solutions abided by these rules, but there was also a need for arbitration that resorted to particularistic criteria: for example, files might not all be allocated through formal channels, and, even when they were, there could be several solutions other than the formal channels to choose from. In addition, resources such as advice and social support were rarely allocated formally. To get access to such resources, members did not entirely rely on formal organization and rules. They were selective in their relational choices, and this selectivity—together with institutional constraints—produced patterns of interest to understanding exchanges in the firm. Members managed their interdependence in their own ways, which are economic and politicized. As seen above, to get access to such resources, members entered exchanges, which were multilateral and multiplex. Thus, they intervened in the process of resource allocation by using formal identities in politicized ways or by introducing other particularistic identities and preoccupations (for example, gender, or law school attended). These attributes, more informal and *ad hoc*, were not necessarily officially recognized by the firm as characteristics that should be used to promote cooperation.

To some extent, dimensions of formal structure of the firm should serve individual members' immediate interests in shaping access to such resources. They should also create room for niches by shaping members' games of identity politics within the firm (Sainsaulieu 1997). In effect, as seen in Chapter 1, the stability that a niche offers in terms of access and exchange of resources comes from introducing time—that is, a long-term perspective—to the exchanges. Identity, via appropriateness judgements in exchanges, is what introduces time in action by defining long-term individual and collective interests. Identity is usually a stable and multidimensional set of attributes that members use to define themselves and get individual and collective recognition as sources of their actions (for credit, accountability, and the definition of a collective purpose) on an ongoing basis.

This raises the issue of how these transfers and exchanges are handled over time. Informed by this understanding of the reasons for choosing some colleagues (as opposed to others) as sources of resources, it is reasonable to expect the existence of social niches. In the next section, I identify these niches at SG&R. Based on the above organizational analysis of resources associated with production, standard sociometric data were collected in the firm. The name generators used to conduct the network study are presented in Appendix A. Analysis of the distribution of key resources shows the existence, at the structural level, of the subsystems that were called niches.

A general methodological indication can be useful at this stage. In this book, the different networks observed in the firm are analysed either stacked together or separately. The first approach (several networks stacked together) is used mainly to identify SG&R's social niches system, but also to understand how access to various kinds of social resources within the firm are interdependent—that is, how interlocked different kinds of multiplex ties can be. The second approach provides cues for several social mechanisms that become particularly visible when specific ties are observed in one single network (as if it had a life of its own).

NICHES IN THE ORGANIZATIONAL EXCHANGE SYSTEM: A VIEW AT THE STRUCTURAL LEVEL

I define a niche analytically as a dense position clustering a subset of approximately structurally equivalent[5] members across as many types of resource networks as needed to work and participate durably in the cooperation system of the organization. It is not simply a 'resource space', but also a quasi-group in which members bring in identity criteria, priorities in partner selection, and eventually bounded solidarity. Technically, this means that a niche is a subset of approximately structurally equivalent members in the organization, across multiple networks (here co-workers', advisers', and friends' networks); these subsets, or positions, are also cliques. They are easily identified on the diagonal of the density tables constructed based on multiple networks (see Appendix B).

An analysis approximating structural equivalence among members of the firm across the three networks provides a simplified overall view, represented in Figure 3.1.[6] The density tables on which this figure is based are presented in Appendix B. To summarize, it shows that the three networks stacked together break down into nine positions of approximately structurally equivalent members. These positions visualize seven niches as defined above; in effect, Positions Four and Eight are not dense enough across the three networks to qualify as social niches. Some niches are more dense than others, reflecting a stronger and richer type of bounded solidarity.

Positions One, Two, and Three are positions of partners; all the others are positions of associates. The thick grey lines—that is, reciprocated advice ties—reflect the backbone of the firm: the positions of three partners and their senior associates. Note that requests for advice converge towards them. One subset of senior associates on the litigation side stands out (among associates) as an important intermediary between litigation associates and litigation partners, especially Position One partners. Many of the relationships between positions are not symmetric. Indeed, the asymmetries in the transfers of resources, along with the dependencies attached to them, reflect the multiplex exchange system in the following way.

Position One was a dominant group of Office I litigation partners who got advice, strong collaboration, and friendship from Positions Two and Five. Theirs was a protected niche: its members got almost what they wanted from the people they chose. Many positions of associates were directly indebted to it for advice and collaboration, but it was not the top performing position (third in average individual dollar collection). Position Two was a group of Office I corporate partners almost in the same dominant situation as Position One, except that it had an exchange of advice for friendship with Position Five. Many positions of associates were directly indebted to it for advice, but not for friendship. It was the top performing position economically. Position Three was a group mixing Office II corporate and litigation partners, in the same category as Positions One and Two in terms of dependence on others for resources. It claimed strong collaboration from Position Two, but unreciprocated in kind: Position Two members tended not to rely on Position Three for strong collaboration, but did so for advice and friendship. Here reciprocity tended also to be direct, but not necessarily in kind. Note that Position Three had direct exchanges of strong collaboration only with two positions of associates, Positions Six and Seven, not with other positions of partners—but cross-selling could still take place, for example, since it was a mixed position. As for Position Two, many positions of associates were directly indebted to it for advice, but not for collaboration or friendship. It ranked second in average individual dollar collection.

To anticipate on further analysis (see below) at the dyadic level, partners' positions were characterized by a comparatively very high proportion of 'Blau ties', (ties in

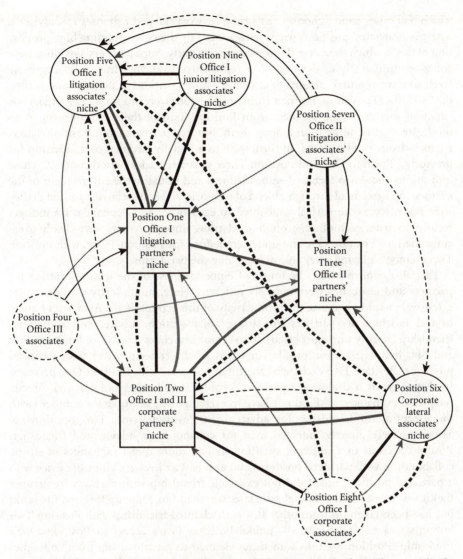

Figure 3.1. *Overall view of transfers and exchanges of resources in the firm: The co-workers',*
advice, and friendship networks superimposed

Note: This figure is a reduction representing the pattern of relationships between positions of approximately structurally equivalent members across the three networks of all attorneys in the firm. Boxes
represent positions of partners. Circles represent positions of associates. Thick lines represent mutual
exchanges of a specific resource. Thin arrows represent unreciprocated transfers of a specific resource.
Black lines represent the co-workers' network. Grey lines represent the advice network. Dotted lines
represent the friendship network. All the positions are social niches, with two exceptions: the dotted
circles representing Positions Four and Eight mean that the latter are not social niches.

Source: Reprinted from E. Lazega, *Réseaux sociaux et structures relationnelles,* p. 71. Copyright 1998 with
permission from Presses Universitaires de France.

which '*i* chooses *j* and *j* chooses *i* as strong co-workers, and *j* chooses *i* as adviser'), whereas associates' positions were characterized by the corresponding high proportion of ties in which they were the advice-seeking party. Such partners' positions were cohesive: mutual triplex ties were over-represented in them. Thus, at the aggregate level, all three resources tended to circulate within positions of partners and among the two Office I positions. Partners from Position One were in a socially advantageous situation for reminding partners from Position Two of their commitment or to moderate status competition among them, but not partners from Position Three. Partners from Position Two, in turn, were in a socially advantageous situation for pressuring Position One and Position Three partners back to good conduct. These indications show two forms of embeddedness and visualize the enforcement of the partnership agreement through a blend of task-oriented and social ties. Although they were not often asymmetrically indebted to each other and dependent on indirect reciprocity from each other, economic relations among partners were clearly over-embedded for Position One and under-embedded for Position Three, with Position Two members playing a key role of balancing the two forms.

This also confirms that the forms of embeddedness of the labour contract for partners and associates were radically different. Here, multiplexity was also more extensively used to enhance the productivity of this economic tie. Associates tended to feel indebted to partners for strong collaboration, advice, and sometimes friendship (mostly unreciprocated). Two senior associates' positions, Positions Five and Six, had a less clear profile (in terms of direct reciprocity) than partners' positions. Position Five exchanged the three resources with Position One partners. In that sense, it had almost a partners' profile. It had other uniplex and directly reciprocal exchanges, and did not have to exchange one resource for another (with the exception of friendship for advice with Position Two). Two positions of associates were directly indebted to it for collaboration, advice, and friendship. Position Six was in a different situation. It had more direct exchanges of strong collaboration with partners' positions and also had a direct exchange of advice with a partners' position. But it did not exchange friendship with partners (remember that it was constituted of lateral associates who had not come up through the ranks but had been taken on from other firms). It claimed friendship with Position Two but this was not reciprocated—unlike Position Five's access to Position One's friendship. Position Six thus sometimes claimed to get friendship from colleagues (Positions Five, Seven, and Eight) other than those to whom it provided it.

Already at this stage of the analysis, small cycles characterizing generalized exchange can be found in this representation of the system: multiplex and local cycles reflecting the existence of highly embedded strong co-workers' task forces existed, for example, among Positions One, Five, and Nine, or among Positions Two, Six, and Eight, or among Positions One, Two, and Four. This is due, in particular, to the fact that indirect reciprocity was at its strongest with less senior associates, who were never in a position, for instance, to reciprocate for advice. They most often had to reciprocate in Blau-type status recognition and strong commitment to work. This reciprocation in commitment to work was not necessarily directed to sources of advice. For example, Position Eight got advice from Position Three, but was only indirectly involved in strong work ties with Position Three through Position Six. Another example is Position Seven, which got the three resources from Position Five but was not in a position to reciprocate directly at all. It thus remained indebted, providing Position Three with a strong commitment to work and friendship. A similar short cycle was also present among Positions Three, Six, and Seven. Position Four was in the same dependent situation as Position Seven with regard to the three partners' positions with which it had ties. Note that it did not get friendship at all from other positions, not even indirectly, which shows that the exchange system failed to provide this resource to some of its members.

A large spectrum of forms of embeddedness were present here to fuel social mechanisms and help them enforce the labour contract for partners and associates. It would be too simple to reduce the situation by saying that performance of individuals was directly affected by these forms of embeddedness because high performers were always involved in very multiplex exchanges and low performers in less multiplex ones, or because resistance to the general circulation rule always produced low performers. For some associates high productivity went hand in hand with strong friendship ties with partners: Positions Five and Seven over-billed and over-collected compared to the other associates. Associates could often feel that they were kept at arm's length, and that 'partners didn't let them in', but here we also see that some partners were nevertheless in a favourable social situation to extract high commitment from these associates. And, at the other extreme, Position Four associates were also highly productive but much less socially connected to the partners they worked with: requests for advice still indicate social embeddedness through status recognition, but partners were less in a position to extract work for friendship. In contrast, junior associates were less productive economically and claimed friendship with one another and with senior associates. Here partners could play on resource dependencies to get commitment from associates in different ways, sometimes indirectly through the dependence of junior associates on senior ones. Senior associates could also play this resource dependence game with strongly socially embedded junior associates (in Position Eight, pure friendship ties were highly over-represented and Position Seven included a record proportion of unreciprocated triplex ties), but not so much with partners. Further descriptions of relationships between embeddedness and performance are presented in Chapter 4.

Still at the dyadic level, reciprocal work tie combined with a unidirectional advice tie (Blau ties) were very frequent in Positions Two and Seven, One and Nine, Two and Four, Three and Six. This compound reflects one of the most frequent types of embeddedness of exchanges in niches. Partners also concentrated requests for advice, as well as unreciprocated citations as friends and advisers, or as co-workers and advisers. Such citations converged towards all partners' positions but were strongly over-represented for Position One. Moreover, associates' positions were much less cohesive, which is confirmed by a low proportion of mutual triplex ties. In Position Three, empty ties and mutual duplex (co-work and advice) ties were over-represented.

In the next section, I identify the forms of status that could be found in the firm and locate them within this system of social niches. This network analysis is *ad hoc* by construction, but its results make sense from a theoretical point of view.

STATUS IN THE ORGANIZATIONAL EXCHANGE SYSTEM: NICHES AND POWER

To identify the forms of status in this firm, Table 3.1 looks at simple correlations between dimensions of importance in this partnership (measurements of centrality[7] in the three different networks, as well as measurements of economic performance that will be elaborated upon further below). This provides a view of the concentration of resources at the structural level.

The three different forms of status identified in the Introduction (finder, minder, and grinder) can be found at SG&R by analysing these correlations: first, obvious finders, who were central in the co-workers, and advice networks, as well as strong performers in terms of time input and fees collected; secondly, minders, who were central in the three networks but not strong performers themselves; and, finally, grinders, who were not central in any of the networks but strong in time input and fees collected. The ways in which these forms of status, which overlapped for a few partners, drove collective action and were important for specific social processes (such as quality control, monitoring and sanctioning, and many others) are presented in detail in the chapters below. The simple existence of such an informal stratification shows that members reached out of their niches and combined maintenance of niche ties with status competition.

In effect, strong and multiplex cohesion among rival members is a defining feature of the collegial phenomenon. It does not mean that status competition is absent from niches. As defined above, this process is built into the blend of collegial relationships; it is more visible when members rely on each other for strong collaboration, or actually work together, but it does not necessarily need to be so. In this section, I describe each niche, its role in the circulation of resources within the firm, whether or not it was very centralized and dominated by key persons, its members

Table 3.1. *Correlations between indicators of status in the firm*

Indicators of status	Mean	SD	1	2	3	4
1. Fees collected	*	*	—			
2. Time input (hours)	1,407	335	0.46			
3. Centrality (advice)	18	12	0.64	0.19	—	
4. Centrality (friendship)	11	7	0.21	0.18	0.60	—
5. Centrality (co-workers)	22	9	0.44	0.23	0.76	0.52

Notes: $N = 71$. SD: standard deviation. Correlation table for measurements of actors' importance in the firm (indicated by centrality in firm's social networks and by economic performance). Centrality scores are computed based on choices of partners and associates. * means that the information may not be disclosed.

with firm-wide status, and its possible difficulties with regard to access to resources or capacity to deal with demand for resources. This description will be useful for analyses in subsequent chapters.

Position One (a niche for Partners 21, 27, 24, 11, 26, 13, 8, 1, 22, 36, 20, and 23, and Associates 38 and 40) was made up of *Office I litigators*, almost all *partners*. This was a very strong niche, including several key characters mentioned in the previous chapter, providing large quantities of work and advice to others. However, its members were not the most central colleagues in the friendship network: in that respect, most Office II partners and firm associates were kept at arm's length. It had no unreciprocated ties and, although it is hard to picture its members, at this level of reduction, as heavily dependent on others for one of the key resources, triplex reciprocated ties with Position Five senior associates indicate strong reliance on them. Absence of work ties with Office II partners and associates reflects the existence of two clearly separate markets and pools of workforce; ties were maintained at the level of exchanges and transfers of advice. At the time of the study, members of Position One did not rely much on Office II or Office III colleagues, and their pattern of ties does suggest a self-contained firm within the firm.

The senior partners in this niche were Partners 1, 8, 11, and 13; medium-seniority partners included the main minders in Office I (such as Partners 20, 24, 26, who, along with Partner 13, had heavy administrative responsibilities at the time of the study) and in particular two senior associates (38 and 40). Indegree centrality scores (reflecting the number of times each member was selected by all the other members) in the co-workers' network were very high for Partners 24, 26, 13, and 22 (members of the associates committee), and Associate 38, a senior associate who was one of the most active brokers between partners and associates on the litigation side; they were among the highest in the advice network, especially for Partners 21, 24, 26, 13, 1, 22, and 20 and for Associate 40; and low in the friendship network (except for Partners 21, 27, 24, 26, and 13, because they sat on the associates' committee (the ATC); or, in the case of Partner 27 because she attracted many citations from women associates). In terms of performance, Partners 21, 26, 13, 8, and 1 were among the fifteen highest fee collectors for the previous year. In terms of associate performance, Associates 38 and 40 were the highest fee collectors for the previous year, in spite of lower hourly rates. Others, such as Partner 1, were typical *finders*.

This niche was very dense: its members exchanged many resources with one another. Members of this niche *worked* a lot with each other; they tended to have reciprocal work ties with members of Positions Two (partners, corporate, Office I), Five (senior associates, litigation, Office I), and Nine (junior associates, mainly litigation, Office I), and tended to be cited as strong co-workers by Position Four (associates, litigation, Office III). Notice that they tended not to cite Office II partners (Position III) as strong co-workers or friends, only as advisers. They had dense *advice ties* with each other, reciprocal ties with Positions Two, Three, and Five, and were sought out for advice by all the other niches except Position Six (senior lateral corporate associates). Members tended to have dense *friendship ties* with each other and reciprocal ties with Positions Two and Five.

Many medium-seniority partners transferred large amounts of the resources examined here, which makes sense, since they had been in charge of running the organization that ultimately produced their larger share of the pie. In many ways, their heavy investments in others were multidimensional. Several partners were examples of that: Partner 22 was a typically focused and hard-working finder on whom a record number of associates relied for work and advice (but not friendship). Partner 27, a very active woman partner, had a specific relational profile in the sense that, in addition, she advised and provided friendship for many women associates. Partner 20's management of resources was of the same type, with a specificity probably related to his being the managing partner: he was intensely sought out for advice and relied upon for cooperation, but these were unreciprocated; and when he mentioned members on whom he could rely for work, from whom he sought advice, or as friends, they often did not reciprocate either.[8]

Some in Position One, such as Partners 1 and 26, managed their transfers and exchanges of resources in common. Partner 1 in general was very much relied upon for provision of work and sought out for advice, although sometimes inaccessible. On big cases, he had worked with seconds, such as Partner 26, who had an entirely different relational profile: he was a hard-working partner, heavily involved in the business of the firm, and this shows in his relational profile: he was the person with most ties in the firm. There were only nineteen people with whom he had no tie of some sort. He was among the record holders for Blau ties, the typical partner–associate relation (a mutual work tie and an advice tie from the associate to the partner), for the very close and dense exchanges with other partners (triplex mutual tie), and for concentrating requests for advice; as for Partner 13, many associates said that they liked him and claimed to be friends with him. He was a work-oriented all-round exchanger and investor of social resources. Another category of partners in this niche, Partners 13, 24, and 31, also had an approximately similar relational profile, with, however, an emphasis on large amounts of dense multi-resource ties with other partners and provision of friendship to associates. They could be called key status competition mitigators. Prototypical of these minders was Partner 13, who, in addition to many instrumental relationships with associates, was involved in many exchanges of advice and friendship—that is, not directly functional or focused on a particular case. An indication of that is that he was among the only partners who mixed work-related and friendship ties, breaking the taboo brought to light by the analysis of the blend of collegial relationships presented below; he was one of the few who did not keep associates at arm's length.

Position Two (a niche for Partners 12, 29, 16, 17, 2, 10, 9, 34, 4, and 15) was made up of *Office I and Office III corporate partners*. This niche was also dense and centralized, although less so than Position One. It also provided work and advice to several other niches, and its members tended to be much closer to Office II partners in the friendship network; here again most associates (except again Position Five members) were kept at some distance. Members tended to rely on Position One for all key resources, but they also diversified their sources of resources more (compared to Position One partners): they did not rely much on Office II colleagues for strong collaboration, but maintained advice and friendship ties with them, which was more than Position One members did.

The senior partners were Partners 2, 4, 9, 10, and 12. The minders at the time of the study were Partners 29 and 34. The finders tended to be Partners 2, 4, 17, and 15. This niche was also very dense or cohesive: its members exchanged all three key resources with one another. Firm-wide status as indicated by indegree centrality scores in the co-worker's network was high for most members, especially for Partners 29, 16, 17, 34, 4, and 15, some of whom sat on the associates' committee; among the highest scores in the advice network were those of Partners 12, 16, 17, 2, 34, and 15; and the niche was low in the friendship network (except for Partner 17). In terms of performance, Partners 12, 2, 4, and 15 were also among the fifteen highest fee collectors for the previous year. As mentioned, they tended to have strong *work ties* within the niche, and reciprocal ties with members of Positions One, Four, Six, and Eight. They were cited as strong co-workers by members of Position Three. They sought each other for *advice*, had reciprocal ties with members of Positions One, Three, and Six (senior and lateral corporate associates), and were sought out for advice by associates from Positions Four, Five, and Eight. They had *friendship ties* with one another, reciprocal ties with members of Positions One and Three, and they tended to cite (unreciprocated) as friends members of Position Five, and to be cited (unreciprocated) by members of Position Six. Note that they tended to have triplex reciprocated ties with members of Position One and that they also tended to have duplex reciprocated (advice and friendship) ties with Office II partners, which was one of the structural features differentiating them from Position One partners. This feature allowed them to act as intermediaries between the two competing positions of litigators (Positions One and Three). In turn, this brokerage function explains the strength of Position Two in spite of the lower revenues brought in by its members (a lower economic performance characterizing SG&R corporate lawyers in general at the time of the study).

Among senior partners, Partners 2 and 4 had a relational profile comparable to that of Partner 1, although less inaccessible and more directly involved in work ties (without a broker such as Partner 26 for Partner 1). The two contributed largely to the exchanges with Position Three. Partner 12 had the specificity of personalizing work relationships so much that he maintained the densest exchanges within the niche and with Position One partners. But the flip side of this involvement was his position as a hanger-on in the friendship network: many of the partners from whom he sought friendship did not reciprocate. Note the presence of Partner 10, one of the least productive partners (whose relational profile will be examined more closely in the next chapter). Again, medium-seniority partners were among the most active circulators of resources. Partner 17 was probably the dominant figure in this niche. The characteristic of his profile was the fact that he maintained ten triplex reciprocated ties, an absolute record in the firm. Others such as Partners 16, 29, and 15 were very work oriented: they mixed very little work and friendship. Partner 15 had a special profile and barely made it into this niche (instead of being lost to the 'residuals'—that is, members who did not belong to any position). He was the only partner in Office III, and his reliance on many partners in Office I and II for strong cooperation was not reciprocated. His efforts to keep ties with other offices was more successful with younger associates who did want to work with him. He also had distant work relationships—that is, not personalized by friendship efforts—with 'his' own associates in Office III. Regardless of whether his efforts paid off, his contribution to the centrality of his position as a whole is clear. Finally, another very active figure was Partner 34, a junior partner who was very much sought out for advice and friendship, and very much relied upon for strong cooperation, but which were unreciprocated. Although a very central figure, she separated very clearly her involvement in the firm from her personal life.

Position Three (a niche for Partners 32, 28, 30, 35, 18, 5, 7, 3, 6, 14, and 25, and Associate 50) was made up of Office II partners (plus one associate), a mix of corporate and litigation attorneys. The niche was dense, but less centralized and dominated by a few partners, as in the previous niches. Senior partners here included Partners 3, 5, 6, 7, and 14. Indegree centrality scores in the co-workers' network were low to average for most members—given the fact that there were fewer attorneys in Office II—but very high for Partners 32, 28 (members of the associate committee), and 30; they were average in the advice network, although very high for Partners 28, 30, and 6; and very low in the friendship network, without exceptions. In terms of performance, Partners 18, 5, and 7 were also among the fifteen highest fee collectors for the previous year. Members relied on each other for *work*, as well as on associates in Positions Six and Seven, and they tended to cite (unreciprocated) as co-workers members of Position Two. They relied on each other for *advice*, as well as on members of Positions One and Two. They were sought out for advice (unreciprocated) by members of Positions Four, Six, and Seven. They relied on each other for *friendship*, and on members of Positions Two and Seven. This position had reciprocated advice and friendship ties with Position Two, and only advice (reciprocated) ties with Position One. From a business perspective, Office II seems to have been less self-contained than Office I. Its corporate partners tended to share the senior and lateral corporate associates of Position Six. With such exceptions as exchanges with (Office I) Positions Two and Six, the position's role in the circulation of resources within the firm was limited to Office II members.

Members with firm-wide status included partners such as Partners 5, 6, 14, 28, and 31. Partner 5 had the same status in Office II as Partner 1 in Office I, although less sought out for advice only, and more involved in many work ties with junior partners and associates (without a second). Partner 6 was also very active in advising junior partners and associates, and in addition had great professional status outside the firm, making him a much sought-out adviser generally, which accounted for a good proportion of the requests for advice received by his position. His relational profile, though, was different from that of Partner 5: he was isolated socially and personally. He had strong work ties, as he considered at least five people as important co-workers, but they did not reciprocate. Partner 28 was very active in exchanges with all three resources: with a record number (six times the mean) of reciprocated work and advice ties to Office I partners, he was an important bridge between the two offices (although not very popular yet), and with five triplex reciprocated ties (twice the mean) he was a key social figure within Office II.[9] Partner 31, who was a very sociable and outgoing member (a cheerleader, as he called himself) of the ATC, was a record breaker for unreciprocated uniplex ties: for example, the number of persons he cited for friendship who did not reciprocate was six times the mean, much like Partner 12. However, he also had a near record number of triplex reciprocated ties with other partners, which accounted for a large part of such ties with Office I (especially Position Two) partners.

Note that a number of the partners in this Office III niche had a less clear profile. Partner 14 was a recent lateral partner, but he nevertheless had an above average number of saturated (that is, triplex reciprocated) ties, including Position One partners. Partner 18 was among the highest performers in the firm for that (and the next) year, but also one of the most isolated persons in the firm, with mostly task-oriented ties. Partner 33 was also a very productive attorney, but with few ties, many of them unreciprocated. Conversely, Partner 25 was one of the lowest performers, and also among the partners who had the fewest ties in the firm; his was a clear case of a partner whose 'insurance-policy' ties against exclusion were neatly identifiable with two saturated (triplex reciprocated) relationships, which stood out in a pool of many unreciprocated social ties.

As already mentioned, gravitating around the first three niches in Figure 3.1, were six positions of associates, who by definition were more dependent than, and on, partners. They were less centralized than the previous three positions, which reflects a lesser capacity for collective action among associates.

Position Four (in which Associates 47, 44, and 37 had approximately the same profile) was made up of the three Office III associates, who were quite marginal in the firm; what characterized them was their absence of ties, even among each other, except to Partner 15, their own Office III partner. Indegree centrality scores were among the lowest in all networks. In terms of associate performance, they were among the average fee collectors for the previous year. They relied on each other for *work*, as well as on Office I partners of Position Two (which included Partner 15); they tended to rely on Position One partners for work, but this was not reciprocated. They did not rely on colleagues for friendship, not even on one another.[10] They sought advice (unreciprocated) from partners in Positions One, Two, and Three. This position was a very weakly cohesive bloc of associates, which had no access to production resources easily, and especially not from Office II, thus remaining extremely dependent on Partner 15.

Position Five (a niche for Associates 52, 41, 57, 43, 49, and 39) was made up of Office I litigation associates, a mix of senior associates and younger ones, mainly defined in this exchange system by their strong triplex reciprocated ties with Position One. Senior associates here included Associates 39, 41, and 43 (recall that two other senior associates on the litigation side were members of Position One itself). Indegree centrality scores in the co-workers' network were high for most members, especially for Associate 52, who was also a broker, for example, for Partners 22, 23, and 24; they were average in the advice network, except for the very central Associate 41; and average in the friendship network (except again for the very central Associate 41). In terms of economic performance, these associates were among the average fee collectors for the previous year, except for Associate 39, who was also a particularly high performer. They relied on each other, and on Position Nine associates, for *work*. They were also cited (unreciprocated) as strong co-workers by Position Seven members (Office II litigation associates). They relied on each other for *advice*, in spite of the fact that they competed for the same partnership spots, not hesitating to give each other signs of recognition of status, for which they also had reciprocal ties with Position One. They tended to seek out Position Two, and to be sought out (unreciprocated) by younger associates in Positions Seven and Nine. They did rely on each other for *friendship*, but also tended to have reciprocal ties with members of Positions One, Six, and Eight. They were cited (unreciprocated) as friends by Positions Seven and Nine. The members of this position developed ties with each other that helped them in managing the other associates for busy partners. Their main role in the circulation of resources within the firm was obviously that of a buffer and as intermediaries between Position One and the rest of the associates (at least in Office I). Close ties with Position II relieved any difficulties with regard to access to all specialities represented in the firm. But absence of direct multiplex reciprocated ties to Position Three litigation partners (in Office II) reflected an informal 'no bypass' rule (with respect to their own litigation partners in position One). Interestingly, desolidarization attempts by partners did not have much effect on this niche: it would have been too difficult for these associates to operate as intermediaries without coordination. In some ways, this density represented a way of keeping close to one's competitors.

Position Six (a niche for Associates 46, 60, and 45) was made up of three lateral corporate associates (in Office I and Office II). In terms of their role in the circulation of resources, they were often sought out by partners, but they could not be compared in importance to Position Five associates on the litigation side: they did not function at the same scale as intermediaries between corporate partners and corporate associates (especially Position Eight), and they did not have the strong friendship ties with partners (owing perhaps to their late arrival in the firm). Indegree centrality scores in the co-workers' network were average except for the very central Associate 45; they were low in the advice network; and low in the friendship network. In terms of performance, the associates were among the average fee collectors for the previous year. But they constituted a closely knit triad, with one of the most complex relational profiles: they relied on each other for *work*, and had reciprocal ties with Positions Two, Three, and Eight—that is, all the positions including corporate attorneys. They relied on each other for *advice*, had reciprocal ties with Position Two, sought out (unreciprocated) Position Three partners, and were sought out (unreciprocated) by Position Eight associates. They relied on each other for *friendship*, and had reciprocal ties with Positions Five, Eight, and Nine; they tended to cite (unreciprocated) Position Two partners, and to be cited (unreciprocated) as friends by Position Seven members. This created a dense niche for technically appreciated associates, but with a slight handicap in comparison to Position Five colleagues, given their lack of personalized friendship ties to partners.

Position Seven (a niche for Partner 33 and Associates 51, 59, and 58) was an Office II litigation niche. Indegree centrality scores were low in all networks. In terms of associate performance, they were among the average fee collectors for the previous year. The niche had reciprocal *work ties* within itself, reciprocal ties with Position Three (Office II partners), and it cited (unreciprocated) Position Five as co-workers. It had *advice ties* within itself, and sought advice (unreciprocated) from Positions One, Three, and Five (the main other litigators in the firm). It had *friendship ties* within itself, and reciprocal ties with partners in Position Three; it cited (unreciprocated) Positions Five and Six, and was cited (unreciprocated) as friends by Position Eight. In this niche, Partner 33, a typical 'baby partner' operated as an intermediary between young associates and more senior litigation partners in the same office. The members of this niche did not have firm-wide status, as Position Five associates did, and they tended to be slightly marginalized (as hangers-on to Office I litigation positions) by the status competition between litigation partners in Positions One and Three.

Position Eight (in which second-year Associates 62, 61, 64, 42, and 70 had approximately the same relational profile) was an Office I corporate position built in reference to Associate 42, a senior associate who was not clustered to Position Six. These associates were survivors from the lay-offs of junior associates that had taken place six months before the fieldwork. Indegree centrality scores were low in all networks, except for Associate 64 in the friendship network (she was older than most young associates and played a role of confidante for many of them). In terms of associate performance, they were among the lowest fee collectors for the previous year. The position had no *work ties* within itself, but had close reciprocal work ties with Positions Two and Six. Members did not seek each other for *advice*, but sought advice (unreciprocated) from Positions One, Two, Three, and Six. It had *friendship ties* within itself, reciprocal ties with Positions Five, Six, and Nine; it cited (unreciprocated) Position Seven. Members were heavily dependent on position Two, and had no access to corporate partners in Office II (again, the 'no-bypass' rule).

Position Nine (a niche for junior Associates 68, 66, 71, 65, 67, 69, 55, 56, and 54) included the young associates (first and second years) in Office I, most likely to become litigators under market pressures at the time of the fieldwork. Indegree centrality scores were low in all networks. In terms of associate performance, they were among the lowest fee collectors for the previous year. The position had reciprocal *work ties* within itself, and reciprocal ties with Positions One and Five (their brokers to partners). It had *advice ties* within itself, and sought advice (unreciprocated) from Positions One and Five. It had *friendship ties* within itself, and reciprocal ties with Positions Six and Eight; it also cited (unreciprocated) Positions Five. This niche of junior associates was heavily dependent on Positions Five and One for most of its resources.

Examples of partners who were either nicheless or very marginal in their niche—that is, with a unique relational profile—include Partner 19 (who was quite central in the co-workers' network and one of the fifteen highest fee collectors for the previous year), who was lost to the 'residuals'[11] by Position Two. His specificity as a partner was that his relational profile had a much more than average proportion of unreciprocated ties (in an unusual direction, especially because he sought advice from associates who did not seek advice from him). He had almost no friendship ties, except two reciprocated triplex ties (his 'insurance policy'). Partner 31 (who was quite central in the friendship network, and an average fee collector) was lost by Position Three; Associate 48 (who was a recent lateral recruit) by Position Six; Associate 53 (who was an average performing 'permanent associate' specializing in tax law) by Position Four; and Associate 63 (who was a relatively high performing junior associate in Office II) by Position Three.

When staying at this structural level, it is easier to get a sense of how exchanges use different resources at the same time, and of the overall pattern of exchanges of the three resources in the firm. However, this representation is inductive. Statistical analysis is needed to confirm the existence of such niches, using at least indications from the dyadic level. The next section summarizes the logic of identification underlying the formation of niches and provides such tests.[12]

CONFIRMING THE EXISTENCE OF NICHES: A VIEW AT THE DYADIC LEVEL

Informed by this understanding of the reasons for choosing some colleagues as opposed to others as sources of resources, it is also reasonable to expect that dimensions of firm structure (indicated by formal and informal attributes of members) had a significant effect on the choices of exchange partners observed in this firm. Here, to confirm the existence of niches, I look at these respective effects of attributes on interactions or access to resources. Specifically, I show how choices of sources of resources were influenced by formal dimensions of firm structure, such as hierarchical status (partner/associate), office membership, and speciality. I assume that members perceived these categories as similarities and used these similarities to guide their choices. I look at these effects for each resource separately. As already seen, exchanges of different resources were not independent of each other, but they did each have a life of their own because they solved different problems.

The effects of formal dimensions of structure (that partly define niches) on choices of *co-workers* were likely to be significant for several reasons. Building such strong work ties could depend on many factors such as availability of work, rules of intake and assignment (since a committee tried to distribute work to associates so as to prevent possible conflicts and to expose associates to different partners), access to partners with appropriate clients, and unchallenged power to choose co-workers. Strong work ties were sometimes built on a common experience of previously working together. Such experiences clearly depended on an opportunity structure (members had different specialities, worked in different offices) and individual preferences for potential co-workers' reputations or other characteristics. In this context, partners had obviously more opportunities to choose associates based on their preferences than the other way around, although the latter situation arose when an associate was much in demand. Thus, in their efforts to access cooperation (work opportunities or colleagues), it was easier for members to obtain it on a day-to-day basis in the same office, and it was more likely that members of the same office would expect long-term solidarity from one another (as opposed to expecting strong cooperative goodwill from members of other offices). Given that they often worked together on the same files, it was more likely that members of the same speciality would expect long-term solidarity from one another (as opposed to members from other specialities). Given the big divide between partners and associates, it was more likely that members of the same hierarchical status would rely on each other for strong cooperation (as opposed to expecting strong cooperative goodwill from members of a different status): in effect, partners knew that associates might not be there for long. For associates, the picture was different, but with the same effect: they might have expected strong cooperation (got sufficient quantities of interesting work, for example) from partners, but they knew that partners called the shots, and that all partners' interests were not the same (for example, that the schedulers tried not to let clientelistic ties get in the way of 'fairness' in access to such cooperation). Therefore, they were likely to fall back on other associates, in spite of efforts by partners to scatter and desolidarize associates. Finally, it would make sense to hypothesize that among business heads gender was not likely to have an effect on the extent to which members relied on each other for strong cooperation—although there could be reasons to hypothesize the opposite. For the same (fragile) reasons, it makes sense to hypothesize that solidarity based on having been to the same law school (that is, having the same level of prestige) was also unlikely to have an effect on the choices of strong co-workers, the latter being too closely associated with actual work and business decisions.[13]

Given the importance of *advice* as a vital resource in this type of knowledge-intensive firm, one could easily believe that flows of advice were 'free' or at least that they did not encounter structural obstacles that would systematically prevent exchanges of intelligence between any two members. However, even in a context that was saturated with advice, several factors created obstacles for exchanges of ideas. In several ways, the same type of reasoning applies to the two other resources. The effects of formal dimensions of structure on choices of advisers were also likely to be significant, because it was easier for members to obtain advice on a day-to-day basis in the same office and in the same speciality—that is, in their own niche. However, advice could be expected to come from more senior, experienced, and authoritative members. Seniority should, therefore, come in as a more discriminant characteristic in describing the flows of this resource. In addition, the importance of status may be connected with the nature of advice as a resource. Advice can include content that is not always predictable in advance. It often happens that advisers reformulate the question asked by advice-seekers, who thus may find themselves in a situation of 'meta-ignorance' (Smithson 1985). In such conditions of uncertainty about the question itself, the latter may include a quest for approval and legitimacy. Given this dimension of advice-seeking behaviour, it made sense for some actors to let face-saving status games or considerations of accountability (that is, covering themselves) frame their advice-seeking behaviour. In addition, advisers too were aware of the fact that questions submitted to them were sometimes controversial and could raise tricky issues of confidentiality. Finally, for the same reasons as for co-workers' goodwill, it makes (fragile) sense not to expect gender and law school attended to have a significant effect on advice seeking.

Finally, constraints of specific dimensions of formal structures on selection of *friends* in a professional firm were likely to be significant for several reasons. As seen above, partners were often friends with other partners from the days of their common associateship. Their selective socializing went well beyond the require-ments of task-related cooperation, although many felt that socializing was hampered by the fact that they did not see each other on a day-to-day basis.[14] However, compared to ties with other members of the firm (associates or partners from other offices), ties with a friendship component were very distinctive. In this case, many reasons could have explained these asymmetries in the selection of friends, especially high sensitivity of members to formal dimensions of the structure. In a situation of status competition where members exposed themselves, they could also want to protect themselves from lack of control by choosing people who were familiar to them with respect to various common characteristics. This is consistent with pre-vious work on the determinants of the formation of friendship: members want people similar to them (McPherson and Smith-Lovin 1987); they choose friends among people with whom long-term exchanges are likely to be easy. Partners knew that it could be painful to be entangled in friendships with associates about whom they would make career decisions. Thus similarity in status was likely to count, although such friendships could also mitigate conflicts arising from exploitation. In addition, it is easier to work when people who think alike, and friends, relative to non-friends, often make similar attributions (Feld 1981; Krackhardt 1992; Krac-khardt and Kilduff 1990; Lincoln and Miller 1979). Friendship induces agreement on important things.[15] Therefore, the effects of formal dimensions of structure on personalization of workplace relationships were likely to be significant for several reasons. It was easier for members to maintain friendship ties with contemporaries whom they met on a day-to-day basis in the same office and with the same status. Since members usually became friends when they entered the firm as junior associates, and since they had not yet specialized then, having the same speciality should have less effect here than for the two previous resources. Here, we would expect characteristics such as gender and law school to have a significant effect on choices of friends, because these were components of members' exogenous iden-tities, which preceded their membership in the firm. Therefore, such identities created precisely the viewpoints needed to produce some role distance from what was being experienced within the firm.

Thus niches are identified by patterns that are predictable by interests analysis if interests are defined as 'long-term' interests—that is, in a way that includes repeated exchanges of various types of resources. Identities are not opposed to interests. They simplify the perception of these interests and make dense and multiplex exchanges easier. Access to resources depends on identities, because members compare themselves to members similar to themselves and use boundary management to create solidarity in barter and multifunctional exchanges characterizing their multiplex ties. Niche building or joining becomes an identity issue, because mutual identifications partly define long-term interests and solidarities. Niches thus allow members to combine short- and long-term interests. In turn, in later chapters, processes such as mitigation of status competition will be expected to depend on the existence of these niches.

Endogenous and exogenous determinants of the distribution of resources

To check and disentangle these effects of identity criteria on the choices of co-workers, advisers, and friends, and therefore on the (re)creation of niches, I use another specific methodology, p_2 models.[16] These models estimate the effects of various covariates on the presence of a tie, controlling for reciprocity and differences between the individual actors in the number of ties in which they are involved. The covariates can be related to the 'sender' or to the 'receiver' of the tie separately, and also be used to express their similarity. These effects control for one another.[17]

Covariates used here are the three dimensions of formal structure of this firm that were expected to be the most important for access to sources of resources, and thus for the process of resource distribution: hierarchical status, speciality, and office membership. The first covariate is hierarchical status, a variable with two levels, partners and associates. This variable is elaborated upon in the second covariate, seniority. This second covariate is a variable with five levels, three of which are possible for a partner, and five for associates. Seniority is defined by the rank of partners in the letterhead, which was mainly based on age and years with the firm (with the exception of four partners who were hired from other firms). Coding of seniority for partners in *senior, medium-seniority,* and *junior* levels is based on cut-offs between Partners 14 and 15 (a difference of eight years in age) and between Partners 27 and 28 (a difference of nine years in age). These categories were explicitly used by the partners themselves. For associates, seniority had the meaning of being a member of a cohort recruited the same year. We can thus look at gradual effects of numerical rank on shaping flows of resources. Office membership and practice are the third and fourth covariates. Office is a variable with three levels, Offices I, II, and III; practice with two levels, litigation and corporate. The next covariates are the other, more exogenous, attributes, of the actors: gender and law school attended. These attributes are included as control variables representing two characteristics of the outside world that could have an influence on shaping flows of resources. Law school attended is a variable with three levels, indicating whether a lawyer went to an Ivy League law school, to a regional non-Ivy League law school, or to another law school. Table 3.2 presents the distribution of lawyers in this firm per variable.

Using these characteristics, several p_2 models were estimated to establish the influence of such dimensions of structure on members' choices of co-workers, advisers, and friends. Analysis of the determinants of sociometric choices are carried

Table 3.2. *Distribution of members per variable*

Variable	Hierarchical status		Total
	Partners	Associates	
Seniority Level 1	14	7	
Seniority Level 2	13	10	
Seniority Level 3	9	5	
Seniority Level 4		7	
Seniority Level 5		6	
Office I	22	26	48
Office II	13	6	19
Office III	1	3	4
Speciality litigation	20	21	41
Speciality corporate	16	14	30
Men	33	20	53
Women	3	15	18
Law school Ivy League	12	3	15
Law school regional non-Ivy League	11	17	28
Law school other	13	15	28
Total	36	35	71

out at the dyadic level.[18] Table 3.3 presents the three best models provided by this analysis, one for each type of resource. The exact definition of each variable in Table 3.3 is provided by Table 3.2 and by Appendix C for derived similarity variables. This chapter focuses on the choices made by both partners and associates[19] at the firm-wide level. The parameter estimates of μ, ρ, etc., are given together with their standard errors. Including other effects did not improve the model. Overall, effects predicted in the previous section are confirmed by the statistical analyses.

Influences on the selection of co-workers

For the co-workers' network, the underlying story behind Table 3.3's figures can be summarized as follows. First, in this firm, overall, differences in status, office, speciality, gender, and law school did not have a significant effect on the propensity to choose strong co-workers. Members of one office did not cite more or less strong co-workers than members of another office did, members of one speciality more or less than members of another, women more or less than men. In general, partners did not choose more or less co-workers than associates—but note the only one significant sender effect, that is, that senior partners tended to cite less strong co-workers than other lawyers did.

Secondly, office, speciality, or gender did not have a significant effect on the fact of being sought out as a strong co-worker. Members of one office were not significantly sought out more or less than members of another office, members of one speciality

Table 3.3. P2 estimates of the effect of various characteristics of partners and associates on their selections of co-workers, advisers, and friends

Dependent variables	Independent variables	Empty model (W)	Final model (W)	Empty model (A)	Final model (A)	Empty model (F)	Final model (F)
Sender	Variance σ_A^2	0.89 (0.12)	0.87 (0.12)	0.58 (0.08)	0.75 (0.11)	0.95 (0.13)	1.14 (0.16)
	Status		0.41 (0.34)				2.41 (0.51)
	Partner seniority level 1		−0.80 (0.38)		−0.92 (0.30)		0.47 (0.20)
	Partner seniority level 2		0.34 (0.38)				0.21 (0.21)
Receiver	Variance σ_B^2	0.48 (0.07)	0.41 (0.06)	0.76 (0.10)	0.49 (0.08)	0.67 (0.10)	0.61 (0.10)
	Status						1.85 (0.64)
	Associate seniority level		−0.19 (0.05)		−0.50 (0.06)		−1.30 (0.75)
Sender–receiver	Covariance σ_{AB}	−0.44 (0.08)	−0.31 (0.07)	−0.25 (0.07)	−0.05 (0.06)	−0.38 (0.09)	−0.28 (0.09)
Density	μ	−2.34 (0.10)	−3.81 (0.22)	−1.87 (0.12)	−3.98 (0.22)	−2.89 (0.13)	−6.85 (0.51)
	Similarity status		0.65 (0.15)				
	Similarity status 1				0.89 (0.22)		
	Similarity status 2						
	Similarity partner seniority						
	Similarity associate seniority				0.98 (0.19)		0.98 (0.16)
	Superiority seniority				−0.29 (0.11)		
	Superiority partner–associate						0.77 (0.19)
	Similarity office		1.03 (0.13)		1.79 (0.11)		1.82 (0.20)
	Similarity office II		0.85 (0.23)				
	Similarity office III		0.35 (0.61)				
	Similarity speciality		1.41 (0.10)		1.60 (0.12)		0.38 (0.08)
	Similarity status* speciality		−0.55 (0.14)				
	Similarity gender				0.29 (0.11)		0.29 (0.10)
	Similarity law school				0.20 (0.09)		0.17 (0.08)
Reciprocity	ρ	3.16 (0.12)	3.16 (0.20)	1.42 (0.13)	1.46 (0.25)	3.28 (0.16)	4.92 (0.52)
	Similarity status		−1.03 (0.26)				
	Similarity speciality						−1.41 (0.39)
	Similarity office				−0.81 (0.28)		−1.32 (0.45)

Notes: Standard errors in parentheses. The definitions of the independent variables are provided in the text and in Appendix C.

Sources: Reprinted from Social Networks, E. Lazega and M. Van Duijn, 'Position in Formal Structure, Personal Characteristics and Choices of Advisors in a Law Firm: A Logistic Regression Model for Dyadic Network Data', 19: 390. Copyright 1997 with permission from Elsevier Science. Reprinted from European Sociological Review, E. Lazega, 'Teaming Up and Out? Cooperation and Solidarity in a Collegial Organization', 16: 253. Copyright 2000 with permission from Oxford University Press.

than members of another, women than men. There is one significant receiver effect, however: it shows that, the more junior the associates, the less they were cited as strong co-workers. The choice of co-workers was, therefore, slightly asymmetric, because it was sensitive to status, as represented by seniority levels: senior partners and junior associates—that is, at both ends—behaved differently from the rest of the members.

Thirdly, various similarities account for many of the differences observed in the choices of strong co-workers. Density effects show that the general activity in this network tended to be significantly higher among attorneys similar in terms of various characteristics. Members tended to choose as strong co-workers lawyers of the same speciality more than those in different specialities (strongest effect), lawyers in the same office (especially in Office II), and lawyers of the same status.[20] Mobilizing similarities in terms of several attributes was perceived by members to be a useful device for creating strong work ties. When controlling for such effects, more personal characteristics of members, such as gender or law school attended, become insignificant. Other effects not quantified here (and which are therefore included in the 'random' part of the model) operated as well.

Finally, these similarities did not account much for direct reciprocity among members. A single extra direct reciprocity effect is significant: it is an effect that qualifies, or 'moderates',[21] the above-mentioned density effect: attorneys similar in status reciprocated their choices of strong co-workers more to each other than to attorneys different in status. The extra reciprocity between lawyers with the same status (which is left 'unexplained' by the corresponding density effect) was larger than between lawyers differing in status. In other words, partners still directly reciprocated more to other partners than to associates, and associates more to associates than to other partners. This means that the probability of having a directly reciprocal strong work relationship among people similar in terms of status was stronger (than between people different in status). With the prudence imposed by the negative reciprocity effect, it is possible to interpret the fact that partners directly reciprocated more to partners than to associates, and associates more to associates than to partners, as meaning that members of the same status considered each other as direct providers of the kind of security represented by strong work ties. Associates relied on each other for a certain kind of security beyond the immediate short term, such as help in carrying out an assignment, in getting access to specific cases; partners counted on other partners for the same purpose (getting access to other clients, mainly, and cooperating in managing and selecting skilled associates)[22] more than they counted on associates. These effects suggest the existence of a complex, two-tiered, and politicized indirect exchange system. The importance of status underlies the differences in resources exchanged for security: help in work among associates, clients and cases among partners.

To summarize, access to strong work relationships thus depended mostly on determinants such as formal characteristics of members. Among these similarity effects, the strongest were speciality, office, and status in decreasing order. Building strong work ties thus happened with colleagues in niches defined by the same speciality, the same office, and the same status. In their exchanges of cooperation, members tended to rely first on homophily based on characteristics defined from within the firm. Members sought similarity of attributes with significant co-workers across a limited number of dimensions. Notice that more personal characteristics such as gender and law school did not have a significant influence on members' citations; they did not contribute significantly in shaping strong work ties when controlling for more work-related attributes. Thus exogenous identities did not have a clear effect on members' access to strong cooperation and building of strong work ties. Overall, members tended to count on colleagues of the same office and the same speciality for strong cooperation. Thus they did tend to create specialized niches in their local office, niches that were nested within their general practice firm. On the one hand, the distribution of resources was thus very functional. But, on the other hand, this suggests a pattern of solidarity in which members exchanged this security vertically as much as horizontally because partners usually worked with and tended to prefer associates, not other partners (relatively weaker status effect). Such a vertical solidarity is precisely an indication of the existence of patronage or clientelism. Choices creating strongly knitted clientelistic niches also created the possibility of firm disintegration. This dilemma will be dealt with in Chapter 6.

Influences on the selection of advisers

The firm's formal structure had to channel knowledge and expertise. Overall, office, speciality, gender, and law school did not have a significant effect on the propensity to seek advice. Members of one office did not seek advice more than members of another office, members of one speciality more than members of another, women more than men. The only strong and significant effect was the status of top partners, who sought advice less than attorneys below them (in terms of seniority). This indicates that there was, in this firm, a Blau-type iron law of status: one does not seek advice from people 'below' (Lazega and Van Duijn 1997). Hence the only significant receiver effect, which shows that associates were sought out for advice much less than partners. Again, the extent to which one was sought out for advice did not depend on one's office, speciality, gender, or law school.

Within this constraint of status, the overall density effects show that general activity in the advice network tended to be significantly higher among people similar in terms of differing characteristics than among people different in terms of those characteristics. Thus, advice relationships existed more between people in the same office than between people in different offices, between people in the same speciality, and also between people similar in status. Among these similarity effects, the strongest are office, speciality, and status in decreasing order. Weaker but significant density effects are also of interest. Lawyers of same gender and same law school did exchange more advice with one another than lawyers differing with regard to these characteristics. As mentioned before, one can hypothesize that these dimensions helped members in mitigating the severity of this iron law of status and seniority. Members could still play on similarities in terms of office, speciality, gender, and law school in order to bypass the seniority rule. For instance, in this firm, litigators had a significantly higher probability of choosing advisers among other litigators rather than among corporate lawyers; a similar trend was observed among the latter. With speciality, members could play on the content of the advice being sought. By playing on similarity in office membership, they could claim that seeking advice from more junior persons in one's own office was better than bypassing one's own local colleagues. Such choices thus did mitigate the severity of status games. Exchanges of advice could become more personalized than exchanges of other, more directly task-related, resources.[23] A single significant reciprocity effect shows that corporate lawyers had a stronger probability of reciprocating to each other than litigators. Absence of reciprocation as an extra effect tended to offset part of the positive effect of speciality similarity as a density effect—that is, the effect of speciality as an identity criterion chosen by members to secure legitimate access to advice.

To summarize, the p_2 model shows how selected dimensions of formal structure of the firm weighed heavily on interactions related to advice. Flows of ideas and intelligence in this collegial firm were indeed affected by status games among members. Advice seeking tends to go upward. As a possible way to mitigate or neutralize such status games, reciprocal exchanges tended to happen much more within niches defined by formal boundaries such as office and speciality areas, or to rely (to a lesser extent) on homogeneity based on characteristics defined from outside the firm, such as gender or law school attended. In turn, such constraints on exchanges of ideas among members were managed in different ways by the members of the firm, which created disadvantages and inequalities among them (see Chapter 4).

Influences on the selection of friends

Even on this more 'intimate' aspect of members' lives, formal structure did have a constraining influence. Access to this type of resource, the way friendships were created, was prearranged by an opportunity structure. Within these constraints, friendship choices aggregated into an informal structure too. What does this structure tell us about the way members helped each other 'be somebody', assert their identity, take some distance by defining their relationship *vis-à-vis* the group, and ultimately reach a position from where they claimed credit and recognition in the firm?

In this firm, differences among attorneys did not have an effect on their propensity to cite friends. For instance, senior partners did not cite fewer friends than junior ones. If it was lonely at the top, it was no less so at the bottom. But partners did tend to be cited as friends more than associates, the latter expecting more support from the former than the other way around.[24] It is interesting to note, again, the massive effect of homophily and similarities in terms of formal attributes, but this time also in terms of personal attributes, on general activity in the friendship network. All the dimensions retained count here, which is unique for the three networks. General activity in the friendship network tended to be significantly higher among people similar in terms of the characteristics retained than among people different in terms of those characteristics. Status differences between partners and associates came first. Among partners, this was more true for senior ones than for more junior ones. Being in the same office was the next strongest determinant of the choice of friends. Two significant reciprocity effects added an extra weight to status and office, whose members cited each other symmetrically more than they cited members of different status and office. Thus in this firm friendship ties were particularly sensitive to similarities.

Being on the same level of seniority, for partners and for associates, was the next most important determinant. But note that, consistent with the status receiver effect mentioned above, this was 'countered' by the fact that members lower in seniority tended to consider members higher in seniority as friends. Friendship citations also tended to go up, although less so than advice citations. Finally, the weaker but significant density effects already noticed above for other resources emerge here again on the firm-wide level. Similarity with respect to speciality, gender, and law school did have a significant effect too, although weaker, on the existence of friendship ties among members. Thus members could play on more attributes (than for other resources) to engage in exchanges of resources attached to friendship (definition of the situation, emotional support, etc.).

In short, these analyses show how all dimensions of the formal structure of the firm, as well as more exogenous attributes, weighed on interactions related to common socializing outside the firm and helped members secure legitimate access to resources offered by this form of socializing outside work.[25] Formal structure and role distance combined in niches. Whereas advice seeking tended to go upward, friendship ties tended to follow members' similarities and to be more horizontal.

To summarize, when taking into account exchanges among all attorneys, characteristics based on formal dimensions of firm structure—similarities in terms of office, speciality, and status respectively and across the three networks—consistently affected exchange interactions and informal allocations of resources needed to produce and survive in this context. In addition to such consistent and strong determinants, some variations also emerge: for example, members also sought advice from more senior colleagues, while selecting friends among colleagues of roughly the same seniority. More personal attributes, such as gender and law school attended prior to joining the firm, had a comparatively weak, but nevertheless significant effect on the circulation of less directly task-oriented resources (advice and friendship-related resources). Reciprocity effects were more consistently dependent on status.

The two attributes that members most consistently and discriminantly activated in their appropriateness judgements were office and speciality. In other words, controlling in each network for the effects of the other dimensions, similarity in terms of *office* counted most for access to all three resources and for the definition of niches. Each office operated as its own exchange subsystem. In particular, the office organized complex horizontal cooperation ties and interdependencies. For example, this driving factor in the choice of co-workers could represent market forces—that is, clients drawing partners together (and perhaps an element of geographical inertia).

The same was true for similarity in terms of *speciality*, which counted for access to all resources among all attorneys, although less strongly than office membership. Within each office, members with the same speciality tended to exchange with one another more than with others. Other discriminant effects, although less consistently so, included similarities in terms of status, gender, and law school attended. Similarity in terms of status counted for access to advice and friendship, not to get cooperation in work. In other words, attorneys seemed to play status games more when advice and friendship were involved than when they were concerned with performing actual work. Attorneys similar in ascribed characteristics such as gender and law school attended tended to be friends and to rely on each other for advice more than on attorneys of the other gender or from a different type of law school. These latest effects were not significant in work relationships, and were the weakest of all effects; they are nevertheless significant in the other networks.[26]

In conclusion, transfers and exchanges of resources at the dyadic level were institutionally driven, based on formal identities, but also personalized ones. In this collegial organization, the relational structure in each network (especially co-workers) resulted both from formal rules taking into account members' interests, and from informal and mutual adjustments made by people.[27] The analysis shows a polarized, specialized, and stratified system, thus statistically confirming the existence of social niches at SG&R. Finally, it is important to show that this exchange system carried with it the social mechanism (that of generalized exchange) that is key to understanding bounded solidarity among rival partners or interdependent entrepreneurs. For that purpose, it is indispensable to reach beyond the dyadic level, at least the triadic one. In the next section, I present an analysis of the co-workers, network that confirms the existence of this mechanism. This analysis uses a model called p^* (Pattison and Wasserman 1999), presented in Appendix E.

THE FIRM AS A WORK-RELATED GENERALIZED EXCHANGE SYSTEM

Using this p^* model,[28] specific local substructures are identified that illustrate various ways in which members cooperated. These dyadic and triadic substructures and their parameter labelling are presented in Figure 3.2. In this section, I focus only on the local *distribution of co-workers' commitment* in such substructures. This distribution is represented in the resulting model presented in Table 3.4.

The co-work relation appears to have had a local structure that is strongly suggestive of both restricted and generalized exchange (e.g. Bearman 1997; Breiger and Ennis 1997). Two of the parameters that are large and positive correspond to configurations in which co-work was exchanged directly among pairs of lawyers—namely, $\tau_{11\_w,w}$ (direct exchange for two individuals) and $\tau_{6\_w,w,w,w}$ (direct exchange of co-work by one lawyer with each of two others). In addition, the parameter for cyclic exchange among a group of three lawyers ($\tau_{10\_w,w,w}$) is also

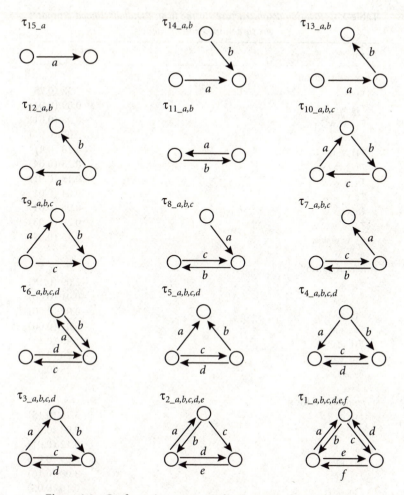

Figure 3.2. *Configurations corresponding to p* model parameters*

Note: The symbols *a, b, c, d, e,* and *f* may refer to any of the uniplex or multiplex relations—namely, W (co-work), A (advice), F (friendship), WA (co-work and advice), WF (co-work and friendship), AF (advice and friendship), WAF (co-work, advice, and friendship).

Source: Reprinted from *Social Networks,* E. Lazega and P. Pattison, 'Multiplexity, Generalized Exchange and Cooperation in Organizations', 21: 81. Copyright 1999 with permission from Elsevier Science.

large and positive.[29] The other positive parameters are $\tau_{12\_W,W}$, $\tau_{14\_W,W}$ and $\tau_{9\_W,W,W}$ and indicate several ways in which co-work ties could occur less symmetrically. In the case of $\tau_{12\_W,W}$ and $\tau_{14\_W,W}$, it appears that some individuals expressed or were nominees for unreciprocated co-work ties with several (unconnected) others. In the case of $\tau_{9\_W,W,W}$, some transitivity in the arrangement

Table 3.4. *Relational substructures in the firm: Pseudolikelihood estimates for three univariate p* models*

Term	PLE
Co-work relation[a]	
τ_{15_W}	−3.32 (0.28)
$\tau_{14\_W,W}$	0.09 (0.01)
$\tau_{13\_W,W}$	−0.08 (0.01)
$\tau_{12\_W,W}$	0.07 (0.01)
$\tau_{11\_W,W}$	4.18 (0.41)
$\tau_{10\_W,W,W}$	0.28 (0.04)
$\tau_{9\_W,W,W}$	0.13 (0.01)
$\tau_{8\_W,W,W}$	−0.04 (0.01)
$\tau_{7\_W,W,W}$	−0.08 (0.01)
$\tau_{6\_W,W,W,W}$	0.20 (0.03)
$\tau_{3\_W,W,W,W}$	−0.13 (0.02)
Advice relation[b]	
τ_{15_A}	−2.09 (0.18)
$\tau_{14\_A,A}$	−0.01 (0.00)
$\tau_{13\_A,A}$	−0.07 (0.00)
$\tau_{12\_A,A}$	−0.01 (0.00)
$\tau_{11\_A,A}$	1.45 (0.13)
$\tau_{10\_A,A,A}$	−0.20 (0.02)
$\tau_{9\_A,A,A}$	0.28 (0.01)
Friendship relation[c]	
τ_{15_F}	−3.25 (0.18)
$\tau_{14\_F,F}$	0.02 (0.01)
$\tau_{13\_F,F}$	−0.12 (0.01)
$\tau_{12\_F,F}$	0.05 (0.01)
$\tau_{11\_F,F}$	3.08 (0.16)
$\tau_{10\_F,F,F}$	−0.18 (0.05)
$\tau_{9\_F,F,F}$	0.32 (0.02)

[a] −2LPL = 2,913.7; MAR = 0.177.
[b] −2LPL = 2,855.6; MAR = 0.17.
[c] −2LPL = 1,795.9; MAR = 0.102.

Notes for the three models: PLE: Pseudolikelihood estimates (approximative standard errors in parentheses). −2LPL: −2 times the log of the maximum pseudolikelihood. MAR: mean absolute residual. See Figure 3.2 for visual representation of τ terms.

Source: Reprinted from *Social Networks*, 'Multiplexity, Generalized Exchange and Cooperation in Organizations', E. Lazega and P. Pattison, 21: 79–80. Copyright 1999 with permission from Elsevier Science.

of co-work ties is evident. The negative estimate for $\tau_{3\_w,w,w,w}$ suggests that configurations that 'break' the exchange balance inherent in the 3-cycle were unlikely. Taken together, these parameters suggest a structure of co-work ties that was consistent, at least in part, with both direct and generalized exchange of co-work.[30] Further, it is clear from configurations such as $\tau_{6\_w,w,w,w}$ that these exchange structures could overlap, and this leads one to view the overall co-work structure as a collection of overlaid smaller exchange substructures. In addition to these structural tendencies, though, it is clear that co-work ties had some properties that would not be expected in a structure whose only 'logic' was that of exchange. These latter properties include a propensity for differentiation among lawyers in the expression and receiving of co-work ties, as well as a weak tendency towards transitivity. These characteristics are further discussed in the context of the multivariate p^* model in Chapter 5.

The existence of this generalized exchange system is consistent with the basic behavioural assumption that members of collegial organizations seek niches where they can rely on various forms of bounded solidarity with otherwise potential competitors (rival partners or associates). The presence of this social mechanism is a first contribution of the structural study of this collegial organization. In the next section, I stress the fact that, although it was useful to the firm as a whole, this mechanism also relied on desolidarization, if not exploitation, of associates.

DESOLIDARIZATION OF ASSOCIATES

In the pattern presented by Figure 3.1, some positions, mainly partners', could use their centrality and the opportunities offered by its derived 'structural holes' (Burt 1992). For example, they could more easily force unconnected associates from different positions to compete for interesting cases, advice, and moral support. Opportunistic behaviour was less accepted within niches where partial suspension of strategic behaviour was required. But in this structure, members of the firm who were not part of one's niche were potentially members that could be more easily played off against each other and exploited. Especially in the crucial advice network, partners in Position One could play that game systematically with associates of Positions Five against Nine; partners of Position Two with associates of Positions Six against Eight; and partners of Position Three with associates of Positions Six against Seven. This list of opportunities to desolidarize and exploit associates does not even take into account the structural holes between them in different offices.

In effect, in spite of being vital for the economic success of the firm, associates were much less autonomous in their practice and not formally involved in regulatory deliberations or in control processes (except perhaps in the monitoring of one another). Many did not get to trial and their practice could easily become tedious and burdened by documents and discovery. For them, the firm was first and foremost a job machine. Recall that the up-or-out 'survival of the fittest' rule was still a central mechanism by which the organization tried to protect its various forms of capital. Partners did not worry much about systematic coaching and training. Associates thus tried to manage their career from a position of weakness. What usually kept them going was high salary and the dream of becoming partners.[31] Valued associates had to perceive a reasonable chance for advancement. They did not want to be blocked by a small but dedicated group of naysayers (Eickemeyer 1988). Any hint that loyal service was becoming a less reliable path to partnership was therefore profoundly demoralizing (for example, when lateral associates were brought into the firm precisely because they had accumulated special expertise somewhere else). During the year of fieldwork for this study, the firm decided to postpone all decisions about new partners, a change that unnerved associates, bringing out explicitly issues of competition between them.

Associates could feel that the generalized and multiplex exchange system described above was forced upon them because they could be dropped out before their returns on investments (in relationships with partners) materialized. In this situation, the source of their exploitation was also less easily detectable than in a dyadic situation (Ekeh 1976: 213). In a way, dealing with this risk was part of their socialization into the difficulties of permanently personalizing and depersonalizing ('embedding' and 'disembedding') business transactions in the company of nominal equals. But the implications of the existence of this multiplex exchange mechanism for associates can be summarized in one word: desolidarization. Two facts provide support for this observation. The first is the nature of patronage. The second is a closer look at associates' niches.

Partners put much pressure on associates to work hard, closely monitored their work, observed their cooperative attitude, socialized them, evaluated their behaviour with clients, and eventually selected a few to become their partners. Relationships between partners and their subordinates were extremely asymmetrical; but they could nevertheless be both very hierarchical and, temporarily, very collegial. As will be closely examined in Chapter 5, whether defending or bringing suit, the client's file needed to be intellectually 'digested' by the task force assigned to the case, explored without too many preconceptions, especially when there was a lot of law on the subject. Attorneys dealing with it needed to probe the issue from scratch. Collegial brainstorming was the key in cases that did not fit regular patterns. Then, much of what survived from this collegial brainstorming as case strategy depended upon the ways in which the partners in charge of that client switched back from collegial, knowledge-intensive work to the hierarchical power allowing them to handle the distribution of tasks (Hazard 1989). Some partners assigned only discrete segments to various members of a team without sharing the whole picture and the overall game plan of the case. As a result, associates often felt frustrated or that they did not know what they were doing.

Thus, they had to try to carve out a place for themselves in this specific social environment, with its strong emphasis on achievement and subsequent expectations and impending frustrations (Blau 1964). They had to learn to recognize, and adjust to, partners' status games and social niche seeking. They had to learn to be careful in their own status games. For example, in their further analyses of this data-set, Robins *et al.* (2000)[32] show a 'ceiling effect' on the number of advice ties that an associate could have towards partners. This confirms the ambiguity of advice seeking for associates: they did not want to seek advice from too many partners because they thought that it might, at some point, suggest to these partners that they (advice-seeking associates) were incompetent. In effect, they sought strong sponsors among these partners, and the latter valued their relationship with other partners more than with associates. Another example: when an associate named a partner a friend, he or she was inevitably considering that partner as a potential help for promotion. To partners, friendship to associates'—if any—was more relative; in the best of cases, they sometimes voted for an associate hoping that the personal relationship with another would not be affected.

A strong cooperation tie to an important partner could be invaluable in the race for partnership. Investing in a relationship to the wrong partner could be damaging. For example, associates saw that junior partners—with whom they worked directly more often than not—were not always treated as they would expect to be by senior partners. In turn, associates feared bad treatment from these 'baby partners', who needed to prove themselves, bring the firm business, show that they could keep associates busy, and do some of more senior partners' 'dirty work'. A true patron was a strong sponsor who stuck up for his or her associates, did not let other lawyers take credit for these associates' ideas, lobbied for support from partners from other specialities, and guaranteed years of good work; but who, in exchange, also required cooperation, loyalty, and support (in status competition) from these associates on a dyadic, one-to-one, basis. As one senior associate put it: 'At the end of the process [the race for partnership], it is a lot of politics.'

In such clientelistic ties, associates were kept uncertain as to their patron's ties to other partners and to other associates. For example, it was difficult for associates (and for observers) to follow partners' power plays concerning staffing task forces or partnership decisions involving back-room deals, if any. Partners used this uncertainty in a subtle divide-and-rule strategy that was typical of patronage. A good example of such a strategy is provided by partners' use of status competition when brainstorming with associates (see Chapter 5). A raw indication of this desolidarization is that density in the strong cooperation network among associates dropped to 0.13 (from 0.22 in the overall network of partners *and* associates). Work ties were strong to partners, but in general associates did not rely that much on each other for cooperation.

Another, but related, indication is that associates alone could not create niches of the same type as partners' niches. As seen earlier in this chapter, associates did create niches of their own to get access to needed resources. But at SG&R, desolidarization was manifest in the fact that there were no niches mixing associates of different levels of seniority, and in the fact that these niches were less multifunctional than partners' ones. Even associates who were very close in terms of seniority levels, speciality, and office membership played status games with each other. They were rational when seeking to create niches among themselves; but status competition interfered with niche building much more than among partners.

Statistical analyses at the dyadic level, combined with information in Figure 3.1, confirmed that niches existed for associates at SG&R, but in a slightly different and looser way than for partners. To summarize the substantive findings, associates tended to rely on cooperation from other associates in the same office and in the same speciality, but not across seniority levels. The same was true for advice ties. There was not much reciprocity in advice relationships, but, among themselves, senior associates similar in terms of office and speciality had a 69 per cent chance of having a reciprocal advice relationship with one another, a 22 per cent chance of having a one-way relationship, and an 8 per cent chance of not having an advice relationship at all. Between senior associates and associates of seniority level 2, the chance of a reciprocal relationship dropped sharply to 29 per cent, the chance of a one-way relationship increased to 36 per cent, and the chance of not having an advice relationship at all increased to 34 per cent. Among themselves, seniority level 2 associates also similar in terms of office and speciality had a 59 per cent chance of having a reciprocal advice relationship with one another, a 27 per cent chance of having a one-way relationship, and a 14 per cent chance of not having an advice relationship at all.

A sharp contrast in this latter respect appears between associates who worked in different offices and different specialities. In terms of advice relationships, they almost lived in two different social worlds. Even among senior associates, two persons now had a virtually zero chance of a reciprocal advice relationship with one another, 9 per cent chance of having a one-way relationship, and a 91 per cent chance of not having an advice relationship at all. This trend increases when differences in levels of seniority are introduced. For instance, a senior litigation associate in Office I was almost entirely unlikely to seek advice from a senior corporate associate in another office, and even more unlikely if the latter was in a lower level of seniority. In sum, associates tended to seek advice from other associates in the same office, in the same speciality, and from more senior associates. Associates were very unlikely to seek advice from someone more junior (that is, someone who had been with the firm for a shorter time, or who was below them in the letterhead). The seniority rule was strong. Concerning friendship ties, associates left to themselves tended to seek friendship from other associates in the same office, in the same seniority level and, after a few years, in the same speciality. Associates were unlikely to establish friendship ties with someone more junior.

It is interesting, however, to see that gender mattered much more among associates at SG&R than among partners. Choices of strong co-workers were more reciprocal when they were in the same gender. A sharp contrast appears between associates of different gender who worked in different offices and different specialities. But this gender-based homophily was also limited in several ways. It was not significant for advice seeking among associates. In addition, although associates tended to mention friendship ties with same-gender associates more than with associates of the other gender, reciprocated friendship ties tended to exist with associates in the other gender more than with same-gender associates. It also turns out that having been to the same law school, another exogenous characteristic, is not statistically important for the choice of co-workers, advisers, and friends among associates at SG&R.

These looser associate niches were easily exploitable by partners but useful in associates' search for resources, for example, in learning the ropes of survival in the clientelistic game—including, sometimes, how to resist it by relying on informal ties with selected other associates. For example, they learned to pay attention to what they did not know, and whom and when to ask, so as not to reveal this ignorance— except perhaps to someone considered to be a friend, and based on exogenous characteristics such as gender. They also learned to strike a fragile balance between cooperation and competition by playing with the (often unspoken) rules: for example, seeking advice from partners not involved in the case at hand. But this in turn tended to be tolerated less for some than for others, thus becoming a double-edge sword.[33]

Cooperation is systematically amenable to structural analyses at the dyadic, triadic, and overall levels. Looking at the firm as a multiplex and multilevel exchange system, in which members vied for resources needed to produce and survive in this environment, provides a realistic view of how such a collegial organization operates. A complex exchange system—which is a politicized social system—is at work in the allocation of these resources. In this specific system, three types of resources (co-worker's goodwill, advice, and friendship) were identified as central. An overall and multiplex view of their exchanges at the structural level was provided, thus allowing for the identification of social niches in which members found bounded solidarity in access to such resources. To confirm the existence of such niches, both formal and particularistic identities of members of the firm were shown to have an effect, at the dyadic level, on the way they accessed such resources and cooperation. Members with long-term interests (represented by identities) in mind built or joined niches reflecting strong structural determinants (but not only formal rules) of resource allocation. Various forms of firm-wide status in this firm—and the partners who achieved them—were described using this network analysis. These tendencies show that cooperation among peers required a specific form of niche building, and a specific social mechanism (generalized exchange). This complex exchange system supported production in this firm. Further below, I show that, without such a social mechanism, in the absence of a credible formal hierarchy, coordination of collective action would raise insoluble difficulties.

Getting durable cooperation among peers is thus a process constrained by formal structure, involving different types of resources, and a form of rationality helping in their multiplex exchange. In turn, this exchange system and its niches sustain other processes in such a knowledge-intensive firm. The next chapter looks at two such social processes: pressure to perform and quality control. The analyses used here show that separate individual networks also reflected partial orders on their own.

4

Economic Performance and Quality Control

Both niche seeking and status competition represent two potentially advantageous micro-political activities for individuals (providing resources and motivation). This chapter focuses on their usefulness in connecting the interests of the individual and that of the firm as a whole—that is, the micro- and macro-levels in the firm. This is done by showing how social niches and status competition have an effect on economic (or quantitative) and professional (or qualitative) forms of performance: by making tenured partners work and by ensuring a form of unobtrusive quality control among peers. Performance in a corporate law firm, as in any knowledge-intensive organization, is related both to the quantity and to the quality of work. Like many such firms, SG&R competed by emphasizing both quality and price:

> You market yourself by saying that we are as good as they are, and cheaper. I mean: you don't want to push cheaper. I don't think marketing on the basis of price is such an excellent idea, but it is a fact and they all know it. I don't know that doing more than that is really useful. Some clients you cannot get anyway, because in-house counsels or vice-presidents for operations want to cover themselves and won't take the risk of hiring someone other than Cravath, Swaine & Moore in New York. (Partner 24)

Among members, concern for quantity was widespread, but the solution was relatively simple: the more partners and associates were pressured to work (especially partners, because their hourly rates were high), the more revenue they brought in. Concern for quality was also permanent, but here the solution could not be standardized (by definition of a profession). Lawyering being knowledge intensive, based partly on a series of information management tasks, formal instruments were available (library, computer memory, standard documents). But there is no pre-defined standard of quality for this type of 'certainty work'. Much of it consists of using past experience to adjust to new problems through individual and collective learning (Favereau 1994; Hatchuel 1994; Starbuck 1992). Thus it had to be done in common: cognitive efforts were more or less shared in brainstorming processes familiar to knowledge-intensive organizations. To avoid using the cognitive psychologists' term of 'distributed cognition', I use here the expression 'distributed knowledge'.[1] Knowledge was shared in two types of situation at least: in common work on cases or in case-related advice relationships. Saying that knowledge was 'shared', however, does not do justice to what really happened in the flows of intelligence and experience. The important characteristic of such flows is shown to be that knowledge as a resource is efficiently distributed/allocated through two processes: selection of exchange partners (niche seeking) and concentration of the authority to know (through status competition). Some members emerge as having the authority to know, although such status was fragile.

Recall that partners, and to a lesser extent associates, were strategic in their effort to choose quality and reliable co-workers. They were constrained by specialization and (other) partners' decisions. Unlike an elusive predefined standard of quality, brainstorming processes included an informal quality control through common monitoring and advice seeking. Finally, this chapter looks at the relationship between distributed knowledge and economic performance at SG&R, thus identifying a few conditions under which the pattern of knowledge flows is most productive for firms stressing quality professional services. Thus economic performance and quality control depend on a social mechanism supporting individual efforts and competencies. The exchange system within and beyond niche boundaries is shown to provide a structural solution to problems of motivation and supervision in the absence of strong hierarchy.

ECONOMIC PERFORMANCE: WHAT MAKES TENURED PARTNERS WORK?

Under their partnership agreement, it was in partners' collective economic interest to produce as much as possible, but it could also be perceived to be in their narrow individual interest to free-ride in the economic sense, especially in an organizational environment where several forms of status were available to individuals who sought to carve out an 'honourable' place for themselves. I argue that niche-level relational pressure and status competition are key processes by which this form of opportunistic behaviour was overcome. They both created various forms of commitment, if not involvement, in projects that were often felt to be too numerous. In effect, niches provided members with a sense of their long-term interest and with resources, but there was also an element of self-entrapment in them. Individual economic performance is shown to be associated with task-force membership.[2] In effect, through status competition, task forces produce social approval and emulation, which in turn reinforce performance. Therefore local substructures such as dense work groups in niches could favourably affect performance when they supported strong commitment. Organizational efficiency depends on the quality and configuration of interpersonal relationships between members (Lewin 1952). Performance also depends on the configuration of these relationships. The multilevel exchange system helped members produce and enhanced individual (and therefore corporate) economic performance. The analysis of the co-workers' network is key to this argument.

Recall that, in this firm, the production process was difficult to routinize. Professional expertise and advice cannot easily be standardized, and therefore 'internal' transaction costs for the firm as a whole could be assumed to be a large part of total costs. As seen in the previous chapter, under such circumstances, high density and cohesion in strong work relationships at the work-group level were represented by a 'locally multiplex' exchange system—that is, a pattern of ties among members that helped them get access to various resources, supported strong work ties and generalized exchange of cooperation, and maintained a specific form of solidarity. Focusing on intra-organizational performance data, this chapter shows that such an exchange system constrained its members—partners and associates—into reaching higher economic performance (mainly defined in terms of number of hours worked and dollar amounts brought into the firm). In other words, the members' 'labour contract' (the partnership agreement for partners and the employment contract for associates) was combined with constraining social ties both at the dyadic and at the structural level.

In effect, in the economic conditions of 1990, it can be assumed that, when performance of partners and associates was good, firm performance was also good. However, in this firm, partners could free-ride and associates could threaten the quality of work. But getting cooperation and keeping production going are also a result of exchanging these resources in a multiplex and flexible way. Therefore, the exchange system can be assumed to have maintained members' commitment and the circulation of social resources in the firm so as to sustain individual and collective performance. To show this, each member's combination of ties (with all the other members) and position in the firm's relational structure are examined below and related to his or her economic performance. Two categories of effects should be expected from this basic principle of economic sociology.

First, the social system should sustain members' commitment to their labour contract: members strongly socially integrated (both through relational investments in the firm and, for example, through norm conformity) should perform well economically, others less well.[3] On the one hand, formal dimensions of structure, in particular status and seniority, should have the greatest influence on economic performance. In general, partners put in less hours but collected more than associates because they charged more; in this firm, the more senior attorneys were, the higher their hourly fees. Associates collected less, although they put in more time than partners. On the other hand, however, the pattern of individual ties should also have an influence on economic performance: since attorneys who were informally sought out for advice and for collaboration by many others (very central ones) charged higher rates, they should also bill and collect more than others. In addition, when the pattern of each member's ties is measured in terms of Burt's constraint scores (1982),[4] results should confirm that members (both partners and associates) with a constraining co-workers' network put in more time, and collected more hours and more dollars. At SG&R, constraint represented the extent to which colleagues could exercise unobtrusive but insistent pressure on a member. The more constraining one's co-workers' network, the higher one's economic performance. High constraint in a specific network means that clique members in that network have high investments in each other and high expectations from each other. The denser a member's personal network of co-workers, the more his co-workers can coordinate their informal efforts at prodding him or her back into performing more. They could, for instance, try to increase their own collaborations with him or her, and exercise this unobtrusive but insistent pressure to put in more time. One can therefore hypothesize that, in the case of this firm, high constraint facilitated high economic performance.[5] Thus, position in informal structure and the pattern of one's personal network in this position should count for explaining performance, although these effects should compete with that of institutionally defined hourly rates.

Secondly, the effect of individual social ties on economic performance should be confirmed by looking more closely, at least at the dyadic level, at specific multiplex combinations of ties that provide a decisive push in performance increase (or that represent a liability that decreases performance). For example, specific configurations of social ties, such as mutual triplex ties, should be strongly correlated with high performance. This would flesh out a positive effect of constraint scores in the co-workers' network. High performers should draw heavily on their social resources, and, in that respect, the firm as a whole should benefit from the networks that some individuals have (dense multiplex networks, especially those constrained at the niche level in the co-workers' network), and suffer from the networks of others (sparser networks, especially those weakly constrained in the co-workers' network).

To put it in Polanyi's terms (and then those of Granovetter 1985 and Uzzi 1997), performance should be higher for members whose work ties are embedded in a way that offers access to advice (which, in this firm, was a form of free collaboration), creating economies of time, providing flexibility in exchanges by allowing a resource of one type to be exchanged for a resource of another type, and helping in forgoing immediate self-gains for a smoother and longer-term collective action. This social structure, to put it in Uzzi's words (1997), should govern the intervening processes that regulate performance outcomes, both positive and negative.

Pricing a tie? A caveat on performance data

Before moving on to test such ideas, a caveat should be made about performance data. In any organization, measurements of performance are intrinsically difficult to interpret and, at SG&R specifically, their informative value could change from one year to another. For example, given the way a partner was compensated at SG&R, looking at the dollar amount actually collected in 1991 does not indicate exactly how productive this attorney was in 1991. Work done in 1990 could be compensated in 1991 (or perhaps even later), and such overlaps make it difficult to disentangle an attorney's productivity in one year as opposed to his or her productivity in another year. Simultaneously, looking at the number of hours billed in 1991 gives an idea of an attorney's productivity in 1991, but does not mean that all the work was done in 1991. Performance data are never as 'hard' and indisputable as one often expects them to be, especially in situations where real productivity gains are difficult to identify. In fact, managers know and learn that such data must be handled with great care. Therefore, using performance measurements as a dependent or independent variable is not easy, and rarely provides spectacular results. In spite of correlation between hourly rates, human capital (years with the firm), and performance, one should not expect easy, strong, and clear-cut correlations between performance and social connections within the firm.

More importantly, given the dependence of economic performance on social processes, the relative contribution of specific individuals to economic performance was a highly political issue. Allocation of credit within task forces (that is, clearly disentangling members' contributions) was often difficult. Thus, looking at how an organization, especially a collegial one, extracts economic performance from its members requires a sociological conception of performance that must pay attention to the micro-political context of members' action and to their strategic behaviour in this context. This approach therefore entails a micro-political conception of economic performance. Narrow econometric conceptions ignore the fact that no measurement of performance in organizations ever goes unchallenged within the organization (Flap *et al.* 1998; Friedberg 1993; Meyer 1994). To some extent, criteria used to measure efficiency of actors were negotiated by members themselves. This negotiation politicized measurements of efficiency. In effect, such measurements are always multidimensional. Practitioners know that it is impossible to find simple measures of performance for organizations with multiple and often conflicting goals. Meyer (1994), for example, shows that performance measures can be considered to be temporary constraints to which members of the organization adjust. It is thus impossible to define absolute measurements of performance outside a strategic context or institutional conventions.

This is also why a direct and quantitative evaluation of social ties in purely economic terms is absurd. Social ties represent conduits for various kinds of resources, and their accumulation represents various forms of status that cannot be reduced to economic power. Rather, a single social tie can be an asset one day, a liability another. It can be a component of social processes enhancing or weakening relationship with work performance. As will be shown in Chapter 5, actual performance often depends, at some stage, on the capacity of the task force to uncouple or disembed the actual work peformance from the social ties that made it possible at an earlier stage.

In the complex context of the law firm examined here, task-force work, autonomy and flexibility in selection of co-workers, and a weak hierarchy unable to force partners to cooperate, all made it harder to provide one ideal measurement of performance by individual employees and task forces. In spite of timekeeping, performance measurement at SG&R was not comparable to Taylorian piece-rate schemes. It was, therefore, difficult to get a reasonable idea of individual productivity differences in such complex production processes. The slope of the SG&R earnings schedule could not come close to reflecting such differences, since it had no formal link to productivity and since partners got their compensation regardless of what they billed. Note that the lockstep system itself was partly explained by the fact that it was difficult to measure actual contributions of each member. The process by which attorneys produced legal services through their collegial interactions was too complex to allow such measurement. This is why, even with SG&R's compensation system, partners often insisted on 'spreading credit around generously', or sharing potential 'blame':

> Our accounting system is designed so that, if you are the billing partner and you rate off time, you can't charge it against a particular timekeeper without doing it to yourself too. The system will rate down things on a pro rata basis without distinguishing between partners and associates working on the file. People do not make themselves look good in that way.   (The managing partner at the time of the study)

Finally, there are several reasons for which variations in financial performance are not entirely explained by the number of hours worked and by hourly rates. For example, billing partners did not bill all the hours worked by their task force. Underlying firm accounts, there was always a permanent preoccupation with client relationships. There were capped service agreements. Payment itself was rarely in full:[6] large firms rarely get 100 per cent of their bills, because clients can threaten to go elsewhere. This went much beyond the behaviour of what some partners called 'crummy clients'. There were various forms of non-chargeable time, and very often there was a negotiation between the firm and the client as to what was an acceptable price for the 'services rendered'. When billing partners billed a client, they could write hours off early, as a courtesy: the billing partner called the client to ask for his or her approval; communication about the bill happened before the bill was sent. Or they could write hours off after the bill was sent, to please a valuable client who reacted negatively.[7] They sometimes wrote off a considerable proportion of hours worked. Like any service firm, corporate law firms have notorious difficulties collecting what has been billed, and many partners choose to live with high account receivables rather than antagonize a client from whom they expect more business in the future. This was considered a serious problem by some very business-minded partners within the firm.

> We have not reached the point where partners can be penalized if their account receivables don't go down fast enough. For instance, someone should come up with a way to reduce the investment we have in receivables and unbilled time and to improve our realization rates. We are not that bad on the realization rates because we are a profitable firm, for a firm of our size, but we'd like to add five or six percentage points to the realization rates, which again is found money. I mean, it's right there, we just have to pick the thing up off the sidewalk where it is sitting, if we can figure out how to do it. Otherwise it's a stupid way to run a business.   (Partner 30)

Another reason was that, to some extent, attorneys could also fudge their time sheets. For some associates, hours worked should also have included time spent at the office (as opposed to time spent on a client)—for example, training time, professional reading time, and so on. But the firm did not always give credit for some of these activities, since they did not include chargeable time. This is why a study of the relationship between social ties and economic performance necessarily leads to issues of fairness (see Chapter 8) and to an examination of the politicized nature of performance measurements.

Many factors accounted for members' individual performance. These factors could be external or environmental (some areas of practice provided more work, some markets were temporarily more lucrative), individual (some attorneys were personally more motivated or hard-working), and relational. In spite of their limited character, the following analyses combine available measurements of members' economic performance—narrowly understood as the number of hours worked and the amount of dollars brought into the firm at the end of the previous year, a few weeks before fieldwork took place—with information on firm structure, work process, and members' social status and intra-organizational ties in early 1991. Following the embeddedness perspective, differences in such performances may be explained, in part, in terms of relationships within the firm—for instance because relational factors could help gain access to needed resources, reduce 'transaction costs' with co-workers, or help pressure colleagues back into more productive behaviour.

Partners' contributions and returns at SG&R

We know that partners' compensation was based exclusively on a seniority lockstep system without any direct link between contribution and returns. The firm did not have a formal peer-review system that could provide intermediate steps between informal control and formal court procedures against free-riders.

> Our compensation system has no built-in peer review process. There is no committee meeting with each partner, no interview devoted to pulling out from that individual his or her state of affairs. With the compensation system there is no built-in financial incentive for people to do things. If you have people who are motivated by other things, like self-respect, pride in craftsmanship, intellectual curiosity, competitiveness, whatever those different personal attributes are, that's not a problem. There are people who aren't as motivated by those other things as certain other people and may wind up resting on their laurels, sitting on their hands, whatever euphemism you want to come up with for becoming lazy both intellectually and how much they are willing to work. (The managing partner at the time of the study)

Great managerial resources were nevertheless devoted to measurement of each partner's performance (time sheets, billing, collecting, expenses, and so on), and this information was available to the whole partnership. A low performance could not be hidden for long. Partners 1 and 5 were the two members of the compensation committee (the 'whack-down' committee) in charge of carrying out exceptional measures preventing a member from reaching the next seniority level on the compensation ladder. It should also be recalled that most partners in this firm managed to have at least one 'safety partner'—that is, a friend who would presumably side with them unconditionally and become their insurance policy against expulsion. Therefore, despite the existence of direct financial controls, the firm did not have many formal ways of dealing with free-loading. This strengthens the suggestion that performance depended also on the social circulation of resources in the firm.

Co-workers' constraints and economic performance: Niches as hell

Based on this discussion, to study the effect of position in firm structure on economic performance, I look at the relationship between measurement of economic performance and various social factors related to firm structure, work process, and members' ties in 1991. I use again as covariates the dimensions of formal structure of this firm that were expected to be the most important (status, office, speciality), as well as two attributes of members defined from outside the firm (gender and law school attended). To locate members in the informal structure of the firm and capture the relevant characteristics of their relational configurations, I use six variables based on the co-workers, advice, and friendship networks. From this data, I derive two types of index. First, individual indegree centrality scores in these networks. As already seen, indegree centrality represents a measurement of the extent to which members were 'popular' in these networks and therefore accumulated resources circulating in them (Wasserman and Faust 1994: 169–219). One can therefore hypothesize that they will be in a better position to perform economically.

Secondly, their individual constraint scores as defined by Burt (1992) in the same networks. In other words, in this type of collegial organization, a constraining network of strong ties, in which members over-invested, tended to create task forces of partners and associates who relied on each other, at least for work. With regard to partners, such task forces represented an element of self-entrapment compensated by status recognition: task forces allowed partners to create emulation and redefine what was an acceptable performance within their work-group, including for themselves. But coordination was also made easier in such work-groups: they brought associates together productively in the kind of intellectually challenging attitude that partners encouraged within their task forces. This does not mean that associates' fate (in terms of making it to partnership) was necessarily improved by this high constraint; but one can hypothesize that economic performance should have been. In effect, structural holes could represent a competitive advantage for associates lobbying for partners' votes, not for partners who could pool colleagues' resources such as knowledge and experience. Thus measurements of relational capital add a set of covariates to the initial model. In this approach, the effect of centrality and of relational constraint on economic performance is expected to be positive.

Using the above-mentioned covariates, several models are estimated to explain quantitative economic performance measured as the amount of fees in dollars brought to the firm (managing partner not included) and the number of hours worked in 1990. It is important to realize that not all the covariates representing various dimensions of position in firm structure can be used at the same time, because of strong dependency between them. This was typically the case for status and seniority; in the following models, the most refined covariate, seniority, is used. In addition, status and seniority overlap, as explanatory variables, with the number of hours worked and hourly rates. The more senior their position in the firm, the more attorneys charged per hour. Associates worked longer hours than partners. Therefore, to avoid this problem, analyses below test the robustness of relational configuration effects using three different models. The dependence between some of the covariates will be taken into account in the interpretation of results. In terms of economic and relational variables, the best overall models predicting the number of hours worked and the amount of fees brought in (and achievable with this dataset) are presented in Table 4.1.

As predicted, Model 1 contains an important effect confirming our expectations. It shows that, in this firm, constraint by task forces of co-workers had a positive and strong effect on the number of hours that members put in. The density of members' network of co-workers helped the latter control and increase the amount of effort invested in hard work. In that respect, the effect of members' relational capital on their performance is confirmed. However, beyond this confirmation, an additional and unexpected dimension of relational configurations also emerges here. Interesting negative effects of dense friendship ties (and centrality in the friendship network) on performance are also apparent. One can speculate about the reasons for

Table 4.1. *Variables explaining economic performance*

Independent variables	Standardized estimates		
	Model 1	Model 2	Model 3
Seniority	0.01	0.76***	
Hourly rates			0.78***
Time input[a]			0.40***
Office	0.24**	0.15*	0.05
Speciality	−0.16*	0.01	0.07
Gender	−0.03	0.00	0.02
Law school attended	−0.14	−0.03	0.02
Centrality co-worker	0.17	0.01	−0.02
Centrality advice	−0.02	0.27*	0.23*
Centrality friendship	−0.27*	−0.11	−0.01
Constraint co-worker	0.23*	0.16*	0.13*
Constraint advice	−0.04	0.05	0.04
Constraint friendship	−0.81***	−0.15	0.11

[a]Including the interaction effect of time input and hourly rates does not provide additional insights here because senior partners who charged high rates were not among the members who put in the greatest number of hours.

Notes: N = 70. ***$p < 0.001$, **$p < 0.01$, *$p < 0.05$. Adjusted r^2 for three models are 0.66, 0.86, and 0.89 respectively. Economic performance is measured by the number of hours worked (Model 1) and by the amount of dollars brought into the firm in fees (Models 2 and 3) in 1990. The managing partner, who concentrated on firm policy and administrative work and was not a timekeeper during his tenure, was not included in the computations of these parameter estimates.

Source: Reprinted from *Corporate Social Capital and Liabilities*, R. Leenders and S. Gabbay (eds.). E. Lazega, 'Generalized Exchange and Economic Performance', 250. Copyright 1999 with permission from Kluwer Academic Publishers.

these effects, such as spending more time on personalizing work relationships outside work than on actual work.[8]

Focusing back on the positive effect of constraint in one's network of strong co-workers, Models 2 and 3—where the weight of economic variables such as hourly rates is more visible—show that such an effect was robust. Indeed, it is also present as a predictor of the amount of fees brought into the firm at the end of the year. It is thus relatively independent of the way performance was measured. In Model 2, status and seniority count heavily. Partners did collect more money than associates, and, the more senior lawyers were, the more money they tended to collect. As already mentioned, in general, partners put in less hours but collected more dollars than associates because they charged more. Associates collected less although they put in more time than partners. The more senior in their status associates were, the more hours they billed and the more they collected. Market circumstances had a mixed effect on economic performance: in terms of office membership, Office II attorneys put in more time than Office I attorneys, and collected more; but in terms of division of work, no speciality (corporate or litigation) seems to have been systematically more lucrative than the other—in spite of a general advantage for litigation in the early 1990s in north-eastern US corporate law firms.

Given our interest in the connection between informal relationships and performance, it makes sense to look into the latter effects in more detail for associates and for partners separately. The following results are then obtained. For partners only, effects considered here for hours billed were either weak, or at best unstable. Practice also had a very weak effect: litigation partners billed slightly more than corporate partners. Again, partners popular as friends tended to bill slightly less. For associates only, centrality in terms of friendship also affected collection negatively. This means that associates who were very active socially and specialized in providing on average more social support to others could have ended up, on average, being handicapped in terms of working and collecting. Obviously the link between the two phenomena is very indirect and remains to be explained, but it exists nevertheless. The more central associates were in terms of their number of co-workers (that is, the more colleagues they worked with), the more hours they billed. The only associates who collected more hours were those who were also central in the co-workers' network (they tended to be senior associates). For associates, seniority was the best predictor of performance in terms of hours collected, but seniority *and* centrality as a co-worker were the best predictors of performance in terms of hours billed.

In this context, the analysis of the effect of individual relational configurations on economic performance also shows that attorneys who were informally sought out for advice and for collaboration by many others tended to bill and collect more than others. This extra effect is partly due to the fact that senior partners were central advisers. As already mentioned, the effect of relational capital measured in terms of Burt's constraint scores is still present in Model 3, in which seniority is replaced by hourly rates and time input. This confirms our expectations: members with a constraining co-workers' network put in more time, collected more hours, and collected more money. The more constraining the co-workers' network, the higher an attorney's economic performance (even measured in such a narrow way). This effect is robust, as shown by the fact that it is still present in Model 3, in which seniority is replaced by hourly rates and time input. Constraint in the advice network and in the friendship network, however, did not have a consistent effect on performance.

Thus, overall, multivariate analyses show that position in informal structure and relational configurations characterizing this position (including niche membership) did count for explaining performance, but these effects were weaker than the weight of seniority or hourly rates as formally defined by the institutional setting. The next sections provide a more detailed illustration of such effects.

Status, self-entrapment, and economic performance

As suggested, in particular, by the effect of constraint in the co-workers' network, economic performance was indeed rooted in the configuration of individual relationships in the firm. This raises the question of the relative weight of specific combinations of ties in providing a decisive push in performance increase (or representing a liability that decreased performance). In this section, I look at similar effects from a different angle by showing that, within a given niche, a specific configuration of social ties was required, at the dyadic level, for high economic performance in this firm. This is due to the fact that maintaining production (collective action) required many kinds of contributions. Describing this configuration is equivalent to understanding how social resources combined with one another to increase or decrease individual performance. Results obtained above are translated into a description of specific configurations of ties that were associated with economic performance. These associations can be measured by the correlations between the frequency of more or less multiplex configurations of dyadic ties for each actor and his or her performance measurements.

Many combinations of ties were possible at the dyadic level in the three networks. For example, the most frequent type of such combinations (besides the 'no-tie' possibility) between two persons in the firm was the Blau tie. Many partners had such ties with themselves as advice distributors and associates as advice-seekers. In contrast, there were no duplex mutual co-work and friendship ties. The complete absence of such ties is not surprising. As will be seen in Chapter 5, although friendship and work could coexist when an advice component was also present, the two resources seemed to be of a very distinct nature and to intervene in the status competition at very different moments.

The extent to which kinds of social ties varied with performance can be measured by the correlations between the frequency of more or less multiplex combinations of types of ties for each actor and his or her performance measurements. Table 4.2 presents correlations between specific configurations of dyadic ties for each individual in the firm and several measurements of performance. Only ties and compounds of ties with a strong correlation with at least one performance index are retained in Table 4.2.

Table 4.2. *The Importance of Blau-ties: Correlation table for performance measurements in 1990 and most frequent types of combination of ties among dyads of actors*

Combination of ties between *i* and *j*	Performance measurements						
	Hourly rates measured in dollars	Time input measured in dollars	Time input measured in hours	Fees billed measured in dollars	Fees billed measured in hours	Fees collected measured in dollars	Fees collected measured in hours
No ties	−0.34	−0.31	−0.08	−0.31	−0.15	−0.31	−0.17
iFj and *jFi*	−0.36	−0.20	0.11	−0.26	0.05	−0.26	0.01
jAi	0.47	0.36	0.11	0.42	0.19	0.41	0.20
jWi and *jAi*	0.36	0.15	−0.08	0.21	−0.01	0.20	0.01
iWj and *jWi* and *jAi (Blau tie)*	0.54	0.44	0.10	0.43	0.18	0.45	0.24
iWj and *jWi* and *iAj*	−0.52	−0.34	0.04	−0.40	−0.05	−0.39	−0.04
iWj and *jWi* and *iAj* and *jAi*	0.22	0.28	0.10	0.24	0.10	0.25	0.16
iWj and *jWi* and *iAj* and *jAi* and *iFj* and *jFi*	0.39	0.43	0.19	0.46	0.25	0.48	0.30

Notes: 'F' refers to Friendship, 'W' to co-worker, 'A' to Advice. '*iFj*' represents a friendship tie from *i* to *j*. '*iFj* and *jFi*' represents a reciprocated friendship choice. For example, having many ties of the '*jAi*' type—which means that many people (*j*) seek out your advice—is strongly and positively correlated (0.41) with collecting high fees measured in dollar amounts.

This exploratory analysis provides several results. First, there was a strong and negative correlation between having many 'no ties' (or many 'empty' ties—that is, potential ties not actually realized) and putting time in, billing, and collecting. The less resources exchanged with others, the lower an attorney's performance. Secondly, there was a strong and positive correlation between having many ties such as 'being sought out (unreciprocated) for advice exclusively' (no co-work or friendship component) and dollar amounts invested (time worked by hourly rate), billed (time billed by hourly rate), and collected (fees actually collected). The same correlation holds when the tie included an unreciprocated friendship component. This is partly related to the fact that senior partners, who were often sought out for advice and cited as friends (without reciprocating), billed and collected more given their higher hourly rates.

Thirdly, and more surprisingly, there are no strong correlations between having a lot of ties that were exclusively reciprocated work ties and any performance index. 'Work-only' relationships were quite neutral in terms of their association with economic performance. Such ties indicate work relationships without status competition. They were more frequent for associates than for partners. However, adding one component to this combination changes this result. Given that partners worked with associates more than with other partners, there are strong and positive correlations between having many such ties with the added component 'being sought out for advice' (unreciprocated), and performance indexes. Such ties were much more frequent for partners than for associates. This confirms that an element of self-entrapment—that is, of strong involvement and commitment that increased with niche density—by partners in small task forces of co-workers within their niche was a good predictor of economic performance compensated, among others, by Blau-type status and professional recognition. When adding friendship components to Blau ties (such as citing the other as a friend or citing each other as friends), positive correlations become stronger, although there were fewer occurrences of that type.

Fourthly, and conversely, there are mostly negative correlations between having ties with components such as 'having a reciprocated work relationship and seeking out advice (unreciprocated)' and dollar amounts put in, billed, and collected. Such ties were more frequent for associates (particularly non-senior ones). Finally, there are strong and positive correlations between having individual triplex mutual reciprocated ties and dollar amounts billed and collected. Dense exchanges of that type were much more frequent among partners. In short, these results translate our previous statements into relational terms. Partners' higher economic performance, for example, shows in the correlation between having, within one's niche, many 'reciprocated work ties with the added component "being sought out for advice" (unreciprocated)' and the amount of money collected.

To illustrate this analysis, I provide examples of low and high economic performers and their specific combinations of social resources. In these examples, each attorney had a relatively different profile, but important common characteristics were related to low or high performance.

Low and high performers

Among low performers (still in terms of dollars brought in 1990), a first—the least productive—partner was a member of Position Two, the Office I corporate niche (see Figure 3.1). He had, in terms of compounds of ties, a higher than average proportion of persons (that he cited as strong co-workers) who did not reciprocate, a much lower than average proportion of Blau ties, and a much lower than average proportion of triplex reciprocated ties. He considered many people to be his friends, but they did not reciprocate. His partners did not listen much to his opinions about firm management and policy issues (that is, he had a low indegree centrality in the influence or 'listening' network presented in Chapter 8). The strong pattern here is the absence of direct reciprocity and multiplexity in most ties. None of the configurations associated with strong economic performance was present in this partner's profile. Recall the managing partner's comments about this partner, which reflect the absence of constraint: '[Jack] is a decent guy on a personal level. He says that under pressure he does things; but he is a corporate lawyer, and there is no pressure on him usually, so he just doesn't do it.'

A roughly similar pattern characterizes a second low-performing partner. He barely made it into the Office II niche: he had a much higher than average proportion of 'no ties' and a higher than average proportion of persons that he cited as strong co-workers but who did not reciprocate; he also had a lower than average proportion of Blau ties. He nevertheless had an average number of reciprocated friendship ties. Most of the partners did not listen much to his opinions about firm management and policy issues. Very few came to him for advice, and he had a relatively low number of co-workers. At the dyadic level, the specificity of this partner's relational profile is the contrast between his very few ties with others in the firm and two very strong (triplex reciprocated) ties with unconditional partners (his insurance policy against expulsion). Recall again the managing partner at the time of the study:

[Frank] was at the low end [of the performance scale] for a long time. Partner 5 went to talk with him. He claims that there isn't anything to do. He says: 'I am a corporate lawyer, my kind of work has dried up, I am out there in the bushes, hustling, doing everything I can.' That is difficult to check. But there is also the fact that some of the people he has worked with do not want to do so again, because they think his competence is in doubt. Partner 17 is extremely good in his field. He once volunteered to go and see this partner to share some work with him. He went to see him, but he says [Frank] did a horrendously poor job.

In sum, the two low performers were marginal members in their own niche and were less involved than others in exchanges of social resources in the firm. They did not create task forces that triggered the commitment and self-entrapment process with associates who could rely on them for work and provide status recognition.

Among high-performing partners, there were broadly speaking two types of relational profiles. The first type included some of the most senior partners, especially favoured by their high hourly rates and by their centrality in their respective niches. Their ties often seemed 'generous'—that is, to combine unreciprocated transfers towards others more than exchanges with them. They were more often sought out than they themselves sought someone out—that is, they were providers rather than beneficiaries. This made economic sense, because they were in charge of running the organization that ultimately produced their larger share of the pie. But it also made sense socially. For example, Partner 1 was highly sought out for advice. He cited few co-workers, because he mainly worked with a junior partner, who acted as a 'foreman', concentrating co-workers' exchanges. Partners 2 and 4 had roughly the same relational profile as Partner 1, except for their more frequent involvement in mutual co-workers' ties and higher than average proportion of Blau ties. In addition to the work-oriented components, Partner 4 had an exceptional five triplex mutual ties with other partners. Thus, in general, unless they worked with a 'foreman', senior high performers were strongly work-oriented persons intensely involved in co-workers' ties and highly sought out for advice. Their compounds did not include many friendship components, except with a very few select other senior partners, with whom reciprocity was taken for granted.[9] They unquestionably always won the status competition. The taboo concerning friendship with associates was also true for young partners, with a few exceptions for contemporaries.

The second type of high-performing partners also included work-oriented persons with an above average proportion of Blau ties. They did, however, diversify their exchanges of resources—that is, their types of ties—more than their more senior partners. They seemed to belong to an old niche while investing efforts in building a new one. Their compounds were more personalized and included more friendship components. Typical of this relational profile was Partner 26. He was hard-working, heavily involved in the business of the firm, one of the people with most ties in the firm altogether, among the record holders for Blau ties and for the triplex mutual ties (with his Office I contemporaries, who—for reasons linked to the history of the firm—formed a very cohesive clique of partners). But, in addition to many mono-resource uniplex ties (such as being often sought out for advice and only for advice, although not as much as Partners 1 and 6), he was involved in many duplex or triplex ties with colleagues who worked with him, but also came to him for advice and friendship (unreciprocated). He was thus more relaxed about personalizing work ties and showed more social openness (than senior partners) to colleagues working with him. He was a work-oriented all-round exchanger and investor of resources.

The contrast between low and high performers' relational profiles shows that high performers (in terms of hours worked and dollars brought in) drew heavily on their social resources and had common specific relational characteristics, in particular those involving them (not surprisingly) in work-related exchanges with associates.

This highlights the fact that, as suggested by the effect of constraint scores in the co-workers' network and by the illustrations above, such configurations of ties (described at the dyadic level) favouring high economic performance were not distributed randomly in the firm. Their distribution depended on the wider pattern of social ties presented in Figure 3.1, the firm's exchange system. As will be described in the next chapter, the structural tendencies in this firm could be summarized by two separable forms of interdependence: first, the interplay of co-worker and advice ties; secondly, the interplay of advice and friendship ties. Mutual strong work ties occurring in conjunction with either unidirectional (associate to partner) Blau ties or mutual advice ties—which were positively correlated with economic performance in Table 4.2—had a higher chance of occurring in niches with constraining co-workers' ties. In that respect, productive co-worker ties were embedded in advice ties. In turn, advice ties were often driven and controlled by more personalized ties. While there was a very weak association between duplex co-worker and friendship ties, [10] there was a strong one between advice and friendship ties. This configuration also had a higher chance of occurring in cohesive niches and it is especially consistent with the strongest positive correlation in Table 4.2 between triplex reciprocated ties and high economic performance. Thus, strong and stimulating (that is, pressuring or constraining) co-workers' ties combined with advice ties or with both advice and friendship ties had a chance of being economically more productive than other ties and more likely to happen in dense niches.

Multi-level embeddedness of the labour contract: A virtuous circle?

It can thus be asserted that, if economic performance is rooted in the configuration of individual social ties, the latter is itself rooted in a collective relational structure encouraging the emergence of work groups. Recall that, given informal constraints guiding the choices of co-workers, advisers, and friends in this firm, and given the existence of such multiplex and local cycles reflecting the existence of highly embedded (in niches) strong co-workers' task forces, givers have a guarantee that they will become receivers, although not necessarily in kind. In other words, the firm had found in this exchange system a structural solution to the problem of cooperation and commitment to the labour contract, a sort of partial 'equilibrium' in the circulation of resources needed to fulfil it. By allowing such a system to exist, this firm maintained certain forms of resource circulation that can be understood more generally as a precondition for group solidarity,[11] but also for individual and collective performance. This social system grew around the formal dimensions of the organization and around constraints imposed by interdependencies in the production process. It was part of this firm's 'corporate social capital': it helped members accept terms of the labour contract that they did not necessarily have a narrow short-term interest in accepting. Performance grew out of this commitment.

In effect, since strong and stimulating (that is, constraining) co-workers' ties combined with advice ties had a chance of being economically more productive than other ties, and of being more likely to occur in dense work groups, the overall structure described in Chapter 3 should be considered, back at the structural level, as a precondition of an individual's productive relational patterns, because it maintained the circulation of social resources in the firm. This structure interlocked work and social ties in a way allowing strongly knitted positions to perform better by extracting and facilitating higher involvement and efforts from their members, often in exchange for status. The forms of embeddedness described above helped enforce the labour contract between partners and associates. It made them more productive by creating chains of mutual obligations and debts, as well as relational taboos. Partners were especially well positioned to play on resource dependencies to get associates' commitment to their labour contract (which was not necessarily in their narrow and short-term self-interest).

Thus, individual commitment to labour contract and individual economic performance were increased by membership in dense niches, which themselves needed a wider, more multiplex and oligarchic exchange system to operate. Individual performance that benefited the firm as a whole was driven by task-force pressure and the social system of the firm: the organization helped its members perform, thereby helping itself through aggregated performances. In many ways this mechanism was good for the firm as a whole as well as for the partner. The configuration of individual relationships transformed itself into corporate advantage because the firm as a whole was more successful in billing and maintaining labour contracts and integration.

For this 'virtuous circle' to operate, however, an important condition needed to be respected. The embeddedness of individual economic performance in a social exchange system again raises the issue of the relative contribution of individual relationships and firm social mechanisms to collective action and performance. When several resources circulate, exploitation is also present but not easily measurable. The fact that this system helps some individual members reach high performance does not mean that it was egalitarian in the distribution of resources and in the provision of structural solutions to individual problems. This will be illustrated in the next section of this chapter by looking at the relative chances of selected senior associates to become partners. In their competition for the attention of partners, associates with the right connections to the right partners had a structural advantage in the highly selective race to partnership. They were 'in the fast lane', because these connections, among other advantages, allowed them to play with organizational rules in an rewarding way, in particular to cross internal boundaries (for example, to seek advice from very senior partners), provided that such 'infractions' were limited and well localized.

Another example of this precondition is that, if the firm social exchange mechanism helps individual members perform economically, then members who participated in building up this social system are also entitled to some of the credit that goes to high performers. In this situation, members' commitment to equality in compensation, their restraint both in keeping track of all their contributions and returns, and in politicizing dramatically the use of measurements, were therefore micro-political conditions for the efficiency of this system. This was especially the case with task forces, where others' behaviour could easily be perceived to be opportunistic. In fact, members' restraint was often weak: many conflicts in corporate law firms or other private professional services firms are disputes about fairness in compensation to individual partners. But many 'cultural' aspects of such organizations, such as an ideology of collegiality, are also explicit exhortations to such restraint.

Thus measuring individual economic performance tells only one side of the story of contribution to collective action. This limiting condition for the efficiency of such a virtuous circle was the reason for managing partners often to emphasize 'spreading credit' as widely as possible. Nevertheless, recognizing and measuring the relative and specific importance of social mechanisms cannot be done without understanding this political negotiation, which enables members to evaluate their contributions. This illustrates the fact that the relative value of social resources is negotiated, and that this negotiation is political. Following in detail these politicized negotiations, and how they tried to disentangle the merits of the firm as opposed to that of its individual members in the production of a specific performance, was not possible and therefore beyond the scope of this book. The principle, however, shows that social mechanisms can be very productive for collegial organizations, but their manipulation can be double-edged.

As mentioned above, measurements of performance are a politicized issue, all the more easily politicized because members can make their relative contribution to firm performance unmeasurable—for example, by bringing more resources into their barters, which was made possible precisely by the existence of a multiplex exchange system. Members of this firm knew that measuring economic performance described only one aspect of their contribution to collective action. In other words, the forms of embeddedness discussed in this chapter did not produce, by themselves, a self-sustaining social order. The structural solution provided by this exchange system raises new problems, that of the fragility of this virtuous circle. For example, niche-level solidarity also threatened the cohesion of the firm: well-knit teams could defect and take away with them valued members and clients (Lazega 1992*b*). This problem had its own structural solution and is dealt with further below (see Chapter 6).

PROFESSIONAL PERFORMANCE: QUALITY CONTROL FOR KNOWLEDGE-INTENSIVE ORGANIZATIONS

The second part of this chapter looks at another effect of the exchange system in the firm: its efficiency in terms of quality control. Maintaining quality through capitalization of authorized knowledge and sharing experience is not an easy process in collegial organizations. A firm such as SG&R was not a (financial) capital intensive organization producing material goods and relying on economies of scale. It produced knowledge-based services evaluated by their level of quality. But quality in 'certainty work' is difficult to measure. There are formal mechanisms, as stressed by Waters (1989), such as official peer review committees, that can perform this task; but these mechanisms often raise suspicions of being too strongly politicized. The question is then: does the firm rely on its exchange system to provide an informal mechanism of overall peer review and quality control? The importance of Blau-ties, i.e. the barter of self-entrapment against status recognition, to economic performance, suggests that it is the case. If so, does it do so by ensuring accumulation and distribution of authorized knowledge and experience?

Lawyers' work is knowledge intensive (see Chapter 2), in the sense of 'knowledge-in-action' accumulated by experience, tacit knowledge, or 'judgement'—a word often used by members to characterize the quality of a colleague's lawyering. This experience is necessary to the provision of legal advice to corporations. This task requires designing new solutions to complex problems, taking risks, and sometimes persuading the client to adopt untested strategies. For this kind of creative work, often invisible and not very spectacular, accumulation of this knowledge-in-action or experience seems indispensable. Managing this capital of expertise means using all the available information technology (libraries, on-line services, a firm electronic memory, and so on), but also—and most importantly—recruiting the best possible attorneys, keeping them, and helping them manage and update their knowledge base. This is often referred to as a firm's 'human capital'. Members must build and convert tacit and innovative knowledge into a shared instrument, and perhaps eventually into more codified and routinized knowledge where pieces of information are already related to one another. Tacit knowledge tends to be mobilized at the local level, in a decentralized way, between individual members. Indeed, if tacit knowledge and what collective learning produces are difficult to capitalize in a central database, actors' 'live' and educated thinking must be taken into account.

In the light of this understanding of professional work, the social distribution of knowledge (as an organizational response to environmental complexity) is supposed to help. Contrary to what is asserted by many specialists in professional services firms, information technology and human capital are not sufficient to ensure a high level of quality. In addition, activities driven only by reaction to market do not necessarily encourage innovation and creativity (Alter 1993; Maister 1993); they can develop short-term adaptation. This raises the issue of quality control as a social process, and that of sharing experience in order to improve the quality of work when needed. The way in which SG&R managed this issue was called 'peer review'. Here I show that many partners at SG&R considered ex post formal peer review committees to be costly, difficult to implement, and inefficient. But informal peer review also took place to try to maintain a high level of quality. Members observed each other's performances and evaluated (mostly informally) each other's production: they praised big successes, and indirectly sanctioned (that is, criticized and gossiped about) blunders and mistakes (on this issue see Bosk 1979; Reynaud 1989; Wittek and Wielers 1998).[12] In the first section, I examine how members of the firm conceived peer review, in particular peer review of the quality of work.

The firm counted on a more proactive form of quality control. By this they meant (1) the fact that its members shared the *whole picture* of the cases with their co-workers, and (2) the fact that they sought each other's *advice* or second opinion and shared their experience before they made decisions or sent opinions out to clients. From the perspective of the organization, relationships between members were necessary to share knowledge and experience. Especially in situations where members worked together, they depended on each other for these resources. Knowledge can be capitalized in members' individual live memory, but its use also depends on their relationships. Indeed reasoning exclusively in terms of human capital, as economists and management theories have done for a long time, presupposes that, once in business, members freely share their knowledge and experience with one another. We know that this is not an obvious fact, especially since Blau (1964) has showed that status is central to such games.[13]

This chapter shows how peer supervision and evaluation of quality was in SG&R's task-related advice network. In order to look at the importance of social exchanges, especially knowledge sharing, for quality control, one has to accept that quality is not a manifest variable (White, forthcoming). It is grasped as an implicit ranking. Transfers and exchanges of advice reflected this specific pecking order and form of status at SG&R—a fragile order, since everyone had been allowed to hope to climb the ladder by impressing his or her colleagues. Indeed, competition for professional status may be one reason why the act of providing advice was kept so distinct from that of collaborating on a case. Moreover, personalized access and multiplex ties to sought-out and selective advisers could help advice-seekers in stretching advice as much as possible before it became collaboration.

In effect, at SG&R, as in many professional services firms, members did meet on a regular basis for updates on the evolution of their knowledge base (the law, regulations, and court decisions). But knowledge was still mainly mobilized and shared while working together. To understand how knowledge and experience were managed in such an organization, it is important to insist on the work process as simplified in Chapters 2 and 5: members work together on cases, and they compete for professional status in the deliberation, or 'brainstorming', process. This takes us back to the question of how members resort to some kind of authority to stop the professional status competition process and take responsibility for quality. The issue of quality is not so much who knows what, but who has the authority to know, and how this authority is negotiated, constructed, and maintained (Lazega 1992a). Indirect control over collective action is often 'epistemic'—that is, related to knowledge construction. Attention to one aspect of a case rather than to another may be the object of a debate. Authority to know helps members impose a certain focus of attention after a deliberation. In the selection of relevant and appropriate information (the interactive elaboration of information), actors need the authority to make an issue salient: people with status can impose that; they are attributed the authority to know. One can, therefore, expect members to share expertise and experience in their niche and to share it in the status games too: knowledge cannot be shared outside such identity politics and status competition. It cannot be shared without an authority argument providing members with the authority to know. Since members tend to work in niches, it is likely that they will find this authority within this niche. But it is also likely that they find it outside the niche, thus using resources provided by the firm as a whole (firm-wide status of specific partners) to manage local quality problems raised by the work process.

Thus, it was in members' collective economic interest to share information and experience as much as possible, but it was also in their individual interest—given the status competition process—to do so while increasing as much as possible their individual credit and stressing the value of their own experience and authority. Knowledge is not only shared under task-force and niche-level relational pressure. It is also shared by the prospect of increasing one's firm-wide and more general professional status. Once they have been provided, by their niche, with resources and with a sense of their interests beyond the short term, members need another level of social approval if they want to increase their status within the firm. This form of status can be called 'professional authority or reputation'. Whereas individual economic performance is strongly associated with task-force membership, professional reputation is also based on the capacity to be recognized out of local niches. The multilevel exchange system was thus a form of productive social mechanism when it helped members reach out of their niches. In this second section, I also look at whether members shared knowledge and how they concentrated the authority to know in the professional status of a few select partners. I argue that much of the proactive quality control was performed by seeking these members' advice on task-related matters. Professional status allowed these central members to push and sometimes impose their standards and criteria of quality.[14]

The main actors in the advice network of the firm—who had acquired a form of status that attracted great deference—are identified below. Several local rules related to the circulation of advice within the firm have already been extracted from the analysis, among which was the most important: one did not seek advice from people 'below'. This concentration of the authority to know may still be puzzling in an organization where members were jealous of their professional discretion and individual intellectual autonomy. It is less so when considering the problems raised by formal peer review of quality of work. The social process of capitalization and of knowledge distribution being inextricably related to quality control through professional status and epistemic alignment, it was necessary, but also costly, to protect this expertise from opportunistic behaviour.[15] The purpose of this chapter is finally to show how such a co-orientation was made possible informally in this type of collegial organization.

A picture of the advice network at the structural level is useful at this point. Indeed, describing the inner workings of the organization as an exchange system for authoritative professional information may help in looking at the connection between individual interests, individual management of knowledge and experience, and firm structure. The distribution of knowledge produced by the multilevel exchange mechanism can be inferred from the overall pattern of the advice network. This structure confirms that co-orientation was achieved and stabilized in the organization through the concentration of the authority to know. The firm's main resource—its expertise and creativity with regard to solving complex legal problems for corporations—was located not only in its mainframe computer, but in the structure of this network (in specific niches and in central advisers). Co-orientation thus happened within and across niches, and requests for advice and professional status recognition—that generated this co-orientation—converged towards positions of partners, with senior associates as exceptions. Seniority and concentration of the authority to know are shown to be important for achieving cognitive alignment or co-orientation, and for the definition of the situation—that is, of the legitimacy of decisions made on cases at hand.

This social solution to the problem of quality control through selective capitalization of socially authorized knowledge, however, also has an effect on other processes in the firm. We know that members also tried to reach out of their niches: to cut across boundaries, to use short cuts to members in other niches, thus increasing their autonomy from a constraining set of niche fellows. For example, this system of circulation of advice favoured a few selected associates in their race towards partnership: through short cuts in the network, it provided them with access to very senior partners. Here again, the exchange system is shown to have been a productive form of social mechanism: it helped members manage valuable experience and learning. But it was also a selection mechanism, because it allocated immaterial resources in an unequal way.

Avoiding formal peer review

Among organizational processes that collegial firms (as well as others) deal with, peer review—that is, the evaluation of one's partners' work—was certainly one of the most sensitive and sometimes upsetting, especially when the review applied to the quality of work, and not only to the economics of productivity. Some firms have a peer evaluation mechanism that looks at every person's 'professionalism' and tries to improve it. Especially under pressure from malpractice insurers, professional firms recognize the need for maintaining or upgrading their overall level of professionalism. Financial incentives are given to firms by these insurers to extend their understanding of collective responsibility and to implement quality control. The financial incentives are tied, for instance, to in-house continuing legal educational courses, or to intake policies that allow the firm to stay out of work that is likely to cause any kind of insurance claim. Despite a tradition of Yankee individualism and a belief that they were part of the elite of the profession, the firm had raised the issue, and was looking for a methodology that would help partners look at what other partners did.

At the time of the study, it had not implemented a formal peer review system for the quality of work in which some partners went and looked through other people's files and determined whether 'they did the matter right'. They relied on a less systematic system (complaints). The main official argument against a more formal system was its high cost. It cost the client or the firm money to put two lawyers on a matter where one sufficed, where one was seen as just serving as a shadow of the other. Resistance to the implementation of formal review mechanisms was widespread. The more senior lawyers did not welcome any change that seemed to detract from the informality of earlier practice. Many partners said that they did not worry about the quality of work of their colleagues, that the problems were with partners who were not working hard enough or taking in lousy business. They saw a peer review as a review of one's contribution to the firm as a partner, as opposed to the quality of the work that went out.

> I think it's a measure of my feeling of respect for my partners. A broad system of peer review, meaning reviewing every major brief, or going in and reviewing files, I think it would be excessively time consuming and that would clearly be an affront to the independence, and I don't think it would reveal much. (Partner 4)

Many were sceptical about quality peer review, either because of such practical difficulties or because of more substantive ones, such as defining the quality of service rendered.

Probably it (control of partner' work by other partners) exists in the most informal way and that informal way would be triggered if someone catastrophically screws up, but I don't know what my partners do, I don't see their correspondence and the briefs that they file, they don't see mine. (a) We are too busy, we are all too busy. (b) It was never that way even twenty-five years ago, they never looked at what the others were doing. I am not aware of any place where partners are looking at what other partners are doing. There is talk about the fact that they should, increasingly for malpractice purposes, for ethical purposes, the fact that we are 'each responsible for each'. Ethically we are liable, from an ethical standpoint before the grievance committee, and from a malpractice standpoint before the court. That does not change; it may change, but I don't see it. I think it might change because people talk about it in the national media and the professional press. And I suspect that there will be firms that will devise structures and methodologies for doing this. And that there will be some catastrophe at some firm and the senior partners will say 'We'd better have something like this, let's borrow what these people do.' One of the problems obviously is that, in order to judge the quality of your work product, you presumably have to know something about the substance, the substantive law, in order to make that judgement. So, because of the specialized nature, you can tell if a letter is sloppily written but I couldn't look at my tax partners' letters and determine whether he has missed the latest IRS rule. It has to be done by other lawyers in their special area in order to be meaningful. And also part of the problem is knowing the fact situation. The example I gave you earlier of sitting with the client and not saying everything you might say because the occasion is not right and you expect an occasion that is right to occur, or because someone else is there, or because you know that based on something that happened two days ago this client would be unreceptive to that suggestion now, but more so later, will persuade you not to say something. The not-saying of that thing may very well in isolation be viewed as malpractice. So strategy, tactics, timing are also part of the decision to give or to withhold advice, or which advice to give when or to whom. The example I gave of that letter: certain things I can say to the top man of the corporation, but the subordinate will not understand and not appreciate, and it might be counterproductive to say it to the subordinate because he will interpret your letter to the top man in such a way as to undercut your ability to persuade the top man once you get there. So it is very difficult for me to judge whether partner X should have mentioned this alternative to client Y in that letter, because maybe there is something else going on, some reason not to use, at that particular time in that particular format, a letter as opposed to an oral point. So there is some inertia: 'If it ain't broke, don't fix it.' I suppose that one can say that, we haven't had that experience. And I suppose that, if the quality of the work is so bad, there is the likelihood that the client will either drop the firm or hopefully not drop it but seek out another partner to say 'This work I have been getting is pretty bad' and that would trigger peer review.   (Partner 6)

The uncertainty surrounding any mechanism of peer evaluation was sometimes the extent to which it would be a perfunctory operation as opposed to a real in-depth look at a whole matter or at a partner's behaviour.

Thus, at the time of the study, SG&R considered officially that the usual financial supervision of partners' productivity represented a sufficiently tight form of control, and that a formal peer review system for quality control was too expensive to install. For instance, there was a debate about whether or not partners should be obliged to reach a certain amount of billable hours. A formal peer review process was to be triggered only when somebody (mainly: a client) complained. SG&R was thinking of creating either a committee reviewing the letters sent out by partners to clients or a procedure by which no formal opinion letter would go out without being reviewed by another partner. The malpractice insurance carrier did provide incentives for an institutionalized opinion committee (by offering a high deductible). Many clearly recognized that they needed to have a review on formal opinions; but opinions that had any potential for difficulty were supposed to be reviewed informally by a second partner. The rationale was that somebody might be so involved with a deal, for example, that he or she could lose the forest for the trees, and it was always useful to have somebody else looking with a fresh mind at one's work.

A committee system was also perceived by some as a good mechanism, because it would avoid shopping practices that occurred in a less formal system where 'people go to the fellow who will give you the right answer'. But, besides formal opinion letters, informal discussions among partners were considered to be frequent enough to constitute a good safeguard, an informal peer review process of getting second opinions. Informal review was seen as part of the cooperative spirit of the firm. If someone was not on the top of his or her game, the managing partner would have to intervene indirectly and informally. People were afraid not so much that their judgement would be called into question by a more formal review system, as much as of the fact that the mechanics of such a system might be difficult to implement, partners being very busy.

> The peer review that we have right now is everyone sits down in the partners' meeting and you have in front of you the print-out that shows you how many hours I worked, how many hours I billed, how many hours I collected, and how outstanding my account receivable is, and then you get people grumbling at the meeting about the account receivables going up and not coming down. But as far as whether I am doing a good job on my work, unless they get a call from a client complaining about me, some kind of peer review as to quality of work, I think that will be hard to implement. I suspect it would be resented by many, and at least at the stage we are at, I don't think I want to be reviewing somebody else's work and decide whether it is good or not. I am too busy, I don't want to do somebody else's work, I want to do my own. The managing partner will have a hard time implementing a systematic second opinion.   (Partner 29)

In summary, the firm still counted on informal and indirect forms of peer review and quality control. It was planning to have at least a formal system for opinion letters, which were reviewed before they went out, but hesitated to go any further in this process of bureaucratization. This issue is further elaborated upon in Chapter 8, because it reflects underlying tensions in precarious professional values. I now look at how the firm managed quality control through the idea that it happened in the process of work-related sharing of knowledge and experience. The characteristics of this mechanism are used to show that quality control takes place through 'co-orientation' and 'epistemic alignment'. In effect, for quality control to be possible in the work process itself, members' brainstorming needed to be based on a form of deliberation that shared the whole picture of the case at hand. In the next section, I focus on members' comments on their cooperation with their declared strong co-workers. I look at how they perceived status competition in their exchanges of background, case-related information in their niches. These comments confirm that the conditions for informal quality control to be possible in task forces were present most of the time.

Sharing the big picture?

How did members of this professional services firm share knowledge with co-workers? In task forces and niches, members combined cooperation, status competition, and knowledge management in various ways, depending on their experience of this competition with specific co-workers. In order to show that quality control was ensured by the multiplex exchange system in the firm, it is important to show that members shared knowledge in the brainstorming process and competed for professional status derived from 'knowing best' in the deliberation. Additional data were collected about this topic, building on the strong co-workers' network analysed above. Specifically, the lawyers were all asked—as mentioned—with whom they had intensive work relationships within the firm; then they were asked to check the names of their co-workers with whom they felt that they usually *shared the whole picture of the cases* on which they worked together (see Appendix A). A sub-network of co-workers, the 'whole-picture network', was thus identified: it includes the subset of colleagues with whom knowledge and expertise were felt to be shared. Arguments were then provided to explain why sharing did or did not take place. These arguments were examined for interpretation focused on status competition.

In other words, members tried to work in niches, but in such niches they combined status competition (hierarchy) and knowledge or information in various ways, depending on their experience with specific co-workers. In a niche, members might or might not share knowledge, but this issue was often connected to that of the authority to know. A partner handling the case was often in a position to select among his colleagues those with whom he or she would allow status competition to take place. When a partner did not share the whole picture of the case with a colleague who also worked on this case, there could not be much deliberation. Someone who did not know enough about a case could not display professional judgement. When a partner shared selectively the whole picture of the case with some colleagues working on this case, but not with others, status competition was usually limited to dyadic tournaments. The following excerpts of members' interviews about 'sharing the whole picture' show that, explicitly or implicitly, status and knowledge were combined in members' attitudes to work. The examples are taken from the arguments provided by respondents to justify their sociometric choices in this vignette.

Several partners did not enter the status competition process. They usually happened to be so senior that such a competition was probably meaningless to them. The main reasons given for this were the costs to the client and the style of practising law:

I don't share the whole picture of the case with my partners. It is shared on an appropriate basis, but not totally. It costs too much to the client. We each have different responsibilities. Same with associates. I also do a lot myself. Partly it is the nature of the practice. I have to learn the case if I am responsible for the case. The way we operate on the litigation matter is at least one partner, one associate, and very consuming, very intensive work.   (Partner 1)

Associate 65 confirmed Partner 1's quote only partly:

The higher up you go on the list, the less they give you details. But most of the time, they end up sharing with you. I am a type of person who learns by working with others. Here you have access to people. If you need it they give you the information. They may not share at the beginning of the case, but they will eventually, even when it is only a narrow part of the project.

Less senior partners, such as Partner 23, sometimes also shared this view:

I don't hold back anything, but I am not going to apply more resources to the case than I can bill. You have to balance the nature of the case and the resources of the firm you mobilize. If I can do that without filling the associate on the whole case, I do that. It is a desirable thing to do, in general, but sometimes inefficient. I can't have everybody rethink everything I have. Time always comes into play. Generally, my clients are not Fortune 500, they are not willing to pay for anything.   (Partner 23)

Some partners acknowledged a more selective attitude as to whom they allowed in the status competition game. They shared the whole picture only with other partners, or only for specific types of cases.

I work in a consultative way with partners; it is generally a matter of dividing and sharing responsibility depending on area of expertise, corporate or litigation. If the matter is in the court, a litigator couldn't do what he is doing without the whole picture. I tend to handle large matters, complicated cases. I have at least one partner who knows as much. I need another head to consider the complications of the matter. With associates, the question is how reliable their judgement is. With associates, I'd say I am more selective. They take pieces out. To think about what to do about a case, I don't rely on what the associate is saying. I define for them the task, and they do that with various levels of sophistication and talent and experience. The associate has a snapshot view of the case. Associates are usually not truly my colleagues. Unless I have tested their judgement and feel comfortable with it. You have to give them the opportunity to learn and grow. But it's not like you have associates to do your work for you. At least 50 per cent of work with associates you could do it quicker and cheaper. You couldn't do everything though.   (Partner 14)

By and large, I do share with other partners. I am looking for their judgement to test my judgement. I also believe that if it's a shared project, I want them to share the upside and the downside of the project. I'll ask an associate to do a discrete task. It would be a waste of my time and his otherwise. My view is I want them to be involved as much as I can, to help their development as lawyers, but often it's a matter of how you're dealing with the reality that there is not enough time.   (Partner 26)

In contrast, many other partners considered that a Taylorian division of labour was difficult to sustain. The whole picture was shared with all, because cases were complex, associates needed training, and that was their style of practising law. Briefing associates (and sometimes paralegals and support staff) on the big picture was therefore perceived to generate interest in the matter and to discourage them from going off on wild tangents.

In general, yes I share. We are working together, and I concede that I don't know everything. Sometimes I want to do something, I get their opinion about whether it is too aggressive. I learned that the advice you get from someone who knows nothing about the case is worth nothing. In terms of managing the case overall, they have to know the nuances of the case. It is only useful then. People do not do a specific limited chore. That's not the nature of my practice. They don't have to know absolutely everything about the case, but their input is better if they know the overall picture. The people with whom I work are good: it does not take a long time to give them the overall picture or to answer questions if they need to. The client won't pay for it if it takes too much time, but you do what the matter requires and over time the bills take care of themselves.   (Partner 5)

All of them. The more they know about the case, the better the job. They are doing analysis for you. The fun of this business is precisely that. I usually hear too much rather than too little on all cases. I need that because I have to persuade the client. My suggestions have to be persuasive. I always say to my partners and associates: 'If you don't agree with me, tell me.' The client has to be persuaded. Persuasion is a big part of this business. Part of this business is making sure clients understand. To the extent that partners and associates are really involved, they do a better job. It's the Japanese style: I need their brains and interest.   (Partner 22)

Traditionally, associates complain about lack of training, about being kept in the dark, about not really knowing how what they do fits into the whole picture of the case. They may work very hard to make urgent deadlines, but they sometimes do not know why things have to be done in a hurry and what was the scope of the project, or the game plan. The decision as to whether they are getting the whole picture was the partners', not theirs. At SG&R, such complaints also reflected the frustration of not being able really to participate in the professional status competition. They came almost exclusively from junior associates, although not from all:

Certain partners like to retain control over a given file. It can be a question of confidence in your ability to do the work for them; or it can be that they are extremely busy. But sometimes it's because they don't let go: ego reasons. It is hard for you to nail them down to get the whole picture. Two of these partners are people who like to keep tight control on their files. They would tell you: here is the problem, here is what I want you to do, go and do it. I never see the client with those two. It also depends on the level of difficulty and intellectual interest of the work. Relinquishing control is difficult. But other partners want more input from you, they are more cautious, they want to see if they have missed a connection. At least if you ask a question, they will tell you.   (Associate 49)

When you first start, cases have sometimes been going on for years. They are too busy to explain what's going on. That stinks. I think it's hard when you start. Often you are given a task in a vacuum; you end up being terribly confused. A lot of it may be because you are new and it's easy to be confused. As a new associate, you learn whom you can approach and whom you should stay away from. Some are personality wise inaccessible.   (Associate 71)

More senior associates usually had the feeling that they participated much more:

When I worked with Partner 17, for example, who is a corporate partner, it was on a limited issue, and I didn't need to know about the whole picture, nor did I care to. But when a case turns into a full-blown litigation, I get the whole picture. I work with remarkably fair people. They all give me adequate information and I am not shy about getting more if I need it. I wouldn't put up with somebody who does not give me enough. I give the whole picture to them. I have limited time too.   (Associate 39)

The partners usually let us in. It is the style of the firm in general. Partners here do not spoon-feed you with things. Sometimes they give you the file, tell you 'read up, find out what it's about, and draft this or that', which is the right way to do it. Most of them give you the whole file. Smallness [of the office] results in a full exchange. There is an element of trust, of familiarity, of being comfortable with you. When the full exchange is not there, it is because the partner is not comfortable with the associate or does not care about what the associate would have to say about the case. Most partners I deal with are interested in what my views are. There are exceptions, of course, but they are difficult to separate from personality issues.   (Associate 50)

Thus, the decision to share was surrounded by reasoning about cost, about personal style, about the nature of the task, and about control. A very unclear division of labour existed in the sharing of background information. The deliberation process was qualified here in various ways, and the ongoing attempts at controlling the authority to know was made explicit several times. Note that partners were never openly accused of mistreating associates. They were sometimes accused of not playing the status competition game in a way that provided the associate with an opportunity to increase his or her professional status.

The analysis of the whole-picture network shows that respondents were selective in their identification of knowledge sharers. But the density of the network was still 0.16, which was not much lower than that of the co-workers' and advice networks (respectively 0.22 and 0.18). Analysis of the aggregated choices shows that sharing knowledge also took place in the niches identified above. The same formal dimensions of firm structure were used as identity criteria by members who felt that they shared knowledge with their co-workers, thus confirming the importance of niches in this process. They tended to feel that they shared the whole picture with same speciality colleagues, in the same office, although this was the case for Office I members much more than for Office II members. Litigators felt that they shared mostly with other litigators, mainly in Office I, and almost equally for partners and associates. The same was true with corporate lawyers, although a little less obviously so. When lawyers felt that they shared with members of other offices, it was mainly with partners. One important result is that status differences did not prevent partners from feeling that they shared within the same office, although it did across office boundaries. At least, overall, partners felt more often that they shared mostly with other partners, but that effect is not statistically significant. It seems that, for partners, status differences did not matter as much as one would expect when sharing the whole picture. Status mattered much more for associates, who felt that partners who worked intensively with them also shared background information much more than other associates (that is, potential competitors) did. Associates who felt that they shared with other associates were mainly litigators from Office I.

Centrality measures in the network show that many partners and senior associates were identified as background information sharers by many others. Senior partners even tended to underestimate the extent to which they shared, when compared to what their younger co-workers felt about the issue: many co-workers considered that these senior partners did share the whole picture with them, whereas the latter thought that they did not. In contrast, a few partners (for example Partners 15, 24, and 26) strongly overestimated the extent to which they shared: they asserted that they shared with almost all their co-workers, whereas only one-third of the latter confirmed it. Status differences seemed to be temporarily downplayed in the deliberation process with one's immediate co-workers and to be more salient (overplayed) with other members of the firm.

These results are quite similar to that of the broader and encompassing co-workers' network. Since individuals tried to harness the advantages of their own social ties and status, and that of the firm itself (the existence of such task forces and niches), they confirmed that members also shared background information in niches of 'same speciality, same office' task forces. Background information was indeed an important task-related resource, and members in this situation did have the feeling that partner–associate status differences tended to be temporarily downplayed in the deliberation process, thus often allowing for minimal levels of informal quality control.

INFORMALLY DISTRIBUTED KNOWLEDGE AND COMPETITION FOR THE AUTHORITY TO KNOW

Quality control depended heavily on the way the firm managed to capitalize and share knowledge and experience in live interactions. This anticipates Chapter 5 (professional brainstorming) and raises the question of how members resort to some kind of authority to stop the professional status competition process—and thus take responsibility for quality. Professional status was recognized in colleagues when they were sought out for advice. As seen above, advice was a key resource in such a knowledge-intensive organization. Members needed it to solve complex legal problems in a creative way. In the advice network, on average, lawyers had in their network twelve colleagues with whom they could exchange basic work-related ideas. We saw earlier that status competition was controlled by the fact that partners held *the authority to know in the deliberation* and that advice was rarely sought out from colleagues 'below'. The issue here, as seen before, was not so much who knew what, but who had the authority to know, and how this authority was negotiated, constructed, and maintained. Attention to one aspect of a case rather than to another could be the object of a debate in the deliberation. Authority to know helped a partner impose a certain temporary focus of attention in a deliberation, although attention could not really be decreed in such a context. In the selection of relevant and appropriate information, members needed this authority to make an issue salient and provide the brainstorming with a conclusion. Indirect control over collective action was often 'epistemic'—that is, related to authority in the management of knowledge (Lazega 2000*d*).

Since members tended to work in niches, it was likely that they would first find this authority within a niche. But it could also happen that they would find it outside the niche, especially if they could not agree on an authority within it. Members did so by expanding their search out of the local task force and niche boundaries to reach and use a firm-wide form of authority and status. They used resources provided by the firm as a whole and created firm-wide professional status for specific partners to manage local problems raised by the work process. Professional and hierarchical forms of status combined to control the production process. This form of status can be called 'professional reputation'. As already stated, whereas individual economic performance was strongly associated with task-force membership, qualitative professional performance was also based on the capacity to reach beyond local substructures and niches. The multilevel exchange system was also a form of productive social mechanism in that it helped members in reaching beyond their niches. The exchange system, this time in spite of its propensity to create niches, provided a structural solution to the problem of quality control by organizing in a credible way the distribution and use of knowledge and experience.

As established above, peer evaluation of quality was in the task-related advice network. The way in which the advice network[16] was shown to be stratified is a useful characteristic for our purpose. Since quality in this context was linked to knowledge and experience, a reputation 'market' was created in the firm. The analysis of the advice network is therefore the key to my argument. In Figure 3.1, it can be seen how exchanges of advice provided a first view of how knowledge was managed within the firm. We already know that the advice network had both hierarchical (or centre–periphery) and clustering tendencies[17] with an emphasis on hierarchical arrangement. Advice was sought within and across niches; requests for advice and professional status recognition converged towards positions of partners, with senior associates as exceptions. Seniority in general was important here for achieving cognitive alignment or co-orientation around a common definition of the situation in collective action—that is, for the legitimacy of a certain course of action. Members rarely sought advice from others below them in the seniority scale: thus the longer you were in the firm, the more people came to you for advice (and the less you sought advice). They also tended to seek advice from others in their own niche—that is, from members similar in office and speciality. However, given the number of seniority levels in the pecking order, it was unlikely that junior associates would seek advice from senior partners. The latter would be overwhelmed with questions below their status. Therefore, it was very likely that members would seek advice from more senior members closer to them on this ladder.

The joint analysis of indegree centrality scores and prominence scores confirms precisely this multilevel dimension of professional status. Indegree centrality scores show that members cited most often (more than twenty five times) were the following: Partners 4, 12, 13, 16, 17, 19, 20, 22, 24, 26, 27, 28, 30, 31, and 34, and Associates 40, 41, 42, 55, 65, and 66. This list includes a few senior partners, in particular those with an open-door policy, either for senior associates, or even, as for Partner 13, for everyone. Senior associates and younger ones with high scores were mostly cited by other associates below or near them, with exceptions who will be examined below. However, Burt's prominence scores (1982), which include a measurement of the importance of the people who cited the focal member, identify Partners 1, 2, 4, 6, 12, 13, 15, 16, 17, 20, 21, 24, 26, 28, and 34 as the most prominent. The difference between the two measures shows that Partners 1, 2, 6, 15, and 21 were cited by few colleagues, but by colleagues who were themselves important ones, mainly partners and senior associates. In addition, prominence scores for top partners were increased by the fact that, while being heavily sought out, they themselves sought out fewer people.[18] Partners 13 and 34 were still in the list but with relatively lower scores because they attracted a heavy volume of associates' citations (women associates for Partner 34, who was one of the three women partners).

In sum, a nested centre–periphery structure shows the existence of firm-wide professional status, an important form of status in knowledge-intensive organizations that count on the capacity of members to innovate and maintain informal quality control. This implies a convergence of requests for knowledge in the system of 'distributed knowledge'. The distribution of the authority to know produced by this exchange mechanism and inferred from the pattern of the advice network provides a clearer picture of the informal quality control process that took place in the firm as a result of avoidance of formal peer review.

It would be too simple, however, to say that just a few central partners and senior associates were key to this form of informal and indirect control. Next, I use an analysis of approximated structural equivalence in this advice network to show that, in a collegial environment, distributed knowledge also means multiplication and competition between professional authorities. Such a multiplication characterizes the learning process in knowledge-intensive firms.

ADVICE FLOWS, DISTRIBUTION, AND CONCENTRATION OF PROFESSIONAL AUTHORITY

Members carefully bounded the set of people from whom they sought advice. They were also included in or excluded from other members' selections. Dimensions of the firm's formal structure also weighed heavily on knowledge sharing and advice-seeking behaviour. This resulted in a relational structure that reflected the existence of the seniority rule (regarding transfers and exchanges of advice) and the joint construction of co-orientation through professional status competition. The pattern describing the shape of flows of advice is described below, using again an analysis approximating structural equivalence between members (Burt 1982, 1991). Eleven clearly different positions were thus identified in the advice network. Figure 4.1 is a reduction providing an overview of the relations between these positions.[19] Appendix D includes the density table from which it is derived and a detailed description of these positions and the relationships between them.

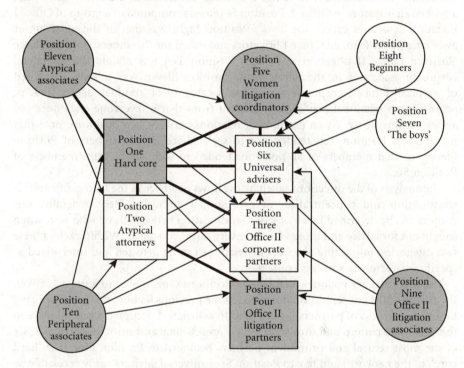

Figure 4.1. *Advice seeking in the firm*

Note: This figure represents the pattern of relationships between positions of approximately structurally equivalent actors in the advice network for all member. Positions represented by a box are composed mainly of partners. Positions represented by a circle are composed mainly of associates. Positions in grey have at least one rival position among the other positions in grey of similar status. Thick lines represent reciprocated advice relationships. For more details about these positions and the relationships among them, see Appendix D. Note that, when analysed separately, each network breaks down into positions that are different from the positions identified when all the networks are superimposed and analysed together to provide a multiplex pattern (Figure 3.1).

Source: Reprinted from *Revue Suisse de Sociologie*, E. Lazega, 'Concurrence, coopération et flux de conseil dans un cabinet américain d'avocats d'affaires: Les échanges d'idées entre collègues', 21: 73. Copyright 1995 with permission from *Revue Suisse de Sociologie*.

Positions represented by a box include mainly partners, and positions represented by a circle mainly associates. Thick lines represent reciprocated advice relationships between positions. As established above in the statistical analysis, partners tended not to seek advice from associates.

To summarize, Position One, the 'hard core' of this network, was composed of Office I partners of all specialities. Position Two clustered the 'atypical' attorneys (either 'laterals'—that is, lawyers recruited from other law firms—or representatives of non-lucrative corporate speciality) from both main offices. Position Three was that of Office II core corporate partners. Position Four was that of Office II core litigation partners. Position Five was that of the 'coordinators', mostly senior women litigation associates in Office I. Position Six clustered the firm's 'universal', advisers, all litigators in Office I. Position Seven was composed of a group of Office I litigation associates called 'the boys'. Position Eight was that of the most junior associates in the firm, all Office I litigators and called the 'beginners'. Position Nine clustered Office II litigation associates. Position Ten was mainly that of lateral corporate associates in the whole firm. Position Eleven was mainly composed of 'atypical' Office I corporate associates. A category of 'residual' actors (that is, actors whose relational profile was different from that of everyone else) does not appear in this figure. As an example of relations between two positions, note that members of Position Ten tended not to seek advice from members of Position Eleven; or that members of all positions tended to seek advice from members of Position Six.

The analysis of the directions taken by the flows of advice in the firm confirms this stratification and concentration of professional authority. Very generally, this context can be described by an obvious stratification between those who were often sought out for advice and those who were very rarely consulted. Within each of these two categories, interesting absences of relations can be detected and interpreted as specific characteristics of this context.

The first category includes members of Positions One to Six in Figure 4.1. Given the nature of the concentration described in the previous section, it is not surprising to find that blocks of partners (as opposed to associates) occupied a central place in this relational pattern and thus represented professional authority. In particular, six of the most central and prominent partners belonged to Position One (the 'hard core', of the network) and five to Position Six (universal advisers easily accessible by associates—often because they belonged to the ATC). As shown by Figure 4.1, the five positions of partners (One, Two, Three, Four, and Five) formed a subset towards which requests for advice converged from all positions. For instance, exchanges with Position One were very frequent; all tended to seek its members for advice, and they often reciprocated, except with Position Four (Office II litigation partners sometimes perceived as rivals). Position Six was potentially the most effective at building 'epistemic alignment' and co-orientation in the firm: its members tended to be sought out for advice by the members of all the other positions, but they tended also to reciprocate only to Positions One and Five (and especially not to Two, Three, and Four).

The second category included members of Positions Seven to Eleven in Figure 4.1. For instance, members of Positions Seven and Eight had access to the rest of the firm through the members of Position Five (the 'coordinators') or Six (the 'universal' advisers). Members of Positions Ten and Eleven were exceptions to this trend. They had direct access to the most important partners in the firm. Such trends can be explained by the ethnography of the firm: we know, for instance, that most associates in Positions Ten and Eleven were laterals; they had not 'grown up' in the firm, and might not have internalized the norms and informal boundaries that inhibited other associates who had come up through the ranks. In addition, given their seniority, they could try to intensify their direct ties with partners to make themselves known and increase their chances of being made a partner.

Figure 4.1 also provides a glimpse into the dynamics of professional status competition between members. Positions in grey had at least one 'rival' position among the other positions in grey of similar status. Absence of mutual relations between positions indicates specific asymmetries in the flows of advice across the firm. They describe the context in which advice seeking occurred in terms of informal stratification (concentration of choices on the 'elite' of advisers and on specific positions in the overall pattern) and polarization (between offices and specialities). The most striking and special aspect of the pattern in Figure 4.1 is the absence of mutual exchanges between certain positions of partners (between Positions One and Four, and between Positions Three/Four and Six). Focusing on the relationships among partners shows both that the One–Six axis was dominant in the control of the flows of advice, and also the absence of reciprocity in these flows, especially among Office I and Office II litigation partners who competed for the best associates, and for status and prestige within the firm. This asymmetry—which could be explained by economic incentives to withhold advice or let other partners down—would be shown even more strongly if Figure 4.1 were simplified to retain only reciprocal relations between positions—that is, truly collective exchanges of advice. Polarization between Offices I and II would still be present, as well as the centrality and prominence of Position One in terms of advice flows. Members of this position, for instance, obviously preferred to seek advice from associates of Position Five rather than from their own partners in Position Four. This structure shows how quality control and co-orientation through knowledge management was achieved and stabilized in the organization through concentration and polarization of the authority to know. This description of the inner workings of the organization as an exchange system for authoritative professional knowledge is informative when one looks at the connection between individual interests, individual management of knowledge and experience, and firm structure.

The distribution of the professional authority to know—produced by the multilevel exchange mechanism and inferred from the pattern of the advice network—provides a clearer picture of the informal quality control process that took place in the firm as a result of avoidance of formal peer review. The next section stresses the fact that professional status and economic performance went hand in hand, which in turn strengthened the informal quality control regime.

DISTRIBUTED KNOWLEDGE AND
ECONOMIC PERFORMANCE

These dynamics driven by concentration and distribution of professional authority underlie the quality control process and are measurably correlated with economic performance. In effect, in this collegial organization, as perhaps for any firm stressing quality professional services, the conditions under which the pattern of knowledge flows was most productive included the existence of at least two processes: first, the selection of exchange partners in the co-workers' network (niche seeking), as seen above; and, secondly, the concentration of the authority to know in the advice network (through a form of professional status competition). The fact that some members emerged as having the authority to know, although such status was fragile, was the result of a micro-political process that seemed to be efficient too. This efficiency can be measured in statistical evidence concerning the relationship between crude measurements of economic performance and position in social networks related to the allocation of knowledge. By going back to Table 4.1 it is possible to test the idea that specific relational patterns shaping the flows of knowledge in the organization were correlated with various measures of economic performance.

The significant effect of centrality in the advice network in Models 2 and 3 suggests that seniority and concentration of requests for knowledge were a determinant of strong performance in this case. This effect is added to that of higher hourly rates for senior partners and to that of constraint in one's work group (or task force). Recall again that members got their advice in social niches, but also outside the niche, among partners with a specific form of status: it was not only technical expertise, but authority based on experience and the pressure to risk an already well-established reputation. Partners with high indegree scores in the advice network had high hourly rates ($r = 0.47$) and brought in more fees (in terms of dollars collected; $r = 0.42$). Being sought out for advice was strongly correlated with being senior ($r = 0.46$), with years spent in the firm ($r = 0.48$), with age ($r = 0.43$), with being a partner (as differentiated from senior associates, who were also sought out for advice; $r = 0.30$) and with coming from an elite law school ($r = 0.28$). Members sought out for advice tended to seek others for advice less (correlation between indegree and outdegree centralities was negative: $r = -0.28$), which confirms a status competition effect (one did not seek advice from people below). In short, processes connected to social status as well as to density of one's work relationships were the key to the efficient distribution of knowledge. Obviously, partners with high professional authority and strong economic performance belonged to the oligarchy of the firm, a strong argument in favour of informal quality control in that firm. The next section stresses the fact that the dynamics underlying this quality control process generated competitive advantages for some associates who were able to reach up and out of their niche. In effect, this was made possible by the fact that—as shown by the pattern—the seniority rule was not as rigid as the expression 'iron law' would suggest.

SHORT CUTS FOR COMPETITIVE ADVANTAGE
AMONG ASSOCIATES

Another form of efficiency of this pattern in the distribution of the authority to know can be derived from the previous analysis, this time for selected associates. In Figure 4.1, absence of advice ties among senior associates is also interesting. For instance, notice that members of Positions Seven, Eight, Nine, and Eleven exchanged advice within their own respective position, but very little with the members of other positions—another sign of patronage where clients were kept apart. This may be explained by the fact that members of each position struck a fragile balance between cooperation and competition. They needed each other for advice, but they also tended to be rivals in their relationships with partners. This was particularly true for the members of Positions Five, Nine, Ten, and Eleven, who were supposed, at the time of the fieldwork, to come up for partnership within the next two years. This competition between associates could result in the design of different relational strategies with regard to the use of professional status. Position Five members, for instance, could try to reduce the number of situations in which the members of other associate positions would get a chance to show their capacity to provide advice—for instance, by insulating them in compartmentalized domains defined by traditional and formal internal boundaries. Similarly, lateral or 'foreign' (from another office) associates could let themselves be used more often, because they were perceived to be easier to exploit or less threatening in terms of loss of status for the advice-seeker.

This pattern also reflects serious structural inequalities among members, which become visible in the differences in their respective individual relational capital. Anticipating Chapter 5 results, the form of interdependence of advice and friendship ties displayed at SG&R was based on the fact that each had a separate local structure, but at the same time a strong propensity for multiplexity and for barter of one for the other. Thus, trading on friendship was an obvious 'short cut'.[20] In such a competitive context, some members had direct access to advice from prominent partners; they could reach these partners within their own niche, thus crossing the hierarchical boundaries identified above. Such infractions to the rules were tolerated for some, and less for others. These others would have had to pay a relatively higher price to get access to the same resources. Such personalized acquaintance with the adviser could be decisive. Members of Position Five, for example, could trade more than members of Position Eleven on personalized ties to get advice and thus obtain a form of professional blessing, even informal, for their work. Their easier access to professional status put them in a position to control the quality of work of their associates. For example, Associates 38, 39, 40, 41, and 43 (among whom 39, 40, and 43 were to become partners very quickly) had a competitive advantage over Associates 42, 48, 53, and 64 (none of whom were partners in 1999). As a consequence, it could be argued that judgements about the quality of their work would not be as clear-cut for Position Eleven associates as it was for Position Five associates: quality would not be guaranteed by the powerful and would thus remain debatable. The distribution of advice as an invisible resource did indeed count for the allocation of credit and promotion.

This system of circulation of advice thus favoured a few selected associates in their race towards partnership: through short cuts in the network, it provided them with access to very senior partners. Thus, the exchange system is again shown to have been a productive form of corporate social capital: it helped members manage knowledge and control quality. But it is also shown to have reflected a selection mechanism, because it allocated immaterial resources in an unequal way. A compartmentalized structure emerges, where some had more or better resources to deal with competition and get access to resources such as advice, whereas others were clearly cornered and dependent on their competitors' judgement. This context of advice seeking was thus constraining in terms of efficiency, but also of control and internal politics.

In sum, the problem of quality control, which was considered to be equivalent to a problem of accumulation and distribution of authoritative knowledge and experience in the firm, was another structural problem to which the exchange system provided a structural solution. Formal peer review being highly problematic, the focus was on yet another way in which this system was productive: by allocating authoritative knowledge and helping members share experience—a crucial resource, too often considered to be exclusively individual 'human capital'—in spite of professional status competition. The exchange system provided a functional equivalent of peer review, an informal mechanism of quality control. The multilevel (from the individual to the relational, then to the collective level) analysis of the pattern of advice network in the firm shows how the distribution of professional status *concentrated the authority to know* and functioned as an informal quality control mechanism providing professional 'co-orientation'.

In such a knowledge-intensive organization, this form of relational mechanism is even more important for collective action than it is in other types of organization. The pattern of advice relationships sustains quality control by *distributing professional authority*, while providing a social solution to the problem of capitalization of knowledge and experience, a crucial problem in such organizations. Flows of advice are not 'free'; they do encounter obstacles, which could systematically prevent exchanges of intelligence between any two members. In spite of the relative density of the advice network (0.18), it is obvious that such flows were socially constrained and structured in a way that solved quality problems more easily for some than for others. This mechanism, consequently, also had an effect on other processes in the firm; in particular, it generated structural inequalities between members in niches including prominent professionals and members who had to pay a heavy price to try to reach out of their niches and access professional advice by bypassing a constraining set of niche fellows.

This chapter has focused on showing how the exchange system helped with economic (or quantitative) and professional (or qualitative) forms of performance: by making tenured partners work and by ensuring a form of quality control among peers. In many ways, the generalized exchange system described above could be expected to prevent tenured partners from free-riding too much (with exceptions such as Partners 10 and 25), in spite of strong incentives to do so. It did so by involving partners in more than one type of exchange. Most partners depended on others for many resources, had to care about others' judgement, and eventually did what was expected from them: that is, participated in status competition, worked hard, and submitted to informal, proactive, and task-related quality control.

Having shown that this exchange system could be productive by helping to solve such problems in collegial organizations—sometimes by cultivating status competition—I turn in the next chapter to a process of mitigation of this status competition. This process of cultivation and mitigation of status competition is shown to be based on the collegial blend of several types of relationships. Indeed, in social niches, articulation of different resources—the intersection of networks—can be explained and symbolized by this process. This will enhance our understanding of participation in collective action among peers by highlighting the combined effect of the three networks that together reflected an order imposed on familiar and chaotic processes such as brainstorming among interdependent professionals.

5

Too Many Chefs?

The solidarity that is provided to members through a generalized exchange system in social niches is fragile, and status competition is a threat to the existence of such a positive social mechanism. This reiterates basic questions: how do niche seeking and status competition coexist, and are they not contradictory drives? This chapter is about this coexistence, as it plays itself out in a process that helps the organization deal with the potentially negative effects of status competition. It describes the way in which the intersection of networks can help a social and informal mechanism that contributes to organizational governance. Multivariate p^* models are used to identify a socially constructed equilibrium between the two drives. They show how multiplex social ties (co-work, advice, and friendship) within niches can be used in such a context both to cultivate *and* to mitigate status competition among professional colleagues. As mentioned before, status competition can get out of hand; but social ties can interlock in substructures, showing that it is mitigated by a delicate process involving advice and friendship ties.

Here, status competition is examined as an 'unbounded' status auction process. Sutton and Hargadon (1996) provided rich descriptions of bounded or segregated[1] status auctions in design firms; the status auction that they described is confined to the brainstorming room and designated brainstorming sessions. Here, I look at 'unbounded' and diffuse status auctions in which status displays and challenges occur throughout the organization. When status auctions cannot be confined or segmented away from day-to-day operations, they need to be governed in some other way.

UNBOUNDED STATUS AUCTIONS AND
THE COLLEGIAL BLEND OF RELATIONSHIPS

The process that combines these resources—that is, that makes multiplexity in exchanges again so important—is the process of mitigation of status competition. Knowledge-intensive work is inextricably mixed with status games (Blau 1964). This type of work in a partner–associates task force is very deliberative. As mentioned earlier, temporary partner–associate task forces at SG&R constituted the core of multifunctional and sometimes multidisciplinary work groups. In such task forces, associates are often expected to brainstorm with higher status members. When deliberating about a case, associates and partners play a temporarily collegial and egalitarian game involving status auctions in which all substantive arguments have equal weight. However, at some point, the partners' greater experience, greater skill and judgement, responsibility to the client, or simply hierarchical position become a justification for stopping these exchanges and making a decision about how the case will be handled and efforts allocated. This is often perceived to be autocratic behaviour of partners imposing idiosyncratic standards of proper practice on frustrated associates, but the latter rarely say so. They hope to advance to the top of the associate pyramid, and to make it to partnership. Among partners, differences are played down and treated as differences in style, and having the final word with associates is considered to be an obvious necessity, either as a service provider, or as a professional educator.

However, status competition can also get out of hand. Status can be endlessly challenged, especially on behalf of different conceptions of professionalism. At SG&R, as in any firm, status competition was thus a double-edged sword. It was both encouraged and contained. This creates management problems for professional, knowledge-intensive organizations, always in danger of unravelling (Olson 1965). It raises the question of how status competition is handled. Economic approaches to labour markets (Frank 1985) assert that incentives such as specific compensation systems take care of the negative effects of status differences. Thus, low performers and low status members tend to be overcompensated relative to the value they produce, whereas high performers and high status members tend to be undercompensated relative to the value they produce: they pay a price for being recognized as high status members. SG&R's lockstep system could, therefore, be considered to be a mitigation device for status competition among partners. A majority of partners supported it because they believed that it prevented yearly conflicts among themselves, especially conflict about each member's value to the firm.

ECONOMIC MITIGATION OF STATUS COMPETITION

If the compensation system was in itself a mitigation mechanism, it was not sufficient, because it was not directly tied to the tasks, the work process, and the relationships between members carrying it out. With the lockstep system, comparisons and relative standing evaluations were frozen. This meant that senior partners had to find younger ones who would accept waiting in order to benefit from postponed reciprocity (hence the tough selection to make it to partnership: selecting people who would work hard, but also stay). In effect, partners engaged in both local and global comparisons. Some of them knew that they could improve their rank and status by 'choosing another pond' (Frank 1985)—that is, by switching to another law firm and defining another group as their peers. But they also knew that they would incur a cost, which sometimes seemed quite high, in the process. Listen to Partner 18, one of the highest collectors for the year:

> Our system costs me money. With a different system, I would have made more money. But not enough more to make me go into a more competitive environment. With people who don't know each other well, you are taking more risks that they would leave. And we don't have such stars that they would make twice as much somewhere

else. We have the type of people who are not concerned with the extra 10 per cent that they would get elsewhere, and the type of people who don't like to fight. It used to be said that in business you shouldn't change jobs unless the change brings you 25 per cent more. Most of us don't have such an opportunity. I operate under that theory. If you give up security relationships and status, you want a substantial increase to justify that. You disrupt your life. I wouldn't even consider moving for less than that kind of increase. It's just easier for me to sit here and be a partner with Partner 8, we don't agree on anything, but I don't have to argue with him about his compensation. If we had a different system, I would be much more worried about his views. Shakespeare: bearing the ills you have rather than fleeing to others that you don't know. The problem is with people who underperform consistently. Do you keep them or not? This is a much more dramatic decision to make. They continue to draw their full compensation until dissatisfaction is such that they are expelled.

This economic mitigation was not obvious at all. In fact it is a rare case that characterized this firm and very few others—which is why it is so interesting for the study of the idealtypical collegial form and its cooperation mechanisms. On the one hand, it was difficult to measure the extent to which Partner 1 or Partner 18 were paid less than the value they produced. But, on the other hand, it was easy to see that Partner 18 and Partner 16 were paid almost the same amount of compensation. Yet, in 1990, Partner 18 brought in around 40 per cent more than Partner 16. In 1991, the difference was close to half a million dollars. What made Partner 18 remain within this firm? Would he not have been better off choosing another pond? The answer to this question was, firstly, as the managing partner said, 'You're hot one year, you're down next year.' So in this firm, relative status did not create a very stable oligarchy; therefore the fact that Partner 18 really belonged to another pond was not easily established. But the answer was also, secondly, because he preferred—as shown above—being a big fish in this smaller firm—that is, experiencing high status compared to lower status partners—to being a smaller fish in a larger pond, in which he would run the risk of being the lower status partner. In this firm, Partner 18 accepted a cut in compensation worth tens (if not more than a hundred) of thousands of dollars in exchange for status and its advantages, including the satisfaction of comparing favourably with others (at least for a few years) who placed a lower value on intra-organizational status and tolerated being lower on the totem pole in exchange for an increase in returns compared to what they brought into the firm.

Members in such a law firm earned much more than the average American income. Therefore, it is safe to assert that they cared more about relative than absolute income.[2] Concerns about relative economic standing, and worries about rank, did exist, but partners could not contest for position, because this position was assigned to them once and for all. Strong restrictions were placed on such contests. There was only one way to gain in formal status: staying with the firm for a longer time. With time, you got status anyway, and you repaid it with loyalty to the firm. On the other hand, members could not suffer a great loss of economic status, unless they were punished for a consistently low economic performance, which was extremely rare. In Frank's terms (1985), they could expend too little effort, but this would not have made them extremely vulnerable or increase dramatically the costs of being lower-rank members. Thus, high performers were indeed very often undercompensated compared to the revenue they brought into the firm, whereas low achievers were often overcompensated with regard to the same comparison.

CULTIVATING AND MITIGATING STATUS COMPETITION: THE BLENDING PROCESS

Professional status competition (among associates, between partners and associates, and among partners) could not be handled in the same way. It was an efficient mechanism for motivating members at work. If receiving social approval from peers is one of Weberian value-oriented actors' goals, allocation of this approval through honours and recognition—along with the privileges of rank in the pecking order—is indeed a powerful motivation device. The following is an example of how partners in this firm typically liked to talk about 'their' associates, and the kind of intellectually challenging attitude (a form of professional status competition) that they encouraged within their task forces:

> Ours is a fascinating structure built on, to some extent, maximizing a certain type of efficiency. All are encouraged to think hard. You look good as an associate if you can convince a partner that he is wrong about something. You have freedom of thought within legal problems.... There is a great intellectual freedom here. An associate yesterday told me that she didn't think that a decision of mine in a file was correct. She stuck to her guns, and fifteen minutes later I called her to tell her that she was right. In other places, if the boss says something, everyone says, 'Good idea, boss.' Not here. (Partner 19)

Since compensation in this firm was tied to seniority, and since each member's rank in the seniority scale was defined once and for all, status competition lost one of its most dangerous stakes: money. But it was thus refocused on other stakes, such as professional involvement, commitment, reputation, and authority in work groups. For example, partners could put down associates through associate reviews, which could also be considered to be humbling rituals, illustrating to associates that there were acceptable limits to challenges to partner status in the work process. The effects of these humbling rituals were softened by comparisons to other associates or by other members who indicated that they would have behaved or handled the case in another way. They nevertheless 'underscored the status differences among their ranks' (Bosk 1979: 143).[3]

I argue that if cooperation is systematically amenable to structural analyses at the dyadic, triadic, and higher-order levels, it is possible to enhance understanding of participation in collective action among status competitors by highlighting the relationship between choices of important sources of resources in any specific organization. At SG&R, this is possible by looking at how the three important production-related resources (co-workers' goodwill—understood as a strong commitment to collaboration—advice, and friendship) were exchanged, or bartered. Specifically, this section formulates expectations about such multiplex exchanges. The next section analyses the interlocking of ties among members to show how this exchange system provided a structural answer to the problem of participation in collective action among competing professional peers.

Given the above understanding of the functioning of work groups in this firm, it is reasonable to expect interdependence of relationships in the work process both to cultivate and to mitigate status competition. Direct exchanges of resources by a pair of lawyers were likely to occur, since such exchanges supported the regularity of their specific joint participation in task forces. In addition, it is also reasonable to think that effective collective participation required interdependencies of transfer and exchange that went beyond direct relations involving a single pair of firm members. Although it is difficult to make precise predictions about the detailed nature of these more complex dependencies, it is nonetheless possible to derive some expectations about their general form. In particular, indirect transfers and exchanges of resources (in triadic chains or cycles of cooperation) were likely to be strong because niches helped members expect that resources transferred to a colleague would eventually come back, either directly or through a third colleague. Thus, extra-dyadic dependencies were also likely to be observed in the circulation of each resource, since it was only dependencies involving three or more lawyers that could provide a structural basis for the coordination of ongoing collective participation.

With regard to the interlocking of the different types of resources, previous argumentation suggests that, to structure the work process, interdependence between co-workers' ties and advice ties was strong in this exchange system. Specifically, members should have mixed work and advice ties so as to bring in status to control the deliberation process. In addition, to mitigate status competition, interdependence between advice ties and friendship ties could be expected to be strong in this exchange system. In other words, members should tend to mix advice and friendship ties so as to soften the potentially negative effects of status competition. Finally, given that partners could always have the upper hand over associates in the same task force, and that partners in the same task force sought out other, usually more senior, partners outside the task force to sort out status competition among themselves, interdependence between co-workers' ties (often mixing partners and associates) and friendship ties should have been relatively weak and infrequent. In other words, members, in general, should have sorted their ties so as not to mix work and friendship directly, even to uncouple them.

Without further analyses, it is difficult to evaluate these expectations about the form of interdependence between resources for the members of this firm, and to understand the ways in which these exchanges help mitigate status competition in collegial organizations. The description and analyses of the exchange system in this firm provide evidence for testing these hypotheses. As mentioned in Appendix E, the p^* class of multivariate random graph models (Frank and Strauss 1986; Pattison 1993; Pattison and Wasserman 1999; Robins *et al.* forthcoming; Strauss and Ikeda 1990; Wasserman and Pattison 1996) were developed specifically for the analysis of tie interdependencies. They are used here to analyse the interplay between the three social resources shaping cooperation among these professionals. They help identify the specific local and multiplex exchange substructures on which this cooperation is based.

SOCIAL MITIGATION OF STATUS COMPETITION: A MULTIPLEX SOCIAL MECHANISM

Substructures and their parameter labelling have already been presented in Figure 3.2. After the local distribution of co-workers' ties were described in Chapter 3, advice and friendship ties were added in such substructures. This distribution is represented in the last two models presented in Table 3.4 (advice, then friendship).

The advice relation has positive parameters for both reciprocity ($\tau_{11\_A,A}$) and transitivity ($\tau_{9\_A,A,A}$), although the reciprocity parameter is not as strong as for the other two relations, mainly because people sought out for advice tended to have equal or superior status to advice-seekers. In addition, the 2-path parameter ($\tau_{13\_A,A}$) and the 3-cycle parameter ($\tau_{10\_A,A,A}$) are large and negative. This pattern of parameter values is consistent with tendencies towards both local clustering and partial ordering. It suggests an advice structure that was globally hierarchical, with some local clustering.

The friendship relation has even larger positive reciprocity ($\tau_{11\_F,F}$) and transitivity ($\tau_{9\_F,F,F}$) parameters than the advice relation. In addition, the 2-path parameter ($\tau_{13\_F,F}$) and the 3-cycle parameter ($\tau_{10\_F,F,F}$) are also negative, suggesting that the friendship relation also displayed strong local clustering as well as some hierarchical organization. In fact, the values of the reciprocity and transitivity parameters suggest that local clustering was stronger for friendship than for advice. The weak but positive 2-out-star parameter ($\tau_{12\_F,F}$) suggests that at least some individuals chose friends who were not tied to one another; thus, at least some friendship ties bridged denser local clusters.

Thus, overall, direct exchanges by a pair of lawyers are shown to have been strong for all resources, enabling joint participation in task forces and availability of advisers and friends for cultivation and mitigation of status competition. However, generalized exchange characterized work relationships much more than any other types of relationship. Transfers and exchanges that went beyond direct relations involving a single pair of firm members were not needed for all resources in order to manage the status competition process. The next section uncovers the kind of interdependencies between the three types of relationships that were able to mitigate status competition among peers. Specific multiplex substructures allowing for this mitigation are identified by an analysis of the interplay of these relationships.

THE INTERPLAY OF RESOURCES AMONG MEMBERS

The number of possible distinct dyadic and triadic substructures involving three relations is very large. As a result, the class of substructures used to define an initial multivariate p^* model was restricted to: dyadic structures of level four or less; triadic structures of level three or less; and the level four triadic substructures identified in the univariate analyses. The pseudolikelihood estimates for parameters in the final model are presented in Table 5.1.

The estimates are organized according to the types of tie involved in the corresponding configurations. A discussion of the structural implications of these estimates follows, but first note that, in addition to the unirelational substructures already described, there are at least three different *types* of multirelational network substructures that are important to modelling the multivariate network. These are: (*a*) multiplex ties linking one lawyer in the firm to another, suggesting some *alignment* of resource dependencies across the different types of resource; (*b*) multiplex dyadic exchange structures in which a pair of lawyers exchanged different types of resource, suggesting some *complementarity* of resource dependence; and (*c*) various triadic configurations involving multiple resource ties, suggesting more complex patterns of structural *interlock* among resource ties. The structures involving each combination of types of tie are discussed in turn, noting the implications that they had for the form of interdependence of ties in the firm.[4]

The parameter estimates in the multivariate model corresponding to multirelational configurations are generally very similar in magnitude to those already discussed for the univariate models. There are just three exceptions to this pattern. The first and arguably most important is the estimate for the co-work transitivity parameter ($\tau_{9\_W,W,W}$): it is small (and negative) in the multivariate model but positive in the univariate model. The absence of a positive transitivity effect in the multivariate model suggests that, once the various associations between co-work and the other two types of tie are taken into account, there was no separate structural tendency for co-work transitivity. In other words, it is possible that the transitive tendency apparent in the univariate model is largely attributable to the entrainment of co-work ties with the highly transitive advice (and, to a lesser extent, friendship) ties. The second exception is the absence of negative 3-cycle parameters for advice and friendship ($\tau_{10\_A,A,A}$ and $\tau_{10\_F,F,F}$): in the multivariate model, these parameters have a less substantial contribution to model fit, presumably because of the associations between the various types of tie (particularly, advice and friendship). The third exception concerns the positive 2-in-star and 2-out-star parameters for advice ($\tau_{14\_A,A}$ and $\tau_{12\_A,A}$) in the multivariate model; these were not evident in the univariate model. The positive parameters in the multivariate model suggest that, once various across-tie dependencies are taken into account, there was a tendency for differentiation among firm members in their seeking and being sought out for advice—but this differentiation is most evident in those advice ties that were not accompanied by co-work and friendship ties.

The large number of parameters in the multivariate model corresponding to configurations comprising both co-work and advice ties suggests that co-work and advice ties were distributed in a highly interdependent manner. We note first that the multiplexity parameter (lawyer *i* sends a duplex tie to lawyer *j*) is large and

Table 5.1. *Multiplexity of ties in the firm: Parameter estimates for final multivariate p^* model*

Co-work		Advice		Friendship	
Term	PLE	Term	PLE	Term	PLE
τ_{15_W}	−3.49 (0.25)	τ_{15_A}	−3.46 (0.25)	τ_{15_F}	−4.65 (0.29)
$\tau_{11\_W,W}$	4.45 (0.47)	$\tau_{11\_A,A}$	1.33 (0.24)	$\tau_{11\_F,F}$	2.91 (0.24)
$\tau_{12\_W,W}$	0.06 (0.01)	$\tau_{12\_A,A}$	0.06 (0.01)	$\tau_{12\_F,F}$	0.07 (0.01)
$\tau_{13\_W,W}$	−0.04 (0.02)	$\tau_{13\_A,A}$	−0.06 (0.01)	$\tau_{13\_F,F}$	−0.06 (0.02)
$\tau_{14\_W,W}$	0.10 (0.02)	$\tau_{14\_A,A}$	0.06 (0.01)	$\tau_{14\_F,F}$	0.03 (0.02)
$\tau_{9\_W,W,W}$	−0.03 (0.02)	$\tau_{9\_A,A,A}$	0.28 (0.02)	$\tau_{9\_F,F,F}$	0.28 (0.02)
$\tau_{10\_W,W,W}$	0.30 (0.06)				
$\tau_{7\_W,W,W}$	−0.09 (0.02)				
$\tau_{8\_W,W,W}$	−0.06 (0.02)				
$\tau_{3\_W,W,W,W}$	−0.11 (0.02)				
$\tau_{6\_W,W,W,W}$	0.21 (0.04)				

Co-work and advice		Co-work and friendship		Advice and friendship	
Term	PLE	Term	PLE	Term	PLE
τ_{15_WA}	2.44 (0.13)	τ_{15_WF}	0.96 (0.17)	τ_{15_AF}	2.42 (0.22)
$\tau_{11\_W,A}$	0.61 (0.21)	$\tau_{11\_W,F}$	0.48 (0.18)	$\tau_{11\_A,F}$	1.30 (0.19)
$\tau_{12\_W,A}$	−0.01 (0.01)				
$\tau_{13\_W,A}$	−0.03 (0.01)	$\tau_{13\_F,W}$	0.01 (0.01)	$\tau_{13\_A,F}$	−0.01 (0.01)
$\tau_{13\_A,W}$	−0.04 (0.01)	$\tau_{13\_W,F}$	−0.00 (0.01)	$\tau_{13\_F,A}$	−0.03 (0.01)
$\tau_{14\_A,W}$	−0.02 (0.01)	$\tau_{14\_W,F}$	−0.01 (0.01)	$\tau_{14\_A,F}$	−0.02 (0.01)
$\tau_{11\_W,AW}$	−0.39 (0.17)	$\tau_{11\_W,FW}$	−1.13 (0.23)	$\tau_{11\_A,AF}$	−0.87 (0.24)
$\tau_{11\_A,AW}$	−0.82 (0.14)			$\tau_{11\_F,AF}$	−0.90 (0.27)
$\tau_{9\_A,A,W}$	−0.08 (0.02)				
$\tau_{9\_A,W,A}$	−0.10 (0.02)			$\tau_{9\_A,F,A}$	0.07 (0.02)
$\tau_{9\_W,A,A}$	−0.12 (0.02)				
$\tau_{9\_A,W,W}$	0.13 (0.02)				
$\tau_{9\_W,A,W}$	0.18 (0.02)	$\tau_{9\_W,F,W}$	0.07 (0.02)		
$\tau_{8\_W,W,A}$	0.03 (0.01)				
		$\tau_{10\_F,F,W}$	−0.13 (0.02)	$\tau_{10\_A,A,F}$	−0.15 (0.02)
				$\tau_{13\_F,AF}$	−0.07 (0.02)
				$\tau_{11\_AF,AF}$	1.55 (0.45)

Co-work, advice, and friendship	
Term	PLE
τ_{15_WA}	−1.00 (0.21)
$\tau_{11\_W,AF}$	−0.30 (0.24)
$\tau_{11\_W,AFW}$	1.51 (0.31)

Notes: PLE: Pseudolikelihood estimates (standard errors in parentheses). For presentation of multi-relational p^* models, see Appendix E.

Source: Reprinted from *Social Networks*, 'Multiplexity, Generalized Exchange and Cooperation in Organizations', E. Lazega and P. Pattison, 21: 83. Copyright 1999 with permission from Elsevier Science.

positive and suggests that the co-occurrence of the two types of tie was likely; to some degree, co-work and advice were aligned in structure. Secondly, the exchange parameter (i sends an advice tie to j, who reciprocates with a work tie) is also positive, reflecting a tendency for the two types of tie to be exchanged. Thirdly, these tendencies towards alignment and exchange were somewhat disjunctive, as is evident from the negative estimates of the parameters $\tau_{11\_W,AW}$ and $\tau_{11\_A,AW}$.[5] Fourthly, there was a clear and interesting form of triadic interdependence for advice and co-work ties: 2-paths comprising one advice and one co-work tie appear to be likely to coincide with a co-work tie, but not with an advice tie. Thus, being a co-worker of an adviser or an adviser of a co-worker was not a sufficient qualification for being a direct adviser. Such indirect ties were more likely to be associated with direct co-worker ties. In this sense, the advice and co-work ties participated in configurations having some of the characteristics of the interlock of strong and weak ties, with advice ties the stronger of the two (Breiger and Pattison 1978; Pattison 1993). It might be hypothesized that advice ties drove the creation of new co-worker ties, in the sense that new co-worker ties could be forged with either the co-workers of one's advisers or the advisers of one's co-workers. Indeed, it is interesting to note that the two triadic advice and co-work configurations with positive parameter estimates contain as substructures two of the few likely co-work forms in which exchange is not evident (namely, $\tau_{12\_W,W}$ and $\tau_{14\_W,W}$). One possibility, therefore, is that the advice tie had a stabilizing role in what otherwise might be a less stable pattern of work distribution in a system driven largely by exchange. That is, the lack of exchange in these configurations could be offset against the opportunity to work with individuals at a higher status; it is in this sense that status-signalling advice ties were strong and helped to articulate the distribution of resources for collective participation. But note that this capacity for work ties to straddle status differences did not extend too far: the advisers of one's advisers were not likely to be co-workers (as the negative estimate for $\tau_{9\_A,A,W}$ indicates). Further, note that status-signalling advice ties played a role in providing access to work opportunities, and that this might have helped mitigate against status games. In all, and as expected, the interdependence between co-worker and advice ties was strong in this exchange system.

Advice and friendship ties also exhibited quite strong interdependence, with substantial multiplexity (i sends a duplex tie to j) and exchange (i sends an advice tie to j, who reciprocates with a friendship tie) effects. In addition, the positive estimate for $\tau_{11\_AF,AF}$ indicates an enhanced reciprocity effect for one type of tie in the presence of a reciprocal tie of the other type; the enhancement was not observed, however, in the presence of an unreciprocated tie of the other type (as the negative estimates for $\tau_{11\_F,AF}$ and $\tau_{11\_A,AF}$ indicate). At the triadic level, the only positive estimate is associated with a triadic structure in which friendship links the advisers j and k of some lawyer i. Arguably, just as advice ties served to articulate co-work relations, so friendship ties may have served a weak articulatory role with respect to advice ties (since configurations in which the friend of an adviser was also an adviser have a positive parameter estimate). It is interesting also to note that in 42 per cent of such triads in which the advice-seeker was an associate, the advisers were both partners. Thus, in these cases where advice was sought by associates from partners who lay outside a current task force, friendship often linked the partners, and helped to offset the difficulties that arose from their giving different advice or from their comparison to one another by a common subordinate.

Negative parameter estimates are associated with 3-cycles comprising two advice ties and a friendship tie (suggesting that, even though the adviser of an adviser was a source of potential advice, such a person was unlikely to return a direct friendship tie). Thus, one might argue that the interdependence of advice and friendship ties can be described largely in the dyadic terms of a propensity for multiplexity and exchange, although there is also a weaker articulatory relationship between friendship and advice ties. These patterns of interdependence of friendship and advice ties can also be interpreted as suggesting that friendship 'softened' the status differences inherent to advice ties, both directly (through multiplexity and exchange effects) and indirectly (by tending to link the advisers of an individual). Thus, these patterns are consistent with the general expectations regarding the role of friendship ties in the mitigation of status competition.[6]

As predicted, the parameters for configurations involving co-work and friendship tend to be much weaker. The multiplexity and exchange parameters are weak but positive, and, since the parameter for the configuration in which a mutual co-work tie occurs in the presence of an asymmetric friendship tie is large and negative, these effects appear to be disjunctive. At the triadic level, cycles comprising two friendship ties and one co-worker tie were unlikely, and there was a weak tendency for friendship ties to link the two lawyers with whom a third claimed co-work ties. This latter effect is similar to, but much weaker than, the pattern by which advice was claimed to help sustain one of the asymmetric co-work configurations. Thus, members tended to sort their ties so as not to mix work and friendship too directly.

Finally, a very small number of dyadic configurations involving co-work, advice, and friendship have large estimated parameters. In particular, the triplex tie from i to j has a negative estimate, whereas the triplex tie accompanied by a reciprocal co-work tie has a positive estimate. This suggests that, even though pairs of lawyers might have been linked by duplex ties more commonly than the overall frequency of individual ties would suggest, the observation of *all three* ties linking a pair was not a common structural form (unless also accompanied by a reciprocal co-work tie).

In conclusion, cooperation between members of an organization can be looked at as routine transfers or exchanges of various kinds of resources. To summarize these structural tendencies, a number of separable forms of interdependence describe the interlocking of the three relations. First, each type of tie appears to have its own characteristic pattern of organizational distribution. Co-work ties were strongly (but not entirely) organized around principles of direct and generalized exchange, whereas advice and friendship ties exhibited a pattern of local clustering and partial ordering (with a greater emphasis on clustering for friendship, and a greater emphasis on a hierarchical distribution for advice). Secondly, despite these apparently quite different organizational principles, there is some evidence for the alignment of the different types of tie, particularly of advice ties with each one of the two others. This provides quite direct evidence for some form of mutual accommodation of the different types of tie.

Thirdly, there is also some evidence for dyadic exchange of different types of tie. This suggests another form of interdependence between the separate tie distributions, but one that might also be expected to have provided a structurally supportive role. As for the alignment effects, the combination of advice with either co-work or friendship yielded the strongest manifestation of this form of tie dependence. Finally, a third type of interdependence links the arrangements of the different types of tie. This third pattern is one in which one type of tie appears to serve as a bridge supporting another. The pattern was strongest for co-work and advice: advice ties linked individuals who were only indirectly connected through (asymmetric) co-work ties. A much weaker version of this pattern is also seen for advice and friendship (with friendship bridging individuals whose advice was sought from a common source) and co-work and friendship (with friendship again in the bridging role).

These results also help to show that cooperation was made possible by a specific generalized exchange system—that is, by the ways in which members exchanged resources connected to their work life in the firm. They also show that such configurations represent the existence of a social mechanism providing a structural solution to a structural problem, here the problem of dealing with status competition among professional members and peers. Such a synthesis contributes to a theory of collective action by developing our understanding of how a collegial organization creates a structure that helps individuals find indirect ways to exercise restraint in the pursuit of status, and thus keep production going. This examination of the firm as an exchange system enhances our understanding of commitment to collective action among members.

THE SOCIAL STRUCTURE OF BARTER

In sum, it is important to note that the generalized exchange system (τ_{10} in the 'co-work only' part of the final model) represented a fragile form of solidarity that could not just stand and last on its own. It needed to be protected both by credible commitments and rules, and by a structural mechanism facilitating individual restraint, which was called mitigation of status competition. Based on these analyses, the process can be summarized by two steps. First, when partners and associates brainstormed together on a complex case to find a solution to a problem, their deliberation could not always reach consensus. At some point, the partner in charge stopped the deliberation without consensus about a solution. This happened often, but it was tricky because 'autocratic' behaviour discouraged the other partners and associates working on the same case from garnering again the enthusiasm that was required to participate in such brainstorms. Therefore, although the decision may have been made, members who disagreed were allowed to seek advice from people outside the task force. They often sought advice from people higher up in terms of status. This is what can be seen behind parameters in the 'co-work and advice' section of the model, in which the member sought out for advice was most often a partner. Bringing status into this type of duplex (co-work–advice) substructures (mainly in the Blau ties) confirms this assertion.

The second step of the status competition process came from the fact that members of the same task force could seek advice from two different advisers. This might mean simply carrying the brainstorm upstairs. This helped only if advisers then agreed, but they might not, and the advisers involved in this second step would then also need help when they tried to reach a solution. This help came from three facts: (1) these advisers were not officially involved in the case (there was less at stake for them); (2) there was generally more pressure on senior people to reach consensus; and (3) they were likely to be connected by a friendship (or an advice) tie. This is how parameter τ_9, in the 'advice and friendship' section of the model, can be interpreted. Bringing status into this type of duplex (advice–friendship) substructures shows that members connected by the friendship tie were often partners. In other words, as long as such ties connect the chefs, the latter are not too many. Barter of resources among them helps mitigate professional status competition. The fragile solidarity that was provided to members through the generalized exchange system in social niches was thus protected from excessive status competition by specific kinds of substructures blending collegial relationships and resources.

These relational substructures characterize barter, a form of 'silent exchange', which was controlled, as mentioned earlier, by politicized boundary management and the existence of social niches. With this view and analyses of multiplexity in social mechanisms, however, Blau's notion (1964) of social exchange takes a more important dimension. The blending process described above is an organized one. A good theory of barter must look at it as a moment in a social process solving specific problems of collective action. If that is not done, the intrinsic efficiency of barter is not recognized and barter itself is conceived only as bilateral and compared unfavourably to market exchange. Thus, a structural approach to participation in collective action in general should examine the interlocks between production-related resources, because they represent the social structure of multiplex barter in different mechanisms that are central to the functioning of work groups and firms, especially collegial ones.

6

Organizational Integration: A Montesquieu Structure

In spite of providing bounded solidarity and generalized and multiplex exchange to its individual members, niche seeking may also be a threat to the organization. In effect, a task force in a social niche can turn itself into a group, team up and out, and start a disintegration process in the firm. In this chapter, I argue that, under specified structural constraints, status competition at the individual level can have positive effects at the collective level. Two processes illustrate such positive effects. First, as noted by Blau (1964), status competition encourages cross-niche exchanges. Secondly, it can help handle opportunistic behaviour encouraged by the niche structure—that is, it can prevent task forces in such social niches from reaching a critical mass necessary for easy defection. This prevention is made possible by a balance of power between two forms of status, a balance characterized by a Montesquieu structure.

Indeed, getting durable cooperation from peers and associates is not a straightforward matter in collegial organizations, where many centrifugal forces are at work. Income equalization has its drawbacks: for example, the lockstep system benefits low performers but not high performers. Nevertheless, workers of different productivity levels coexist under the same roof. Social mitigation of status competition works best within niches precisely because members can find in them a form of economic and social solidarity—that is, some of the resources needed both to produce knowledge-intensive services and to get cooperation in the long term. Recall that, even in constraining niches, members combine selected forms of identification to each other to ease access to, or barter of, these multiple resources.

However, niches are still insufficient in themselves to solve problems of resource allocation and rule enforcement, and they represent a risk. Their contribution to collective action comes at a price: that of endangering the cohesion of the organization. In this context, the integration of the firm is a puzzle. The niche solution to the structural problems of resource dependencies and status competition generates a new, higher-level structural problem. What makes a heterogeneous peer group hang together durably in spite of many centrifugal forces?

CENTRIFUGAL FORCES AND CROSS-BOUNDARY EXCHANGES: RELATIONAL STITCHES

The structural contribution to the study of the social integration of collegial organizations remains at the informal organizational level. Economic factors are very important to explain the cohesion of an organization, and the formal decision-making structure—that is, the committee system—can also have the same effect when it actually works (Musselin 1990). However, this chapter does not focus on such factors. Instead, it looks at patterns of relationships among the members of the firm as a basis for integration.

Using the information collected on the three different types of ties among members, I show that aspects of the informal structure integrated the firm beyond niches and across its formal boundaries because strong interpersonal ties were created without respect to these boundaries. By formal boundaries I mean horizontal differentiation (that is, division of work, represented by type of practice: litigation or corporate), vertical differentiation (that is, hierarchy, represented by partner/associate status), and geographical differentiation (which actually represented different markets and client bases, and was represented by the three offices of the firm).

As seen in Chapter 3, these internal differentiations had an effect on the way members built reliable work relationships, advice relationships, and friendship ties. Hierarchical status, office, and practice all influenced such choices among partners and associates, thus creating niches: in the aggregate, there was an 'inbreeding' bias along these three boundaries. Geographical distances had the strongest influence on the creation and maintenance of all types of relationships. They were followed by differences in status; differences in type of practice had the weakest influence. These internal boundaries were no mystery to the members of the firm. The question addressed here is how did the firm deal with the centrifugal threat represented by such boundaries?

A closer look at the patterns of relationships, as they emerge from a series of cohesion analyses,[1] shows that each network created by these relationships was segmented into dyads or very small groups of members strongly tied to each other by long-term repeated interactions. Such substructures were 'stitches' that brought together two sides of the firm separated by these internal boundaries. In the co-workers' network, this cohesion analysis shows that almost all the members of the firm had strong work ties within the firm. With a few exceptions, these strong working relationships did not cut across the geographical boundaries, or across the practice boundaries. But, not surprisingly, they almost always cut across the hierarchical status boundary; they mixed partners and associates, and in some cases senior and junior associates. All the members did not belong to such groups. They did have significant work relationships with others, but these ties did not aggregate into small 'cliques'.

The same trend was observed in the friendship network. Many small dyads or groups of two or three partners and slightly larger groups of three or four associates can be identified as groups of persons who socialized outside work together. There were eight persons (out of seventy-one), mostly junior associates, who did not socialize with anybody within the firm. With a few exceptions, these strong friendships did not cut across the geographical boundaries, or the status boundary. But most did cut across the practice boundary—that is, included litigators and corporate lawyers. This was explained in Chapter 3 by the dynamics of friendship formation in such firms via common associateship. The members who did not belong to these subgroups did socialize with others, but these ties were weaker.

In the advice network, the same pattern was again observed. Many small dyads or groups emerged, within which members exchanged basic advice with one another. Six persons were isolated in this network. With a few exceptions, these strong advice relationships did not cut across the status boundaries, or across the practice boundaries. But they did cut across the geographical (or market) boundary much more than other relationships; they mixed members in the three offices. The members who did not belong to these subgroups did have advice relationships with others, but these ties were weaker; these members tended to spread their advice relationships among many other colleagues, which reduced the strength of each specific tie with each particular source of advice.

In sum, strong ties were available to be used to bridge organizational boundaries when a problem emerged, a process also spotted in other firms (Baker 1992; Maister 1993; Stevenson 1990). Dyads or small groups of co-workers cut across status boundaries and countered the centrifugal effects of stratification. Small cliques of mutual advisers cut across geographical boundaries and countered the effects of distance and differences between offices. Small cliques of friends cut across practice boundaries and countered the effect of the division of work. This shows that, at least in the informal structure of the firm, there was no single strongest relational basis for integration of the organization. Each type of relationship contributed in a specific way to the cohesion of the firm. Specific ties observed in each network were important for cutting across internal boundaries. They kept together the great number of different and strongly cohesive small groups within the firm. They also increased the flexibility and adaptability of the informal structure of the firm.

Figure 6.1 summarizes the strong ties and cohesive subsets that could be activated to solve problems or deal with tensions involving such differences among members.

Two examples can illustrate the integrative role of such cohesive subsets. The first is about hierarchical status differences. Chances for associates to become partners depended, among other criteria, on the firm's financial basis, a situation about

| | Internal boundaries | | |
	Status	Office	Speciality
Co-worker	X		
Advice		X	
Friendship			X

Strong ties { Co-worker, Advice, Friendship }

Figure 6.1. *Relational stitches: Strong ties cross-cutting internal boundaries in the firm*

Source: Reprinted from *Revue Française de Sociologie*, E. Lazega, 'Analyse de réseaux d'une organisation collégiale: les avocats d'affaires', 33: 575. Copyright 1992 with permission from *Revue Française de Sociologie*.

which they often did not have official information. This created tensions between partners and associates, especially before the partnership decision was made for the most senior cohort. Strong work ties between partners and associates then seemed important to manage these tensions in a credible way—for example, in reassuring associates that their chances were not compromised. Regular and strong work ties seemed to have the capacity to overcome associates' mistrust in *pro domo* official discourse addressed to clients as much as to personnel.

The second example concerns the differences between offices—that is, between client bases. It was not rare for Office I and Office II interests to diverge. One office was more lucrative than the other for several years in a row. A partner from Office II could have a legal or a 'political' conflict of interests with a partner from Office I if they happened to represent strongly opposed clients; one of the two might have to disqualify him- or herself and give up an important client. Such situations generated tensions that revived short-term comparisons between offices (which were not considered profit centres by SG&R's accounting system). A reminder of the various resources, chief of which was advice, circulating between offices was an important way of taming tempers in such situations. Advisers from the other side were in a key position to achieve such signalling.

Thus, the firm was integrated across its formal boundaries of horizontal, vertical, and geographical differentiation when interpersonal ties were created without respect to these boundaries. One of the first lessons of this result is that, in the firm as a whole, horizontal, vertical, and spatial differentiation impeded overall integration, but strong cross-niches ties (stitches) contributed to the integration of the firm across these formal boundaries. At the informal level, integration was secured differently, by different types of relationships, in different corners of the organization. Cohesion-based integration relied on exchanges criss-crossing niche boundaries.

In the following sections of this chapter, I focus on another integration process, one that was made possible, paradoxically, by status competition. I show that integration was also based on surveillance of choices of exchange partners within or outside niches. This was particularly visible with the exchanges of task-related cooperation and goodwill among members. In effect, given their responsibilities for staffing and scheduling, minders tried to impose additional constraints on members' choices of strong co-workers, especially on finders' choices. This second process of firm integration was based on two different forms of solidarity (welfare and patronage) organized by different forms of status. In turn, the coexistence of the two forms of solidarity was based on the control of one form of status by the other. Maintaining heterogeneity of status thus helped deal with the danger of disintegration created by social niches.

TWO FORMS OF SOLIDARITY: WELFARE AND PATRONAGE IN MANAGING WORKFLOW

Professional members valued the ideology of autonomous action and consensus. In such a situation, social solidarity and control mechanisms for maintaining cooperation were of particular interest. They were produced by the combination of formal 'intake and assignment' procedures and informal elective choices of co-workers made—partly autonomously—by the members themselves.

To support this argument, a multilevel approach is necessary. I look at a specific kind of solidary behaviour at the individual (using interests or strategic analysis), dyadic, and structural levels (using network analysis). At the dyadic level (Lindenberg 1997), this behaviour meant that a member was prepared to help out another member who found him or herself in a difficult situation. Such solidary behaviour (see examples in Chapter 1) led to the existence, *at the structural level*, of mechanisms of control that help to explain the integration of this firm. It did so by creating a pattern of exchanges and durable cooperation that prevented members from reaching situations in which they were ready to defect easily. Individual interests, solidarity at the dyadic level (help, whether mutual or not) between interdependent members, combined with organizational rules, provided an unexpected social order that created another kind of solidarity (prevention of exit) at the structural level, a form of integration that had a clear political dimension.

How could this solidary behaviour be related to intake and assignment procedures? The latter are extremely important in a corporate law partnership, as in any professional services firm (Maister 1993: 156). As seen in Chapter 3, to do their work and survive in such an organization, interdependent members of the firm needed access to resources such as work for clients and goodwill from cooperative co-workers. But work was not always very easy to find at the beginning of the 1990s, a period of economic downturn in north-eastern USA: levels of future demand were not easily predictable. The organization helped members get access to such resources. It conducted its affairs based on a formal structure and formal rules, which expressed choices among policy options, and allocated, directly and indirectly, these resources to members. Authority to handle new files or clients (intake) or to allocate this new work among colleagues (assignment) was distributed more or less formally (see Chapter 2). For many members (partners and associates), access to work opportunities depended on such procedures. A basic 'welfare system' was established—that is, a committee that allocated such resources across professional members of the firm and helped organize cooperation (the ATC).

In theory, members of the firm knew about these rules. But partnerships did not function like formal and hierarchical bureaucracies, even when they had a strong administrative component. As mentioned in Chapter 2, rules were not always followed, and getting cooperation remained a delicate matter. In reality members of the firm often behaved differently; they did not necessarily trust or count on the welfare system to get cooperation from one another and provide solidarity. They had an interest and 'political' incentives in not trusting the welfare system. Clientelistic ties and more selective solidarities were established among partners, and between partners and associates. The welfare system was thus intertwined with an informal patronage system. Each system (welfare and patronage) responded to members' interests and solved their problem differently, although the clientelistic match-making process was not formally allowed.

The two forms of solidarity coexisted in a collegial organization such as SG&R. In fact, each type of solidarity was organized by partners with a different form of status. The first was organized by minders, the second by finders. The study of the two forms of solidarity addresses directly the issue of durable relations because, as already mentioned, in such professional partnerships, the existence of patronage often represents a danger of firm disintegration. In effect, clientelistic solidarity between partners and associates could create stable work groups that could defect from the firm, taking lucrative clients away with them. This process was a result of members' tendency to build or join social niches. Here I first provide a strategic analysis of workflow and, secondly, look at the selection of strong co-workers made under such criteria and conceptions of interests.

SCHEDULERS AND RAINMAKERS

As described in Chapter 2, the firm's formal structure attempted to coordinate the work process. In its effort to organize its practice, SG&R formally regulated intake and assignment. There were many reasons for implementing such policies. In particular, the firm wanted to be sure that it was not using its resources on work that was either less interesting or less profitable than other work that it might have been able to get. According to SG&R's intake procedure, new clients should be cleared with the managing partner. But recall that this requirement was not systematically respected. Some partners did not even seem to know about it. Others acknowledged that they had problems saying 'no' to people. Clients whose work had been turned away might not call again. Partners took in the work, knowing that some colleagues were cooperative and would help with the workload. Unless there was an obvious reason to think about a political conflict (a conflict of interest with another partner or a client represented by another partner), they just went ahead.

Assignments were more formally organized for associates, through the ATC, also called the associate committee. Assignment procedures were *match-making* and *match-breaking* procedures. In general, a file (a case) was handled by at least two lawyers, one partner and one associate. Assignments, however, were also often distributed by the partners who brought in the client. Some partners were so used to assigning work themselves (without resorting to the ATC) that they often complained about problems—especially in this multi-city firm—with identifying partners and associates with the right expertise, and with putting together the right task force to work on a case. I will call this informal assignment procedure a *patronage*, or clientelistic, one: partners and associates chose one another based on more strategic and status or 'reputation'-based criteria (Raub and Weesie 1990).

Such a situation is not surprising in a firm that was not departmentalized and where compensation was based on a strict lockstep seniority system. The firm counted on the cooperative spirit of its partners to smooth difficulties with workflow. But the limitations and flexibility of intake and assignment procedures also came, in part, from the fact that some members tended to be more in need of access to work on an ongoing basis, and others—who controlled access to lucrative clients—more in need of cooperation from colleagues. Finders and grinders needed each other. Finders were even interdependent among themselves. As mentioned above, a good way of keeping a client is to cross-sell services that can be provided by partners of different specialities. This increases revenues and retains clients. As seen in Chapter 4, some partners—often finders—were much more 'productive' than others in terms of dollar amounts billed and collected. It made sense for other attorneys in need of (good) work to build strong, secure, and durable work relationships with such rewarding partners, who needed reliable peers and associates to carry out the actual work.

Thus, business interdependence in the practice of law was as strong (if not stronger) a determinant of the management of work as the commitment to professional values and philosophy of apprenticeship. The form of cooperation was thus dictated, among other determinants, by the requirements of the market. Therefore, firm official policy was not enforced exactly as it was formally meant to be. Client intake and assignment procedures did not really change the organization of work into a highly regulated process. Flexibility with control and organization of the two-step workflow was forced upon the firm by personal ties between finders and the client. Partner 6 formulated this clearly: 'I don't think of my clients as my clients in an economic sense; but I think of them as my clients in a personal way. The people I am doing work for, that I have a personal relationship with, that I know as friends or whatever. It would be foolish for a firm to ignore that relationship.'

Under these organizational arrangements, the main preoccupations of time-keeping members (getting a continuous flow of good work from clients or from (other) partners, and getting cooperation from colleagues to perform this work) were also solved by a system of patronage. Partners had some leeway in choosing co-workers and in building up temporary task forces—that is, choosing one another and associates to work on a case. Recall that, given the fact that interdependence among attorneys working together on a file could be strong for weeks, and then weak for months; given the flexibility needed to accommodate clients' needs; and given the size and complexity of some files, a reliable co-worker was a highly valued resource for individual attorneys.[2] In this situation, members' interest, as perceived by them, was in building strong ties to selected others. Such strong work ties, members thought, should be a better guarantee for goodwill and cooperation than weaker work ties. Strong work ties were perceived to be an insurance policy against absence of (good) work and/or scarcity of workforce. They meant more than short-term security. They meant that efforts would be actually shared (that is, everyone would pull their weight), and that one's own work would be recognized (that is, colleagues would not grab all the credit for themselves in successful cases). For associates, for instance, they could mean access to partnership.

As an example, Associate 37 considered that there was a tacit contract between himself and Partner 15, his obvious patron. His dependence on Partner 15, and his distrust of the assignment committee, came across clearly in his interview:

> Any partner wants to have his associates next door, to be able to go down the hall and talk to them about their files. I have been here for five years and it's been that way from

day one. I have heard partners say, year after year, 'We need to get Associate 37 to work with partners from other offices,' and it doesn't happen. For example, I had an associate review last August. One of the things which was said was that the corporate ATC indicated that they wanted me to work with other partners, and they made a commitment to do that. During the five months since then, I have worked with only one new partner. It takes time, a concerted disciplined effort to see that I get that kind of work, to make sure that all partners are advised that it is worthwhile to work with me. Partner 15 is quite supportive, and he would never do anything against my working with others, but he leaves it to me. That's a touchy issue. And I have probably not taken enough initiative in the past. Because of the way the firm is structured [ATCs], I cannot pick up the phone and call partners one by one and ask them if they have work for me. I have to go through the ATC. My hesitation in the past is that I didn't want to annoy them, to pester them, to bug them, and also to annoy Partner 15. But after the review I realized that I couldn't afford any more lip service. I have decided to call up the ATC and ask, 'Which new partner do you want me to work with this week?' The firm did not help me acquire a speciality which makes me indispensable. I received assignments from Alan, I assisted him on his files, and then the clients began to call me directly, and I became their primary contact. Work for Alan and work for these clients represent most of my work. Whether this will help next year with the partnership decision, I don't really know.

In the more general terms of Blau (1964: 21–2) and Flap (1990), members of an organization have four possible alternatives to becoming someone's client (in a patronage system), that is, to be deferential and promise future services in return: immediate reciprocation with a service that the patron immediately needs; securing the needed service elsewhere, with another patron; coercing the other into providing the service; or doing without the service. Associates at SG&R could try the first and second solutions, but with difficulty—the original situation being one of unequal access to diverse resources, and also the number of patrons being limited. Strong opposition from one of them could ruin one's chances of becoming a partner. But not the last two: clients compete for special treatment, and there is always another potential client willing to take the place of an unwilling one (Flap 1990). Therefore, clientage was the only secure option, apart from the welfare system of the ATC. Desolidarized associates needed a champion, and no enemies (Burt 1992). In the case of SG&R, there was more than one partner, and associates could try to align with other partners, using a factional structure. But they could not do it too often without sinking costs and building a reputation of instability. It would not have improved their prospects much, given the number of other clients, the scarcity of the ultimate reward, and the limit defined by patrons to their own competition.

Although it was certainly unpleasant for partners serving on the ATC, the coexistence of the two match-making procedures was not really a puzzle to anybody. It is well known that, in professional services firms, schedulers and rainmakers often challenge each others' staffing requests (Maister 1993). A short interest analysis for partners and associates clarifies this point. Partners were interested in looking for the best associates, who were close and easily accessible, and knew as much as possible about the issue. Some got used to specific associates with whom they liked to brainstorm, and ATC choices did not always respond to such selection criteria. As partners grew in stature, they became more involved in non-chargeable marketing; their rates increased as their time sheets grew in non-billable hours: their immediate preoccupation was with making the client happy by organizing their work themselves. Recall Partner 6 expressing disagreement with the firm's minders as to whether or not the formal assignment process worked efficiently ('This is supposed to go through the associate committee . . . but I think the committee does not really work very well. Associates do generally get work directly from their partners'). Associates' main interest was in becoming a partner. They knew that they were expected to bill at least 1,800 hours a year, or to gross three times what they earned as a salary. 'If you work hard, you are in demand as an associate. If fees are collected, that means that you were given good work and that you carried it out well. The client perceives value and has money to pay. You get judged first on your collection rate' (a former associate).

Under this kind of pressure, a regular flow of good work was most welcome, but—as mentioned by Associate 37—associates were also in a bind about how to get this work. ATC members—called the 'schedulers' by another associate—could provide this work, and they also evaluated associates twice a year: associates had to listen to them and abide by their rule. However, if associates followed the schedulers systematically, they could often get stuck with assignments from which they would not learn enough, or with a partner who would not introduce them to other partners, thus reducing their chances in the internal labour market. Associate loyalty to the ATC was good for insurance, but not so good for learning and relational capital. Many wanted the best work from the best clients, not run-of-the-mill work from the scheduler. The scheduler could provide diversity and access to many partners, but, the more successful associates were, the more they became strategic, tended to avoid the scheduler, and tried to manage their careers in a more 'intrapreneurial' way. They ended up saying yes to partners who could sometimes guarantee years of good work (that is, work in which they learned something) for good clients, instead of turning them down and seeking the schedulers' approval. Of course, the minders might step in, but then associates counted on their patron to solve the problem.

We do not know what the structure of assignments would have looked like if work had been allocated exclusively by some sort of internal 'market' and reputation process—that is, if the clientelistic match-making process had been undisturbed by ATC schedulers. Nor do we know what would have happened if the official ATC match-making process had been undisturbed by patronage interference.[3] Precise information was not made available about the number of hours actually worked by each associate for each partner, and about options before ATC members and their colleagues when the matches took place. But this assignment and match-making problem obviously led to another problem, that of the relationship between ATC partners and partners who did not abide by the official rule. My interest here is in firm integration. In short, and to simplify, the problem of assignment is interesting here because the coexistence of the welfare system and the patronage system reflects the control relationship between two forms of status, that of the minders and that of the finders. Seen from this perspective, the issue of assignment and match-making is indeed an issue of firm integration.

Finders and minders had both common and different interests. Both forms of status were indispensable to run the organization. There was an obvious trade-off between them. Finders tolerated the lower economic contribution of the minders as an exchange for the minders carrying some of the costs of control within the firm. If the finders could not rely on the minders to keep everything running reasonably smoothly, then they would have had to devote more time to this themselves and forgo income anyway. In turn, minders tolerated finders' attempts to create permanent task forces, which also explains why the ATC was relatively flexible about assignments. The ATC functioned as a 'welfare system', even though this expression rang somewhat awkwardly, given that ATC members also evaluated associates and played an important role in their selection for partnership. It was true that associates too close to one big finder often did not make it. But in several ways, what the official structure of assignment was doing was not so much providing opportunities to associates, but suppressing and desolidarizing them. Associates wanted good work and more experience, and formally the ATC was there to help them; but another effect was the dismantling of close collaborations between associates and the creation of a stratification among them. Indeed, if as an associate you needed the schedulers' help, you might be in trouble already.[4] The firm did not have a formal rotating rule, because the ATC needed the cooperation of all the partners in its evaluation of associates and in the process of their selection for promotion to partnership. The internal labour market would not work if ATC members were blind to strong relationships between partners and associates, or to associates' reputations—that is, if their evaluation of associates were to focus exclusively, for example, on the number of hours worked and the results of the training programme. As in any internal labour market, SG&R's could be understood only if human *and* relational capital were considered together.

However, the two forms of status could also conflict, and the issue of firm integration became a problem of a balance of power. Finders controlled (often temporarily) resources such as access to important clients. What was at stake in the intake and assignment process was also the capacity of the minders to control another key resource in the firm: the allocation of workforce. From this perspective, the use of the phrase 'welfare system' for the ATC was again a bit questionable, unless one considers that it was part of 'welfare' to establish a balance of powers and keep the finders in check. In effect, the clientelistic exchange system, and its underlying social discipline, represented a 'neat kind of social plumbing' (White 1985, cited by Flap 1990; see also Centeno 1992 or Lomnitz 1988 for prototypical examples of the coexistence of patronage and bureaucracy from the perspective of political sociology). It allowed individual members to 'trade horses', team up, and build strong, presumably repeated, more secure and reliable work relationships with others, partners or associates, who would also pull their weight, recognize one's contribution, and share credit and responsibility among themselves. But the firm tried not to allow these work groups to stabilize and grow sufficiently to defect to another firm. In this situation, the Montesquieu structure reflected the existence of both a differentiation and an integration process.

This danger of defection was clearly on partners' mind, as shown by the following declaration:

> There are client loyalties to individual lawyers within the firm; but among ourselves I view all clients as clients of the firm. And indeed, if you are an individual to whom the client has demonstrated a great degree of loyalty, one of your responsibilities is to make sure that there are other partners to whom that client may also look and rely upon. Not necessarily on an ongoing basis. But if for some reason, for example if I am away, if I were suddenly to decide to go pump gas for the rest of my life, any number of things, that client loyalty is not an asset that belongs to me. If I were to go to another firm, if I have done my job well here at SG&R, if I call my client and say 'I want you to know that I am in firm DE&F now', that client's response should be 'Whom at SG&R should I call now?', it shouldn't be 'What's your new number?' Whether that would be the case in all cases, who knows, that's what ideally it should be.   (The managing partner at the time of the study)

This was confirmed by Partner 7's story of two partners who left Office II before the merger that created SG&R:

> I socialized [with my colleagues] until Salto and Branfield left the firm, young partners. I think that cast a spell on the social life of the people in this office. I thought they were good friends, then I found out they had planned to leave for a long time, and they took valuable clients with them. I think I felt that our trust had been betrayed. There was a sense of betrayal because when you are partners you send your clients to another partner because he can solve their problems. This is part of the job of a senior partner: to bring in work and turn it over to young partners. They cultivated the client on a social basis knowing that they would leave, with that purpose in mind. You cannot do anything against that. You can't plan your life around distrust. Everyone is free to go where they want to. Since that time, there hasn't been an active social life among senior partners at the office. The younger yes, not the older who have not made the effort to host parties and include younger people in social events.

Because they induced two forms of exchange, the welfare and the patronage systems provided two different bases for limited solidarity.[5] The two forms of solidarity or match-making system, and the two types of status (finders and minders), could compete, conflict, and/or complement each other. However, for lack of information, following the emergence of this coexistence was not easy. The establishment of strong ties depended on many factors other than rules of intake and assignment. It depended on how the ATC operated, on availability of work, on access to partners or associates with good reputations, on access to partners with appropriate clients or with unchallenged power to choose their co-workers, on previous experience of cooperation. Therefore, I look instead at the pattern of strong work ties among members and interpret it as a representation of this coexistence.

The transition from an interests analysis at the individual level to the dyadic then structural levels provides a method for exposing the multilevel phenomenon of the firm's integration and durability.

TEAMING UP AND OUT?

Examining the ways in which the two forms of solidarity coexisted shows that the firm provided a second structural solution to this problem of integration. It remained one firm because the coexistence of the two solidarity systems was actually based on a process of control and counter-control between finders and minders. The two intertwined systems created a specific and stable pattern of work relationships. I have called this pattern (along with Kuty 1998) a *Montesquieu structure*, for one of its main characteristics was that it established a balance of powers within the firm, allowing the partners who tried to manage the firm's workforce to keep in check the partners who managed the firm's lucrative clientele.

The Montesquieu structure reflected the existence of a partial political order, an order already visible in status consistency measures provided in Chapter 3 (and again in Chapter 8 below). This order functioned as a stabilizing force by trying to prevent potential work groups from becoming niches and from mustering all the resources needed to defect easily (in particular direct access to pools of workforce). One of the goals of intake and assignment procedures was thus also to prevent the creation of work groups that were 'ready for easy defection' (RED). Ultimately, democracy among the partners was necessary to the coexistence of the two solidarity systems and to the durable maintenance of this structure. Otherwise there would have been no power to keep the welfare system in place, and the finders would either defect or be on the committee that controlled the welfare system. Interests analysis and structural analysis are thus combined here to look at this new picture of the work process and at the structural solution provided by the minders of a collegial organization to the problem of firm solidarity and integration.

As seen in Chapter 3, choosing co-workers in this collegial context was a delicate operation. Associates competed for the attention of partners. Partners competed for the best associates and for prestige within and outside the firm. Partners and associates recognized each other as strong co-workers based on long-term calculations and identity criteria, giving rise to socially constructed niches. These niches could be stable work groups of attorneys who had specialized in the same area and were able to defect from the firm in which they were nesting, and establish themselves elsewhere as specialized 'boutiques'.

The fact that members found strong co-workers in such niches helps explain the coexistence of welfare and clientelism. First, the niches were partly a product of the two combined systems. Secondly, choices of strong co-workers aggregated and combined, at the structural level, into a pattern of exchanges that created a balance between the two systems. This balance was essential to firm integration. To show this, it is necessary to use other methods where the individual (and not the dyad) remains the unit of analysis. Specifically, the exchange system is described by an analysis of the co-workers' network in terms of approximated structural equivalence. It establishes a partial order, which helps account for the 'political' integration of the firm.

RED SETS OUT OF NICHES?
A MONTESQUIEU STRUCTURE

Analysis of the co-workers' network[6] shows that the collective action system of this firm was made of ten different sets of approximately structurally equivalent actors. Figure 6.2 represents these sets, their members, and relationships between the sets. It is based on the density table that is presented in Appendix F, along with a detailed description of Figure 6.2.

Members of each set, or position, were partners and/or associates occupying an approximately similar position in this structure of strong co-workers' ties; they had approximately the same relational profile, approximately similar work ties with firm members outside this position, and often had strong ties within the position too. The configuration describes the system of interdependencies, which was partly clientelistic and partly official, and which was explained by the nature of legal work, by members' common niche-seeking strategies, by power relations among members, and by the ways in which the finders–minders relationship played itself out in the two different specialities. The method helps to detect subsets that might have been able to team up permanently (alone or with others), and create—within their niche—stable work groups bringing together finders with direct access to their own associates.

A first split[7] reflects the strong influence of speciality within the firm: corporate lawyers on the left of Figure 6.2, litigators on the right. Each speciality—particularly litigation during the early 1990s—could indeed have left the firm and created a firm of its own. But none could be certain that the market could bear it; 'boutiques' of that size needed a highly concentrated market, such as that in New York City. The next split is more illuminating with respect to the issue at hand. Breakaway threats could presumably exist for all positions including partners—that is, Positions One, Two, Four, Six, Eight, and Ten. An actual breakaway threat existed particularly for Position One, and was lower for the other positions. Some of the reasons for which firm integration was nonetheless maintained in this situation are outlined below.

I qualify as 'Ready for Easy Defection' (RED in short) a subset or a position in Figure 6.2 that had three characteristics. First, it had a high enough average income, which represented its capacity to be immediately 'in business' outside the firm, and thus the kind of revenue that compared with the income achieved at SG&R.[8] Secondly, it was a stable team with high cohesion (that is, with strong work relationships among its members) and sufficient size to be immediately operational outside the firm. To this form of economic and relational capital (clients and reliable workforce), I will add a third condition—that its individual members have not had a lifelong investment in the firm as a whole; such an investment in economic and relational capital—with the compensation system rewarding loyalty with the highest

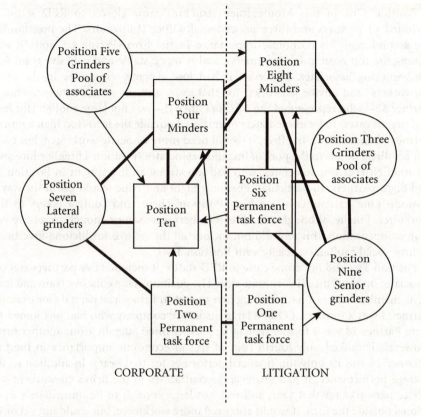

CORPORATE   LITIGATION

Figure 6.2. *Access to cooperative colleagues: A Montesquieu structure*

Note: This figure represents the pattern of relationships between positions of approximately structurally equivalent actors in the strong co-workers' network. Thick lines indicate mutual ties. For a detailed description of positions and their members, see Appendix F. Note that, when analysed separately, each network breaks down into positions that are different from the positions identified when all the networks are superimposed and analysed together to provide a multiplex pattern (Figure 3.1.)

Source: Reprinted from *Revue Française de Sociologie*, E. Lazega, 'Analyse de réseaux d'une organisation collégiale: les avocats d'affaires', 33: 578. Copyright 1992 with permission from *Revue Française de Sociologie*.

incomes—could pay off only if one stayed within the firm. This means that positions with finders in them (such as Ten and Six) do not necessarily qualify for RED status. In effect, such finders, especially if they were very senior in that firm, had too strong incentives to stay. Moreover, the positions may not have included good associates willing to follow them elsewhere. Remember that associates were very strategic about whom they wanted to work with, and being too close to a single rainmaker could sometimes be counter-productive in terms of career. When reviewing partners' positions to check for these criteria, none had RED status.

Position One in this Montesquieu structure came closest to RED status. It included six partners and three associates, all Office II litigators. The position had the second rank for economic importance in the firm (Partners 5 and 18 were among the top economic performers), and it was a stable and cohesive team with hard-working associates. However, it had low average centralities in the firm's co-workers' and advice networks[9] for that year, and, in spite of the presence of Partner 32—who represented the ATC in Office II—was not large enough (for large and urgent cases) to be immediately operational outside the firm (too high a ratio of partners to associates). In effect, it would need more associate workforce, but could not get direct access to the pool of litigation associates (Position Three) or lure away Position Nine senior associates, who had too strong an investment in Position Six and Eight partners. In particular, Positions Eight and Nine would get in the way of Position One's attempts at reaching Position Three, and control access to that workforce. Finally, although two of its members were senior enough to receive very high compensation, this rent did not include all the returns for lifelong investment in firm social capital, especially with Position Two.

Position Two did not come close to RED status. It included five partners and two associates on the Office II corporate side. The position was a cohesive team and most of its members did not have lifelong investment in firm social capital (for example, Partner 3 was a former CEO of a large insurance company who had just joined the firm; Partner 14 was a former managing partner hired laterally from another firm). However, it ranked only fourth (out of six) in economic importance in the firm (Partner 14 was its only top financial performer for that year). In addition to this average performance, it had low average centralities in the firm's co-workers' and advice networks for that year, and was not large enough to be immediately operational outside the firm. It would also need more workforce, but could not get direct access to the pool of corporate associates of Position Five. Position Four controlled access to that workforce and would get in the way.

Position Six did not come close to RED status. In contrast to the two previous subsets, it did have direct access to a reserve of workforce in the pool of associates. But it was a weakly cohesive (in the co-workers' network) Office I position and, in spite of counting highly prominent and top performing Partner 1, grossed a relatively low average amount of fees (it ranked fifth in that respect). Its members did work closely with Positions Eight and Nine, but it was difficult to conceive of this subset as defecting without Partner 1 being at the origin of that move. For financial, social, and historical reasons, however, it was also difficult to conceive of him leaving. He derived too much of his social status as 'the Monarch' from speaking on behalf of the firm and representing its sense of professionalism.

Position Ten came closer to RED status than Position Six. It was indeed a powerhouse: it was the highest grossing position in the firm for that year, mainly thanks to Partner 4's performance, and it had high average centrality in the co-workers' network. However, many reasons prevented defection from happening. Its three partners relied very little on one another for work, and their subset was not a cohesive team. The position would not defect without the leadership of Partner 4, who had access to large clients and provided many colleagues with work; but—as for Partner 1—he was at the top of his firm, with one of the highest incomes, and a lifelong investment in the firm and its members. The three were simply so senior that they would not bother leaving. Finally, it would be hard pressed to grow in size sufficiently quickly: the pool of associates on the corporate side (Position Five) was 'shielded' from these powerful partners by Position Four partners.

Finally, Positions Four and Eight were in special situations. Position Four could come close to RED status. It included six Office I corporate partners, among whom Partners 12, 17, and 19 were top performers. Partners 16, 17, 19, 29, and 34 were also highly central, owing to their ties with associates. It grossed an average amount of fees and had a high average centrality in both task-related networks. However, it was a cohesive position because members cooperated on firm management tasks—not so much on large cases. It concentrated administrative authority, but did not have enough of its own clientele yet. It did not include associates systematically, because corporate work often did not mobilize as much workforce for long periods of time as did litigation work. It had direct access to Position Five and Seven workforce, but as much in its members' capacity as ATC officials as because of their rainmaking power.

The situation was somewhat different for Position Eight. It was not able to defect easily. It included Office I partners, mainly litigators, who were recognized as truly good citizens by other partners. They were in charge of the welfare system for associates on the litigation side, and did not seem to groom their own clients. It was the lowest performing group of partners in economic terms (in spite of the presence of top performers Partners 13 and 26). It had the highest average centrality scores in the two task-related networks, but this was due to its ATC responsibilities rather than its rainmaking capacity. It had direct access to Position Three and Nine workforce, but again as minders.

By trying to be strategic in their choices of partners, associates[10] may also play a role in preventing some partners' positions from reaching RED status. Senior associates in Positions Seven and Nine, for example, could help some partners' positions grow sufficiently quickly to be operational elsewhere without delay. But, in order to increase their chances of making partner, they had learned to divide their loyalties between, and invest in ties with, many partners (here at least between two positions of partners); they may have hesitated too much between losing an important broker position (for Position Nine) and helping defectors.

Thus, although many positions could defect, and seriously harm the business of the firm, the fact that not a single one of them had RED status meant that it could not do so easily or advantageously for its senior members.[11] Within the niches where they found easy access to the resources needed to work and survive in the firm, members would find it difficult to create stable and RED subsets. The basic criteria for that purpose—high enough average income, sufficient size, the right type of relational capital (high cohesion, workforce, few lifelong investments in the firm as a whole)—made it more difficult to defect in such a context than is usually acknowledged. For example, based on their own declarations, as shown in Figure 6.2, Positions One and Ten did not have systematic and direct access to pools of additional workforce (Positions Three, Five, and Seven) and could not grow rapidly enough to become serious threats. For that purpose, they would have needed to go through Positions Four and Eight, which were minders acting as welfare state and selection committees for the associates. Recall that they included partners in charge of the ATC who followed associates' level of activity and monitored their work, even when these associates collaborated with other partners.

As mentioned above, this system of interdependencies for strong cooperation is partly a clientelistic one, partly a 'welfare' one. Welfare was mainly represented by Positions Four and Eight. Patronage was particularly likely with Positions One, Two, and Ten. In this light, the welfare system appears to have had the function of a political device for preventing stable RED work-group development, and therefore for preventing firm disintegration. The ATC function was indeed as much a *match-breaking* device as it was a match-making one. It prevented finders from building many direct strong work ties with grinders.

Finally, the fact that the ATC considered both the possibility of colleagues' defection and associate training or overload was not official policy. It was never acknowledged explicitly that the role of the ATC was to prevent defection. But the danger of defection, as already mentioned, was obvious in such a firm. Enough unobtrusive and circumstantial evidence was gathered that that was a serious concern. As in any professional services firm, partners did perceive the creation of stable work groups as a threat of opportunistic behaviour. Some partners were more upfront about acknowledging it than others. Lawyers who did not commingle their assets could take away with them a large volume of business, and continue to handle that business somewhere else. Recall the words of the managing partner and of Partner 7 above.

With this pattern of strong work relationships, the firm provided a structural solution to a classical collective action problem, that of integration. The firm remained one firm because the coexistence of the two intertwined solidarity systems, the welfare system and the patronage system, created a specific and stable pattern of work relationships. This balance between welfare and patronage imposed restrictions on the behavioural alternatives of actors, thus leading to political integration and foreclosing violent conflict in such an institutional context (Flap 1988, 1990). I called this structure a *Montesquieu structure* because of its main characteristic— that is, because of the balance of powers between two types of strong statuses within this collegial organization (minders and finders), each representing a different solidarity system. In many ways, the power that made the Montesquieu structure itself survive (by keeping the welfare system in place) was the partnership as a whole. One could easily imagine that finders could have 'infiltrated' the assignment committee; but the members of this committee were elected by the committee of the whole at partnership meetings that operated under the one-partner-one-vote rule. One step removed, democracy among the partners was thus the real answer to the coexistence of the two solidarity and control systems, to the maintenance of firm integration and durable work relationships.

˙STATUS HETEROGENEITY AND THE BALANCE OF POWERS AMONG OLIGARCHS IN COLLEGIAL STRUCTURES

In sum, this chapter has examined two processes of social integration helping members of collegial organizations ensure durable cooperation from peers and associates. We know that internal differentiations created niches and weakened the integration of the firm. However, members competing for status also reached out of their niches. By doing so, they both gained some autonomy and created, at the overall level, a cohesion-based integration process of 'stitches' bridging sides separated by internal boundaries. Integration was thus partly ensured by different types of relationships reaching various corners of the structure. In the second process, two forms of social solidarity (a formal welfare system and an informal patronage system) competed and intertwined to create a specific form of firm integration through allocation of different members to different forms of status. Status heterogeneity and the articulation of the two solidarity systems helped maintain cooperation in this partnership. It was produced by the combination of formal 'intake and assignment' procedures and informal elective choices of strong co-workers made by the members themselves.

Given that members could manage their interdependence in their own ways (which were strongly politicized)—as opposed to the ways imposed by the welfare system—they could also create niches including both partners and associates and defect from the firm, taking lucrative clients away with them. The firm provided a structural solution to this collective action problem. An analysis of the network of co-workers shows a pattern of strong work relationships providing a new picture of the work process, one that takes into account this politicized dimension of collective action—that is, issues of power in the allocation of this resource. This pattern shows that the social construction of clientelistic ties around the welfare system produced a partial political order. This order functioned as a stabilizing force by trying to prevent potential teams from getting direct access to additional pools of workforce. It offered the possibility for the two forms of solidarity to coexist in the firm. This informal political order could thus become a necessary condition for the production of a collective good such as social order in a collegial firm. The data collected do not allow me to assert that this order was a stable one. However, since it offered a structural solution to a heavy structural problem in this type of firms, it seems reasonable to hypothesize the stability of the process.

Cooperation in such collegial settings was shaped by the ways in which this organization structured itself and balanced different sources of power, as much as by professional ideology (idealization of work well done, unconditional allegiance to the law, priority of ethical considerations over business pressures). Durable relations in and between social niches were made possible by status heterogeneity and a division of powers within an oligarchy. This oligarchy was divided, and it was precisely this division that provided the structural solution to the collective action problem of maintaining durable work relations among peers in a relatively flat and knowledge-intensive organization.

These results confirm that generalized exchange and status competition between finders and minders in the firm were not sufficient in themselves to explain a collegial compliance with the rules, especially prevention of potentially opportunistic behaviour. At this stage, the issue of constraint with regard to performance and conformity remains abstract. For example, to say simply that the exchange system was sufficient in itself to ensure conformity to previous agreement would be to rely too much on the economic 'self-enforcement' theories. In the next chapter I show that this firm developed another social mechanism, a horizontal control regime that is specific to collegial organizations and that helped enforce the rules of the game, especially in a firm that had an aggregation rule and a lockstep management of partner compensation.

Pressuring Partners Back to Good Order: A Lateral Control Regime

This chapter examines another social mechanism, that of protection of common resources against free-loading. Recall that, at SG&R, signing the partnership agreement was a strong commitment to rules, cooperation, and collective responsibility. The firm was nevertheless confronted with the fact that some partners were perceived to be systematically neglecting this commitment, while still deriving *de facto* benefits from sharing common resources. As seen in Chapter 1, the democratic method of government through deliberation that allows members to conciliate interests also needs self-policing to enforce such rules and common decisions. At least at an early stage of the control process, this collegial organization policed itself in a specific way: colleagues themselves reminded deviant partners of the need for conformity to rules.

Structural characteristics of the collegial organization have been shown above to help deal with opportunistic behaviour: for example, niche building is associated with a partial suspension of calculating behaviour, co-workers' constraint with a spiralling involvement in work, or the Montesquieu balance of powers with the protection of the integration of the organization. Such processes, however, do not preclude the use of controls. Niche seeking and status competition among colleagues are again important components of the control mechanism. The issue here is no longer one of easy access to resources needed for production. It is rather one of dealing with a form of social taxation. An individual partner's dilemma was between 'spending' or 'not spending' his or her own social resources for the protection of the common good. In effect, niches provided relational paths for lowering such control expenses; status competition among peers was based on a form of status heterogeneity that allowed new forms of status to emerge, including one of 'protector of the common good' to whom such expenses could be shifted.

This mechanism, called 'lateral control regime', is based on a counter-intuitive complementarity between niche seeking and status competition. It helps most peers exercise early monitoring and sanctioning by reducing their individual costs of control. It maintains low costs through appropriate use of relationships between members. In other words, sanctioners are chosen, or expected to act as such, because they are structurally close to the infractors. However, such a proximity also means that situations can arise in which infractors would be reserved preferential treatment because they are too close to pressure—that is, because they control resources too important to their close sanctioners. Then the special form of status called 'protector of the common good' becomes useful: some of the costs of control are shown to be shifted to uncontroversial partners who (for reasons to be understood, including that of reaching this form of status) accept that they will incur such costs.

While direct command or use of administrative hierarchy were considered inappropriate means for exercising influence at SG&R, partners closely monitored everyone's performance. As part of what Waters calls 'decision processes' (ratification, normative arrangements, compliance relationships, control patterns), the firm had a formal control system. Associates were reviewed systematically by the ATC. For partners, this formal control system was limited to a broad monthly review of each partner's figures by the partnership meeting. But, as suggested by measurements of constraint in Chapter 4, collegial controls were also informal and indirect. When every member has regulatory interests, all can be expected to participate in the control system, if only in an unobtrusive or 'stealthy' way—for example, by monitoring and formulating expectations about who should be brought back to good conduct, and how. Such expectations were seriously constraining at SG&R: partners had strong incentives to monitor and sanction each other, because they were personally liable for the actions of the other partners, and because they often depended on them for resources.

In the expression 'lateral control regime', 'lateral' is equivalent to both 'horizontal' and 'indirect', but for a context without formal hierarchy, and therefore no resort to hierarchical superiors. A lateral control regime thus reflects a specific organization of enforcement of rules and decisions using third parties, or *leverage* (Gargiulo 1993; Lazega and Vari 1992). In addition to suggesting how the niche system helped members put pressure on each other to maintain productivity (Chapter 4), this vocabulary characterizes this control regime as part of a niche-related and status-based mechanism that partly accounted for members' conformity to their commitment. This process helped them compel each other informally, unobtrusively, and often cheaply, to contribute the required efforts and resources.

Network analysis and a vignette study show that, as part of this enforcement mechanism, SG&R gave rise to specifiable *pathways for lateral control* through which partners in this firm asserted that they would prod each other into cooperation at an early but crucial stage, before formal and well-defined court procedures were used, and without external intervention. Lateral control is a form of 'influence'.[1] These pathways, as perceived by individual partners, aggregated into a specific pattern characterizing the firm. This pattern reflected members' *convergent expectations* concerning who should put pressure on whom, and thus dispositions for action; such expectations constituted standards that they must live up to in order to get their colleague's approval (Blau 1964; Merton 1957). It was, therefore, inextricably, both structural and normative.[2] In effect, if everyone expects me to do something, the likelihood that I will comply is higher than if this pressure is not exercised on me. The pattern was closely anchored in key dimensions of formal and informal structure of the firm, and thus reflected a credible niche-related mechanism for helping members find ways of exercising lateral control. Knowledge of this mechanism helps in understanding how members kept monitoring costs low, and therefore kept themselves motivated to carry on monitoring each other. It thus offers a solution to the so-called second-order free-rider problem in formally egalitarian interdependent groups—that is, the problem of who will enforce previous agreements.

In this chapter, the complex relational pattern reflecting the lateral control regime is simplified and made visible by the aggregation of individual choices of 'levers' (or 'sanctioners')—that is, envoys of the firm in charge of pressuring deviant partners ('targets' or 'infractors') back to good conduct.[3] The study of this firm's lateral control regime can thus show that it was also based on both the existence of niches and the concentration of lateral control in the hands of a few partners with a specific form of status, whom the rest of the partnership often chose as levers. I describe the role and characteristics of these main levers, the social 'territory' in which each of them was expected to exercise control, and how they were expected to control each other—that is, the issue of who guards the guardians. This control regime can thus be considered to be a strong component of the governance system of this type of organization, one that ensures that cooperation remains possible.

ETHNOGRAPHIC EVIDENCE OF LATERAL SANCTIONING

As seen in the previous chapter, behaviour perceived to be opportunistic is always a preoccupation in private professional services firms. But at the time of the study SG&R made little formal effort to protect itself (its various forms of capital) against opportunistic behaviour:

> [Opportunistic behaviour] is always a threat. I don't try to cover it. Partners come under the partnership agreement, and the partnership agreement doesn't speak in terms of protection along those lines, except in certain specified areas. I don't have an invest-ment in real estate, so there's no protection there in terms of if somebody leaves, what happens and so on. In terms of clients and all that stuff, I also have no built-in protec-tions; I have always relied on, and probably will continue to rely on, the fact that once you're here, you want to stay. As a practical matter I'm not so sure that if I really ran into somebody who wanted to leave although they were being treated fairly, I'm not so sure I'd want him here as my partner anyway. The system got us this far. (The managing partner at the time of the study)

As indicated by Partner 7's story (see Chapter 6, p. 192), it came out during ethnographic fieldwork that the firm had recently been confronted with behaviour, by several partners, perceived to be opportunistic. Although they did not agree to describe in detail what had happened, several partners mentioned that informal and indirect control had been used and a mediator chosen to go and talk to the uncooperative colleagues. The following interview of a second former partner presents another case (told by the target himself who was perceived as behaving opportunistically because he was seeking more freedom in his choice of a speciality within the firm). It illustrates the existence of early informal relational pressure, which helped the firm to deal unobtrusively with this kind of behaviour.

> I came into the firm in 1963. Bill Henderson hired me, I was in the same class as Partner 8. I became a partner in 1969. At the beginning, I did a lot of trial work, medical malpractice litigation, I worked with the Mayor on city planning. Then Bill Henderson came to see me and offered me to do probate work. I refused. He said, 'You won't have to do it forever.' And I still do this to this day. Henderson left around 1970. I continued to develop the clientele and a reputation. In 1976, I became very restless. I did not find a lot of satisfaction in what I was doing. I was concerned with the lack of associates who were specializing in this area. There was no commitment of the firm to that area of practice. It can be very lucrative if you run it well.... In 1980, I was the only one left doing this kind of work in the firm. Still no associates. I had a lot of work and responsibilities on my shoulders. I was asking myself, 'Do I want to be this firm's senior and only trust and estate lawyer?' Partner 2 was doing some, but not enough. I wanted to get out of this area and do something else. *I had lunch with Partner 2.* I said, 'I want out; I want to do something else'; Henderson had said, 'You won't have to do it forever.' I talked to him as a friend who was the only one who had a clue about what this speciality was about. Nothing happened. Then came the committee meeting about how many associates to hire for the coming year. I said: 'You ought to hire a couple of probate to replace me. I am not going to do this anymore. I need either two people who have had some expertise, or four people without expertise.' Everone's jaws dropped: 'What happened to Partner X?' *The next day Partner 4, one of the big billers, came to see me.* He wanted to know if I was sick. I said no. I wanted to do something else, move into a different area of practice, go back to trial work. He said: 'It is a very selfish idea, and it would never work in any organization.' It dragged on. I announced that I was going to take a leave of absence for a year, that was in the fall of 1980. I said, 'I am leaving.' *I had a meeting with the managing partner to discuss this.* He said, 'A law firm is not a university.' They wanted to schedule three other meetings with me for the following year, but I asked that the partnership take a vote for or against a leave of absence. I said, 'I need to step aside, take some perspective, the firm needs to get other people to do this work.' *At the partnership meeting I got very limited support.* Partners 8,9,11, my contemporaries, did not stand up to support me. Three spoke in my favour, among which was Partner 13. I was turned down. So I said, 'I am going anyway.' There were a number of attempts to talk me out of it. *Partner 4 came to offer a newly vacated office.* A large office. That was ridiculous. So I finally left. ... They had left open the possibility that maybe they would take me back. I came back a year later. *Partner 4 invited me to lunch.* He was the one who was the most curious and probably jealous of what I had done. They had not hired other people to do this work. I insisted on practising in another area of law. The managing partner sent the first angry letter, 'I do not want you to count on coming back.' ... So I went solo. I decided to use my expertise and do it on my own. It would be more satisfying. It has been very successful.... There has been no socializing with members of the firm since then. Before, it used to be like a fraternity. Now some of the partners I hired (while at SG&R) still send me work when they have a conflict [of interest]. I now represent so many relatives of the partners of this firm, including the wives of some of these partners who give me their real estate work, that I sometimes feel uncomfortable about this. I refer them to other people. (Former Partner No. 2)

The existence of such pressures brings us back again to the classical idea that organizational efficiency depends on the quality and configuration of interpersonal relationships between members (Lewin 1952).[4] But the control mechanism created by such pressures has not been thoroughly studied in the sociological literature. Just as relationships between members are important to performance, they are also important to enforcement of previous agreement. Following Freidson's work (Freidson 1975; Freidson and Rhea 1963), Charles Bosk (1979) characterizes such collegial settings by their 'atrophy of corporate self-control' and 'hypertrophy of professional self-control' of individual members. The study of SG&R, while not ignoring the reasons for the existence of this 'atrophy', shows that there is among peers at least one informal corporate mechanism for early sanctioning, specifically the lateral control regime.

A STRUCTURAL VIEW ON THE SECOND-ORDER FREE-RIDER PROBLEM

As theorized in Chapter 1, enforcement through negative sanctions can be costly for the sanctioner, particularly when control is mobilized for the protection of the common good in a formally egalitarian body. The relationship between cost of control and choices of suitable sanctioners in a collegial organization plays itself out in the following ways. Members are interested in getting the infractor going again to the degree that they are dependent on resources controlled by the infractor. Thus, at SG&R, partners were interested in sanctioning that was likely to happen and that was likely to work. Based on this argument, niches should count in the choices of levers: one can hypothesize that, the more similar members were to infractors in terms of their formal organizational attributes, the more likely they were to be chosen to act as sanctioners for these infractors. Then, if costs of inter-action are reduced by structural proximity in such niches, it can be argued that sanctioning is also more likely to happen if cost of control interaction is also lowered by easy access to the infractor. Therefore, members connected to infractors through personal ties must have been more likely than others to be chosen to act as sanctioners for these infractors.

Since partners were also interested in sanctioning that was likely to work, we can also predict that the relative seniority level of sanctioner and infractor was an important variable. Seniority is often considered to be a substitute for hierarchy and formal status (Black and Baumgartner 1983). Being sanctioned by people 'from below' would have been considered a loss of status and would have increased the cost of intervention. In addition, senior partners often had more incentives than others to act as sanctioners (because their compensation system rewarded seniority). Therefore, the more partners are equal or superior to the infractor in terms of seniority, the more likely they are to be chosen to act as sanctioners. Partners at SG&R had a strong interest in motivating the malfunctioning partner and in preventing damage to him or her because they depended on him for resources. Therefore, they must have chosen as sanctioners other partners with whom they had a close relationship so as better to control the process. When they were not so close to the sanctioners, one may predict that they would have chosen as sanctioner someone who was powerful, so as to fend off interference from other partners and shift the costs to the powerful levers. In other words, the more personal ties members have with an infractor, the more likely they are to choose as sanctioners other members to whom they are also personally close. In addition, the more control partners have over resources in the firm, the more likely they are to be chosen as sanctioners.

Finally, this concentration of leverage in the hands of a few partners in charge of bringing their peers back to good conduct raises the classical issue of 'who guards the guardians'—that is, who will perform early monitoring and sanctioning of partners with this specific type of status. From a structural perspective it makes sense to assert that this elite of levers will police itself. In effect, this is the cheapest way to deal with the extra costs potentially incurred with control of partners with this type of status. This solution, however, is a fragile one: this form of self-supervision by oligarchs may sometimes amount to no supervision at all. One can speculate that more formal sanctioning mechanisms would be used under such circumstances. But the conditions under which this informal way is a robust way to guard the guardians can also be safely specified with the same structural approach if we look at the meaning of status heterogeneity (see Chapter 6).

METHODOLOGY

In order to test these hypotheses, a data-set on lateral control was collected at SG&R. I relied mainly on network analysis and a vignette study to examine these channels of lateral control. Analysis of this data-set combined four types of information. First, to identify a partner's expectations, I used a vignette to conduct a network study derived from Krackhardt's technique (1987) to elicit three-dimensional data on manipulation of relationships among partners. This vignette was used, owing to the limited access (in time and possibility of following the thirty-six partners systematically) provided by the firm. It confronted partners with socio-emotional problems having repercussions on productivity, mainly because partners found it inappropriate to discuss tougher issues of 'deviance' involving other partners. It asked each partner to match levers and deviant partners, or targets, in the firm for lateral control purposes, and to justify their choices of levers. These justifications are also used here as qualitative material to illustrate how partners presumed that lateral control operated. Secondly, the standard sociometric data on partners' ties with one another were used to locate the partners in the informal structure of their firm, for specification of the pathways of lateral control, and for correlations between choices of levers and partners' management of social resources. Thirdly, information on individual characteristics of partners (such as speciality, office membership, centrality scores in the sociometric networks, and performance measurements) was used to describe the lateral control regime in its relation to specific dimensions of formal structure. Finally, ethnographic information collected during fieldwork was also used to make sense of many of the results. The analysis presented below combines quantitative and qualitative methods to describe the lateral control regime.

As mentioned before, it came out during ethnographic fieldwork that the firm had recently been confronted with behaviour by at least two partners that was perceived to be opportunistic. Several other partners mentioned that informal and indirect control had been used and a mediator chosen to go and talk to the uncooperative colleagues. A vignette was designed to use this event for research purposes, as an analyser for the description of pathways for lateral control. The data were elicited from all partners using the following scenario:

Here is the list of all the partners in the firm. I would like you to imagine that you are the managing partner. You notice that X is having personal problems. It could be anything, from alcohol to depression, or divorce. But it has repercussions on his or her performance. As a managing partner, it is your job to do something about it. You are looking for colleagues of his or hers among the other partners of the firm to intercede on a discreet and confidential basis, to go and talk to him or her, see what's going on, what the firm can do to help, and give unsolicited advice. You don't want to do this yourself because you want to keep it informal, and your position would be in the way. My question is: who are the persons among all the other partners whom you would ask to approach X, and why would you delegate this task to them? What if this person were Y, or Z, etc.?

Each partner (or 'respondent') was thus asked to choose one or a set of colleagues (or 'levers') who would be in charge of handling, at this early stage, the problem created by a specific partner (or 'target').[5] This design elicited information on each partner observed as a respondent, as a target, and as a lever. It provided two types of data at the individual level: one matrix per respondent matching one or several levers for each target, and arguments justifying the choices. Each partner was asked about *all* the other partners as targets. All partners performed the task. As with Krackhardt's type of data, I collected one 'lever-by-target' matrix per partner, as well as arguments justifying the choice of each lever. These matrices can be viewed as representing 'delegation networks' (White 1992) centred around targets for social control. The result was a set of thirty-six networks of control relationships, one per partner, and a set of arguments, one per lever used. Altogether, 3,043 paths of lateral control were defined in the data. One knows, therefore, who would have expected whom to perform this control task and collegial responsibility on whom, and why. Partners were free to delegate this task to one or to several levers simultaneously, thus often building task forces of social control.

Here are two examples of arguments provided by the partners to justify their choice of each lever:

To see Partner X, I would send Partner 8 and Partner 11. They are close friends of his. If you have to make communication not threatening, you have to find someone close. You know intimately and best the person of your age in the firm. That applies at any age. Having been associates at the same time, having grown through such uniformity of experience, creates strong links. The camaraderie born of that is important here. You don't want someone who shows up as an envoy of the firm. It has to follow from some everyday discussion. I could also send Partner 27. She is his wife. But I may not, it could be unfair on her to have to deal with this, assuming that she knows what's going on. If she doesn't it would make things worse.   (Partner 21)

If you send a friend, it can ruin the friendship and the friendship can trouble your judgement. Partner X has very close friends here. Too close to go on behalf of the firm. I would send Partner 1: they have reciprocal respect but are not as close in terms of friendship. You can dispatch Partner 1 depending on the problem and level of concern. To see Partner 1 getting into your office to tell you to pull yourself together, the shock should be enough to straighten you out! What would happen if he leaves! (Partner 13)

The design of the question also used the fact that the position of managing partner did not imply an especially strong status in this particular firm—for instance, in terms of controlling big clients, making long-term decisions, or having a particularly strong professional reputation—while still representing partners' preoccupation with the common good (ultimately their individual interest) and willingness to participate and act on behalf of the firm. In other words, given that the position of managing partner was a short-term administrative job, it was simply used to help partners worry about their common good, express potentially convergent expectations, and thus identify dispositions based on which they were likely to act. The vignette relied on each partner's capacity to think of this common good and to design a relational strategy to protect it. In effect, partners had a strong interest in monitoring the situation (and might easily one day themselves serve as managing partner). They were asked not to get involved directly (which would not be realistic) and to reconstitute their expectations and conception of how lateral control would be efficiently exercised in the firm. With its mix of personal and work-related issues, the vignette was received as a real-life question about free-loading and collegiality.[6]

The task assumed that information about the trouble was available; as seen above, information about partners' performance was systematically collected and distributed to the whole partnership. Given this great visibility of individual performance, a problem partner was quickly detected. It also assumed that, in such a position, differences (between respondents) in terms of access to levers would disappear, since they acted on behalf of the common good. As the question was designed to make all partners feel entitled to intervene on behalf of the firm, not on their own behalf, it strongly reduced the individual cost of asking levers to intervene. Corporate lawyers in general are used to performing such tasks: for instance, it bears similarities with staffing a case when opening a file, and with representing the whole partnership when writing an opinion.

The analyses below combine the different kinds of data collected. For example, choices of sanctioners are combined with information on sociometric ties. The dependence of the choices of sanctioners on the existence of interdependencies between respondent and sanctioner, or between respondent and infractor, can thus be assessed. These data are also used to locate the partners in the informal structure of their firm and for correlations between importance as a sanctioner and importance in the control of such resources.

CONCEPTIONS OF HOW EXPECTATIONS CONVERGE ON LEVERS AND ON TARGETS

Using these data, it is useful to summarize partners' assumptions about how indirect influence would have been exercised at SG&R. As shown by examples of answers selected below, respondents' arguments provided clear insights into the micro-politics of their firm

A. 'To talk to Partner 1? Who would dare? Who would go tell Partner 1 "You've got a problem"? I think when you are that senior and important to the firm as he is now, you can only send someone who has approximately the same age, seniority, who is not a litigator to avoid some sort of competition. I would pick Partner 3. But if you need also a litigator who understands the consequences of the problem, who knows the clients, and so on, then I would also send the deputy managing partner.'

B. 'To talk to partner 6? I'd send Partner 5, the deputy managing partner. Partner 6 is a more formal kind of person than anybody else on this list. So I would give him the structure, the official presence. Partner 5 is a good choice if I wanted more authority brought to the meeting, and I would give Partner 5 a large bottle of scotch when it's over.'

C. 'I would send Partner 1: they have reciprocal respect but are not as close in terms of friendship. You can dispatch Partner 1 depending on the problem and level of concern. To see Partner 1 getting into your office to tell you to pull yourself together, the shock should be enough to straighten you out! What would happen if he leaves! Both Partner 1 and Partner 5, anyone in the firm must think: "This is serious if he comes to me." '

D. 'To see Partner 19, I'd send Partner 20, because Partner 19 has a history of emotional problems, which would require a lot of meetings, someone with a lot of time to spend. And someone who is also a psychiatrist. Partner 20 is a good psychiatrist. He would be seen as supportive.'

E. 'To see Partner 16, I'd send Partner 20. He is less confrontational than others. He has a good temperament for dealing with these issues; that means that he gives the impression that it hurts him as much as it hurts the other person.'

F. 'Partner 2 is a senior, very thoughtful, respected, and fine person. An unusual person, a man of breadth, judgement, and compassion. He would be received well for any kind of judgemental matter like this and would handle it very well.'

G. 'Partner 2 would be a good person to counsel with. You have to have a good amount of humanity if you want people to take your advice.'

H. 'Maybe it is old-fashioned to think of this in this way, but it seems that in work relations, if you have a personal problem, you are likely to listen to someone who is a contemporary if you are 30 as well as if you are in the 50s. You tend to get a sympathetic audience with people your age. It would be harder to take it from a younger person for instance.'

I. 'To talk to Partner 3? Partner 1 and Partner 9. Partner 3 started in the City I office in the 1950s, then became CEO of [a large company], then to our office in City II. Partner 1 and Partner 9, because they made the deal to get him back here.'

J. 'On this question, you want someone who is at the same time a friend but also a good reporter back, someone who would keep in mind the accuracy of the information and its helpfulness to you as a managing partner. Plus a good relation to the target. Some would see it in a rose-coloured way or maybe cover up a few things. I want someone who relates well to the person but who also gets good information.'

As illustrated by answers A and B, partners as *targets* (that is, as free-riders) were presented as more or less difficult (costly) to handle for different reasons, mainly personality and status within the firm. This was the case, for instance, with Partners 1 and 6. A second category included partners who were perceived as easy to pressure, because there was an obvious choice of levers to match with them. This was the case, for instance, with Partners 5 and 18, who would most likely be sent to deal with each other. As illustrated in examples C to G, partners as *levers* (that is, envoys of the firm in charge of pressuring deviant partners back into good conduct) were most often presented either in terms of personal qualities and authority as emissaries, or in terms of easy access to the target. This was how Partner 2 and Partner 20 were almost unanimously presented in these illustrations. Both were often chosen as levers when respondents did not know about the personal relationships of the target, or were unable to think of anybody else. Regarding access to the target, respondents talked about leverage in terms of a personal or special relationship with the target, in terms of having something in common with the target: being contemporaries (same age or seniority), litigators, friends, having expressed mutual respect, could serve as a foot in the target's office door. This is particularly clear in answers reported in examples H to I.

In respondents' answers, trust from the firm and access to the target were the two explicit dimensions of the efficient lever. Thus the main dilemma was between sending a lever who represented the firm and spoke reliably on its behalf, and sending a lever who was close to the target. Partner 15 summarized the dilemma in example J. The special relationship between targets and levers was an important factor, but it was presented as problematic when left unchecked, because the lever might end up siding with the target at the expense of the firm. At least as long as it remained informal, leverage was often presumed to be exercised through a 'soft cop, tough cop' approach. It worked through both friendly discussion and persuasion, provision of professional and impersonal support, but also pressure through the use of intimidating partners with status and reputation. Partners' expectations thus reflected a specifically 'collegial' know-how, a strategic and micropolitical culture.

SOCIAL NICHES AND LATERAL CONTROL

If we look at peers' conceptions of lateral control at the level of individual partners, it becomes easier to understand how they allocated costs of lateral control. The following illustrations are provided to show that, for each member, this form of cost management brought in niches through three preoccupations.

1. Investing one's own relational capital in the lateral control process or shifting the costs of control by playing on others' (the lever's or target's) relational capital (that is, resource dependencies). Good relationships with colleagues (a form of individual relational capital) being both fragile and unequally distributed within the firm, a partner had a choice, when selecting a lever, between using his or her own social resources or not.
2. When shifting, spreading the costs of control among many members or concentrating these costs on a few specialized members.
3. When shifting and spreading, bringing in niches by paying particular attention to various similarities among protagonists, so as to try to 'smooth' the control process by using formal dimensions of firm structure.[7]

The fragmentation of lateral control

Partners had a comprehensive picture of the network of lateral control, which could consist of several components or be all connected. For instance, Figure 7.1 shows that Partner 35 thought, with very few exceptions, that Office I targets should be taken care of by Office I levers, and Office II targets by Office II levers. A strongly discriminant office boundary thus fragments this structure.

For instance, to pressure Partner 1 (Office I's most senior partner), Partner 35, who was an Office II partner, would use Partner 26, saying: 'He was brought up in Partner 1's world, he is his protégé. Partner 26 is also my catch-all on the litigation side.' To pressure Partner 6, Office II's prima donna partner, he would send Partner 5, Office II's most senior partner, saying: 'They are both here in Office II, both are pre-merger, they knew the founder of the firm, they have known each other for a long time.' In this perception, each office represented a world of its own, dominated by a few heavyweights, but also identified by the existence of close ties among some of its members. This line of argument was pushed further by partners who detected 'groups' among other partners and used them for leverage purpose. For instance:

> To talk to Partner 23, I'd send Partner 24, Partner 25, and Partner 26. They were all associates together, all are competent, well perceived by each other. I would turn them loose on him. Then I would stick him back on the others.   (Partner 4)

> To talk to Partner 4, I'd send Partner 9. They are the two most senior corporate lawyers in Office I. Bright but groupy. They drink hard, they play hard, they work hard.   (Partner 30)

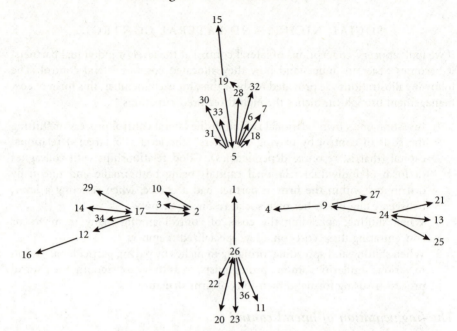

Figure 7.1. *Partner 35's expectations concerning leverage in the firm*

Source: Reprinted from *Quality and Quantity*, E. Lazega and D. Krackhardt, 'Spreading and Shifting Costs of Lateral Control in a Law Partnership: A Structural Analysis at the Individual Level', 34: 159. Copyright 2000 with permission from Kluwer Academic Publishers.

Thus, perceptions of small groups based on different types of ties between levers and targets also influenced the extent to which members spread control costs.

Fragmentation also occured in other ways. In Partner 33's picture (Figure 7.2), it is the presence of several couples of target and lever mutually chosen to control each other that explains his low connectivity score (one of Krackhardt's 1994 indexes). Partner 33 defined several worlds by choosing one heavyweight as a representative for each, and by matching, within each world, levers and targets based on personal considerations. He rarely crossed the office boundary and did not raise personal considerations about the target or the lever when doing so. Thus, since partners were closer to other partners in the same office, the leverage network created by this respondent ended up being disconnected. This fragmented view of lateral control also came from respect for other internal boundaries within the firm (speciality, seniority groups). An additional reason for this fragmented view is that some partners chose few levers for each target. Thus low connectivity was correlated with high scores of 'hierarchy'. I find that respondents who saw a fragmented or dis-connected world of influence, a structure made of many components (low con-nectivity scores), were new to the partnership (Partners 3, 21, 30, 31, 33, 35), or far from it (Partner 15), with three exceptions: Partners 1, 8, and 26.

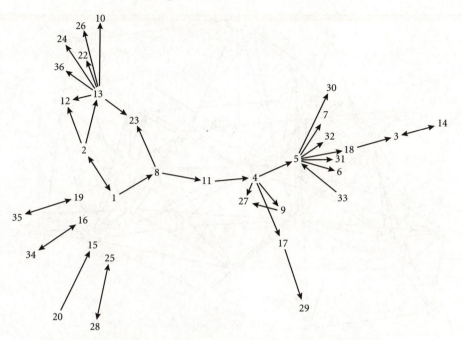

Figure 7.2. *Partner 33's expectations concerning leverage in the firm*

Source: Reprinted from *Quality and Quantity*, E. Lazega and D. Krackhardt, 'Spreading and Shifting Costs of Lateral Control in a Law Partnership: A Structural Analysis at the Individual Level', 34: 160. Copyright 2000 with permission from Kluwer Academic Publishers.

The 'overkill' strategy: Leverage as a collective effort

One way of reducing individual costs of control was to spread these costs between several levers, each taking part of the responsibility for exercising sanctions. Respondents were free to choose one or several levers for a given target. Respondents differed in the extent to which they used one or several levers for each target. This could vary from very lean paths of influence to an 'overkill' strategy. It is measured by an index called graph efficiency (Krackhardt 1994), which relates to the extent to which members used redundancy. High graph efficiency means using partners sparingly to control one target. Respondents could systematically stress either the lean, confidential, or discrete effort in leverage, or the more public and collective effort. In the latter case, it was mainly because they did not trust one single path of influence (for good feedback purposes, for instance), because they had a 'good-guy–bad-guy' conception of leverage, because they did not know what was going on in the other office (and therefore chose many senior levers), or because they wanted to be protective of some partners. Among such respondents, I found several firm minders, such as Partners 5 and 20, but also partners recruited from other firms who played it safe by choosing several levers for each target (because they did not feel absolutely sure of

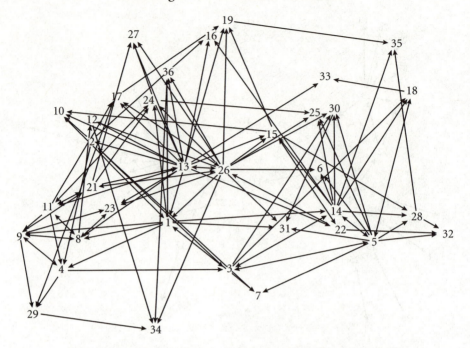

Figure 7.3. *Partner 20's expectations concerning leverage in the firm*

Source: Reprinted from *Quality and Quantity*, E. Lazega and D. Krackhardt, 'Spreading and Shifting Costs of Lateral Control in a Law Partnership: A Structural Analysis at the Individual Level', 34: 161. Copyright 2000 with permission from Kluwer Academic Publishers.

their choice; this was the case, for example, with Partners 14, 22, and 25). Figure 7.3 represents Partner 20's conception of the leverage structure and shows that he chose systematically three or four levers to be sent to deal with each target. This does not mean that, in these structures, all partners were chosen equally often as levers. Partner 20's approach to the choices of levers was explained by his own arguments:

> Some of this is clearly office-based, some of it is work-related, and in a few instances it is friendship-based. And also sometimes authority-based: the target would look to them [*levers*] as having authority. Some of it will have to do with age differences, but not necessarily. I give you in general people who know best the person in trouble, to whom the target would not react negatively. Plus those who know his business. In another firm, it would sometimes be difficult to find a single person. Here you always have three or four persons you can think of.   (Partner 20)

Partner 24 reasoned in the same way:

> To talk to Partner 8, I would send Partner 17. They are close friends. He would know how to get through to him without being too threatening, making him too defensive. But I would also send Partner 2, because I don't think that Partner 17 would really be able to deal with the business aspect of the situation.   (Partner 24)

Statistical confirmation

The fact that control was overwhelmingly expected to be exercised in niches is demonstrated by the fact that important dimensions of the formal structure of the firm had a clear influence on respondents' choices of levers. At the individual level, the effect of a limited set of attributes derived from position in the formal structure was analysed across the thirty-six actors. It tested the effect of each variable on each partner's set of choices. Variables representing the use of similarities (and their significance—as presented above—in terms of lesser effort, increased competence, and higher legitimacy of access to resources) to smooth the control process were introduced by taking into account formal structural dimensions of the organization relevant to respondents when matching levers and targets. The value of each hypothesis was tested by including in a regression model the following effects:

1. lever and target were in the same office;
2. lever and target had the same speciality;
3. lever and target were in the same level of seniority;
4. respondent and lever were in the same office;
5. respondent and lever had the same speciality;
6. respondent and lever were in the same level of seniority;
7. respondent and target were in the same office;
8. respondent and target had the same speciality;
9. respondent and target were in the same level of seniority.

Multiple regression analyses including variables 1 to 9 were replicated across the thirty-six partners. Appendix G displays the distribution of strongly significant determinants for each respondent. Two effects are of particular interest to our study of management of costs of control at the individual level. Many respondents looked for similarities between lever and target in terms of office location and in terms of level of seniority. Thus, they tried to smooth the lateral control process by allocating the control costs to targets close to the levers, both geographically and in terms of experience (but not speciality), while still counting on the levers' use of the target's dependence on such resources.

The niche effect in the design of pathways for lateral control is also confirmed at the aggregate level. Table 7.1 shows that respondents matched levers significantly more often with targets similar in their formal attributes, such as practice, office, and level of seniority, than with targets differing in these attributes.

All the variables included in the table significantly affect the choices of levers for a given target. Office I levers were chosen significantly more often to control Office I targets than Office II targets.[8] Symmetrically, and even more strongly, Office II levers were chosen significantly more to take care of Office II targets than Office I targets. Thus, partners of one office were chosen to control each other, and comparatively rarely to control partners in the other office. In the arguments, this was often explained by two reasons: first, it was more convenient to ask a lever to intervene who was located in the room next door to the target rather than to ask a partner in

Table 7.1. *Effects of selected dimensions of firm formal structure on the choices of levers*

Independent variables	Models				
	1	2	3	4	5
Office similarity	0.31***				0.30***
Practice similarity		0.13***			0.14***
Seniority similarity			0.18***		0.29***
Seniority superiority				0.09*	0.25***

Notes: *$p < 0.05$, ***$p < 0.001$, one-tailed tests. Coefficients are standardized in Model 5. For Model 5, $r^2 = 0.2$. Number of usable permutations: 999. Significance levels were determined by the multiple regression quadratic assignment procedure (Krackhardt 1988). For details about the procedure used in these analyses, see Lazega and Krackhardt (2000).

Source: Reprinted from *Organisation Studies*, E. Lazega, 'Enforcing Rules among Peers: A Lateral Control Regime', 21: 201. Copyright 2000 with permission from Aldine-de Gruyter.

another city; secondly, targets from one office were also likely to perceive control efforts from 'foreign' levers as intrusive.

Litigators were chosen significantly more often to control other litigators than corporate targets. Symmetrically, corporate levers were expected to take significantly more care of corporate targets than of litigation ones. The arguments provided two main reasons for such a symmetry. One was that levers with the same speciality as their targets were supposed to know their targets and understand their business situation better than levers from other specialities. Another reason is to be found in the differences in professional 'subcultures': corporate lawyers had a reputation for being more conciliatory and quieter, and litigators for being more combative and more aggressive; thus, they were not perceived to be good matches with one another.

Finally, the ten most junior partners were rarely chosen as levers, and were more likely to be chosen to control junior targets rather than more senior ones. Medium-seniority levers were chosen to control junior and medium-seniority targets. Senior levers were chosen much more systematically, and were not chosen to control any one level of seniority significantly more often than any other. Most notably, the coefficients for both seniority variables go up in the multiple regression as compared with the simple regression. This confirms that senior levers were chosen more often than medium-seniority partners, and much more often than junior ones. Many reasons were provided for this strong asymmetry and descending hierarchical structure. Particularly, junior partners did not know older partners as well as their contemporaries did, and were not perceived as carrying the necessary weight to impress more senior partners. In general, partners said that they did not trust junior partners for this type of task as much as they would trust more senior levers.

Overall, office location, division of work, and seniority boundaries shaped respondents' expectations. The weight of these internal differentiations can be interpreted as a clear influence of the formal structure on the pattern of the lateral control. This embeddedness in formal structure increased the chances of lateral control being an efficient solution to the second-order free-rider problem in such niches. As such, it strongly points at niches as a fundamental component of an organizational control regime.

Multiplex social ties and leverage in niches

The next question with regard to management of costs of lateral control is whether or not the existence of niches had an effect on respondents' propensity to invest their own relational capital in the lateral control process. The answer should be obvious, since we know that members in general tended to find their co-workers, advisers, and friends in their niche. Another series of independent variables was used to look more closely at the determinants of choices of levers at the individual level. This was done mainly by looking at the relationship between choices of levers and informal ties among partners, specifically at the effect of relations between respondent, lever, and target on the choices of levers. The analysis was again replicated across the thirty-six actors. For confirmation purposes, variables representing issues of cost of control in terms of investment of relational capital were introduced by the analytical question, 'Whose friends, advisers, and co-workers does the respondent mobilize to put pressure on the target? His or her own ties? The lever's ties? The target's ties?'

The value of each hypothesis can be tested by including in a regression model the following effects:

10. respondent saw the lever as a friend;
11. respondent saw the lever as a co-worker;
12. respondent went to the lever for advice;
13. lever saw the target as a friend;
14. lever went to the target for advice;
15. lever saw the target as a co-worker;
16. target went to the lever for advice;
17. target saw the lever as a friend;
18. target saw the lever as a co-worker;
19. respondent saw the target as a friend;
20. respondent saw the target as a co-worker;
21. respondent went to the target for advice.

Partner 14's responses illustrate this analysis in Table 7.2. There is only one significant effect in this example: Partner 14, in his conception of lateral control, was sensitive to the fact that the target sought advice from the lever, and that such a dependence could be used to put pressure on the target. He chose to make use of the target's relational capital to monitor and sanction him or her. More generally, Appendix G displays the results of this series of regression models and shows that two effects are of particular interest to our study of management of costs of control at the individual level. First, the fact that 'target went to the lever for advice' and that 'target saw the lever as a friend' were important criteria: dependence of the target on the lever for those resources was perceived to be a major way of reducing control

Table 7.2. *An example of the effects of an individual partner's pre-existing ties on his choices of levers: The case of Partner 14*

Independent variables	Parameter estimates
10. Respondent saw the lever as a friend	0.01
11. Respondent saw the lever as a co-worker	−0.05
12. Respondent went to the lever for advice	−0.12
13. Lever saw the target as a friend	0.10
14. Lever went to the target a for advice	0.04
15. Lever saw the target as a co-worker	−0.04
16. Target went to the lever for advice	0.14**
17. Target saw the lever as a friend	0.05
18. Target saw the lever as a co-worker	0.00
19. Respondent saw the target as a friend	−0.03
20. Respondent saw the target as a co-worker	−0.01
21. Respondent went to the target for advice	−0.00

Notes: $N = 1,260$. $**p < 0.01$, one-tailed tests. Coefficients are standardized, $r^2 = 0.08$. Number of usable permutations: 999. Results of multiple regression quadratic assignment procedure (Krackhardt 1988). Independent variables are numbered as in the text.

Source: Reprinted from *Organisation Studies*, E. Lazega, 'Enforcing Rules among Peers: A Lateral Control Regime', 21: 203. Copyright 2000 with permission from Aldine-de Gruyter.

costs. This suggests that many members did play on others' (target's) relational capital, especially on their dependence for advice and friendship. This conception of lateral control tended to shift the costs of control to the target—that is, the person responsible for the infraction. At the aggregate level, a general classification of choices of levers is presented in Table 7.3.

This table could again suggest that, in absolute numbers, the general trend in this firm was to use personal ties (considered separately one type at a time) very little for lateral pressure. For example, in the first sub-table of Table 7.3, members used levers whom they considered to be friends in 29.9 per cent of the cases. These relatively low rates of 'conversion' of personal social resources into relational pressure could come from the fact that the goal of such manipulations was to protect the common good, not immediate individual interest. Members would have left it to others to invest their social resources for that purpose, rather than 'sacrifice' their own.

However, the analyses at the individual level and the reading of absolute figures at the aggregate level can provide a misleading view of what went on in niches. In the next section, I show that, in fact, given the general density of the observed network, respondents overused their own social ties, particularly in their niches. In effect, size and density of each network in the firm defined limits to the number of choices of levers: all actors did not necessarily have enough friends, co-workers, and advisers to 'cover' all their partners. If the 'possible' was thus constituted by taking for each pair of respondent–target all the theoretically available influence paths (thirty four of them), there were always, among the actually 'observed'—that is, defined by respondents—paths, more personalized relations than one would expect.

Table 7.3. *Selection of levers: Conditions under which respondents invest their own relational capital to exercise lateral control for the common good*

		Regardless of relationship with the target	Target friend of respondent		Target co-worker of respondent		Target adviser of respondent	
			No	Yes	No	Yes	No	Yes
Lever friend of respondent	No	2,133 (70.1)	1,787 (76.6)	346 (48.7)	1,483 (72.9)	650 (64.4)	1,453 (73.3)	680 (64.1)
	Yes	910 (29.9)	545 (23.4)	365 (51.3)	551 (27.1)	359 (35.6)	529 (26.7)	381 (35.9)
Lever co-worker of respondent	No	1,895 (62.3)	1,509 (64.7)	386 (54.3)	1,441 (70.8)	454 (45.0)	1,361 (68.7)	534 (50.3)
	Yes	1,148 (37.7)	823 (35.3)	325 (45.7)	593 (29.2)	555 (55.0)	621 (31.3)	527 (49.7)
Lever adviser of respondent	No	1,614 (53.0)	1,306 (56.0)	308 (43.3)	1,198 (58.9)	416 (41.2)	1,192 (60.1)	422 (39.8)
	Yes	1,429 (47.0)	1,026 (44.0)	403 (56.7)	836 (41.1)	593 (58.8)	790 (39.9)	639 (60.2)
Regardless of relationship with the lever			2,332 (76.6)	711 (23.4)	2,034 (66.8)	1,009 (33.2)	1,982 (65.1)	1,061 (34.9)

Notes: $N = 3,043$. Numbers in the table are counts, and percentages (in parentheses) are column percentages. The unit of analysis is the choice of a sanctioner by a respondent for a given infractor. Example: When the target is not a friend, respondent chooses a lever who is a friend in 23.4% of the cases.

Source: Reprinted from *Revue Française de Sociologie*, E. Lazega and M.-O. Lebeaux, 'Capital social et contrainte latérale', 36: 764. Copyright 1995 with permission from *Revue Française de Sociologie*.

Actors can therefore be said to have used their social resources *more* than general densities would suggest.[9] This, in many ways, amounts to a form of 'privatization' of lateral control.

The privatization of lateral control

Privatization of lateral pressures is first suggested by the fact that choices of sanctioners varied with the types of mobilized ties. When partners 'invested' their own ties for the protection of the common good, they tended to mobilize their advisers more than their co-workers and friends. The proportion of personal social ties converted and 'expended' for control (personalized paths), compared to all the non-personalized paths (independent of the tie between respondent and target), varied with the type of relationship: partners tended to be more 'stingy' with colleagues they considered to be friends than with colleagues they cited as advisers. Thus, on average, 30 per cent of the choices of levers by respondents mobilized the latter's friends, 38 per cent their co-workers, and 47 per cent their advisers. The higher rate for advisers can be explained by the fact that different networks had different densities and that partners central in the advice network were often senior and experienced partners. This confirms that they were therefore often chosen to represent the interests of the firm in front of the targets. Mobilization was all the easier here since the advice for which they were sought out was usually 'free'; when representing the firm in front of the target, advisers could more easily carry on advising him or her, this time unsolicited.

This relative compartmentalization of ties by members—that is, this variation of rates of conversion by type of tie—suggests that over-utilization of relational capital (compared to the general density of each network) mentioned above was even more pronounced when each type of relation is considered separately and when the tie between respondent and target is taken into account. Table 7.4 presents a first analysis taking into account this relationship with the target. It provides the odds ratios of the nine sub-tables in Table 7.3. The diagonal in Table 7.4 shows that friendship ties were the 'purest,' before co-worker ties. Ties among advisers were a little less strong, more fuzzy and dispersed. Thus, when the choices of levers are analysed, taking into account the tie between respondent and target, the conversion of relational capital into lateral constraint appears to have been very selective.

This selectivity suggests that attention to the relationships between, on the one hand, respondents and levers and, on the other hand, respondents and targets should provide additional insights on how this lateral control regime helps in overcoming the second-order free-rider problem. I first checked whether each lever chosen by a respondent was or was not mentioned by him or her as a friend, adviser, or co-worker. I then looked at the extent to which the existence of a tie between the respondent and the target had an effect on the respondent's choice of levers who were part of his or her relational capital. Table 7.5 shows that partners chose to invest their own relational capital for lateral control purposes, but mainly to protect their *own* personal relational capital—that is, targets who were also part of their relational capital.

In this table, the dependent variables were constructed as follows. For the first model ('Respondent chooses the levers among his/her friends'), a dichotomous variable with 3,043 observations was created in which the value is 1 each time respondent *i* chooses a lever *k and* mentions *k* as a friend in the sociometric

Table 7.4. *Table of odds ratios of the nine sub-tables of Table 7.3*

	Target friend of respondent	Target co-worker of respondent	Target adviser of respondent
Lever friend of respondent	3.46	1.49	1.54
Lever co-worker of respondent	1.54	2.97	2.16
Lever adviser of respondent	1.67	2.04	2.28

Source: Reprinted from *Revue Française de Sociologie*, E. Lazega and M.-O. Lebeaux, 'Capital social et contrainte latérale', 36: 765. Copyright 1995 with permission from *Revue Française de Sociologie*.

Table 7.5. *Logit analysis of the effect of relationships between respondents and targets and between targets and levers on respondents' choices of levers among their own friends, co-workers, and advisers*

Independent variables	Models		
	Respondent chooses the levers among his/her:		
	Friends	Co-workers	Advisers
Target is a co-worker of the respondent (according to respondent)	0.10 (0.10)	0.93 (0.10)	0.35 (0.09)
Target is an adviser of the respondent (according to respondent)	−0.03 (0.11)	0.25 (0.10)	0.60 (0.09)
Target is a friend of the respondent (according to respondent)	1.20 (0.10)	0.09 (0.10)	0.18 (0.09)
Target is a co-worker of the lever (according to lever)	−0.05 (0.09)	0.17 (0.09)	−0.06 (0.08)
Target is an adviser of the lever (according to lever)	−0.02 (0.10)	−0.28 (0.09)	−0.04 (0.09)
Target is a friend of the lever (according to lever)	0.28 (0.09)	−0.20 (0.08)	−0.11 (0.08)

Notes: $N = 3{,}043$. Unstandardized coefficients, standard errors in parentheses. For details about the combination of sociometric choices and selections of levers, see the text.

Source: Reprinted from *Revue Française de Sociologie*, E. Lazega and M.-O. Lebeaux, 'Capital social et contrainte latérale', 36: 765. Copyright 1995 with permission from *Revue Française de Sociologie*.

friendship matrix, and 0 when i chooses a lever k *and* does not mention k as a friend in the sociometric friendship matrix. Dependent variables for the next two models ('Respondent chooses the levers among his/her co-workers/advisers') were recoded in the same way. Independent variables were reconstructed in the same way. For instance, for the variable 'Target is a friend of the respondent (according to respondent)', a variable with 3,043 observations was constructed in which the value is 1 each time respondent i chooses a lever for a target j *and* mentions target j as a friend in the sociometric friendship matrix, and 0 when i chooses a lever for a target j *and* does not mention j as a friend in the sociometric friendship matrix.

These parameters show that choosing a friend as a lever (rather than a non-friend) is explained by being friends with the target. This selectivity characterized what could be called a relative homogenization of social control in function of type of tie: respondents tended to favour choices of friends to put pressure on friends, advisers to put pressure on advisers, co-workers to constrain co-workers. This conversion was thus characterized by the fact that respondents tended to 'protect' their relational capital. The same holds for the fact that the lever was friends with the target (according to the lever). The type of conversion that emerged here required the creation of a group of friends with cliquelike features—that is, choosing each other mutually to deal with their own problems themselves, in a privatized manner.

Choosing a co-worker (rather than a non-co-worker) as a lever is explained by the fact that one was a co-worker of the target, but also by the fact that the target was not an adviser of the lever (according to the lever). This type of conversion may be based on the tendency for respondents to contain the difficulties created by work ties within the realm of such work ties, as well as on resistance of levers to this strategy when the target was one of their advisers. The fact that respondents chose one of their own advisers (rather than a non-adviser) as lever is mainly explained by the fact that they sought advice from the target and that they were also co-workers of the target. Having a strong professional tie, at least duplex, with the target (as adviser and co-worker) explains the choice of an adviser as lever. This type of conversion illustrates the idea that relational capital constituted by advisers, although very precious, was more generally 'expended' than relational capital of levers considered as friends and collaborators.

In sum, partners pressured one another using their own personal ties more than one would expect. To this relative privatization of lateral pressure, one can add the fact that actors chose their levers among their advisers rather than from other networks. They tended to prefer the choice of an adviser regardless of their own ties to the target, whereas in the other cases they stayed within the sphere or type of tie that they had with the target. They also used their own social relations (friends, co-workers, advisers) more to exercise constraint on peers when the latter were also part of their relational capital. Type of tie by type of tie, these strategies show that members tried to stay *en famille* more frequently in the friendship or in the co-workers networks than in the advice network (the latter's ties being more easily interlocked with each one of the other ties, as seen in Chapter 5). This selectivity can be explained by the will to protect this capital, type of tie by type of tie, in the sense of not investing it in a random way, thus avoiding the potentially negative effects of the exercise of power among peers. The conversion of relational capital into lateral constraint thus followed a specific know-how or set of rules, in particular a norm that had an 'economic' dimension. Efficiency of pressures, as it was anticipated by partners, depended on the type of resource circulating in each network and on their desire to protect their relational capital.

Borrowing others' connections

If partners were disposed towards using their own relational capital for control within their niche, they were *also* disposed towards borrowing others' resources for the same purpose. The existence of these different modalities of conversion, which varied according to the type of relational capital and according to the type of target, made some influence paths more likely than others. Table 7.6 describes the distribution of the different types of lateral influence paths reconstituted based on these data. Recall that these paths were comprised of two segments, the first being the relation (or absence of relation) between respondent and lever, the second being the relation (or absence of relation) between target and lever. When choosing a lever to put pressure on a target, a respondent could often count on the fact that there

Table 7.6. *Distribution of the different types of two-step control paths, according to the type of tie used in each step*

First step: Ties between respondent and lever (according to the respondent)	Second step: Ties between lever and target (according to the lever)								Total	Baseline frequencies
	No tie	Friendship	Co-work	Friendship and co-work	Advice	Advice and friendship	Advice and co-work	Advice, friendship, and co-work		
No tie	410 (13.47)	101 (3.32)	122 (4.01)	40 (1.31)	91 (2.99)	112 (3.68)	84 (2.76)	259 (8.51)	1,219 (40.06)	50.0
Friendship	72 (2.37)	26 (0.85)	11 (0.36)	9 (0.30)	20 (0.66)	36 (1.18)	11 (0.36)	44 (1.45)	229 (7.53)	5.9
Co-work	46 (1.51)	9 (0.30)	10 (0.33)	3 (0.10)	7 (0.23)	11 (0.36)	14 (0.46)	37 (1.22)	137 (4.50)	7.0
Friendship and co-work	9 (0.30)	2 (0.07)	3 (0.10)	1 (0.03)	2 (0.07)	6 (0.20)	0 (0.00)	6 (0.20)	29 (0.95)	1.4
Advice	109 (3.58)	21 (0.69)	22 (0.72)	10 (0.33)	22 (0.72)	23 (0.76)	19 (0.62)	53 (1.74)	279 (9.17)	7.4
Advice and friendship	42 (1.38)	10 (0.33)	14 (0.46)	9 (0.30)	10 (0.33)	11 (0.36)	15 (0.49)	57 (1.87)	168 (5.52)	3.5
Advice and co-work	205 (6.74)	42 (1.38)	29 (0.95)	6 (0.20)	25 (0.82)	43 (1.41)	44 (1.45)	104 (3.42)	498 (16.37)	12.8
Advice, friendship, and co-work	152 (5.00)	33 (1.08)	51 (1.68)	21 (0.69)	35 (1.15)	49 (1.61)	44 (1.45)	99 (3.25)	484 (15.91)	11.7
Total	1,045 (34.34)	244 (8.02)	262 (8.61)	99 (3.25)	212 (6.97)	291 (9.56)	231 (7.59)	659 (21.66)	3,043 (100.00)	
% column	56.5	6.0	6.8	1.6	6.5	4.1	6.9	11.7		
Baseline frequencies										

Notes: $N = 3,043$. Figures in the table are counts, with percentages in parentheses.

Source: Reprinted from *Revue Française de Sociologie*, E. Lazega and M.-O. Lebeaux, 'Capital social et contrainte latérale', 36: 769. Copyright 1995 with permission from *Revue Française de Sociologie*.

were one or more types of relation between this lever and that target. Respondents may not have always been conscious of the fact that they dug into the lever's relational capital, but the arguments provided to justify these choices show that they were actually often conscious of it. In one case or another, the respondent still depended, by construction, when exercising lateral constraints, on this relationship between lever and target. We must focus on the nature of these relationships to reconstitute the paths of lateral influence.

Choices of levers by respondents are distributed into eight categories of paths constituted by the eight possible combinations, according to whether the lever was considered by the respondent as his or her adviser, co-worker, and/or friend. For example, the choices of levers that could be called impersonal—where the lever chosen by the respondent was not one of his or her advisers, co-workers, or friends—constituted 40 per cent of all the choices of levers by the respondents. In absolute numbers, influence paths in which levers were at the same time advisers, co-workers, and friends of the respondent constituted 15.9 per cent of all the choices of levers. Still, in absolute numbers, the choices that could be considered entirely personalized, where respondents invested the strongest and most precious triplex ties in their relational capital, were thus more than twice as rare as the impersonal choices. The same prudence, however, as in the reading of Table 7.3 is necessary here. These absolute numbers do not mean that respondents were not disposed towards investing much of their relational capital in this lateral control.

Generally, paths went through either the relational capital of the respondent or that of the lever. In other words, the most frequent types of paths did not combine personalized ties between respondent and lever with personalized ties between lever and target. This is easily visible in the fact that completely impersonal paths constitute 13.5 per cent of all paths and that 60 per cent of all chosen paths belong either to the first row or to the first column of Table 7.6. For example, the paths going through the very personal ties of the lever (that is, without personalized relationship between respondent and lever, but with a triplex relationship between the lever and the target) are the second most frequent case in the table (8.5 per cent of all observed paths). Out of the two possible cases of triplex relations, paths combining all personalized ties between lever and target were more numerous than paths combining the personalized ties between respondent and lever.[10]

Table 7.6 confirms that paths went through advisers more often than through friends or co-workers. One finds thus a primacy of paths in which the first segment was impersonal, then paths in which there was an advice tie between respondent and lever (separated from or coupled with the two other types of tie). Advice ties seem, once again, to have characterized personalized paths.

Relationships between levers and targets were also distributed into eight categories constituted by the same possible combinations. As already seen, impersonal relations—where the lever chosen by the respondent did not seek advice from the target, did not work with the target, and did not have a friendship tie with the target—constituted 34.3 per cent of all recorded choices. This constituted an underutilization of impersonal paths compared to the 'baseline' distribution. When choosing levers, respondents were likely, one time out of three, to exercise impersonal pressure on the target. In this case, the lever did not invest his or her own relational capital. In contrast, ties that could be considered entirely personalized between lever and target—where the lever sought advice from the target, worked with the target and considered him or herself friends with the target—constitute 21.7 per cent of all recorded influence choices, which corresponds to an over-utilization of this type of path. It is interesting to note that the difference decreases between these two extreme cases when compared to the relationships between respondent and lever: this confirms that, consciously or not, respondents constructed paths that mobilized more easily other partners' relational capital (that is, levers' relational capital) than their own. Thus it is all the more apparent that respondents seemed less discriminating and less careful with regard to the nature of other partners' capital than when they invested their own. In effect, among paths that involved only one type of tie between lever and target, those mobilizing a co-worker tie with the target (8.6 per cent), or a friendship tie with the target (8 per cent), or an advice tie with the target (7 per cent), were approximately equally frequent, which was not the case in the relationship between respondent and lever.

In order to understand these paths from the partners' perspective, in particular this difference between the use of one's own relational capital and the use of others' relational capital (that of the lever), we need an analysis that re-introduces the relationship between the respondent and the target. For this purpose, Table 7.6 was simplified by measuring the strength of ties among all protagonists with a scale going from absence of tie to presence of the three types of tie, and thus by grouping paths into four categories. This approach helps in analysing the expenditure of the lever's relational capital. It is summarized in Table 7.7, which represents the tests of the models that try to check that the relationship between the lever and the target was not independent from the two other relationships in the triplet.

There was a strong interaction between the respondent–target relationship (R_T in Table 7.7) and the respondent–lever relationship (R_L). But there was also a stronger interaction between the lever–target relationship (L_T) and the respondent–target relationship (R_T) than between the lever–target relationship (L_T) and the respondent–lever relationship (R_L). Among the level 2 interactions, notice that $R_T R_L$ interaction was the strongest (its corresponding R is 67.4 per cent). The triple interaction was also significant, although more moderately so (it corresponds to 17.9 per cent of the chi-square of the baseline model).

The fact that the relationship between the lever and the target was not independent from the relationship between respondent and target shows that respondents expected the levers to use their own relational capital regardless of the strength of the tie that respondents had with the lever or with the target. More precisely, levers were expected to 'spend' their relational capital in an undifferentiated manner, whereas respondents—as seen above—tended to 'invest' their relational capital more when they wanted to protect their own relational capital (that is, more carefully). Respondents tended to expect levers to be less strategic with their use of their ties.

Table 7.7. *Log-linear modelling of ties between respondents, targets, and levers*

Models	Degrees of freedom	L^2	Test	R (%)
1. Baseline model				
(R_T) (R_L) (L_T)	54	393.37	$p < 0.0001$	
2. $(R_T R_L)$ (L_T)	45	128.26	$p < 0.0001$	67.4
Test of $(R_T R_L)$: (1) − (2)	9	265.11	$p < 0.0001$	
3. (R_T) $(R_L L_T)$	45	377.43	$p < 0.0001$	4.1
Test of $(R_L L_T)$: (1) − (3)	9	15.94	$p = 0.0681$	
4. $(R_T L_T)$ (R_L)	45	353.55	$p < 0.0001$	13.1
Test of $(R_T L_T)$: (1) − (4)	9	39.82	$p < 0.0001$	
5. $(R_T R_L)$ $(R_L L_T)$ $(R_T L_T)$	27	70.40	$p < 0.0001$	82.1
6. $(R_T R_L L_T)$	0	0		
Test of $(R_T R_L L_T)$: (5) − (6)	27	70.40	$p < 0.0001$	

Notes: R_T represents the strength of the tie between respondent and the target; R_L between respondent and the lever; L_T between the lever and the target. For the meaning of the expression 'strength of tie', refer to the text. L^2 is the chi-square of the likelihood ratio representing the difference between the observed values and the values estimated under the appropriate hypothesis. 'R' is interpreted as the proportion of the chi-square of the baseline model that is explained by fitting a more complex model.

Source: Reprinted from *Revue Française de Sociologie*, E. Lazega and M.-O. Lebeaux, 'Capital social et contrainte latérale', 36: 773. Copyright 1995 with permission from *Revue Française de Sociologie*.

The fact that the triple interaction is significant means that levers were expected to spend their relational capital in a less discriminating way, although still in a *weakly* discriminating way. Respondents did not expect levers to use their relational capital entirely 'randomly'. The difference may be described by the fact that respondents, when they had no relationship to the target, chose in 52 per cent of the cases a lever who had no relationship to them (respondents), but who also had no relationship to the target in only 36 per cent of the cases. The path between lever and target was expected to be personalized in two out of three interventions, and in one out of two interventions between respondent and lever. Respondents tended to choose a lever who spent overall more personal relational capital than they (respondents) would when there was no personalized tie between themselves and the target. When they were relatively external, distant, and personally unconcerned, respondents tended to choose a lever with personalized ties to the target. They got personally involved in one out of two cases and expected the lever to get personally involved in two out of three cases.

In contrast, when respondents had a very strong tie with the target, they tended to choose a lever with no personal tie to the target (impersonal path) in only 22 per cent of the cases (that is, a personalized path in 78 per cent of the cases), whereas the lever had an impersonal tie to the target only in 29 per cent of the cases. The lever had impersonal ties to the target that varied only within the interval of 36 per cent and 29 per cent, whereas respondents had impersonal ties with the lever that varied between 52 per cent and 22 per cent. If we assume that respondents knew whether or not there was a relationship between the lever and the target—which is a reasonable

assumption given the type of arguments provided to justify the choices of levers—
then respondents had a strategy of choices of levers that left less leeway to the lever in
the choice of whether or not to risk his or her relational capital for the common
good. Levers were chosen so as to get more personally involved in policing (compared to the respondent), especially when the respondent had no personal tie to the
target. Levers were thus expected to be more indifferent to their own personal
interests in terms of managing their relational capital within the firm.

These results converge to suggest that much lateral control happened in niches and
that, within such niches, members spent both their own and the sanctioners' relational capital for protection of the common good. Indeed, this may explain the
frequencies of 'unsafe' and 'expensive' choices of levers (between 7 per cent and
9 per cent depending on the type of tie).[11] Such strategies lost some of their riskiness
when they were deployed within niches, where members did not measure their efforts
in the same way. However, keeping costs of control low by choosing sanctioners who
were structurally close to the infractor left at least two problems connected to the
second-order free-rider issue unsolved: that of preferential treatment within niches,
and that of infractors outside the respondent's and the sanctioner's niche. Recall that
when respondents' choices of levers were analysed taking into account the link
between respondent and target, they appeared to be highly selective. Choosing a
friend as a lever (rather than a non-friend) was explained by the fact that the
respondent was a friend of the target. This selectivity shows that lateral control would
tend to create cliquelike formations of friends who chose one another to solve their
difficulties in a 'privatized' way. To go back to Table 7.5, partners tended to choose
members of their own relational capital (friends, co-workers, and advisers) to put
pressure on peers who were part of their relational capital. This selectivity could be
explained by the 'economics' of relational capital—that is, the wish to protect this
capital in the sense of not expending or investing it randomly, thus limiting the
potentially negative effects of exercising this type of lateral constraint.

But in addition, partners were not only reluctant to invest systematically their
own personal ties for the protection of the common good when the target was not
part of their own relational capital. As already mentioned, they also did not have
enough friends, co-workers, or advisers to cover the entire partnership. They were
thus willing or forced to make choices outside their personal network. Therefore I
argue that a few members operating as informal 'whips', whom I call 'multi-target
levers' (MTLs), or 'protectors of the common good', were granted a specific form of
status in the social organization of individual and collective responsibility. They
were chosen to represent the interests of the firm and talk on its behalf to targets who
were not part of the respondent's niche or relational capital.

PROTECTORS OF THE COMMON GOOD:
STATUS AND LATERAL CONTROL

The delegation of responsibility to a few MTLs, which is shown here to be at the core
of this lateral control regime, makes sense from the perspective of individual

partners' management of social resources, but also from the firm's perspective. Partners indeed thought that MTLs would both reduce their own control costs and increase the safety of the sanction. In the next section, I illustrate this perspective at the individual level. In the subsequent sections, I look at who these MTLs were, the social 'territory' that each covered, and at the related question of who would exercise control on them—that is, who would guard the guardians.

The stratification of lateral control

Respondents varied in the extent to which they perceived and expected a lateral control structure that was clearly stratified. This can also be measured by another Krackhardt (1994) index, called hierarchy score, which refers to the extent to which a network allows cycles of influence. This can be interpreted as an indication that respondents believed that status mattered for leverage. Figure 7.4 shows Partner 18's perception of the leverage structure. In this perception two main levers dominate: Partner 20 and Partner 5, the managing partner at the time of the study (Office I) and his Office II deputy. Each of them was expected to control more than ten targets directly without being controlled by them in return. Notice that Partners

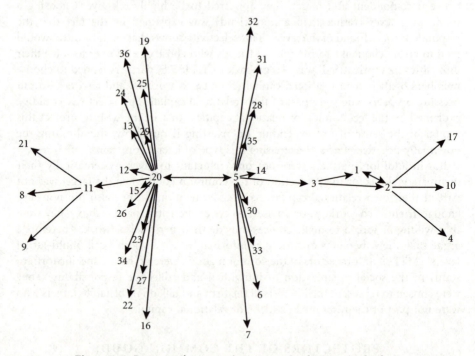

Figure 7.4. *Partner 18's expectations concerning leverage in the firm*

Source: Reprinted from *Quality and Quantity*, E. Lazega and D. Krackhardt, 'Spreading and Shifting Costs of Lateral Control in a Law Partnership: A Structural Analysis at the Individual Level', 34: 162. Copyright 2000 with permission from Kluwer Academic Publishers.

5 and 20 were chosen to control each other. This was explicit in Partner 18's arguments, such as:

> To handle Partner 6, I would send Partner 5. He is the most senior Office II attorney. He has worked with him for many years. He has respect for him, and he would do it effectively.... To talk to Partner 11, I would send Partner 20, the managing partner. He is in the same office, less confrontational as somebody of Partner 1's seniority. And he has a good temperament for dealing with these issues.

The status of Partner 5 and Partner 20 was recognized throughout the partnership, which is more sharply illustrated by statements concerning difficult targets, such as Partner 1 (recall Partner 13's exclamation, cited on p. 209, argument A) or Partner 6:

> To talk to Partner 6, I'd send Partner 5. Partner 6 is a prima donna. He wouldn't listen to anyone who is not a real peer, someone with as much seniority. I am not sure he actually thinks he has a peer in this firm! (Partner 30)

In other cases, different heavyweight levers were chosen. Partner 32 chose Partner 22 to control everyone else in a pure starlike structure (see Figure 7.5). High

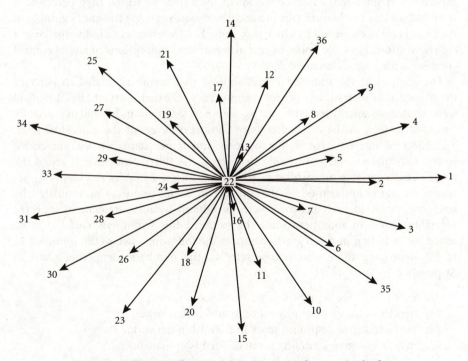

Figure 7.5. *Partner 32's expectations concerning leverage in the firm*

Source: Reprinted from *Quality and Quantity*, E. Lazega and D. Krackhardt, 'Spreading and Shifting Costs of Lateral Control in a Law Partnership: A Structural Analysis at the Individual Level', 34: 163. Copyright 2000 with permission from Kluwer Academic Publishers.

hierarchy scores often mean that MTLs were almost exclusively chosen. The reason for such a belief in status may be the perceived safety of such paths of lateral control, which was explicit in Partner 32's argument:

> Partner 22 for everybody. He did it successfully once. There is the personal problem and then the firm issue. You can't put blinders on either. As a managing partner you would have to focus on the second issue. The institution comes first. [Partner 22] is an ex-marine, well-organized and efficient, able to get it done immediately. He would not let his personal feelings influence him. He would handle the task of putting the institution first. He is very much respected by everyone in the firm.   (Partner 32)

Partner 6 also chose Partner 2 as an almost universal lever:

> To talk to all of them, I would ask Partner 2. I have a great deal of respect for him. He would be able to handle the situation. When I don't chose Partner 2, it means that I think that the two persons are more attuned to each other, and they understand what drives the other well enough, so that it overrides my feeling for Partner 2 as the best person.   (Partner 6)

To summarize, partners differed in the extent to which they perceived and expected a fragmented influence world, in the extent to which they perceived a stratified control mechanism (for instance, by choosing an MTL at the beginning of the chain) and in the extent to which they thought of leverage as an individual or as a collective effort. How did issues of cost and partners' conceptions of lateral control combine with such differences?

The analyses at the individual level showed that members tended to perceive the existence of a stratified control regime. To verify that costs of lateral control were shifted to members with status, another series of independent variables was used to look at the determinants of choices of levers at the individual level. The effect of interest here is that of lever and target status on the choices of levers. The analysis was again replicated across the thirty-six actors. It tested the effect of each variable on each set of partner's choices. Variables representing variations in status understood as the amount of social resources accumulated by lever and target in each network were introduced by measurement of indegree centrality scores in four networks. The value of this hypothesis could thus be tested by including in the regression model the following effects (the numbers 22 to 29 identifying these effects here refer to the numbers identifying them in Appendix G):

22. lever's indegree centrality score in advice network;
23. target's indegree centrality score in advice network;
24. lever's indegree centrality score in friendship network;
25. target's indegree centrality score in friendship network;
26. lever's indegree centrality score in co-workers' network;
27. target's indegree centrality score in co-workers' network;
28. lever's indegree centrality score in influence network;
29. target's indegree centrality score in influence network.

Results, also displayed in Appendix G, show that, at the individual level, conceptions of control did not vary strongly based on the amounts of members' relational capital and status in the firm—that is, on the position of the protagonists of the control drama in the pecking order of the firm. One weak exception to this statement is the levers' centrality score in the influence network. Members to whom partners tended to listen at partnership meetings when discussing firm management issues were more likely than others to be chosen as main sanctioners and to incur more costs of lateral control. Shifting these costs to them was seen as a legitimate move, especially since many of them tended to have administrative responsibilities in the firm. However, the lever's or the target's status as measured by their indegree scores in the co-workers', advice, and friendship networks did not weigh heavily on the choices of levers when examined at the individual level. Additional insights are thus needed to understand what made someone apt to be a 'protector of the common good'.

Status and the concentration of leverage

At the structural level, there was also a centralization of lateral control in the hands of a few partners with a specific form of status. The raw aggregated data show that, for some targets, consensus as to who should be the lever was very strong. As already mentioned, for example, Partner 5 was chosen thirty times to deal with Partner 18; Partners 1 and 2 were chosen twenty-four times to deal with each other. For other targets the regime was less clear as to who should be the appropriate lever: for example, Partners 25 or 29, as targets, were not matched with 'obvious' levers. The ethnography of the firm shows that, in these cases as in many others, the absence of high levels of consensus concerned targets whose status was atypical (for instance, lateral[12] partners, women partners), or difficult to handle (for instance, partners married to one another, partners notorious for behaving like a prima donna).

Network analytic techniques show a pattern in these data. Measurements of centrality of levers show that an informal hierarchy was a key feature of this control regime. Overall, some partners—mostly senior ones—were expected to act as levers much more often than others. Partners 1, 2, 4, 5, 9, 11, 12, 13, 17, 20, and 26 were the most popular levers. The control network was thus stratified and less than a third of the partners emerged as key players in the regime. Within this 'elite' of levers, additional distinctions were of interest. Some were 'single-target levers', others were MTLs. As an example of the first type, Partners 8 and 21 were not very popular levers, but locally specialized, and their role could be crucial; for example, Partner 21 was the partner who was most often chosen to control Partner 20, the most central and universal lever of all. Then several partners, such as Partners 1, 2, 4, 5, 9, 20, or 26 were boundary-spanning partners performing a role of MTL for many (up to ten) targets.

It is important not only to identify MTLs, but also to show that they were chosen in a discriminant way—that is, to exercise control on a specific set of targets. Figure 7.6 provides an example of MTLs' specialization in a specific 'territory' of

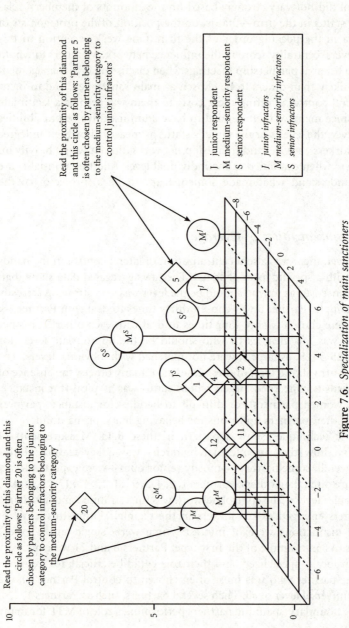

Read the proximity of this diamond and this circle as follows: 'Partner 20 is often chosen by partners belonging to the junior category to control infractors belonging to the medium-seniority category'

Read the proximity of this diamond and this circle as follows: 'Partner 5 is often chosen by partners belonging to the medium-seniority category to control junior infractors'

J	junior respondent
M	medium-seniority respondent
S	senior respondent
J	junior infractors
M	medium-seniority infractors
S	senior infractors

Figure 7.6. *Specialization of main sanctioners*

Note: This figure contains two kinds of objects: important sanctioners (represented by a diamond) and groups of respondents and infractors (represented by a circle) collapsed together based on their respective level of seniority. The way in which sanctioners and groups are located in this space is explained in Appendix H. The figure shows that the main sanctioners (in diamonds), or protectors of the common good', were chosen in a very selective way by their partners, i.e. they were chosen most often to exercise control on a specific set of infractors.

Source: Reprinted from *Bulletin de Méthodologie Sociologique*, E. Lazega and S. Vari, 'Acteurs, cibles et leviers: Analyse factorielle des relations de contrôle indirect dans une firme américaine d'avocats d'affaires', 37: 49. Copyright 1992 with permission from *Bulletin de Méthodologie Sociologique*.

lateral control. Seniority—as will be confirmed below—was chosen as a criterion for its particular importance as a dimension of formal structure. The figure is based on a principal component analysis, which is necessary to represent respondents, levers, and targets *in the same space*, and to stress the differences between the ways MTLs were chosen (for a detailed description of the procedure used, see Appendix H). It demonstrates that a few partners were chosen much more often than others as levers, by all levels of seniority and to deal with targets of different seniority levels.

This figure stresses the *contrasts* between the ways in which important MTLs (Partners 1, 2, 4, 5, 9, 11, 12, and 20) were chosen as levers.[13] Proximity in this space reflects the fact that they tended to be chosen together: for instance, Partners 2 and 4 are close to Partner 1, and were thus often chosen together by the same respondents to deal with the same targets. The large distance between Partner 20 and Partner 5 represents the fact that they were rarely chosen simultaneously as levers to control the same target. It was also rare that a respondent used simultaneously Partners 1 and 5. Respondents and targets were collapsed in groups (circles) according to three levels of seniority. The proximity between a group and a lever in this space thus indicates the existence of a culturally established and specialized pathway for the flow of lateral control within the firm.

The figure shows that the main sanctioners (in diamonds), or 'protectors of the common good', were chosen in a very discriminating way by their partners—that is, they were chosen most often to exercise control on a specific set of infractors. For example, Partner 20 was often chosen by senior partners to go and 'talk to' medium-seniority infractors. Partner 5 was often chosen by junior partners to go and talk to junior infractors. In this figure, the three axes locate the main sanctioners in a way that shows these contrasted specializations. Again, a great distance between sanctioners (diamonds) means that they were rarely chosen together by the same respondents to go and talk to the same infractors. Axis 1 expresses the contrast between choosing Partner 20 and choosing Partner 5 as a sanctioner: these two sanctioners are separated by a large distance in the picture, which means that they were very rarely chosen together as sanctioners (that is, by the same respondents and to control the same infractors). Axis 2 expresses the same kind of contrast, this time between choosing Partner 1 and choosing Partner 5 as sanctioners. Finally, Axis 3 displays the contrast between choosing any one of the main sanctioners represented in the picture versus all the other partners who were not chosen often enough to qualify as a protector of the common good. When a group is close to a sanctioner in that space, it means that respondents in this group chose this sanctioner very frequently to go and talk to infractors in that same group. I interpret this result as an indication that, according to the respondents, this important sanctioner was specialized in a specific category of infractors and thus had his or her territory of social control.

Heavy and widely cited levers were thus specialized in a specific social 'territory', a particular category of target. For instance, Partners 1, 2, and 4 would be sent by most respondents to control senior partners across the firm. They were chosen by all partners to control senior partners (S^J is to be read as 'senior targets as indicated by junior respondents'; S^M as 'senior targets as indicated by medium-seniority respondents', and so on). Thus, an important difference emerges from this analysis between Partner 5, who was chosen by most respondents to control young partners (mostly in Office II), and all the other main levers. Another difference is between all the main levers and Partner 20, who was a medium-seniority lever chosen to pressure medium-seniority partners. Especially concerning Partner 20, the managing partner at the time of the study, this contrast seems very clear in terms of internal politics. As seen above, he was presented as a default option by many respondents. Choosing him was perceived as an 'apolitical' strategy, one that could cut across speciality and office boundaries. In the next section, I look more closely at the characteristics of the MTLs.

Uncontroversial partners avoiding conflict escalation

Additional data are particularly useful to establish the relationship between this specific lateral control pattern and more obvious sources of power in the organization. As already suggested, there were two types of main levers. The first type was important in terms of administrative responsibilities and control of workforce. This appears in Table 7.8, which shows that partners who were popular levers were neither systematically central in the main sociometric networks (and therefore informally powerful), nor systematically important in terms of revenue brought in during the previous year.

Ordinary least-squares regression coefficients describing the effect of indegree centrality scores in the friendship, co-workers', and advice networks on outdegree centrality in the control network are below significance level. Overall, members' performance as measured by amount of revenue brought into the firm did not have a significant effect on popularity as a lever. However, one can better predict

Table 7.8. *Effect of partners' importance in the firm on the number of times they are chosen as levers*

Independent variables	Parameter estimates	Standardized estimates
Advice centrality	24.1 (15.3)	0.25
Influence centrality	49.9 (10.3)	0.69
Friendship centrality	3.0 (12.8)	0.02
Co-worker centrality	−36.6 (17.2)	−0.28
Business performance	−0.0 (0.0)	−0.00

Notes: $N = 35$. Standard errors in parentheses. $r^2 = 0.68$. Indicators of partners' importance are indegree centrality scores in the advice, influence, friendship, and co-worker networks, as well as partners' business performance. Previous year business performance is measured here by the dollars amount actually brought into the firm by each partner at the end of the previous year.

Source: Reprinted from *Organisation Studies*, E. Lazega, 'Enforcing Rules among Peers: A Lateral Control Regime', 21: 206. Copyright 2000 with permission from Aldine-de Gruyter.

a member's popularity as a lever knowing his or her indegree centrality score in the influence network: being listened to by many partners on matters of firm management and policy was a relatively good predictor of being chosen often to be sent as a lever, and thus of being an MTL. This confirms the prevalent role of minders as MTLs over that of many heavy client-getters and billers in the firm. Two explanations may account for the fact that MTLs were chosen among partners who were minders and not necessarily powerful in terms of access to important clients. First, the use of levers who did not control such key resources was less threatening. These levers drew their authority from the fact that they were senior but at the same time *not perceived as controversial* (for instance, not involved in potentially cut-throat power struggles focusing on the bottom line), could legitimately speak on behalf of the common interest, and thus could prevent tensions from escalating, especially between partners of different practices and offices. Secondly, heavy billers or rainmakers could be perceived as less likely to accept being used as levers, which could be unpleasant. This analysis suggests that the lateral control regime fulfilled its function in a way compatible with Freidson's 'rule of the collegium' (1975): partners' norm of avoidance of open controversies. Indeed, what seemed to be shared by MTLs was a *firm-specific status* that was different from status as described by, for example, Bucher (1970) (based on professional recognition and reputation as the primary dimension of power in a medical faculty) or by Nelson (1988) (based on control of clients).

A second category included partners who did have high scores in key networks, such as Partners 1 and 2, who had close relationships to lucrative clients, and were important in terms of business and revenue brought in. However, they were also autonomous, uncommitted to any clique, and therefore perceived as objective and capable of negotiating on behalf of the firm. They were freer partners, who could be chosen as levers because they were not locked in a constituency. Powerful actors could be sought out in key networks by multiple constituencies (Burt 1982); they tried to control the whole system. This type of MTL would have the power to exercise pressure in many dyads in spite of internal divisions. This is exemplified with Partner 1, who was the authority figure, the most senior person in the firm. Recall that he 'commands respect', was called by some 'the Monarch', although not perceived as potentially offensive to targets, and would bring some formality to a meeting without creating an antagonistic situation.

By allowing partners to avoid conflict escalation and to reduce individual enforcement costs, this lateral control regime becomes a credible component of the collegial governance structure. It helped partners manage early monitoring and sanctioning so as to solve the second-order free-riding problem and the threat that it represented to collective action.

The concentration of leverage in the hands of a minority of specialized partners raised the key issue of how this lateral control regime solved the classical problem 'Who is chosen to control the main controllers?' The next section uses measurement of approximated structural equivalence to answer this question.

Who guards the guardians?

A lateral control regime is an informal social mechanism, and thus fragile. Its very existence was threatened by the fact that its main sanctioners, some of whom were part of the oligarchy of the firm, could make themselves immune from control, thus enforcing rules that they themselves would not be pressured to respect. It makes sense to extend previous reasoning to the specific case of main sanctioners as potential infractors and to look at how members asserted that they would keep oligarchs in check. The classical question of who guards the guardians is thus important here, and so is the structural solution provided by this social mechanism.

Specifically, in this section, I analyse the choices of levers used to influence such oligarchs. This helps in identifying a structure of lateral control that reflects two types of firm protection strategy. In the first, oligarchs were mainly divided into several subgroups, which were then selected to control each other; theirs was not a cohesive position of enforcers, but a fragmented one. In the second, some members of the firm, with little status but personally close to some of the oligarchs, were also used to monitor the latters' behaviour. Evidence of this upward 'divide-and-rule' strategy is provided by showing that such channels of lateral control, as derived from individual partners' convergent expectations, reflect a specific network pattern. In turn, this pattern shows that the lateral control regime also provided a structural answer to the structural problem of guarding the guardians.

If partners with status and resources were more likely to be chosen as early and specialized sanctioners in general, they were also more likely to be chosen as early sanctioners specialized in each other. In effect, one can argue that only important partners carried enough weight (controlled enough resources and attracted enough deference) to impress other important partners, and that peers would choose segments of this elite to control each other in a circular way. This extension can be facilitated by the fact that main sanctioners did tend to share a similar general role with regard to the rest of the partnership. They could not be strictly structurally equivalent (especially if they were specialized in different types of infractors), but they could still be perceived to be closer to each other in the lateral control network (and thus exercise influence on each other) than to the rest of the partnership.[14] This provides the basis for the idea that partners chosen as main sanctioners were also more likely than others to be chosen to control each other.

Measurement of approximated structural equivalence among partners is useful to test this assertion, because it includes a description of how lateral control would operate among the most central levers. Strong levels of structural equivalence among partners in the control network created control positions. Figure 7.7 clusters approximately structurally equivalent partners into such positions. This procedure identifies what can be called the 'leverage structure' with six positions, the members of each position, and the relations among positions. For a detailed description of the procedure and the pattern emerging from the analysis, see Appendix I.

The overall pattern in the flows of lateral control described by this figure is not simply that of a stratified centre–periphery structure; it also shows what happened

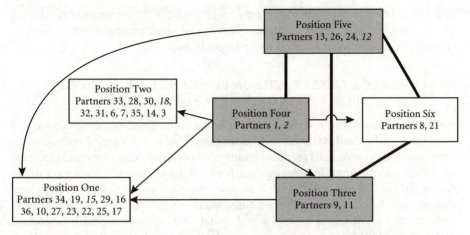

Residual partners: *4*, *5*, 20

Figure 7.7. *Who guards the guardians?*

Note: This figure represents the pattern of relationships between positions of approximately structurally equivalent partners in the lateral control network. Boxes in grey indicate that members of these positions were expected to control each other. Thick lines represent mutual control ties. Numbers in italic represent partners who made a big difference in terms of revenue during the previous year. For details about the procedure used to construct this figure, see Appendix I.

Source: Reprinted from *Research in the Sociology of Organizations*, E. Lazega, 'Who Guards the Guardians? Protecting a Lateral Control Mechanism from its own Oligarchs', 18: 279. Copyright 2001 with permission from Elsevier Science.

within the 'elite' at the top. Several central positions, occupied by a few actors each, were often chosen to control each other as well as many others. The oligarchy was fragmented into different kinds. First, there were the partners with heavy administrative responsibilities, the minders—for instance the managing partner, the deputy managing partner, and partners sitting on committees such as the associate committee, who were MTLs (mainly Position Five); minders had an important responsibility, since they were chosen to control the highly central finders and boundary-spanners in Position Four. Secondly, there were the senior MTLs who were finders (Position Four); thirdly, the three top levers who were lost to the 'residual' category; fourthly, two partners with special status in Office I (Position Three); and, fifthly, members of Position Six, Partners 8 and 21, single-target levers mainly chosen to control MTLs 11 and 20. Thus the lateral control regime divided the MTLs at the top—preventing this stratification from becoming too pyramidal— and chose segments of this oligarchy to control each other in an approximately circular way.

In summary, a few mostly senior partners and minders concentrated a great deal of leverage in their hands, cut across formal boundaries, and were chosen to exercise control on a fairly specific social 'territory'. The lateral control regime protected itself from the destructive effects of potential 'immunity' of MTLs by solving the problem of who guards the guardians in a specific way. It chose members of this elite to control each other using a complex division of work among minders, finders, structurally unique partners, and single-target levers.

LEVERAGE STYLES: THE IMPORTANCE OF SENIORITY FOR COLLECTIVE RESPONSIBILITY

Finally, it is interesting to come back to a synthesis of members' different ways of combining niches and status in their management of lateral control costs. Several 'leverage styles' (patterns of preoccupations of respondents when they made leverage decisions) can be broadly distinguished from taking an overall view of results in Appendix G.[15] These styles tended to combine various ways of spreading and shifting such costs, and characterized three levels of seniority. In effect, in partners' conceptions of how lateral control would operate in their firm, the main differences that could be relied upon to show the complementarity of niche seeking and status competition in the lateral control mechanism were between senior, medium-seniority, and junior partners. Seniority appears to be a key variable for actors' views of unobtrusive protection of common resources among peers.

In these conceptions of leverage, senior partners tended to use resource dependence and to be business oriented. They tended to concentrate rather than spread the costs of control, and to shift them to a few safe and specialized levers or to carefully selected and personally involved levers. They were relatively more sensitive to the fact that the target saw the lever as a friend, and tended to use this resource dependence. They cared less than others about similarities between lever and target, especially in terms of seniority and speciality, and therefore about 'smoothing' devices. Since they actually did not all always know very well who the junior partners were, they instead relied on more levers. This way of managing costs of control may assume that senior partners tended to have more relational capital within the firm than younger ones (which was not always confirmed, since they tended to cite less friends than others). Since they thought of themselves as more central in most networks, they also thought that senior levers could afford to use their ties to 'live up to their status'. Senior partners believed in status and in the 'muscle' theory of relational capital: the more you use it, the more efficient it is. Note that, since most MTLs were senior, this conception of control was also presumably self-serving and dominant among the guardians of the guardians.

Medium-seniority partners, mostly in Office I, tended to think as integrators of the firm—that is, in terms of avoiding conflicts—more than others. They did use resource dependencies, since they were sensitive to the fact that the target seeks advice from the lever. But they would rather spread the costs of control—even if this meant using an 'overkill' strategy—and smooth the process by stressing, more than others, niches and similarity in terms of office, seniority, and speciality. They tended, more than others, to choose as levers partners central in the influence network, since many of them were precisely very central in this network. This fact suggests that they did not tend to shift the costs of control to others, but accepted investment of their own social resources (which was not scarcer than that of senior partners) for that purpose. This does not mean that they relied less on MTLs than other partners, but that they tended to combine their use with that of niche pathways.

Junior partners tended to be more hesitant in their choices of levers, and more careful with their own scant relational capital. They were especially sensitive to their own relationships to the lever and to the target—for instance, to the fact that they considered the target to be their friend. The 'lever saw the target as a friend' effect was often important to them, which means that they tended not to shift such costs to levers unless the levers had a personal incentive to get involved. Most junior partners were in Office II, which meant a tendency to concentrate leverage in the hands of a few MTLs and shift the costs of lateral control to them, rather than spread the costs or invest their own relational capital for that purpose. In spite of many differences in terms of commanding relational capital, they seemed to be closer in their conception of management of costs of control to senior rather than to medium-seniority partners.

This analysis also suggests that a combined theory of management of costs of control expressed in terms of potential losses in relational capital, of resource dependencies, and of symbolic recognition of identities and similarities, explains why partners shared a common conception of how lateral control operates in their own collegial organization. Niche seeking and status competition help peers use various but identifiable forms of manipulation of relations among themselves to create a social order in an informal, indirect, and relatively unobtrusive way.

THE SOCIAL STRUCTURE OF COLLECTIVE RESPONSIBILITY

To summarize, the firm stood to gain 'quasi-voluntary compliance' with its rules and agreements by reducing members' costs of intervening on behalf of the common good. A lateral control regime was described that spread the control costs among members, thus organizing collective responsibility. Partners had a strong interest in motivating their deviant or malfunctioning partners and in preventing damage to them because they depended on them for resources. Therefore, partners were interested in sanctioning that was likely to take place and that was likely to work. It is shown that it was more likely to take place if the cost of interaction was lowered by easy access to the infractor and by the existence of personal ties between sanctioner and infractor in social niches. In their choices of sanctioners, partners relied on various commonalities of interests and identities among protagonists of the control situation. It is also shown that it was likely to work if sanctioners tended to be more senior than infractors and if they were powerful in uncontroversial ways. This means that the costs of enforcement, a serious problem associated with collective provision of group solidarity in delicately calibrated institutions (Hechter 1987), which plague every collegium (Freidson 1975), were reduced for most partners and for the firm because they were shifted to members with a specific form of status.

A great deal of lateral control responsibility was informally concentrated in the hands of a few 'protectors of the common good', to whom the rest of the partnership often delegated this task. However, the kind of status that these sanctioners had suggests that they were also chosen so as to prevent the possible preferential treatment for some infractors that was induced by close relationships with them. In particular, in such an institutional context, these important sanctioners were less controversial and more likely to live up to this form of status: they could speak on behalf of the firm without triggering additional and escalating conflicts, or being suspected of representing specific coalitions, and without individually benefiting from exercising pressure on infractors. This lateral control regime could thus help members find an early solution to the so-called second-order free-rider problem in formally egalitarian interdependent groups—that is, the problem of who should bear the costs of enforcing previous agreements. Because it offered a specific organization of early enforcement of rules and decisions, it helped in ensuring that cooperation remained possible. It can be said to be a credible component of the governance structure in this type of firm.

Finally, this reconstitution of a pattern of lateral control using network analysis required field-related and methodological choices that define three clear limitations of the approach used in this chapter, both substantive and methodological. These limitations prevent quick generalization from this study.

First, it should be noted that the lateral control regime described here would not by itself prevent some partners from reaping free-loading gains. It was only one informal mechanism helping partners choose sanctioners to compel each other, at an early stage, to contribute the required efforts and resources before they decided to switch to more formal disciplinary mechanisms (committees, votes, and so on). I do not explore when exactly lateral control was needed (as opposed to more direct control) (Wittek, 1999). I deal only partially with the second-order free-rider problem, because I assume that partners had enough motivations and incentives (other partners' convergent expectations created a strong constraint based on resource dependencies; it was in their economic interest; in their social niche, they had enough investments in relational capital to protect) to let themselves be used as sanctioners. However, I did not, in addition to ethnographic evidence, have a chance to observe the conditions under which this pressure on partners to be sanctioners was actually efficient.

Secondly, the character of the management problem used as a tracer for the lateral control regime means that the logic of how this problem was handled in this firm may be specific to its socio-emotional, or expressive, character—as opposed to a more instrumental, task-oriented problem. As a result, the lateral control regime in this firm may not be completely investigated. For instance, partners could empathize with social emotional problems and perhaps mobilize personal ties for leverage purposes more easily than for more instrumental problems. One can hypothesize that, if they had to deal with such instrumental issues, partners would systematically choose sanctioners senior in advice giving so as to coach the infractor more closely. They could hesitate less, presumably, to cross over to the other side in a polarized system, in terms of boundaries such as office membership or the division of work. Moreover, when dealing with issues such as professional mistakes of the kind that Freidson (1975) calls 'inexcusable mistakes', the influence of certain dimensions of the formal structure on the choices of sanctioners and on the flow of lateral control could become significantly stronger: speciality could become even more salient, whereas office similarity and seniority superiority could lose some of their importance. Similarly, the control pattern building up around instrumental problems could have more controversial rainmakers at the top, who might interfere much more brutally with more politically charged strategies, such as speeding up formal peer-review processes. The elite of sanctioners might then play a different role—for instance, guaranteeing the fairness of a peer-review committee. Such hypotheses clearly need further investigation. The extent to which this lateral control regime covered different types of infractions remains to be assessed in studies using different tasks as analysers.

In the next chapter, I look at the ways in which oligarchic processes stabilized the rules of the games, just as they were contributing (see Chapter 6) to firm integration. Management of potential tensions between different norms and policies is shown to take place through politicization of exchanges in a way that is typical of collegial organizations—that is, in the negotiation of 'precarious values' by members with status. This helps combine a structural and institutional approach to collegial organizations. In this case, the mechanism is not derived from the work process itself, and reflects a relative autonomy of firm 'political processes'.

8

Multi-Status Oligarchs and the Negotiation of Precarious Values

This chapter shows that the form taken by status competition at SG&R stabilized its regulatory process and reinforced the *status quo*, particularly in the debates about compensation. Rules, and underlying norms and values, count for economic and political actors not simply through moral virtue but through negotiation of terms of exchanges. Renegotiating *precarious values* is the ultimate way for members to politicize their exchanges. Because they are strategic, they could—in a collegial context—be arguing endlessly about changes in the rules of the game. But members called *multi-status oligarchs*, with relatively loosely coupled—or 'inconsistent'—forms of status, are shown to control the regulatory process. The source of their influence is both control of resources and legitimacy. Since any such change means broken promises, they are in a better position than others to handle the effects of these changes among their peers. They can legitimize them by sacrificing resources of their own for the collective good,[1] thus reaching a position where they can ask for similar sacrifices from others as well. Taking this high road, however, may not be efficient in itself (the losing party may object that 'similar losses' are relative, and may not be equally bearable by all), which is why multi-status oligarchs are also in a position to force these changes by using their control of resource dependencies. Both legitimacy and power go hand in hand in the management of social change among peers.

As seen in previous chapters, several dimensions of status can be described in such a firm: one derived from professional reputation, but also that of members controlling access to important clients, and of those spending energy on administrative matters (often overlapping with the 'protector of the common good' status). Values of efficiency, loyalty, respect of members' autonomy, and defence of the common good could all be invoked ideally to guide collective action and exchanges at SG&R. In this chapter, the role played by members cumulating such heterogeneous and inconsistent forms of status is shown to be the key in the regulatory process as a social mechanism. Inconsistency, or at least loose-connectedness, of the multiple forms of status is functional. In effect, it allows oligarchs to lose resources along one dimension, while still maintaining prominence and concentration of resources along other dimensions. Correlations between forms of centrality in the firm, as well as the existence of a Montesquieu structure (identified in Chapter 6 as an integration device), showed that these loosely coupled forms of status were present in the firm (as in any small community or large society). Note that inconsistency does not mean incompatibility. It means that oligarchs are in an uneasy position involving role strain, another form of price to pay for those involved in status competition and seeking to be *primus inter pares*.

POLICY ISSUES AND UNDERLYING VALUE ORIENTATIONS

Looking at the redefinition of precarious values from a broadly conceived structural perspective is done by following several aspects of debates on firm management policies, and by exploring the structural constraints shaping these debates. As seen in Chapter 2, SG&R had formal rules written in its partnership agreement and informal rules that members learned when they were first assimilated as associates, then as partners. At some point, participation in collective action and regulatory activity reached a discussion of such rules and underlying values, often presented as a discussion about professionalism and firm culture.

As also mentioned before, negotiating precarious values was a sophisticated way for members to politicize their exchanges. For some, this meant trying to redefine the rules of the game in a way that favoured their own interests more directly. For example, it made sense for younger partners at SG&R to want to change the compensation system. Instead of waiting (for a whole generation) for their turn to reap the highest profits, they wanted to introduce more merit-based criteria in the annual sharing. However, to do this in a context of strong pressure towards consensus, they needed to promote the 'entrepreneurial' values that would legitimize such a change. In order to renegotiate their participation in collective action, members have to abide by the rules of regulatory deliberation. At this stage, a strategy based exclusively on threats of leaving, for example, could be costly and insufficient in itself.

Preoccupations with values in regulatory deliberations were obvious in the ideology of collegiality that permeated partners' discourse on the 'culture' and 'uniqueness stories' of their firm. Discussion about collegiality and the quality of the social atmosphere in which they practised was permanent among them. It was a basic form of social self-monitoring and self-critique (Walzer 1965). For example, Partner 19 discussed collegiality in mixing business and values:

> We don't like puffy people who put on a lot of airs. No business-getters who don't practise. Everyone does his own writing. Sometimes you'll even see Partner 1 in the library, doing his own research. We all have strong lawyerly skills, write very well, speak well, analyse problems well. It is an innovative and imaginative firm too. All the basic ingredients. Very ethical firm too. We fired two partners because of unethical behaviour. And it required unanimous consent. Trustworthiness and honesty are essential. Intelligence too. We have the reputation of a mixed group of people, with different religious backgrounds and lifestyles, as opposed for instance to Henderson & Robinson across the street, who are more homogeneously Yankee Protestants.

However, it was in debates about policy options that the negotiation of precarious values was the most visible. SG&R's explicit or implicit policy choices reflected its dominant sense of professionalism. Based on qualitative interviews, I first look at some of the main issues discussed by the members of SG&R about firm policy. Echoing Nelson (1988), who showed that policy choices do reflect values, especially that of the elite in power, I connect these debates to the structural features of the firm.

Seron (1992) contrasts several 'value orientations' within legal services. In the case that she studies—that of the 'new providers' such as legal services with prepaid plans—she suggests that delivering legal services revolves around three relatively different tasks and value orientations that do not all complement the traditional professional model. These tasks are those of the manager, the entrepreneur, and the professional. In their effort to find the most appropriate organizational arrangement for ensuring the completion of assignments, managers value supervision, accounting, efficiency, and predictability. Entrepreneurs value innovation, getting business, social skills, networking and politicking, risk taking, and political commitment. Professionals try to resist managerial standardization and entrepreneurial social skills becoming more important than legal expertise *per se*. In the context studied by Seron, they value control of the case, working in a small office, private lawyer–client relations, and working alone. In the context of a firm such as SG&R, the emphasis is lower on the 'working-alone' aspect. Seron also argues that managerial and professional values share an anti-risk-taking orientation; managerial and entrepreneurial values share an anti-substantive orientation; and professional and entrepreneurial values share an anti-hierarchical orientation. This synthetic approach is useful in the description of values described by members of this firm.

In the following pages I look at four such managerial policy issues as indicators of ongoing debates or discussions of values in the firm. Significant options existed among managerial policies, which could more or less reshape the nature of the practice. Four examples are considered: workflow, compensation, marketing, and peer review.

Workflow

As seen before, the organization of work in the firm was based on a two-step workflow: intake (mainly, who decides whether or not to take in a case, and based on what criteria) and assignment (mainly, who will do the work) procedures could be more or less formal and flexible. Flexibility, at least in the implementation of one of the two steps, seemed to be imperative, because the workflow depended on the nature of the practice, the source of work, and sometimes on the client's requirements. The extent of this flexibility was a matter of discussion at SG&R. Should management be flexible on both procedures? Be flexible on one procedure only and inflexible on the other—for instance, inflexible on intake but flexible on assignments? The procedures in place were flexible about both steps. A new matter had to be approved by a lawyer with managerial responsibilities, especially in the fields that were most crucial to firm's profits, but many said that this was not automatic. The way to staff a case was often negotiated by the initiator of the matter within the limits defined by specialization.

Some thought that real departments in the firm would impose more discipline on their lawyers at different stages of the workflow. This would help the firm in using its resources on work that was either even more interesting or even more profitable than other work that it got.

> People walk down the hall and they'd see a litigator and say, 'Hey I need some help.' It's not so easy to educate your partners, but it's getting better. Someone should be responsible for taking matters in, decide whether they are appropriate cases for us to handle—we want to upgrade our practice—whether we are going to get paid, and so on. It's hard to be disciplined about those things, but someone should be responsible to the rest of the partners to make this a more efficient and profitable good operation with good reputation.   (Partner 32)

The firm was also preoccupied with situations that were not technical conflicts of interest, but that were not desirable in business terms. There were various reasons to implement assignment policies, such as increasing the productivity of a firm by using people and human capital more efficiently, or ensuring fairness of the distribution of the workload.

> The firm should not take on a litigation matter unless the managing partner signs off on it. The managing partner should approve all new business that comes into the firm. You have to have someone with a global view of what's going on. Just because we don't have a conflict of interest does not mean it's something that is appropriate for us to handle. Someone has to be aware of it. Some of our clients could get upset. For example, a big case we know is going to happen. I said nobody should accept a case involving this issue because we want to see whether we get contacted by one, two, three, or four [sides] and we may want to make a decision based on that. But the way we resolve that is to have the rule that every case comes to the managing partner. That may happen some day. As you get bigger it's just hard to keep the information flow. But when I say I decide things, it's really kind of more consensus building and persuading, more than it is that I issue a decision and people walk off shaking their heads; that's not really the way it works. If somebody comes in and they have a client who wants to do work with them, we won't, as long as the work is in the individual's field, we generally won't step in the way. But you've got to have the buck stop somewhere, and I am one of the stops.   (The managing partner at the time of the study)

Many partners, on the other hand, favoured a 'free-for-all' approach (Maister 1993: 156). They said that workflow also depended upon where the work came from and upon historically developed patterns. Therefore, they argued, bureaucratic procedures should not be tightened:

> An awful lot of the firm's practice, at least on the business side, relates to ongoing clients with which we have had a relationship and for which we handle either all of their work or a particular kind of their work on an ongoing basis. I think, to a certain extent, that is less true of the litigation side, where there may be more of a one-time flavour to it. . . . Patterns tend to develop. The client expects that when he's got a tax problem it's going to go to that tax lawyer, and when he's got a real-estate problem it's going to go that real-estate lawyer. That client will very quickly develop a pattern of going directly to the person who has worked with him in the past. Some of our larger clients develop that

subsidiary set of workflow pattern. There should always remain a partner who is more involved with the direct hands-on client responsibility, who is ultimately responsible for the client, and if there were a problem with the work that was being done at any other level, that person would hear about it.... So it really just depends on the way the patterns have developed historically. If ATC partners were to become too heavy-handed in their interventions, I think you might have some clients rather upset about what they might view as arbitrary decisions being made on who their lawyers will be. We have to look at it from a firm perspective, of course, but we don't want to necessarily interfere with the natural patterns.   (Partner 26)

Thus, in spite of an overall trend towards more formally organized workflow, there was a great deal of variance in the way partners understood how intake should work and the amount of autonomy that members should have in the organization of their practice. Clearly, managerial value orientations competed here with market and professional value orientations.

Compensation

Compensation is a second example. In the organizational and broadly conceived structural approach advocated here, members' rationality is assumed to be guided first by the characteristics of the production process—that is, complex, non-routine, and knowledge-intensive work. Analytically, constraints imposed by this process shape subsequent decisions made by members about the terms of their production-related investments, exchanges or sharing rules. In particular, fairness judgements stressing equality or equity are contingent on the complexity of resource dependencies among members, itself a variable correlated to the type of work. At SG&R, complexity with work was combined with *procedural* simplicity in the distribution of rewards (equality among partners), a traditional solution that was being questioned by other models provided by the environment.

The distribution of income could follow many different patterns. There was discussion at SG&R on changing the criteria for distributing economic rewards. The growth of firms in previous decades (the 1970s and the 1980s) had worked to the advantage of most senior members. They had reaped profits from the efforts of the growing number of lawyers in the firm who were their juniors in terms of years and client responsibility. Many were strongly attached to the lockstep seniority system, in which their share of profits was slightly larger; it also avoided open confrontations about intangible worth and tricky performance measurements:

I believe that compensation criteria should not change. People should do what they have to do. Some adjustments to be made in individual cases where they don't carry their weight. I deal with it on a negative basis. There should be a penalty system for those not performing in one way or another, rather than a rewards inducement system which would fracture the framework.   (Partner 1)

Others took another stand:

On the compensation issue, I think that the criteria will change, but I wouldn't start out there. If it changes, I would not endorse a drastic change, a slight one yes. This is a congenial, laid-back place, too congenial. But we have new challenges. Old ways of doing business won't work in the 1990s. But changing a compensation system is not that easy. It is like privatization in Russia. Before you do that, you need also greater accessibility from partners on who are their clients, what they have done in the last year to retain their clients, what new clients are they looking for, what billing will they do on a monthly basis, and establish criteria for each partner to meet relative to firm administration, to billing, etc. Inside and outside, people should have different goals to meet and be accountable. Individual goals and more accountability to each other. Changing the compensation system means increasing accountability.   (Partner 4)

Some medium-seniority partners also favoured this system; they expected to benefit from it soon. Recall Partner 18, the main collector for that year ('Our system costs me money. With a different system, I would have made more money. But not enough more to make me go into a more competitive environment...'). Others wanted to adopt a more entrepreneurial approach, to go with the general trend towards compensation systems that weighed client responsibility more heavily. For the firm to keep its 'hotshots' and 'client-getters', or to attract partners laterally, they argued that the partnership agreement must move away from a purely seniority-based system to a system that also pegged partnership shares to revenue production.[2] There were pressures towards taking into account merit, client responsibility, and productivity. Younger partners especially pushed for taking into account both seniority and merit. Some wanted changes by taking merit into consideration in 'marginal' ways, such as modest discretionary bonuses awarded for outstanding work in a particular year; or the definition of an acceptable window of performance. This was recognized by the managing partner: 'Some younger people are unwilling to wait, and they can threaten to go somewhere else.' They wanted a special committee that rewarded a mixture of contributions such as seniority, productivity, generating business, and management responsibilities. Performance could be measured against previously defined objectives. Partners would be penalized if what they did last year did not correspond, within certain limits, to their individual targets. Voicing more directly younger partners' position, Partner 30 also said:

Seniority lockstep: a dinosaur system. There are law firms where you eat what you kill. Here we want to go less far. I inject myself a lot in policy issues. I have written memos to Partner 20 [the managing partner at the time of the study] about issues of partners' economic responsibilities, and means of inducing them. There is a great disparity among partners. Coercion has not been tried, but I think that's the only thing which would work. That's the real problem of collegiality to me.... Our managing partner should be more aggressive. We don't have incentives for partners' performance. Outstanding performances are grossly under-compensated. Partner 1 makes half as much as Jackson [the most senior partner at the firm across the street, SG&R's main competitor], but he is twice the lawyer Jackson is.

Many partners did not welcome the prospect of a finance committee allocating each year a percentage of firm's profits to each partner. They argued that, if the percentage were to be adjusted up or down from year to year depending on performance, merit would be evaluated in a way that was not very precisely known to the partners, and often challenged. Even in very sophisticated systems where compensation was tied to individual marketing targets and plans, purely mathematical formulas were rare, and committees had to rely on subjective judgements.

This debate had Rawlsian dimensions because members went to great lengths to construct a rationale for equalizing incomes that was independent of concerns about contribution and relative standing. This was done mainly through control of status competition and long-term equalization of contributions ('You're hot one year, you're down next year'). For a majority of lawyers interviewed in this firm, an equality-based compensation weighted by seniority protected a cooperative environment. Introducing merit and equity criteria or a bonus system meant creating incentives for grabbing clients or associates, compensation-bred competition among lawyers. Despite the fact that clients were unequivocally clients of the firm, practically speaking the partners knew that the major clients were used to dealing with certain people (their 'primary lawyers'). Clearly, managerial value orientations again conflicted with entrepreneurial and professional ones.

Marketing

Marketing issues are a third example. As seen above, built-in pressures to grow in size in medium-sized firms could become a threat by getting out of hand. To control this possibility firms could try to 'listen to the market', predict future needs, and plan systematically how, and to what extent, they wanted to grow (Maister 1993). However, several factors (the uncertainty in the economy, client behaviour, turnover) made this difficult. At the time of the study, SG&R partners were divided between two attitudes. On the one hand, there was resistance to the pressure to grow. Some did not want their firm to become larger. They believed that their size allowed them to staff the most complex litigation or corporate transaction in the region. The problem then became how to deal with associates when they felt that their chances to become partners were based on economic criteria instead of professional judgement applied to each individual's work. A brutal way of controlling growth could threaten the ways in which the lawyers cooperated within the firm. Other partners, subscribing to a more entrepreneurial approach to growth, wanted their firm to expand, but in a centralized and controlled way. They thought that leverage was not the key to success when growth is divorced from demand: there must be a certain client base to support a larger firm.

Partners with each value orientation nevertheless agreed on hiring as little as possible. Under such a policy, maintaining profits could mainly be done by moving more heavily into booming and lucrative specialities. Instead of hiring, the firm tried to steer associates and partners into more profitable areas of practice. But here again, members disagreed on the extent to which the firm should reshape the nature of the practice in terms of specialities. Those who pushed for a more systematic and centralized analysis of the market also pushed for subsequent adjustments that would require more flexibility from partners, more efforts on refocusing, new decisions about where to put one's priorities in terms of existing personnel and the hiring process. This meant identifying strengths, weaknesses, specific areas in which the firm wanted to grow, while acknowledging the effort and costs involved in switching to a more lucrative specialization. For instance, as seen in Chapter 2, some in the firm hesitated between dropping insurance defence work (based on contingency fees) and developing expertise in the areas of international law, environmental law, and bankruptcy law. This policy met with strong resistance. Partners opposed to such changes favoured traditional forms of marketing and argued that the firm was committed to remaining general practice and that it was in its long-term interest to provide individual freedom to choose one's area of practice, even in a context encouraging growth by specialization.

> Marketing is a chicken and egg question. Part of it is looking at your skills and seeing who out there could use your services. And the parallel way of doing it is looking for clients out there by reading the business newspapers, by being involved in the community and knowing what's out there. And then see if you can tailor your lawyers and your skills to meet their needs. You have to see that environmental law issues are increasingly important in corporate transactions, in real-estate transactions, and see whether your firm has people who are trained in that area so that then you can go and say, 'Hey folks have you ever thought of us as environmental lawyers.' You do that by sending out brochures, you can do that by getting one client let you run one seminar or that sort of thing. (Partner 6)

The issue of 'tailoring oneself' to new specialities could create serious conflicts in such a firm. Recall Former Partner No. 2 (see p. 204), who experienced a kind of pressure by the firm that was similar to the pressure that would be exercised on members of the firm who would be asked to switch specialities. In this case, though, the pressure was on a partner *not* to switch.

Each position required an emphasis on a different type of marketing. Officially, the firm thought about marketing in traditional terms. There was no formal requirement from individual lawyers to participate in centralized marketing, only a diffuse encouragement to get more involved in the community. There were no real financial incentives offered to individual lawyers to go out and get new clients. The philosophy was that a law firm makes itself different from other firms by the reputation of its individual lawyers or groups of lawyers in specific specialities. They differentiated themselves by being known as the best at something. At the time of fieldwork, like all the other firms, SG&R worked on generating an image of the firm as a young, dynamic, busy, high-visibility litigation firm.[3] However, partners did vary in the extent to which they wanted to systematize their marketing activities and reorganize themselves with that purpose in mind. Most lawyers' thoughts about marketing were informal and *ad hoc*, in terms of whether it was better to join clubs or to give lectures and seminars and count on the reputation of giving the best-quality service to the client.

> We do not have the same incentives to do that as other firms do because of the compensation system. But we have been trying to encourage people to do more marketing that includes lots of different things, I mean participate more in bar

association activities, put on seminars and other kinds of programmes. Take prospective clients out to lunch, play golf, all of those things. But apart from trying to keep our clients happy, by doing high-quality work, I personally have done almost none of it. (Partner 13)

We don't have to be out doing marketing, we don't do a lot of marketing, we don't do a good job at marketing ourselves, we don't wine and dine clients, we don't send them boxes of cigars. I know other law firms would buy seats for the Yankee Stadium and give them to the clients, we just haven't done that kind of stuff. I don't know whether that's good or bad, but we just haven't done it. (Partner 6)

Others pushed for the creation of a more centralized infrastructure to support individual lawyers' 'bottom-up' marketing activities (a marketing director whose job would be to help each professional develop a personal strategic plan, to get him or her placed on boards and on committees where the publicity value was considerable, and to plan ahead of time) and for 'more guidance offered by the firm' (Partner 29). Clearly, managerial and entrepreneurial value orientations conflicted here with traditional professional ones (for example autonomy).

Peer review

Finally, peer review is also an example of a policy issue that was on the discussion agenda, especially under the pressure from malpractice insurers, and certainly one of the most sensitive. Some feared that peer review might trigger dangerous personality attacks:

My partners are intelligent, straightforward, innovative and responsible. If they say that they'll do it, they'll do it. There is a similar mold to that extent. But the fabric that holds it together is delicate. Like an egg, it depends where the pressure comes from. The strain is the strain of the work. But I think what could break it are personality attacks. There is no mechanism for clearing the air for personality problems. People remember problems of years ago. It is not like a family. That's a threat. It can take a lot of pressure on job matters, not on personal things. That's visible in the fact that they don't bring up personal issues. They are too afraid to do that. Example: the quality of someone's work, things which would be taken personally. Very few compliments are given here. It is a lonely atmosphere. We rarely have partners telling other partners, 'Hey you did a good job.' It's traditional Yankee reluctance. Very few expressions of affection, but similarly very few expressions of dislike. Very little emotional connection, even with your mentor. As long as you are dealing with the usual conflicts linked to legal problems, there is a lot of stress and risk, but the firm holds best. It is very strong in a strict legal context. If someone sued the firm, the lawyers would band together like one person. But if one of us were to say: 'Mr X, you are not working hard enough,' then it would break the egg. (Partner 19)

Partners varied in the extent to which they thought that the firm should look more closely at partners' quantitative and qualitative contribution. Some thought that managerial and financial controls (standard computer outputs distributed at partnership meetings) constituted an ongoing and sufficiently tight peer review; they would focus the debate on what could be considered an acceptable window of quantitative performance. Methods for assessing partners' contributions were being discussed. Recall that the firm already had the possibility of preventing a partner from reaching the next level of compensation. This system was understood as a substitute for the absence of built-in incentives for productivity in the compensation system. Partners focusing the debate on this quantitative aspect of performance usually opposed formal peer review about the quality of partners' work:

> Judgement about the quality of work for other partners may happen through the procedure of identifying the appropriate staffing on matters which often involve more than one partner. So there are checks and balances that simply happen naturally because on anything that is sophisticated or complex it would be rare that there was only one person who was involved. Indirectly it is peer review. (Partner 13)

As seen in Chapter 4, many were sceptical about quality peer review. Some thought that formal peer review of quality went against respect for one's partners. Some were not so much afraid that their judgement would be called into question, as convinced that a broad and formal system of peer review would be too expensive and difficult to install (sometimes specialities were not even duplicated within the firm), excessively time consuming (people were very busy), and not very revealing (substantive difficulties inherent to ex-post reviews of a case and to defining the quality of service rendered). A formal peer review should be triggered only when a client complained. Problems stemmed more from a partner who was not working hard enough, or taking in undesirable business. As part of the cooperative spirit of the firm, informal discussions among partners were frequent anyway, which constituted an informal peer-review process by getting a second-opinion. Once formalized and separated from the ongoing practice, a second opinion procedure (reviewing an opinion letter before it goes out, for example) would become a perfunctory operation.

Other partners thought that, since there had never been a compensation process with an aura of peer review, a periodic review mechanism would allow the firm to assess each partner's performance against goals—for example, every five years—and to provide constructive advice. This would include a look at a sample of each partner's work product and billing figures, talks with people who worked with the person within the firm, and talks with clients. They focused the debate on the methodology: who should sit on a committee that would monitor the quality of partners' work more formally. Management also underplayed the threatening aspects of these reviews: they would be quite superficial and useful only as a way to tip the institution about partners who had personal problems. A partner in favour of more peer review described how the review committee should work:

> Nobody would be immune, we should be able to sit down with everyone and talk. We should have a committee of primarily senior but uniformly highly respected partners, because it's important that people think that this process is real and that it's not a lynch mob. It would gather comments about each of the partners, almost like an associate review, and then would sit down with the partner and talk about it. Hoping that it would be a dialogue, not a monologue and that the partner will be able to talk about things

that he or she is concerned about, where they hope their practice will be going in the future. If it turns out that there's a consensus that the person is being overpaid, the person shouldn't go to the next level of compensation.   (Partner 30)

Again, managerial value orientations conflicted here with professional ones.

POLARIZATION OF POLICY PREFERENCES AND STATUS QUO

According to the questions on management policies presented in the questionnaire (see Appendix A), the partnership was mixed with respect to the defence of values that should orient its practice. With regard to workflow, 44 per cent of the partners (sixteen out of thirty-six) thought that it should change: finders thought that it should be less controlled; minders that it should be more controlled. Fifty-six per cent favoured the more flexible status quo. To come back to Seron's classification of value orientations, the majority here was more entrepreneurial than managerial. With regard to compensation, 72 per cent of the partners favoured the status quo. This reflected more managerial than entrepreneurial values. With regard to organizing marketing at the individual level, 50 per cent of the partners thought that everyone should become more entrepreneurial. With regard to peer review, 64 per cent of the partners refused a more formal system; the others favoured more peer review, especially if the compensation criteria were not changed. Here the partnership remained more entrepreneurial. Figure 8.1 represents the polarization of the partnership in terms of policy preferences.

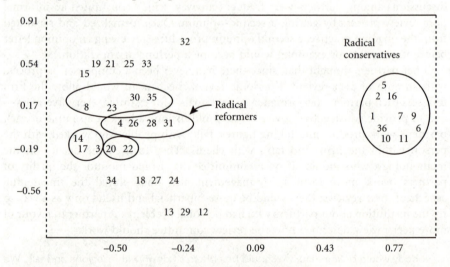

Figure 8.1. *Polarization of policy preferences among partners*

Note: Each number represents a partner. Partners close in this space have similar policy preferences. This figure comes out of multidimensional scaling of a one-mode table representing partners' similarities with regard to policy options. Subgroups displayed are identified by hierarchical cluster analysis.

Figure 8.1 clusters members based on shared positions with regard to changes in firm management policies. A first split distinguishes two groups of partners. Note mainly the distance separating the cluster of 'radical conservative' partners (defending the status quo) from that of combined and 'radical reformers' (pushing for a different partnership agreement) and other partners in favour of just 'tinkering' with the partnership agreement. The first group (including Partners 1, 2, 5, 6, 7, 9, 10, 11, 16, and 36) represents the defence of the status quo. Its members were mostly senior and conservative partners who did not want any change in firm policies. The other group represents partners who favoured a change with regard to at least one policy issue. Further splits in this second group display the existence of several subgroups representing different combinations of policy positions and values. It shows that there were four core subgroups favouring substantial changes: a first subgroup includes Partners 4, 26, 28, and 31, who supported changes in the four policy issues at hand; they could be called 'radical reformers'. The second subgroup included Partners 8, 23, 30, and 35: they supported changes in three policies, with an emphasis on policies underlain by entrepreneurial values (compensation, marketing, peer review). The third subgroup included Partners 20 and 22: they also supported changes in three policies, but with an emphasis on policies underlain by managerial values (workflow, marketing, peer review). A fourth subgroup included Partners 3, 14, and 17, who also supported changes in policies underlain by managerial values (workflow, marketing). Other subgroups were more inclined to support change along one policy issue only, usually for a policy underlain by managerial values; they were closer to conservatives than shown in the figure.

Each combination of policies/values made sense to its defenders. Senior partners such as Partners 1, 2, and 5 had no incentive to change a system that benefited them the most, in particular the lockstep seniority compensation system. A comment of Partner 1 was typical of this approach, 'Our compensation system is something that we want to preserve because it eliminates a lot of back-stabbing . . . '. These partners controlled access to many clients already and emphasizing individual marketing activities would not introduce a change for them. They did not wish to depend on inflexible intake and assignment procedures, or face the problems raised by more intrusive peer review, even as arbitrators. At the other end of the spectrum, Partners 4 and 26 championed changes in all firm policies. They represented more entrepreneurial values of mostly junior partners who wanted their firm to follow the trends followed by other firms in the USA. As mentioned above, younger partners in particular tended to be more in favour of strong change: they were not prepared to wait in an uncertain environment for their turn to reap the benefits of seniority. Note that Partner 4's support for radical changes did not go against his own immediate economic interests, but put him in an awkward position *vis-à-vis* his senior peers. His status provided younger partners with the legitimacy that they needed to propose changes in the rules of the game in a socially acceptable way. Slightly less pushy, but still in the avant-garde of change, was the managing partner, who advocated combinations of policies that tried to promote change more discretely, while still preventing the emergence of conflicts within the firm, mainly by opposing changes in the equality-based compensation system.

In between the extremes, more moderate combinations represented attempts to change the firm within the framework as it was. Partners 14 and 17 invoked changes in workflow and marketing that required more individual mobilization and discipline without providing good citizens with more incentives than they already had. Such medium-seniority partners were willing to wait for a few more years until their share of the pie would become the biggest. Few, however, carried with them the two orientations (managerial and entrepreneurial). Closer to conservatives, Partner 15 advocated a firm with a slightly more entrepreneurial touch; he considered that this would be enough to secure its long-term survival and growth. Even more prudent, Partner 13 was mainly concerned with changes in the enforcement of workflow policy. Note also that, apart from the subgroup of members who wanted to change the system entirely, partners tended not to think both that the compensation system should be changed and that the workflow should be put under more surveillance (more bureaucratized). Few were both more entrepreneurial and more managerial at the same time.

During the year of fieldwork, the partnership meetings discussed these changes but opted for the status quo: no changes at all were introduced in the basic agreement of the firm.[4] Figure 8.1 confirms the existence of different value systems, but it does not create a link between structure and the negotiation of such precarious values. In particular, it does not introduce status differences between interests and values. Members are grouped based on their choices, their common way of thinking, or common value system. But these discussions about professionalism could turn into endless theological debates without a structure that helped them establish a legitimate, though always questionable, set of policies. I turn to structural analysis to show that this normative order was supported by specific types of relationships. Even when participation in the regulatory process is formally equalized to mitigate status competition among partners, democracy is always a form of polycracy. Theories such as that of Waters tend to underestimate this structural and strategic dimension of the negotiation of values, in particular its relationship to status competition based on various forms of relational status, and to personalization of power (Bourricaud 1964).

To combine a normative and structural approach to the collegial negotiation of values, the interesting issue here is to look at what maintains the status quo in spite of the fact that, as shown in Figure 8.1, there was much pressure towards change. The argument above is that, in the uncertainty surrounding regulatory changes and their consequences, it was not enough to say that partners with status decided on matters of policy. I have argued that partners with *multiple and locally inconsistent (that is, not easily combined) forms of status* had the strongest influence on producing stability or change. The task now is therefore to identify these multi-status oligarchs and the kind of status inconsistency that made a difference in the policy decisions. To do this, it is important to look more closely at where the regulatory debates took place in this firm. I first examine the functioning of the partnership meeting, the firm's main decision-making and ratification body, especially at attention allocation in this central committee of the whole. Then, I look at relationships in which more informal discussions take place—that is, friendship ties. This approach will identify twenty-two partners who could be considered to be multi-status partners in this firm (out of thirty-six). When one looks more closely at their policy preferences, the balance against changes becomes sixteen against six, which reduced the weight of reformers considerably.

FORMAL AND INFORMAL REGULATORY DELIBERATIONS

Following the discussion of values in partnership meetings would have been ideal. But I did not have access to these meetings. Studying the transformation of individual preferences into a common political will, and its subsequent formalization into a rule—through negotiations, perhaps blackmail and bluffs, lateral pressures, bullying tactics, persuasion and argumentation styles—was beyond reach. Instead, I collected interview descriptions about the dynamics of these meetings, as well as sociometric data about attention allocation in them (who listened to whom, as indicated in Appendix A). I use these data to look into structural constraints on the negotiation of precarious values. These constraints came from relationships that were key to regulatory work, not directly task related in the sense adopted in Chapter 3. I can thus examine the ways in which debates tended to become restricted to the voices of firm oligarchs, mainly through this attention allocation to opinion leaders.

Centrality in each type of network provides a specific types of status. Together with partners already known to be prominent in the firm, an oligarchy of partners is identified that was informally vested with representation of precarious values, along with the resulting outcome of the negotiation—that is, oscillation leading to status quo in the definition of firm policies.

The partnership meeting

The partnership meeting was the collegial organ *par excellence*, the 'committee of the whole', exclusively composed of partners, and the formal arena for regulatory deliberation. The confidential character of its deliberations was part of partners' code of deontology. This forum had a communication and information function, but also a strong symbolic function. It stressed clearly the differences in hierarchical status between partners and associates (who were not allowed in the meetings). Its deliberations signalled whether the firm was integrated or not. Partnership meetings then also became places where values, norms, and attitudes were reasserted and consensus about them re-expressed (Etzioni 1961). Very often, the committee of the whole just ratified what had been decided elsewhere. Sometimes it decided by itself. It represented the institutional order that was based on equality and formal collegiality, on the one hand, and on equality and subordination (of associates among themselves), on the other. According to several partners, decisions in the past had been reached by consensus, and people would defer to a dissenting minority.

> From 1971 to the late 1970s, there was an emphasis on collegiality and cohesiveness to the point that I don't remember a decision made at the time which was not based on consensus. Dissent never happened, because dissenting people would withdraw, or the majority would defer to the minority. The foremost concern was not to disrupt the style and the cohesion. Not a single issue was permitted to interfere with that. The firm at the time had lots and lots of institutional clients, it was not under the kind of financial stress that began at the early 1980s, chasing clients, etc. There was an awful lot of socializing outside the firm, partners and associates alike, at the end of the 1960s and beginning of 1970s. At least once a month the entire firm went out together. . . . Now the bottom line is that formal votes are taken with more frequency. People don't defer any more to the wishes of minorities. People are far less willing to do it. Even back in the early days in terms of deference, there were people who were more important when they exposed a view on an issue. People who did not have their status did not challenge their views. At this stage, the lines between the important and less important partners are not as clearly drawn, so that contributes. You have thirty-six people whose basic interest is try to earn a livelihood and maximize their remuneration, which is, up to this point at least, based on seniority. The process can be said to be collegial, in the sense that confrontations, guided by a modicum of civility, can take place among people who know each other well. (Partner 11)

An important characteristic of debates in partnership meetings, one that also explains the influence of members with status, was the time pressure.

> Over time, you develop a political sense of how to be effective in a partnership meeting. You focus on consensus raising, you don't want to have a fractious debate. Takes too long. We would be there all night. (Partner 28)

Well attended meetings were thus perceived to be important monthly occasions, whether to review firm figures or to scrutinize the managing partner's ideas, even for routine matters, sometimes to decide what to say to help the associates tackle difficult and confusing issues. As already mentioned, information available to all partners sorted out the firm's data by most important criteria: speciality, client, billings, collecting, and so on. The extent to which this was also a truly deliberative assembly, not simply a monitoring and ratification body, was difficult to evaluate. Open confrontations could sometimes be avoided by creating subcommittees made of a cross-section of the firm and members representing all the sides. But partners acknowledged that debates were very rarely taken in such sub-committees, and that corridors were not crammed with plotting members. The managing partner, who controlled the agenda, was not backed by a whole team of administrative officials.

This committee of the whole was perceived to be efficient within the limited expectations that partners had. Speeches were rarely pure theatre. Partners said that they had little patience for high-blown vacuous set-piece contributions.

> At partnership meetings, you speak only when you have something to say. The group is tough if you are trumpeting the obvious. You may get laughed down and told to be

quiet. Lawyers like to make fun of other people, draw a little bit of blood. The discussion tends to be harsh. Say: 'With all due respect' and then make fun, as long as it is not direct personal attack. Never seen *ad hominem* happen in the partnership meeting. So, by and large, people who speak have given it a thought and have a point to make. This firm has only one prima donna type: Partner X. Not a team player at all. We try to accommodate him as best as we can. I got out of my way to ask for his advice and make him feel good about things. But you cannot absorb more than two or three like that. He stands up in partnership meetings and 'I would not tolerate this' and 'I would not tolerate that'. . . . Most people here have big egos, but they are not prima donna types, they don't take themselves too seriously. Bad feelings between people exist, but they are fairly limited. If you do have conflicts, they are likely to be solvable because most people are of that type, capable of taking criticism even if they don't like it. Partner 14 [a lateral partner who came in from another firm] says that we don't generally take ourselves quite seriously. We are not pompous lawyers who think of themselves as important, central in the clients' life, at the centre of the universe. Not here. You won't have large blow-ups over personalities alone. There is also a safety valve: if a partner feels very strongly about something to the point of becoming emotional, upset, generally people will defer, back down, and be sensitive. There are negative votes, and close votes. But there is an implicit rule: if you care enough to put yourself on the line, if you stand out after a vote and say, 'I am going to resign if . . .', the firm will accommodate you, as long as you don't do it too often, say, more than once every five years.   (Partner 19)

Politics were said to take place across office boundaries, and across age and speciality divides. Professional and economic status games were many: partners could find it offensive that their performance be judged by others as low, or inadequate. Fear of being penalized if you did not perform by others' standards was not strong, but fears of irritation, of resentment among one's colleagues, and of marginalization, still mattered according to the managing partner. Disagreement was not perceived as undermining his authority. People disengaged from struggles because it was unpleasant to be at odds with their partners.

At SG&R, claims to leadership by members of the oligarchy were subject to more complex constraints, and their relationship to precarious values did not seem to be as elusive as Nelson (1988) would suggest. In order to look at the connection between such claims and the negotiation of precarious values in this context, I elicited from partners an identification of their opinion leaders among their peers. I was allowed to ask each partner to whom he or she seriously listened in this body—that is, to whom he or she paid particular attention when discussing policy issues. In effect, as seen above, partners attending formal meetings were sometimes irritated by their lengthiness, and might or might not take very seriously some of their colleagues and their views. Power was personalized. Attention was focused and influence was structured. Among equals, there were some people whose views and expectations one tried to find out (especially what they expected from you); one often had to second-guess them. This elite of partners most 'listened to' (which, in the euphemistic vocabulary of these lawyers, means 'influential') in debates about policy issues and professionalism was thus ultimately expected to maintain a certain continuity in the management of the firm. This can be shown by looking at the structure of attention allocation in these meetings. One would expect that this form of status would be strongly correlated to other forms, and that a partner who—at least at the time of the discussion—kept many lawyers busy had more influence than others (was more listened to) in partnership meetings. Others would hesitate to challenge him or her.

All partners answered the same question about this topic (see Appendix A). Here is an example of an answer:

> I listen to what the most senior people have to say about that. The compensation is based on seniority, and doesn't involve any merit assessment. From time to time that issue is revisited. I view Partners 1 and 4 as two of the most significant producers of new, existing, and repeat business. They have been with the firm for so long, that they grew up with the firm, they understand its ethic.   (Partner 25)

These data help to combine this approach to firm discussion of precarious values with more structural dimensions of the firm. Partners with both status and active leadership claims can be identified by looking at the members cited most often as listened to (indegree centrality score of 20 or more) in these meetings. They were, in order, Partner 20 (the managing partner), Partner 4 (who was to become the next managing partner), Partner 1, Partner 26, and Partner 14, mostly from Office I.[5] Note that this form of popularity favoured identification of Office I partners as partners with leadership claims, since there had always been more partners in that office. Therefore special attention was paid to the position of the most central Office II partners in this structure, including Partner 14 and 5. These six partners, who can be called oligarchs, could also be considered among the most influential in regulatory debates, in the sense that they framed the issues that were discussed in the partnership meetings, and were listened to. As already seen above, these influential opinion leaders based their claim to leadership on different forms of status, and the way in which they emphasized various policy orientations and value systems was not random. As seen above, their voices carried and framed the negotiation of precarious values in identifiable ways. To simplify, Partners 1 and 5 defended the status quo. Partners 4 and 26 challenged the status quo based on more entrepreneurial values. The other oligarchs were looking for compromise by challenging the status quo based on more moderate managerial principles. The social mechanism by which the debate became restricted to the voices of firm oligarchs can be further explored by analysing in more detail this pattern of attention allocation.

Attention allocation in partnership meetings

Structural constraints that weighed on the debates at SG&R partnership meetings can be grasped by looking at the pattern of attention allocation in these meetings. This helps to get a better sense of what went on in the negotiation of precarious values. The density table presented in Appendix J shows that this dense network[6] can be represented with four positions of approximately structurally

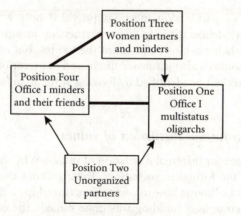

Figure 8.2. *Attention allocation in partnership meetings*

> *Note:* This figure represents the pattern of relationships between positions of approximately structurally equivalent partners in the 'listening-at-the-partnership-meeting' network. Thick lines represent mutual ties. For a detailed description of positions and their members, see Appendix J.

equivalent partners. Figure 8.2 visualizes the way in which the positions were related to one another.

This centralized and deceptively simple pattern shows the existence of an oligarchy of leaders in Position One carrying firm-wide values and representing different forms of status. This structure signals the high concentration of partners' attention on what these specific oligarchs had to say. Notice for example Position Two partners, an unorganized set of Office I and II members who listened to the oligarchy of minders, but unreciprocated. One particular feature of this pattern suggests that, in this partnership, discussion of values also took place informally in more personalized relationships, based on more exogenous identity criteria. Also central in this structure are Position Four minders and their friends. Note that this segmentation of the partnership no longer reflected the niche system, because specialities did not count that much, but overall seniority and office membership did, as well as gender. Women partners (two of whom minders), for example, made a separate position. Recall Figure 6.1 showing that strong ties cutting across speciality lines were friendship ties, understood as sources of role distance and a definition of the situation. Recall also p_2 models (Chapter 3), showing that more exogenous—that is, informal—identity criteria counted as a basis for selection of friends. This suggests that the close connection between influence and friendship had both inclusive and exclusive effects. This could mean that informal and more personalized discussions of precarious values also contributed to shape policy and explain, for example, Partner 17's presence in Position One, among the oligarchs. But it could also mean that women partners would have been part of Position Four if they had been listened to by Position One multistatus oligarchs—for example if they had had strong friendship ties with them (Ibarra 1992).

Formal debates in partnership meetings provided only a partial view of the process of regulatory deliberation. In effect, partnership meetings were a forum for members to assert their positions and count their votes. But other, more informal and personalized, contexts also witnessed discussion of precarious values and policy issues. Such contexts can be identified by looking at the friendship network among partners.

Friendship and informal discussion of values

Why was there a need for informal discussion of values? Why should this discussion take place outside the formal organization? Talking about the managing partner, Partner 19 said that he 'knows how to court the partnership ahead of time', meaning that much of the consensus building was done outside the official forum of the partnership meeting. A distance must be constructed to redefine individual interests and to evaluate day-to-day operations and firm policies. As emphasized by Bourricaud, there is a 'decentring' process in any form of democracy. In collegial contexts, friendship ties helped create, by definition, such a decentring.[7]

Recall the terms in which partners talked about friendship in Chapter 3. In task-oriented brainstorming and its characteristic status competition, role-distance ties had an important function: they helped mitigate the potentially negative effects of the use of hierarchical authority in a professional context, such as open confrontations. In that respect, they did not just represent chit-chat among members; they helped stabilize the deliberation by maintaining a social fabric, especially among senior advisers, that was vital even—perhaps especially—in a very pressuring firm. In this section, I argue that role-distance ties also helped members achieve this result by providing an informal forum to discuss regulatory changes and to fine-tune precarious values. This implies that members very central in the friendship network may also be considered members of the regulatory oligarchy.

This is not a digression about collegial 'altruism'. Recall the importance of unconditional friends as an insurance policy against expulsion from SG&R. In addition, friendship ties were consistent with the three aspects of collective action among peers discussed in Chapter 1. First, there was the fact that the labour contract, particularly the lockstep compensation system, worked best when partners had a long duration in mind, actually the perspective of a lifetime loyalty to the firm. Secondly, partners who succeeded in this forum were often partners who had the patience for building consensus, for discussing issues with one partner after another months in advance, working things out slowly, avoiding treading on toes unnecessarily, emphasizing what held people together and not what divided them.[8] This worked also because of physical and social proximity during non-working hours (such as athletic facilities). The reference group of members of this kind of firm was much more heavily composed of co-workers than was the case for a typical American worker (Frank 1985). Recall again Former Partner No. 2 saying that he felt socially isolated now that he was no longer a partner at SG&R. Thirdly, there was the personalization of power among peers.

For the purpose of policy-oriented deliberation about precarious values, only friendship ties among *partners* are of direct interest here. Associates at SG&R were almost never consulted about policy. Density was relatively high (0.21, compared with overall density in the friendship network (0.12); or with density in the friendship network among associates only (0.15)). The partners cited most often as friends by other partners (indegree centrality score of 15 times or more) were Partners 26, 17, 27, 9, and 4. All were also from Office I. Note the absence of Partners 13 and 24, who were very central in the friendship network for the whole firm because they were cited very often by associates. This, for example, adds credibility to the inclusion of Partner 17 into the small circle of opinion leaders ('a compromise man' who played an important role in connecting the blocks of partners represented in Figure 3.1, and so ensuring the generalized nature of exchanges).[9] Through informal ties, he brought together members with different forms of status and carrying different values.

In sum, in this firm, the 'listening' and the friendship ties affected the debate between value orientations. Figure 8.1 confirmed the existence of different value systems, but created only a minimal link between structure and the negotiation of such precarious values by showing that a majority of partners stood for some changes—while no changes occurred for five years after fieldwork. But it did not introduce status differences that could mediate between interests and values. Members were grouped based on their choices, their common way of thinking, or common value system. But these discussions about professionalism could become endless without a status structure that helped them establish a legitimate, though always questionable, set of policies.

Few members belonged to the multistatus oligarchy that was particularly involved and exposed in policy deliberations. They were Partners 1, 4, 5, 14, 17, 20, and 26. What characterized their social profile was that they all cumulated at least three forms of 'importance'. Partner 1 was a top money-maker, adviser, reliable co-worker, and multi-target lever. Partner 4 was a top money-maker, co-worker, and very central friend. Partner 5 was a top performer, multi-target lever, and an active minder. Partner 14 was a top co-worker, adviser and minder. Partners 17 and 26 were top co-workers, advisers, and friends. Partner 20 was the ultimate minder, multi-target lever, and adviser.[10] In the next section, I look at which specific forms of status existed among partners only and at how these multi-status oligarchs were successful at preserving the status quo in a situation where most partners did want at least some changes.

THE OLIGARCHS FRAMING DELIBERATION ON PRECARIOUS VALUES

The fact that regulatory deliberation is dominated by important members is not sufficient in itself to account for the social mechanism of negotiation of precarious values. In effect, issues of status consistency must be brought in.[11] As suggested by Frank (1985), the price of status is high when members interact intensively. In the context of SG&R, cumulating several forms of status was therefore even more difficult. Very specific correlations between measurements of importance were needed to build a status system that drove the negotiation of precarious values (since—as theorized above—multi-status members could muster extra-legitimacy by showing that they 'sacrificed' resources when siding with specific—and costly to some—policy options). Table 8.1 identifies three basic kinds of status in this firm. It looks at the correlations between all the dimensions of importance in this partnership, thus providing an additional view of the structural context in which the debate on precarious values took place.

Table 8.1 confirms that, overall, partners at this firm tended to be allocated across the three familiar different forms of status (which overlapped only exceptionally in the six members of the oligarchy identified above). First, members influential in policy discussions in partnership meetings tended also to be cited as important professional advisers and important protectors of the common good, and were considered by many to be friends. These were minders. Secondly, members—including young and entrepreneurial partners—considered important to others as strong co-workers in the production process tended also to be sought out often as professional advisers, but did not put in many billable hours. These were often rainmakers or finders who were in a position to distribute large amounts of work to others. Finally, there were solo operators who happened to bill and collect individually enormous amounts during that year, but tended to be prima donnas, especially not protectors of the common good (significant negative correlation). Part of this overall picture echoes the interdependence of elites and balance of powers *à la Montesquieu*. Policy remained a matter discussed by all, but seriously framed by officials in charge (minders) and by finders who were also rainmakers. This approach identifies a switch in the representation of constituencies based on exclusion of partners without multiple forms of status. In spite of the 'one-person-one-vote' rule and of constituency support, they did not have their ticket into the actual circle of influential decision-makers.

Table 8.1. *Correlations between dimensions of status among partners*

Indicators of status	Mean	SD	1	2	3	4	5	6
1. Fees collected	*	*						
2. Time input (hours)	1,380	328	0.51	—				
3. Centrality (influence)	3.26	1.12	0.15	−0.22	—			
4. Centrality (advice)	3.20	0.87	0.26	−0.16	0.58	—		
5. Centrality (friendship)	2.62	0.75	−0.09	−0.13	0.41	0.28	—	
6. Centrality (co-workers)	3.09	0.65	0.06	−0.00	0.16	0.58	0.17	—
7. Centrality (leverage)	22.40	16.70	0.15	−0.31	0.77	0.51	0.37	0.04

Notes: $N = 36$ partners. SD: standard deviation. Correlation table for measurements of partners' 'importance' in the firm as indicated by their respective centrality in firm social networks and by their economic performance. * means that the information may not be disclosed.

STATUS INCONSISTENCY AND STATUS QUO: STIFLED ENTREPRENEURIAL VALUES

Having identified these endogenous forms of status in the organization, it is possible to re-identify the oligarchs, their policy choices, and their effect on the deliberations. Once attention to status inconsistency is introduced in the identification of multi-status oligarchs, their circle can be enlarged as follows. Among the multi-status partners, some combined three different and inconsistent forms of status: Partners 1, 14, 15, 17, and 27 opposed important changes; Partners 4, 26, and 30 favoured them. Among bi-status partners, Partners 2, 5, 8, 9, 12, 13, 16, 20, 21, 22, and 24 opposed them, whereas Partners 28, 31, and 34 favoured them. Using this information, Table 8.2 presents a different view of the relationship between structure and culture as understood here—that is, forms of status and values underlying policy preferences in the firm. Each form of status is separately, then jointly, correlated to these preferences.

Minder, finder, and collector are each a form of status identified in Table 8.1. Minder status is measured by centrality in the advice, discussion about management policy issues, friendship, and lateral control networks. Finder status is measured by centrality in the strong co-workers' and advice networks. Collector status is measured as rank in two types of economic performance measurements: number of hours worked and amount of fees collected by each partner during the year of fieldwork. In Table 8.2 each status variable was derived from counting the number of consistent dimensions of status that were accumulated by each partner. This was done by ranking each partner along the compatible centrality scores. Regardless of issues of status consistency, a partner central in all these networks, plus hard working for lucrative clients, could accumulate seven forms of 'importance' in the firm (mean is 2.9, standard deviation is 1.8). Within each consistent form of status, cut-off points were chosen based on large drops in the values between two partners or based on reputation (that is, ethnographic knowledge of the way in which partners themselves perceived each other's prominence).

Table 8.2. *Correlations between having one or several forms of inconsistent dimensions of status and preferences with regard to changes in management policies*

Suggested policy change concerning:	Multi-status oligarchs	Minder status	Finder status	Collector status	1	2	3
1. Workflow	0.36	0.16	0.40	0.08	—		
2. Compensation	0.02	−0.22	0.21	0.02	0.07	—	
3. Marketing	0.13	0.11	0.06	0.06	0.11	0.37	—
4. Peer review	0.13	0.04	0.25	−0.07	0.38	0.57	0.40

Notes: N = 36 partners. In this table, multi-status oligarchs are partners accumulating two or three inconsistent forms of status, for example 'minder and finder', or 'minder and collector', or 'finder and collector'.

This look at the effect of the structural context on the debate on precarious values confirms that indeed policy remained a matter discussed by all, but seriously shaped by multi-status oligarchs identified above as influential in policy deliberations. They tended to accumulate forms of status that, overall, remained inconsistent in this firm. Members shaping the debate on precarious values were partners who bridged particularly the first and second categories of status. Note again that members with only the third type of status, that derived from bringing in much more than their share of the revenue (big individual collectors), were not much listened to. Hence the absence of Partner 18, the big collector who ranked third on the performance scale in terms of dollars brought in that year (and first the next year); he did not have high centrality scores in any of the firm's networks.

Looking jointly at Figure 8.1 and at Table 8.1, it becomes clear that the social mechanism by which the debate became restricted to the voices of these specific firm oligarchs had the expected effect on the firm's policies. It helped to maintain the status quo, not to promote change. Recall that Partners 1 and 5 defended the status quo, particularly with regard to compensation. Partners 4 and 26 challenged the status quo based on more entrepreneurial values. The other oligarchs were looking for compromise by challenging the status quo based on more moderate managerial principles. Thus the main voices in these discussions did not represent together the whole spectrum of forms of status. Exceptions such as Partner 1 belonged at the same time to all categories, and were very conservative. Partner 4 was lobbying for changes, but his status was more that of the first and third type. Partner 26 covered almost all three types, but he was not a multi-target lever, which meant not a confirmed minder; he was closer to Partner 4's profile than to Partner 1's. Thus managerial conservatism was backed by minders. Entrepreneurial values tended to be backed by finders.

This form of status inconsistency (for oligarchs)—already detected in Chapter 6 (finders in a RED set are not minders)—helped maintain the status quo. It meant an awkward position for multi-status oligarchs—another price to pay for status. But its main effect was to prevent challengers from becoming minders and minders from mustering alone enough legitimacy to challenge efficiently the rules of the game. Workflow, compensation, marketing, and peer-review policies were therefore challenged, but not strongly enough. The first remained flexible, the second remained committed to the lockstep system, the third remained a matter of individual goodwill, and the fourth remained entirely informal. The partners who were listened to in the deliberations were in the majority the partners who wanted the status quo, except Partners 4 and 26. Thanks to the latter, the values and policy options carried by younger partners had to be considered legitimate and put on the agenda, and the compensation system was obviously in danger. But, given the connection between the specific forms of status inconsistency found in this firm, chances of new values to win more legitimacy and be adopted as priorities for that year were low. Under this form of status consistency and structural arrangement, conservative minders win out. Five out of seven opinion leaders stood for small changes, if any. The sharing of profits arrangement—the most important rule of the game—was not dangerously questioned by the elite of that year.

Structural constraints on the discussion of precarious values are established. They derive their strength from the mechanism of maintenance of status heterogeneity described in Chapter 6. Most partners at SG&R did not feel left out of the decision-making process. But key partners emerged as important to regulatory deliberation. Members with two or three inconsistent forms of status had a stronger normative function; they were expected to define the terms under which exchanges took place, the 'rules of the game'. In particular, minders tended to defend equal distribution of income for all partners (weighted by seniority—that is, loyalty to the firm), strict rules with regard to the grey areas of multiple representation (political conflicts of interest), or the introduction of a more formal peer-review process. Finders tended to push for more merit-based compensation criteria and a more risk-taking attitude to multiple representation (for example, by seeking client waivers as often as possible), and to oppose a more formal peer-review process (as inevitably political).

Finally, it is useful to provide an example of how multi-status oligarchs 'sacrificed' resources for the common good. The only 'constituencies' that expressed clear preferences between these policies were senior and junior partners. As a constituency, senior partners favoured the status quo for three policies (workflow, compensation, and peer review; their client base being established already, they did not need to oppose individual marketing efforts that would not be carried out at their own expense). As a constituency, junior partners tended to favour the changes. No other characteristic of partners has such a systematic effect on policy choices as seniority does.[12]

Looking only at such constituencies as the end of the story misses an important point. Recall that in this firm partners' values did not entirely mirror their narrow economic interests. Some multi-status oligarchs who represented constituencies stood up for the values that promoted their immediate and personal advantage, but some did not. Partner 1 defended the status quo; according to many, he would certainly have fared better under a different compensation regime. Partner 4, who had approximately the same interests, defended entrepreneurial values. Partner 33 favoured a single managerial change (more individual work devoted to marketing) that would not have increased his revenue from what he received under the compensation regime as it was. Thus the logic of values was not entirely consistent with the logic of short-term economic interests.

THE STRUCTURAL BASIS OF NORMATIVE ORDER

To summarize, in this partnership, multi-status members, who cumulated several loosely coupled forms of status, were in a position to arbitrate in the negotiation of precarious values. It was only those oligarchs who were senior, productive, respected, and active in management (that is, with uneasily combined forms of status) who could hope to muster enough credibility (both resources and legitimacy) to impress their colleagues in the deliberation about new rules. Uni-status members (for example, a highly productive partner who championed one single value—say, 'merit' in the distribution of compensation) were not influential among their peers in debates about policy. Thus, the form taken by status competition at SG&R stabilized its regulatory process and tended to reinforce the status quo—to stifle entrepreneurial values, stressing more managerial and professional ones. The notions of precarious values, status inconsistency, and multi-status oligarchs are thus useful for combining legitimacy and resources dependencies in the explanation of organizational change (or lack thereof). They bring together institutional and broadly conceived structural approaches to the regulatory deliberations.

Thus, data analysis found evidence for specific structural constraints on negotiation of precarious values. It provides an exploratory analysis of the structural basis of normative orders. This procedural approach to the regulatory debate in this collegial organization explains how the rules of the game were maintained or changed. The debate on precarious values took place in a context that was structurally well defined, and among members who were allowed to personalize a form of status at the time of the deliberation. The structural mechanism kept in check the discussion of values among peers by allowing some, and not others, to participate in a credible way in the debate. This supports the idea that the relationships between interests, values, and policies are not direct and straightforward among peers. A social mechanism characterizing the regulatory deliberation introduces complex status games that weigh on their policy decisions. In particular, any organization authorizes certain forms of status heterogeneity that help maintain an ongoing debate about professionalism.[13]

Conclusion

The purpose of this book was to develop a broadly conceived structural approach that can account for collective action among peers confronted by complex, knowledge-intensive tasks, in both its formal and informal dimensions. I have attempted to show that this approach improves on previous understanding of this form of cooperation, the 'collegial phenomenon'. I did so by arguing that members organize their work as niche-building entrepreneurs valuing a form of work-related bounded solidarity, and as status competitors participating in regulatory activities. Such characteristics help expose three generic social mechanisms that allow collegial organizations to operate and to solve typical problems of collective action and collective responsibility among rival partners, or interdependent entrepreneurs. These mechanisms sometimes make use of particularistic ties for the benefit of such organizations' informal self-governance. They include a generalized exchange system, a lateral control regime, and a process of renegotiation of precarious values among multi-status oligarchs.

Beyond the issue of durable cooperation among peers, this approach is of interest to more general sociological theory because it shows that such mechanisms can be understood only when rational choice and strategic analysis are combined with structural analysis. It also gives a new purpose to studies of 'embeddedness' in economic sociology. A multilevel structural analysis, one that recognizes that the micro–macro link is above all a political and politicized issue, can thus be brought back into theories of solidarity, control, and regulation in the organizational society.

THE SCOPE OF THE COLLEGIAL FORM

The collegial form and its characteristic social mechanisms remain idealtypical. Generalization of mechanisms observed systematically in a law partnership remains hypothetical. Here, I have assumed that all collegial organizations will have the problems of production, exchange, control, and regulation described above. Whether different types of collegial organizations will have different types of solution to these problems is still a matter for verification.

Two variables suggest a path to follow for generalization. First, the nature of complex specialized knowledge, identified, for example, by the objectives of peers' common activity, or by the measurability of the product, can vary widely. Usually, the specialized knowledge of a task force of surgeons can be verified more quickly than that of a religious or even judiciary council. Therefore, forms of status competition should vary with the type of knowledge-intensive activity. Secondly, resources exchanged by peers during the production process, and with them the type of niche that is built and the type of status for which members compete, can vary too: for example, controlling access to clients may provide more status to lawyers than to medical doctors when there is less shortage of clients for the latter. Exchange and control mechanisms may also vary as a consequence. The nature of knowledge and the types of resources involved must have an important effect on the solutions found by these organizations to their common problems. In addition, the relationships between members of the oligarchy of firms can be much more volatile than that observed at SG&R. In these domains, much remains to be done.

One example of direction for future research is the enforcement of contracts and the protection of cooperative institutions through lateral control, and organizations' ability to induce their members to honour their obligations. First, given that this case study is unique, I am not in a position to generalize these exact results to other organizations based on the findings reported. Although the lateral control regime described here was consistent with specific formal characteristics of adhocracies, other similar organizations might not be able to help their members deal with the second-order free-rider problem by mobilizing sanctioners with enough incentives and/or legitimacy to reduce costs of control sufficiently. It remains to be seen whether or not this pattern has relevance for other types of collegial organizations. In professional business partnerships—for instance, in medicine, engineering, accounting, and universities—one could also find a reluctance to pull rank and use formal procedures, as well as similar incentives and similar 'protectors of the common good'. Other law firms with different partnership agreements have different and often harsher ways of sanctioning partners who do not comply with the norms. But one can hypothesize that, as long as such organizations can be characterized by formal equality and interdependence among professionals, such a lateral control regime will always emerge to help with early monitoring and sanctioning, thus performing a function essential to collective action.

Secondly, given that the lateral control described here takes into account key dimensions of formal structure, it remains to be seen to what extent such a pattern changes in more bureaucratized professional firms (Morrill 1995; Wallace 1995; Wittek 1999) as well as in pyramidal environments (that is, among non-professionals), especially in bureaucracies with reduced numbers of hierarchical levels, or in 'inner circles' (Useem 1986) examined at the level of groups of large firms. For instance, because power relations in collegial firms are often both denied and limited by the ideology of collegiality, more bureaucratized firms may not have to rely on lateral control as much as the firm examined here. In such firms, the lateral control pattern may allocate the costs of monitoring and sanctioning in a different way (for instance, to formal department heads, in which case it loses its 'lateral' dimension). Further research should determine under what conditions these findings on lateral control are relevant in other, especially larger and more bureaucratic organizations preoccupied with altering tall structures, increasing the professionalization of the workforce, and setting up autonomous, empowered, and knowledge-intensive work groups or teams

(Hodson *et al*. 1993). This dimension of collective action may be important for explaining success or failure of experiences in organizational democracy (Dahl 1985; Hechter 1987; Rothschild and Whitt 1986; Sainsaulieu *et al*. 1983; Swidler 1979).

Since they stem from more general collective action problems, the generic social mechanisms identified by a broadly conceived structural approach make sense even in knowledge-intensive organizations that do not benefit from the support of organized professions. As mentioned in the Introduction, the fact that this analysis was carried out on data collected in a relatively traditional corporate law firm does not mean, in my view, that such social mechanisms are waning. They may take different forms in local offices of global firms, but their existence is a necessary consequence of cooperation in knowledge-intensive work. Development of knowledge-intensive firms through multinational expansion does not invalidate the study of social mechanisms at the local level. Local establishments that are allowed to self-regulate must also witness such mechanisms, perhaps in different ways that remain to be researched, and that are imposed by the specific bureaucratic constraints of the global level. Rather, further work could use this structural approach to explain variations in these mechanisms, as well as provide answers to more practical questions, such as why professional services firms fall apart or what happens when they merge.

Finally, the issue of collegiality as an idealtype is not limited to a specifically collegial organizational form. In Waters's view, as in that of many others, 'pure' collegial organizations can develop only in the most limited conditions, where scale and functional complexity are relatively low. But sociologists such as Sciulli (1986) or Baylis (1989) argue that collegiality has come to represent a value capable of creating restraints on instrumental action and the arbitrary exercise of collective powers in society at large—that is, in all deliberative bodies typically comprised of heterogeneous actors and competing (that is, non-consensual) groups. Their reasoning opens up the collegial phenomenon not only to organizations other than professional ones, but also to cooperation among all kinds of interdependent entrepreneurs, such as individualistic craftsmen or subcontractors trying to coordinate their work and set up structures of collective responsibility for their economic survival. Collegiality serves both to deny an authority system and to limit its strength. This helps maintain high levels of commitment and cohesiveness in any potentially volatile organization where power has this quality of 'now you see it, now you don't'. Formal equality and collegiality come mainly from complexity of tasks to be performed and from the willingness to share risks. The more people are needed to crack a complex and non-standard problem in an economy of quality (White, forthcoming), the more collegial the organization becomes. Research focusing on the extent to which social mechanisms associated with collegial organizations (such as partnerships) can be extended to collegial pockets within large bureaucracies—especially those shortening and weakening hierarchical channels to do knowledge-intensive work—seems particularly promising. In the situation of decentralization of large organizations, and generalization of project forms of management, power also has a collegial component, and it is much stronger than is usually acknowledged. As soon as experts cooperate, some collegial mechanisms, sometimes based on particularistic ties, may be triggered.

This comparative perspective also raises the issue of the existence of the same social mechanisms in organizations where incentives are designed differently. In this book, the nature of the task to perform in common is considered a much more powerful determinant of the shape of social mechanisms than the criterion used to provide incentives to members. The complexity and knowledge-intensive nature of the task is the most important factor distinguishing collegial organizations from more bureaucratic ones. But are the mechanisms examined here limited to situations of equality, much less frequent than organizations where various forms of equity are the norm? There are reasons to doubt it. First, SG&R is not an egalitarian organization: an approximation of formal equality exists among partners only, with all the feelings of relative deprivation that come attached nevertheless, and that heavily influence interactions. Equality is mainly procedural. Secondly, equity criteria are not rigidly and directly coupled with specific types of interaction among actors (Kellerhals *et al.* 1988), and therefore with the form taken by generic social mechanisms. Distinguishing structures simply by equality or equity is too situational an approach, not structural and organizational enough. A longitudinal study of SG&R could have provided insights into this question. A rigorously conducted comparison between social mechanisms in organizations using different incentive schemes would be useful structural research on conceptions of justice and collective action.

In addition, it remains to be seen to what extent such mechanisms can exist only where risk of economic failure provides the energy to kick and sustain them—which is not the case, for example, in many public-sector organizations. When this threat is less obvious, interdependence may not be as strong, and the result may be a notorious indifference to collective or mutual accountability, and hence a switch towards more bureaucratized forms of collective action. This would entail a reassessment of the extent to which they are significantly influenced by their environment.

Parts of this approach thus require further thoughts and research into the collegial form, its generic mechanisms, and its variable scope at any time in history. Collecting evidence for such hypotheses in various types of organizations should prove to be a productive area of research. In addition, this approach shows that the collegial form raises social problems that challenge both the sociology of organizations and the sociology of the professions.

HOLDING ONE'S OWN IN THE COMPANY OF PEERS

This form of organization offers its members many ways to carve a place for themselves in the group. They compete for a great variety of forms of status, which is socially integrative—as long as they are focused on work. However, in spite of what more idealistic approaches to cooperation would assert (Desroche 1976; Meister

1972), it is at the same time a socially very constraining environment (Barker 1993). The social discipline and forms of collective responsibility underlying collective action among peers are important components of knowledge-intensive work and of flat organizations. But they are also very demanding. Particularistic ties matter for governance of organizations in a systematic way when a balance between niche seeking and status competition is maintained so as to help generic social mechanisms. Such a balance is difficult to achieve. Knowledge-intensive collective actors are not suited to kinder gentler coordination. They are generally organizations in which rival partners or interdependent entrepreneurs need to become even more strategic (in areas of their lives that were left outside the standard work relationships in more typical bureaucracies), and then find niches where strategic and opportunistic behaviour can be suspended.

The issues of multidimensionality of status and status competition, in particular, change the relationship between the individual and the group in collegial settings, when compared to more monocratic and bureaucratic ones. Status is not only based on seniority and money; it has a particularly strong dimension of prestige, of symbolic recognition of a member's contribution, and of ongoing critical judgements about members' quality. To define their place in the group, members need to invest in a form of status, cultivate status competition and learn how to mitigate it, and defend a conception of 'professionalism'. Whether or not they try to become a *primus inter pares* in some way (economic, managerial, professional), they always need to get involved in the complex task-oriented exchange system of the firm. This is a much more stressful form of organizational assimilation than in many bureaucratic organizations, one that requires adjustments to highly complex and personalized mechanisms for solidarity and control.

Partnerships or their functional equivalent bring together partners with great incentives to run their business well and invest in the group. It is less easy for such members to stay away from the risks of participation. Withdrawal from the group is less likely than in bureaucratic organizations, even if collegial and participationist utopias have their limits. The existence of social niches means that one must learn to personalize (embed) and depersonalize (disembed) work relationships and business transactions. This may amount to increased exploitation, as in the case of associates, if they can be dropped before reaping the return on such—often ambiguous and demanding—relational investments. It becomes increasingly difficult to externalize social costs in such organizations. Often, there are not many persons outside the organization (such as family or friends) ready to incur such costs when they reach a certain level. More research is thus needed on how actors can hold their own in such a context of intense personalization and depersonalization of work relationships for exchange, control, and regulation.

A broadly conceived structural approach assumes that members have to become political players in order to hold their own and defend their interests in such collegial organizations. Since professional practitioners in knowledge-intensive organizations are often formally equal, they have to allow each other to speak on behalf of the collective and recognize each other's regulatory interests. This implies that informal authority of members with status is based not only on control of all sorts of resources (important clients, workforce, day-to-day operations, technical competence, experience), but also on their capacity to manipulate relationships to create consensus, on their firm-specific strategic culture. By this I mean a political know-how allowing them to be players in a power game de-emphasizing unilateral impositions of strength and encouraging learning and mutual prescription in negotiations. This requires a capacity to share with others a certain code of collegial relations and an ideology of collegiality (Frischkopf 1973)—that is, a certain conception of professionalism. For example, the mix of an adversarial and pushy professional culture, on the one hand, and of personalized and unobtrusive lateral control, on the other hand, are not always easy to combine for partners in a corporate law firm. This also requires rhetorical manipulation of an ideology of collegiality in debates about professionalism, especially when members with market power try to pressure others for consensus around their own conception of professionalism.

Forwarding one's own interests while at the same time contributing to the protection of common resources, and to the maintenance of long-term institutional arrangements, is a difficult task. Seen from the outside of collegial organizations, strategies for handling potentially negative effects of status competition—such as preventing task forces from being too stable, relying on mitigating friendship ties, plotting peer-driven 'police' intervention on behalf of collective interests—may seem unrealistic or paradoxical. From within, they must be learned and shrewdly used. Similarly, understanding interdependencies is the key to establishing a partial order at the structural level through manipulations of relationships and subsequent social mechanisms. For example, niche members' 'bounded solidarity' picks up their structural equivalence and makes it indispensable for firm-level solidarity. Although niche-building/seeking members are entitled to participate in regulatory activity, to speak up in partnership meetings, and to claim their share of status, they also have to subscribe to priorities among many common goals, learn how to exchange in highly multiplex and personalized situations, and do all this in ways considered acceptable and legitimate by their peers. In other words, cooperating peers have to be willing and able to play politics—the complexity of which is only sketched in this book.

In sum, a combined neo-Weberian and structural approach clearly raises and disentangles key questions with regard to collective action among peers in modern societies. But one of the main questions raised by this approach is that of the willingness of individuals to invest so much in their professional lives. This points to the problem of a new relationship to work in a knowledge-intensive, organizational society characterized by 'flexible' labour markets and multilateral relationships between all sorts of 'stakeholders'. I argue that failure to take into account the social mechanisms that help rival peers design structural solutions to problems of collective action would mean failure of economic sociology to understand how an increasing number of individuals defend their interests in this organizational society.

THE ETHICAL PROBLEM OF CONFLICTS OF INTERESTS

Finally, the issue of polycracy and collegiality has serious regulatory implications too, ones that should also be of closer interest to the sociology of the professions and economic sociology. In other words, the social discipline and mechanisms at work here raise questions about the capacity of professions to respect their ethical commitments and to regulate themselves in the business world. In Waters's view, this organizational form helped professions in maintaining their closure and forms of monopoly. Because professions practise and struggle for jurisdiction and rights in a society that is much more organizational than usually acknowledged by the sociology of the professions (Abbott 1988; Perrow 1991), collegial self-governance and collective responsibility often conflict with professional rules of ethics on behalf of the profession's economic privileges. Ethical commitments are a key area on which a broadly conceived structural approach to collegial organizations, particularly professional services firms, can shed some light.[1] A specific example is the treatment of conflicts of interests.

In corporate law firms, and in professional and knowledge-intensive organizations in general, this issue reflects the limits of professional self-regulation in the business world. The problem of conflicts of interest is a classic ethical preoccupation for all the professions, especially for lawyers, whose adversarial business often involves choices between suing or not suing client A (one of their own clients), or one of client A's subsidiaries, on behalf of client B. In this situation, the lawyer risks being disloyal to one of the parties, and to favour the interests of the more lucrative one.

The profession has traditionally tried to deal with this problem by formulating codes of ethics that are meant to protect confidentiality and secrecy in the relationship between the professional and the client. However, pressure to disregard or change these codes comes from the growth of firms employing professionals and semi-professionals (law firms, hospitals, advertising agencies, financial institutions); from the fact that firms imposing collective responsibility and liability expand and take on an increasingly broad range of businesses; from the fact that clients spread their business around; from the changing characteristics of modern career paths and the mobility and flexibility of members; from the fact that many firms are multi-city; from the complexity of many financial transactions; and from the likelihood of cross-ownership, the acceptance of partial payment with stock, and cross-selling (Dezalay 1992). All this contributes to the intensification of this problem and increases the ethical difficulty of multiple representation.[2] As most of the lawyers I interviewed admitted, conflicts of interest were everywhere, large law firms ran into themselves all the time; but—to my knowledge—reliable figures are not available on this issue.

What kind of insight does a structural approach provide on such ethical issues? It is important to remember that conflicts are imputed throughout the firm (the legal entity being the firm, and, if a lawyer who is a partner in the firm is disqualified by the court for a conflict, the whole firm is disqualified). Large law firms deal with conflicts of interests arising with former and with current clients by using one of three organizational solutions. First, they can screen clients when opening a file, using computerized 'adversity checks'. Practically, before opening a file, a lawyer can check for conflicts by looking at whether other parties to the new matter are former clients. Secondly, they can raise formal 'Chinese walls' between members of the firm representing the conflicting clients. Thirdly, deliberation in ethics committees can lead to the self-disqualification of the firm—that is, to the giving-up of representation of one of the two parties to another firm. This may entail heavy sunk costs, especially when the conflicts are hard to uncover (Hazard 1987).

Given what we know about the ways in which work is taken in and allocated in such firms (see Chapters 2 and 6), it is unlikely that the first solution functions as a credible organizational device. Examination of the control of workflow showed that intake procedures were not respected by many rainmakers. Lawyers in general do not like to turn work away. Since responsibility is collective throughout the firm, a conscientious lawyer would have to conduct these checks for all former clients of every lawyer in the firm. One would have to do this usually before opening a file— that is, before the full scope of the new matter is known, often without really knowing the precise information to look for. When a firm has dozens (if not hundreds or thousands) of lawyers in three, five, ten offices, this becomes next to impossible. That more or less forces the firms to overlook many conflicts that they conveniently call 'theoretical'.

Another solution is to disclose the potential matter conflict, because clients are often willing to waive conflict issues in many areas of practice, or when there is a risk that the firm representing the other side has special and sensitive inside knowledge about these clients' company. One incentive for the client to waive the conflict is the knowledge that the firm guarantees to set up a Chinese wall (a 'safe-harbor' exclusion from the abstinence requirement for multi-service firms) between the lawyers who represent the potentially conflicting sides. For instance, when a lawyer leaves a firm for another firm, the firm's conflicts do not travel with him or her if he or she is screened from participation in the particular matter giving rise to the conflict within his or her new firm. Given what we know about social niches and the ways in which bounded solidarity is established in collegial organizations, it becomes difficult to believe in members' respect for these Chinese walls: for example, heavy reliance on others' advice, intellectual challenges, unbounded status auctions and reliance on partners outside the case for mitigation of status competition, use of cases for the training of associates. Porosity of internal boundaries is also an issue: for example, at SG&R, the ties that would cut across Chinese walls between specialities were the friendship ties, which are the least visible ones and the least subject to any form of control.

Finally, a third solution is to self-disqualify. But this means that one of two partners has to give up his or her client. As mentioned in Chapter 2, some of the biggest fights that people told me about in these firms were precisely about lawyers who had to give up a client to another lawyer, or just let the client go after it appeared that there might be a visible conflict that could not be handled.

Professional services firms such as corporate law firms are often furnished with thick carpets in luxurious buildings, creating a deceptively quiet atmosphere, an impression of 'being in control', where people try to avoid such open fights. Especially when compensation systems weigh merit, client responsibility, and productivity more heavily than other factors, status competition among partners within the same firm incites them to use the organization for their personal benefit more than for the interests of the collective, including its ethical reputation. Therefore there is an incentive to avoid discussing a potential conflict and disclosing it to the client, or to disclose it in such a way that it does not seem threatening.[3]

All these organizational features of collegial organizations strongly question, in my opinion, the efficiency of the 'solutions' offered by large firms to the problem of conflicts of interests. Being more ethical thus necessarily sets a limit to the growth of the firms. This is why, for example, large law firms have long tried to redefine and loosen the rules of ethics in such a way that appearance of conflict in the eye of the most cynical observer will not be enough to disqualify a lawyer. Medium-sized and large firms seem to accept a form of business competition that escapes the control of the profession, until they are able to redefine the ethical rules of the profession itself (Nelson 1988; Nelson *et al.* 1992).

Using conflicts of interests as an analyser, it becomes obvious that collegial organizations and their social discipline often contradict traditional ethical rules of the profession, ones that were thought—paradoxically—to find in collegiality a guarantee of professionalism. Such an issue belongs to the more general reflection on social control of organizational life (Reiss 1984, 1988), on the balance between external and self-regulation of all sorts of knowledge-intensive and professional services firms. When it reaches the level of a fully-fledged organizational form, collegial self-regulation, in many ways, conflicts with professional self-regulation. Such issues are raised by the study of the collegial form and deserve further research in economic sociology and the sociology of the professions, which have to adapt their approaches to the fact that professions practise and struggle for jurisdiction and rights in an organizational society.

In spite of the difficulties raised by durable cooperation among rival peers, knowledge of such mechanisms can help members of collegial settings, whether recognized professionals or not. Many social mechanisms are not beyond the control of interdependent entrepreneurs involved in unstandardized decision-making or production. This knowledge can help manage and lower the costs of many moments of workplace democracy that they can achieve. There should also be much to learn from extending this broadly conceived structural approach to any formally democratic system, action, and regulatory change. In my view, this kind of knowledge would generally contribute to more democracy and accountability in the organizational society.

Appendix A. *Fieldwork and Questionnaire*

This structural study is exploratory and inductive, although systematic; it is both qualitative and quantitative. It combines a qualitative approach such as that of Glaser and Strauss (1968) and Crozier (1963), and a more formalized approach using network analysis. Data collection was based on qualitative interviews with several open-ended questions, on sociometric questionnaires filled out in my presence, and on systematic documents provided by the administration of the firm (such as performance data for the year before and after fieldwork, or the partnership agreement). However, in spite of this relative openness compared to other law firms, access was limited. I did not see firm's files or attend a partnership meeting.

The data were collected between October 1989 and June 1991. Research was carried out in two stages. During the first stage, I interviewed forty lawyers with managerial responsibilities (managing partners, members of committees, heads of departments), administrators and business officers in six of the largest law firms (between 60 and 250 lawyers) in a north-eastern US state. Professor Geoffrey Hazard, at Yale Law School, helped by supporting the project and making the first phone call. A senior partner of one of the six firms, Spencer, Grace & Robbins, agreed to be interviewed, and then to introduce me to other partners in his firm. The managing partner of SG&R then introduced me to managing partners in other firms. The first stage of the project snowballed its way through. These interviews were about the formal structure of the firms and their respective organizational policies. This exploratory fieldwork provided a clear picture of how they dealt with the changes in the US market for legal services and in the US legal profession in the early 1990s. It also focused on their attempts to find new organizational forms better suited to this environment, mainly in order to control the partner–associate spirale and increase their flexibility for the development of new practice areas. In addition, I conducted interviews in New York firms for comparative purposes.

The research proposal sent out to these firms for the first stage stressed that the study was concerned with the management of law firms, that it focused on issues such as the structure of the firm, its policies concerning specialization, compensation, recruitment and admission to partnership, growth, division of labour, personal working styles, and relationships between colleagues (for instance, exchanges of expertise). It offered insights into the organization of the firm that could assist evaluation of future strategy. It presented the study as relying on in-depth interviews that would cover the areas mentioned above. It also mentioned further developments of this project, which could include collecting quantitative data and statistical analysis. Confidentiality was guaranteed by the fact that I was concerned with organizational and managerial issues, not with specific cases and substantive areas of law. It was agreed that participation in this project would not threaten any privileged relation with clients. Individual interviews with members of the firm would not be made available to other persons in the firm. The name of the firm, the names of its clients (if they happened to be mentioned), would be kept strictly confidential.

The second stage of fieldwork, the network study at SG&R, took place in January and February 1991, with tests conducted on name generators and the vignette a few months earlier. This was negotiated with the firm as a study of its level of collegiality. The firm provided an office and authorized me to contact all its attorneys to seek an appointment. The managing partner sent a memo to all the members of the firm, supporting the project. To take me in meant a strong political commitment from him. All agreed to be interviewed. It was also agreed upon that an interview would not last more than forty-five minutes. Many partners, however, opened their door for longer discussions. In addition to Geoffrey Hazard's support, advice from Kenneth Mann and Stanley Wheeler at Yale Law School, from Miguel Centeno and Albert Reiss at Yale Sociology, from Ursula Cassani at Cravath, Swaine & Moore, and from Bill Felstiner at the American Bar Foundation in Chicago, was also very helpful in handling this negotiation so as not to be considered a threat or a waste of time. Interviews with former partners and associates were also helpful in the interpretation of results.

A report on the informal mechanisms of firm integration was sent to the firm in April 1991. Later discussions with the managing partner showed that the firm was interested, at the time, in the fact that, in the firm as a whole, horizontal, vertical, and spatial differentiation impeded integration, while both strong and weak ties integrated the firm across formal boundaries created by this differentiation. Integration was secured differently, by different types of relationships, all compounded—at the time—under the name of 'collegial relationships', in different corners of the structure. Years later, as a former managing partner, he was interested enough in the idea of this book to discuss the findings and to provide more information that the firm was not prepared to share at the time of fieldwork, such as a copy of the partnership agreement and firm accounts measuring individual members' economic performance for the years of fieldwork. He read the drafts of the papers written based on this study and provided helpful criticism and suggestions, as well as confirmation of the validity of the results.

The questionnaire used for systematic data collection included sociometric name generators used to reconstitute co-workers, whole-picture, advice, friendship, and influence networks. All interviewees were presented with a list of all the members (attorneys) of their firm. Interviewees were asked to annotate the lists of names based on the following questions.

Co-workers' network: 'Because most firms like yours are also organized very informally, it is difficult to get a clear idea of how the members really work together. Think back over the past year, consider all the lawyers in your firm. Would you go through this list and check the names of those whom you have worked with. (By "worked with" I mean that you have spent time together on at least one case, that you have been assigned to the same case, that they read or used your work product or that you have read or used their work product; this includes professional work done within the firm like Bar association work, administration, etc.)'

Whole-picture network: 'Now look at your list of all the members that you just checked as a strong co-worker. When you work on a case, you have or make up your own picture of the case, think about how to handle it, and about what is going on in it. My question is the following: when you work on a case with each of these persons, do you usually feel that you share the whole picture of the case with him or her? If yes, why? If not, why not? (For each justification, make sure that the answer contains an indication about why sharing or not sharing is legitimate.)'

Basic advice network: 'Think back over the past year, consider all the lawyers in your firm. To whom did you go for basic professional advice? For instance, you want to make sure that you are handling a case right, making a proper decision, and you want to consult someone whose professional opinions are in general of great value to you. By advice I do not mean simply technical advice.'

Friendship network: 'Would you go through this list, and check the names of those you socialize with outside work. You know their family, they know yours, for instance. I do not mean all the people you are simply on a friendly level with, or people you happen to meet at firm functions.'

[For partners only] Influence (or 'listening') network: 'Would you go through this list of your partners, and check the names of those you consider as influential for important decisions made in the firm, on matters of firm policy; this could include partners you pay special attention to when they speak up at partnership meetings, for instance.'

[For partners only] Lateral control scenario: 'Here is the list of all the partners in the firm. I would like you to imagine that you are the managing partner. You notice that X is having personal problems. It could be anything, from alcohol to depression, or divorce. But it has repercussions on his or her performance. As a managing partner, it is your job to do something about it. You are looking for colleagues of his or hers among the other partners of the firm to intercede on a discreet and confidential basis, to go and talk to him or her, see what's going on, what the firm can do to help, and give unsolicited advice. You don't want to do this yourself because you want to keep it informal, and your position would be in the way. My question is: who are the persons among all the other partners whom you would ask to approach X, and why would you delegate this task to them? What if this person were Y, or Z, etc.?'

The questionnaire ended with a question on management policies: 'What is your position with regard to each of the four policy issues being discussed today in your firm: workflow, marketing, compensation, peer review? Should the firm change its policies?'

In-depth interviews on the firm, its history, and the meaning of collegiality were conducted with partners particularly interested in the project and quoted more often than others in the text.

Appendix B. *Density Tables for Figure 3.1 across the Co-Workers', Advice, and Friendship Networks of all the Lawyers in the Firm*

All density tables below were constructed with Structure 4.1 software (Burt 1991). For more details about this type of analysis, see Burt (1982, 1991). Such tables are themselves matrices, and could be analysed as such. The tradition, however, is to call them tables, because they are the final product of a procedure designed, in part, to represent a complex network (or several stacked networks) in a simplified way.

Table B1. *Density table for the co-workers' network in Figure 3.1*

Position	Position									
	One	Two	Three	Four	Five	Six	Seven	Eight	Nine	Residual
One	0.317	0.249	0.107	0.123	0.405	0.128	0.112	0.148	0.325	0.102
Two	0.259	0.517	0.175	0.277	0.125	0.382	0.020	0.353	0.086	0.306
Three	0.174	0.257	0.522	0.150	0.131	0.311	0.458	0.165	0.100	0.340
Four	0.246	0.389	0.178	0.293	0.113	0.146	0.140	0.161	0.129	0.213
Five	0.448	0.194	0.108	0.087	0.349	0.128	0.110	0.159	0.299	0.083
Six	0.161	0.447	0.253	0.194	0.110	0.704	0.075	0.305	0.100	0.315
Seven	0.226	0.164	0.489	0.095	0.275	0.184	0.741	0.085	0.215	0.241
Eight	0.169	0.558	0.126	0.072	0.151	0.281	0.041	0.120	0.082	0.323
Nine	0.423	0.156	0.123	0.070	0.457	0.104	0.154	0.146	0.275	0.098
Residual	0.210	0.405	0.349	0.108	0.113	0.216	0.142	0.263	0.132	0.223

Table B2. *Density table for the advice network in Figure 3.1*

Position	Position									
	One	Two	Three	Four	Five	Six	Seven	Eight	Nine	Residual
One	0.551	0.529	0.318	0.068	0.350	0.215	0.070	0.146	0.048	0.266
Two	0.433	0.623	0.359	0.136	0.215	0.339	0.061	0.176	0.040	0.348
Three	0.314	0.410	0.554	0.070	0.152	0.296	0.197	0.140	0.027	0.335
Four	0.406	0.560	0.480	0.281	0.164	0.256	0.162	0.109	0.033	0.273
Five	0.589	0.323	0.228	0.059	0.601	0.210	0.059	0.182	0.142	0.234
Six	0.245	0.501	0.371	0.123	0.193	0.654	0.106	0.290	0.030	0.404
Seven	0.318	0.187	0.505	0.021	0.378	0.212	0.563	0.073	0.106	0.254
Eight	0.344	0.502	0.309	0.186	0.268	0.481	0.063	0.198	0.076	0.305
Nine	0.453	0.210	0.162	0.031	0.531	0.096	0.159	0.255	0.438	0.135
Residual	0.357	0.491	0.448	0.132	0.241	0.474	0.164	0.237	0.037	0.269

Table B3. *Density table for the friendship network in Figure 3.1*

Position	Position									
	One	Two	Three	Four	Five	Six	Seven	Eight	Nine	Residual
One	0.610	0.551	0.243	0.015	0.516	0.156	0.104	0.225	0.069	0.202
Two	0.589	0.629	0.296	0.088	0.419	0.199	0.128	0.185	0.066	0.234
Three	0.277	0.312	0.456	0.020	0.189	0.229	0.426	0.125	0.090	0.193
Four	0.000	0.000	0.000	0.000	0.000	0.000	0.000	0.000	0.000	0.000
Five	0.449	0.261	0.112	0.005	0.629	0.294	0.226	0.444	0.268	0.203
Six	0.284	0.302	0.170	0.005	0.573	0.540	0.241	0.604	0.330	0.356
Seven	0.245	0.200	0.527	0.006	0.377	0.290	0.571	0.232	0.238	0.246
Eight	0.253	0.152	0.126	0.005	0.620	0.546	0.340	0.613	0.543	0.245
Nine	0.250	0.109	0.110	0.003	0.503	0.326	0.256	0.461	0.556	0.163
Residual	0.367	0.351	0.284	0.005	0.359	0.371	0.365	0.353	0.220	0.159

Table B1 shows the density table for the co-workers' network, where cell i, j is the average relation from someone occupying Position I to someone in Position J. The average relation between any two people in the network was 0.237. Representation of this table uses this value as a cut-off point.

Table B2 shows the density table for the advice network, where cell i, j is the average relation from someone occupying position I to someone in position J. The average relation between any two people in the network was 0.300. Representation of this table uses this value as a cut-off point.

Table B3 shows the density table for the friendship network, where cell i, j is the average relation from someone occupying Position I to someone in Position J. The average relation between any two people in the network was 0.289. Representation of this table uses this value as a cut-off point.

Appendix C. *Definition of Variables Presented in Table 3.3*

The similarity variables used in Table 3.3 are (in increasing refinement): *similarity in status*, taking value 1 if both actors in the dyad were partners or if they were both associates; *partner similarity*, 1 if they were both partners; *seniority 1 similarity*, 1 if they were both partners with seniority 1; *seniority 2 similarity*, 1 if they were both partners with seniority 2; *associate similarity*, 1 if they were both associates with the same level of seniority. The first constructed and most general asymmetric variable is *superiority*, which takes value 1 if the relation is directed from i to j and i has a lower level of seniority than j; it takes value -1 if the relation is directed from j to i and i has a lower level of seniority than j. A similar definition is given to partner superiority, where i and j both have to be partners, for associate superiority where i and j both have to be associates, and for 'partner–associate superiority', where i is associate and j is partner. It is important to realize that not all of these covariates can be used at the same time, because of dependency between them. For instance, when only status is used to distinguish formal positions of partners, then status similarity or partner similarity and superiority or 'partner–associate superiority' can be used for modelling the density parameter.

A forward selection procedure was used to reach the best model presented in Table 3.3. It carefully inspects all possible effects taken individually. After selecting the most significant explanatory variables for the four parameters, the model is estimated again with these variables. Variables that are no longer significant in the joint model are removed. For all models, the variance components and the 'general' density parameter μ and reciprocity parameter ρ are part of the model. In these networks, few sender or receiver or extra-reciprocity effects are significant; the variance parameters for sender effects and receiver effects, as well as the 'constant' term for extra reciprocity, do not change much in the empty and final models. For example, for the advice network, adding explanatory variables for the density parameter has reduced the 'constant' term for density, μ, thus accounting for a good part of the differences among attorneys in this network. The covariance between sender and receiver parameters shows a certain amount of negative correlation: the tendency to select advisers is negatively related to the tendency for being sought out as an adviser. For a detailed description of the model selection procedure, see Lazega and Van Duijn (1997).

Appendix D. *Professional Authority and the Distribution of the Authority to Know*

This is a detailed presentation of Figure 4.1. Table D1 constructed with Structure 4.1 (Burt 1991) shows the density table for the advice network, where cell i, j is the average relation from someone occupying Position I to someone in Position J. The average relation between any two people in the network was 0.302. Representation of this table uses this value as a cut-off point.

The positions defined based on the analysis of this single network are not the same as the positions defined based on the three networks stacked together in Figure 3.1 and Appendix B. Examining the paths followed by actors specifically to get access to a single resource, such as advice, helps identify additional, usually more subtle aspects of the structure of the firm. All Office I and Office III senior partners, including the managing partner and two more junior partners, of all specialities, occupied Position One (Partners 1, 2, 4, 8, 9, 10, 11, 12, 15, 16, 17, 20, 29, and 34). They exchanged advice among themselves and sought advice from partners from Positions Two, Three, and Six, mixing all specialities and offices, as well as from Office I associates of Positions Five and Eleven. Note that they did not directly seek out Office II litigation partners, or Office II litigation associates with little experience or seniority. However, their advice was sought out by the members of the positions they sought out (Two, Three, Five, Six, and Eleven), and also by members of Positions Four (Office II litigation partners) and Ten (atypical associates from all offices). This confirms an asymmetry between Office I and Office II partners within the same speciality. This asymmetry was probably caused by a status competition between the main litigators of these offices, by the critical mass—in terms of the number of litigators—reached by Office I, but also perhaps by what Office II attorneys felt to be a certain 'arrogance' of its members. This is suggested by their prominence scores (Burt 1991). More than half of the most prominent partners in the firm (in the advice

Table D1. *Density table for the advice network in Figure 4.1*

Position	Position											
	One	Two	Three	Four	Five	Six	Seven	Eight	Nine	Ten	Eleven	Residual
One	0.597	0.327	0.469	0.265	0.346	0.511	0.092	0.000	0.046	0.092	0.319	0.267
Two	0.447	0.436	0.571	0.466	0.238	0.317	0.067	0.000	0.134	0.162	0.272	0.285
Three	0.408	0.489	0.693	0.610	0.243	0.316	0.054	0.000	0.143	0.123	0.215	0.357
Four	0.415	0.320	0.628	0.658	0.252	0.479	0.098	0.000	0.167	0.067	0.169	0.431
Five	0.454	0.173	0.228	0.331	0.340	0.725	0.289	0.000	0.045	0.036	0.279	0.305
Six	0.493	0.210	0.256	0.301	0.545	0.711	0.185	0.000	0.065	0.040	0.270	0.283
Seven	0.298	0.163	0.169	0.259	0.465	0.649	0.425	0.000	0.119	0.029	0.204	0.312
Eight	0.201	0.104	0.158	0.152	0.409	0.478	0.633	0.674	0.087	0.165	0.262	0.213
Nine	0.165	0.247	0.452	0.778	0.313	0.340	0.272	0.000	0.674	0.040	0.051	0.348
Ten	0.520	0.420	0.484	0.361	0.294	0.408	0.080	0.000	0.100	0.089	0.292	0.330
Eleven	0.522	0.384	0.383	0.216	0.438	0.453	0.108	0.000	0.044	0.094	0.433	0.248
Residual	0.412	0.293	0.478	0.488	0.279	0.402	0.067	0.000	0.088	0.100	0.138	0.289

network) belonged to this position. Therefore I call it the 'hard core' of the firm. Its members were more often sought out and listened to than others.

Position Two clusters 'atypical' (non-lucrative speciality and lateral recruitment, for example) mainly corporate partners and associates from both offices (3, 7, 19, 25, 45, 46, 50, and 60). This does not mean that their advice was not sought out. On the contrary, they exchanged advice among themselves and sought out partners from Positions One, Three, Four, and Six, mixing specialities and offices. They did not seek out any associate in the firm, thus playing more status games than members of Position One. Their advice was sought out by partners from Positions One, Three, and Four, but not Six, as well as by atypical associates from both the largest offices (Positions Ten and Eleven). It is interesting to remember that lateral associates had to rely almost exclusively on their competence to become partner, and that they might consequently have a more instrumental attitude in exchanges of advice. They had less time than other associates to make themselves known by partners, and could take advantage of these exchanges to meet them more systematically. They were also members of both offices, and constituted an unexpected bridge between them. They almost never sought out associates from other positions, but were sought out by the latter (especially from Positions Ten and Eleven). Atypical partners and associates thus tended to exchange ideas more often with one another than with more typical colleagues. This particular circuit in the advice flows may explain why Position Two cut systematically across speciality and office boundaries. I call it the position of 'atypical' attorneys.

Position Three clustered exclusively Office II corporate partners (14, 28, 32, and 35), who exchanged advice among themselves and sought out partners from all the other positions (One, Two, Four, and Six), but almost never associates. This is perhaps due to the fact that there were few corporate associates in Office II, and that direct access to Office I corporate associates was a delicate matter, unless through Office I partners, which introduced a strong dependence. Their advice was sought out by partners from Positions One, Two, and Four (but not Position Six), as well as by associates from Positions Nine, Ten, and Eleven—that is, atypical associates from all offices and Office II litigation associates. Note that Office I corporate associates did not seek out these Office II partners of the same speciality. I call this position the position of the Office II corporate partners.

The fourth position was composed exclusively of Office II litigation partners (5, 18, 30, and 31), who exchanged advice among themselves and sought out partners from all the other positions (Position One, Two, Three, and Six) but again very rarely from associates. Their advice was sought out in return by the members of Positions Two, Three, and Six, but not One, the Office I 'hard-core' litigators. One finds here again the status and prestige competition, the critical mass and independence of Office I, the perception of arrogance described above. Office II litigation associates (Position Nine) sought them out as well as the Office I litigation associates of Position Five (who played a broker role between litigation partners and associates in the whole firm) and Position Ten. Associates from Positions Seven, Eight, and Eleven did not have direct access to these Position Four partners, from whom they were separated by status and office boundaries. I call this position that of Office II litigation partners.

The fifth position was exclusively composed of women litigators in Office I (27, 38, 39, and 43): the most senior woman partner in the firm and the three most senior women associates in the firm. They exchanged advice among themselves and sought advice from partners in Positions One, Four, and Six, mainly the most prominent partners in the advice network, Office I and Office II litigation partners. They were very close to the most prominent position in the network and focused exclusively on advice relationships with other litigators; they did not seek out other associates, corporate partners, or the atypical partners described above. They did, however, exchange ideas with Office II litigation partners (Position Four), which may have been a sign of independence or distance from Position One partners. Their advice was, however, sought out by members of six positions (One, Six, Seven, Eight, Nine, and Eleven). They centralized many requests and even Office I partners (corporate as well as litigation partners) asked for their advice, as did all the litigation associates in the firm. Notice that even Office II litigation associates (Position Nine) sought them out for advice, which could have allowed them not to bypass their own Office II litigation partners and take less risk with their reputation there (they did not have to go for advice to their own direct and local 'bosses'). This position was also clearly a bridge between prominent Position One partners and firm litigation associates who did not have access to them directly (for instance, Positions Seven and Eight). Finally, members of this Position Five had very few advice relationships with the atypical lawyers in the firm and with the corporate side of the firm. They were a pure product of Office I, its training and promotion system. I call this position that of the women litigation coordinators.

Position Six was made up of the partners most active in firm administrative committees (managing partners and deputy managing partners excepted), that of the minders, as well as two of the most senior male associates in the firm (13, 21, 24, 26, 40, and 41). All were litigators from Office I. They exchanged advice among themselves and sought out Position One partners and Position Five associates, thus confining themselves within their own office. All were among the most prominent lawyers in the firm, and their position was the most central in the whole pattern. Their advice was sought out by the members of all the other positions. They were the most 'universal' and reachable advisers in the firm: they were sought out by lawyers regardless of status, office, or speciality. Note that, although it was very much populated by Office I persons, this position was different from Position One precisely because of its high reachability and homogeneity (it was exclusively composed of litigators). I call this position that of the universal advisers.

Position Seven was exclusively made up of Office I medium-seniority (three or four years with the firm) male litigation associates whom other associates called 'the boys' (49, 52, 54, 55, 56, 57, 62, 65, and 68). They exchanged advice among themselves and sought out Position Five associates and Position Six partners, all litigators. Note that they did not have direct access to Position One partners, despite being also pure products of Office I. Thus, in terms of exchange of ideas and advice, they were relatively isolated from the rest of the firm. They were themselves sought out only by more junior associates (Position Eight). I call this position that of 'the boys'.

The most junior associates in the firm (66, 67, 69, and 71), recruited six months before the interviews, all Office I litigators, also had a Position of their own, Position Eight. They exchanged advice among themselves and sought out Position Five, Six, and Seven members, mostly more senior associates and the 'universal' advisers (who were partly in charge of associates). They did not dare to bother other partners and stuck to senior associates of their own office and speciality. Nobody sought them out in the advice network. This relative isolation was a classic charateristic of first-year associates in law firms. I call them the 'beginners'.

A ninth position was composed excusively of Office II litigation medium-seniority (three or four years with the firm) associates (51, 58, and 59). They exchanged advice among themselves and sought out litigation and corporate partners in Office II (Positions Three and Four), as well as the coordinators and universal advisers in Office I (Positions Five and Six). It is obvious that associates in Office II had more direct access to partners in their office than their peers in Office I did. This may have been due to the smaller size of Office II and to its specific relational climate. Like the majority of Office I associates, though, they could not have direct access to partners of the other office, and had to use intermediaries. Seeking them out directly would have been perceived as deliberate bypassing of (and lack of trust in) partners in their own office. Nobody sought out their advice. I call this position that of Office II litigation associates.

Position Ten was composed of relatively marginal associates in the firm (44, 47, 61, and 70)—that is, the corporate laterals or members of the small Office III (at the time of the fieldwork). They did not exchange advice among themselves and sought out directly partners from Positions One, Two, Three, Four, and Six, who did not reciprocate. Just like the members of Position Two, they contributed in blurring internal speciality and office boundaries. No one sought them out for advice. I call them the 'peripheral associates'.

Finally, Position Eleven was composed of Office I corporate associates (42, 48, 53, and 64), also relatively atypical in the firm (one lateral, one 'permanent associate', and so on). They exchanged advice among themselves and sought out members of Positions One, Two, Three, Five, and Six. The main difference between these associates and the others of similar profile (such as Position Ten associates, for instance) was that partners from Position One, one of the most prominent in the firm, sought out their advice. I call this position that of Office I 'atypical' corporate associates.

A 'residual' category included seven members (6, 22, 23, 33, 36, 37, and 63) whose relational profile in this advice network was very different from that of any other member in the firm.

Appendix E. *Presentation of Multirelational p* Models*

Models within the multivariate p^* class are probability models for multirelational networks (Pattison and Wasserman 1999; Wasserman and Pattison, forthcoming). In their most general form, p^* models express the probability of an overall multirelational network structure in terms of parameters associated with particular network substructures. *A substructure* is considered here as a specific hypothetical configuration of network ties linking a small set of network members—for instance, a pair of lawyers joined by mutual co-work ties or a trio of lawyers, two of whom were linked by mutual advice ties and a third linked by friendship to one of these two. The substructures appearing in the model are determined by the independence assumptions that one makes: specifically, the substructures are defined by sets of possible ties, each pair of which is assumed to be conditionally dependent, given the remaining ties. (The number of possible ties in a particular substructure is termed the *level* of the substructure.) Pattison and Wasserman (1999) have argued that the multivariate Markov assumption permits one to examine many of the forms of interdependence among ties that have been proposed in the network analysis literature. These forms are associated with notions of role set, exchange, path dependence, structural position, and actor effects. The multivariate Markov assumption specifies that two possible network ties are conditionally independent, given all remaining ties, unless the pair of possible ties has a lawyer in common. The consequence of this assumption is that multiplex ties and multiplex dyadic and triadic configurations are all potentially critical in modelling the overall network structure. In the case of a multirelational Markov assumption, the model for the network is expressed in relation to substructures of a multivariate triad, or of a multivariate *star* of order $n-1$ (for a network of n nodes; see Pattison and Wasserman, 1999). Analyses of the role of higher-order stars of order three or more (that is, of substructures comprising three or more ties directed to or from a member of the firm) are not reported here, since preliminary investigations suggested that higher-order stars play a much less substantial role than the multivariate triadic configurations on which this analysis focuses here.

In order to describe the exchange system of the firm, analyses based on the p^* class of models are presented in two stages. In the first stage, a reduced univariate Markov random graph model (Wasserman and Pattison 1996) is identified (see Table 3.4) for each of the three network relations (co-work, advice, friendship). These models analyse the network distribution of each kind of resource in the firm in terms of local dyadic and triadic characteristics. In the second stage, a multivariate p^* model (see Table 5.1) is derived for the three network relations simultaneously. This model is based on the multivariate Markov assumption and allows interdependencies among the three types of relations to be evaluated at the level of ties, dyads, and triads.

If a substructure has a large positive parameter in a p^* model, then the presence of the substructure enhances the likelihood of the overall network. All models presented here are homogeneous in the sense of assuming that a relational substructure of a given form (a pair of reciprocal friendship ties, or some particular triadic structure) has a constant effect on the likelihood of the overall network structure and is not dependent on attributes of the participating nodes. As a result, the models have a single parameter corresponding to each possible substructure.

Parameters are estimated in all cases using pseudolikelihood estimation (Pattison and Wasserman 1999; Strauss and Ikeda 1990). The approximate standard errors that accompany the pseudolikelihood estimates are given only for guidance as to likely order of magnitude; all comparisons among models are based on two indices of model fit—namely −2 times the log of the maximized pseudolikelihood, and the mean absolute residual for each possible network.

Appendix F. *A Montesquieu Structure: Spotting RED ('Ready-for-Easy-Defection') Subsets*

This is a density table for Figure 6.2 and a description of positions of approximately structurally equivalent members in the strong co-workers' network. Table F1 shows the density table for the co-workers' network: cell i, j is the average relation from someone occupying Position I to someone in Position J. The average relation between any two people in the network was 0.237. Representation of this table uses this value as a cut-off point. Figure 6.2 represents the best (i.e. 'cleanest') split into positions approximating structural equivalence between members in this network.

Position One included six partners and three associates, all Office II litigators. Average amounts collected per partner ranked second when compared to that of other positions (first being that of Position Ten), average indegree centrality was 16 and 15 for partners in the co-workers' and advice networks respectively (which was high for Office II members). Among them, Partners 5 and 18 were among the top performers in the firm, and Partner 32—who represented the ATC in Office II—among the most central partners in the co-workers' network. They worked together closely, forming a more or less permanent team. They also worked with Position Two members (same office, different speciality), with Position Eight (high status partners, same speciality, different office) and Position Nine (senior associates, same speciality, different office). Through Positions Eight and Nine, they could get access—when additional manpower was needed on large and urgent cases—to Position Three members, a pool of more junior litigation associates in the other office. Associates 51, 58, and 59 could be considered to be clients of Position One partners, especially 5 and 18. In this network, they also benefited from their proximity with Partner 32.

Table F1. *Density table for Figure 6.2*

Position	Position										
	One	Two	Three	Four	Five	Six	Seven	Eight	Nine	Ten	Residual
One	0.715	0.397	0.130	0.124	0.060	0.162	0.214	0.259	0.369	0.203	0.231
Two	0.368	0.647	0.057	0.380	0.131	0.071	0.392	0.187	0.108	0.304	0.340
Three	0.092	0.088	0.420	0.174	0.095	0.418	0.144	0.582	0.344	0.178	0.209
Four	0.081	0.234	0.154	0.639	0.418	0.116	0.325	0.281	0.182	0.556	0.228
Five	0.067	0.149	0.108	0.636	0.291	0.089	0.184	0.279	0.199	0.374	0.217
Six	0.131	0.086	0.368	0.210	0.128	0.313	0.149	0.460	0.456	0.277	0.233
Seven	0.133	0.286	0.127	0.583	0.164	0.129	0.643	0.126	0.100	0.526	0.157
Eight	0.176	0.093	0.471	0.276	0.140	0.315	0.134	0.232	0.492	0.253	0.179
Nine	0.235	0.052	0.285	0.214	0.138	0.406	0.108	0.522	0.122	0.183	0.231
Ten	0.100	0.147	0.136	0.477	0.224	0.183	0.563	0.331	0.041	0.204	0.256
Residual	0.232	0.229	0.113	0.210	0.161	0.099	0.116	0.338	0.231	0.231	0.278

Position Two included five partners and two associates, all Office II corporate lawyers, among which were Partner 14, a top performer, and Partner 28, a very central partner in the network. Average amounts collected per partner ranked fourth when compared to that of other positions; average indegree centrality was 16 and 14 for partners in the co-workers' and advice networks respectively (which was high for Office II members). Members worked together, as well as with Position One litigators (same office, different speciality), with Positions Four and Ten (high-status partners, same speciality, different office), and with Position Seven (a set of highly competent lateral associates, same speciality, different office). Through Position Four and Seven, Position Two could get access—when needed—to the Position Five pool of more junior corporate associates in the other office. Associates 50 and 63 could be considered to be clients of this position partners, especially 14 and 28.

Position Three included one partner (Partner 21, a top performer) and eight associates, all Office I litigators. This was a less cohesive position, in which members worked with one another less than members of the previous positions. They constituted a pool of manpower working mainly for Positions Six and Eight—i.e. Office I litigation partners and their Position Nine brokers (senior associates in the same office). Position Three members show that the patronage system was a two-tiered system; they were clients of clients who did not (yet) belong to close-knit stable teams.

Position Four included six Office I corporate partners, among which Partners 12, 17, and 19 were top performers, and Partners 16, 17, 19, 29, and 34 were highly central. Average amounts collected per partner ranked third when compared to that of other positions; average indegree centrality was 24 and 20 in the co-workers' and advice networks respectively. They distributed work to Position Five associates (same office, same speciality), and to their senior and lateral associates of Position Seven (same office, same speciality). They worked with Position Eight partners (same office, different speciality) and with Position Ten partners (same office, same speciality). This position was highly cohesive and concentrated much power, but did not seem to have its own clientele. Positions Five's and Position Seven's associates were shared with other partners, especially from Positions Eight and Ten. They did not consider Position Two members (same speciality, different office) as strong co-workers: there were more people in Office I, and thus more different specialities represented, and they did not feel that they needed to strengthen the Office II corporate group.

Position Five included mainly corporate associates in Office I and Office III, mixed with associates working mainly with Office I Positions Four and Ten (same office, same speciality partners) and with Position Eight (same office, different speciality partners). Partner 2, a top performer, was also a member of this position. This was mainly another manpower pool in which it was difficult to distinguish close clientelistic ties with specific partners. In particular, senior corporate associates of Position Seven, mostly laterals, did not operate as brokers between these associates and the partners; in addition, just as Position Three associates, they did not work much for Office II corporate partners.

Position Six included closely tied Office I litigation partners (among which were Partner 1, a top performer and the lawyer with most prestige in the firm, two other partners working with him, and Associate 52, a very central broker between Partner 1 or Partner 23 and other associates)—another stable team in the firm. Average amounts collected per partner ranked fifth when compared to that of other positions; average indegree centrality was 12 and 16 in the co-workers' and advice networks respectively. Partners in this position controlled large clients and provided their own associates, as well as Position Eight partners and Position Three associates, with work. They used Position Nine senior associates to collaborate with corporate partners in their own office (Position Ten), but not with Position Four. This stable team subcontracted a lot of work, but not to Office II litigators, with whom they did not feel much solidarity.

Position Seven included senior corporate associates in the firm, almost all laterals, among whom was Associate 45, one of the most central attorneys in the firm. They were not part of a stable team, nor did they seem to be clients of specific partners. They were more senior than most Position Five associates, and had a specific structural position in that they worked with/ for the three positions of corporate partners in the firm (Positions Two, Four, and Ten), without exception: they were hired based on their indispensable specialities. Because they had not 'grown up' in the firm, they seemed to have more autonomy in their choices of colla-borators, depending less on one or two specific patrons. Their relationship with the other lawyers in the firm was more impersonal and functional.

Position Eight included Office I partners, mainly litigators, who had in common that they were closer to most associates in the firm, because they belonged to the associate committee on the litigation side (one of their duties being to match associates, partners, and new files). They included two top performers, Partners 13 and 26, and four among the most central lawyers in the firm, Partners 13, 22, 24, and 26. Average amounts collected per partner ranked sixth (i.e. last) when compared to that of other partner positions; average indegree centrality was 24 and 26 in the co-workers' and advice networks respectively. They worked with many positions, although more with litigators in Office I, Positions Three and Six (same speciality, same office), and corporate lawyers in Office I (Positions Four and Ten) than with those in Office II, and they used Position Nine's senior associates. They were recognized as repre-sentatives of the good citizens in the firm, in charge of the welfare system for associates, and did not seem to groom their own clients.

Position Nine members included senior litigation associates in Office I. As with Position Seven's senior corporate associates, they worked very little together. But they were very central intermediaries between partners and more junior associates in this network. One of them, Associate 38, reached one of the highest scores in that respect. They redistributed work mainly among Position Three associates, worked directly with Positions Six and Eight partners, and controlled a considerable part of partners' access to manpower, particularly in Office II, where they depended less on partners for their promotion to partnership than in their own office (Office I), where partners were twice as many. They therefore had to maintain a fragile balance between several 'constituencies' (with regard to the forthcoming partnership vote).

The last position, Position Ten, included three senior corporate partners in Office I, among whom was Partner 4, both a top performer and one of the highest centrality scores in this network. Average amounts collected per partner ranked first when compared to that of other positions of partners; average indegree centrality was 20 and 11 in the co-workers' and advice networks respectively. They did not work together, but collaborated with members of Posi-tions Two, Four, Five, Seven, and Eight. Contributing to their position as a powerhouse within the firm, and to the explanation of why they had a position of their own, was the fact that they also represented a structural bridge between corporate and litigation lawyers.

A 'residual' category included seven partners, including the managing partner of the firm, and one associate. Three of the partners, Partners 7, 8, and 15, were among the top perfor-mers, and two, Partners 15 and 30, were among the highest centrality scores. Some worked mostly alone, whereas others were highly active in the work distribution process.

Appendix G. *Overall Distribution of the Significant*
Effects on Each Respondent's Choices of Levers
Analysed Separately in Chapter 7

Partners	Effects																												
	1	2	3	4	5	6	7	8	9	10	11	12	13	14	15	16	17	18	19	20	21	22	23	24	25	26	27	28	29
1	0	0	0	0	0	0	0	0	0	0	0	0	0	0	0	0	0	0	1	1	0	0	0	0	0	0	0	0	0
2	1	0	1	0	0	0	0	1	0	1	0	0	0	1	0	0	0	1	0	0	0	0	0	0	0	0	0	1	0
3	1	0	0	0	0	0	1	0	0	0	0	0	0	0	0	0	0	0	0	0	0	0	0	0	0	0	0	0	0
4	1	0	1	0	0	0	0	0	0	0	0	0	0	0	0	0	1	0	0	0	0	0	0	1	0	0	0	0	0
5	0	1	0	1	0	0	0	0	1	0	0	0	0	0	0	1	0	0	0	0	0	0	0	0	0	0	0	0	0
6	1	0	0	0	0	0	1	1	0	0	0	0	0	0	0	0	0	0	0	0	0	0	0	0	0	0	0	0	0
7	1	0	1	0	0	0	1	0	0	0	0	0	0	0	0	0	1	0	0	1	0	0	0	0	1	0	0	0	0
8	1	0	1	0	0	0	1	0	1	0	0	0	0	0	0	0	0	0	0	0	0	0	0	0	0	0	0	1	0
9	0	0	1	0	0	0	0	0	0	0	0	0	0	0	0	0	1	0	0	0	0	0	0	0	0	0	0	1	0
10	1	0	1	0	0	0	0	0	1	1	0	0	0	0	0	0	1	0	0	0	0	0	0	1	0	0	0	0	0
11	0	0	0	0	0	1	1	0	0	0	0	0	0	0	0	0	0	0	0	0	0	0	0	0	1	0	0	0	0
12	1	1	1	0	0	0	0	0	1	0	0	0	0	0	0	1	1	0	0	0	0	0	0	0	0	0	0	1	0
13	1	0	1	0	0	0	0	0	0	0	0	0	0	0	0	1	1	0	0	0	0	0	0	0	0	1	0	0	0
14	1	1	0	0	0	0	0	0	0	0	0	0	0	0	0	1	0	0	0	0	0	0	0	0	0	0	0	0	0
15	1	1	1	0	0	0	0	0	0	0	0	0	1	0	0	1	0	0	1	0	0	0	0	0	0	0	0	0	0
16	1	0	1	0	0	0	0	0	0	0	0	0	0	0	0	1	1	0	0	0	0	0	0	0	0	0	0	1	0
17	1	0	1	0	0	1	0	0	0	0	0	0	0	0	0	1	0	0	0	0	0	0	0	0	0	0	0	1	0
18	1	0	1	0	0	0	0	0	0	0	0	0	0	0	0	1	0	0	0	0	0	0	0	0	0	0	0	0	0
19	1	0	1	0	0	0	0	0	0	0	0	0	0	0	0	1	0	0	0	0	0	0	0	0	0	0	0	1	0
20	1	1	1	0	0	0	1	0	0	0	0	0	0	0	0	1	1	0	0	0	0	0	0	0	0	0	0	0	0
21	0	0	0	0	0	0	0	0	0	0	1	0	0	0	0	0	1	0	0	0	0	0	0	0	1	0	0	0	0
22	1	1	0	0	0	0	1	0	0	0	0	0	0	0	0	0	0	0	0	0	0	0	0	0	0	0	0	0	0
23	0	0	1	0	0	0	0	0	1	0	0	0	0	0	0	0	0	0	0	0	0	0	0	0	0	0	1	0	0
24	1	0	1	0	0	0	0	0	0	0	0	0	0	0	0	1	1	0	1	1	0	0	0	0	0	0	0	0	0
25	1	1	0	0	0	1	0	0	0	0	0	0	0	0	0	1	0	0	0	0	0	0	0	0	0	0	0	1	0
26	1	0	1	0	0	0	0	0	0	0	0	0	0	0	0	0	1	0	0	0	1	0	0	0	0	0	0	0	0
27	1	1	0	0	0	0	0	0	0	0	0	0	0	0	0	1	1	0	1	0	1	0	0	0	0	0	0	0	0
28	1	1	0	0	0	0	0	0	0	0	0	0	1	0	0	1	0	0	0	0	0	0	0	0	0	0	0	1	0
29	1	1	1	0	0	0	1	0	1	0	0	0	0	0	0	0	1	0	0	0	0	0	0	0	0	0	0	0	0
30	1	0	1	0	0	0	0	0	0	0	0	0	1	0	0	0	1	0	0	0	0	0	0	0	0	0	0	0	0
31	1	0	1	0	0	0	0	0	1	0	0	0	1	0	0	0	1	0	0	0	0	0	0	0	0	0	0	0	0
32	0	0	0	0	0	0	0	0	0	0	0	0	0	0	0	0	0	0	0	0	0	0	0	0	0	0	0	0	0
33	1	0	0	0	0	0	1	0	0	0	1	0	0	0	1	1	0	0	0	0	0	0	0	0	0	0	0	0	0
34	1	1	1	0	0	0	0	0	0	0	0	0	1	0	0	1	1	0	0	1	0	0	0	0	1	0	1	0	0
35	1	1	0	0	0	0	0	0	0	0	1	0	0	0	1	0	0	0	0	0	0	0	0	0	0	0	0	0	0
36	1	0	1	0	0	0	0	0	0	0	0	0	0	0	0	0	1	0	1	0	1	0	0	0	0	0	0	1	0

Notes: This table lists the thirty-six partners and summarizes the results of the three rounds of regressions presented in Chapter 7, testing the effect of variables 1–9, then 10–21, and finally 22–29, on the choices of levers by each of these individual partners. Thus, for example, for Partner 1 (first row of this table), only two variables seem to have had an effect of his choices of levers: effects 19 and 20; that is, the fact that he saw the target as a friend and the fact that he saw the target as a co-worker.

  1 = significant at least at $p < 0.01$; else 0. To identify each effect, refer to Chapter 7. Only such strongly significant effects were taken into consideration for inclusion in this table and for interpretation.

Source: Reprinted from *Quality and Quantity*, E. Lazega and D. Krackhardt, 'Spreading and Shifting Costs of Lateral Control in a Law Partnership: A Structural Analysis at the Individual Level', 34: 169. Copyright 2000 with permission from Kluwer Academic Publishers.

Appendix H. *Specialization of the Main Levers: Procedure Followed to Construct Figure 7.6*

Figure 7.6 is the result of principal component analysis. This method is a type of factor analysis that is similar to correspondence analysis. It differs from correspondence analysis, among other features, in that it does not use any weighting in the analysis of the raw target by lever matrix that is used as data input. The absence of weighting strengthens the effect of numerically important columns in the extraction of factors. Thanks to this particular sensitivity, this method is especially well adapted to this data-set, because it is precisely the position of the main levers (i.e. those selected most often as indicated in the columns of this matrix) that must be identified and located in a three-dimensional space. In addition, correspondence analysis was not used because it is too sensitive to little cohesive groups of levers and targets, whereas a principal component analysis on the positive deviations from the independence matrix offers more massive overall effects.

The figure contains two kinds of objects: important sanctioners (represented by a diamond) and groups of respondents and infractors (represented by a circle) collapsed together based on their respective level of seniority. The figure shows that the main sanctioners (in diamonds), or 'protectors of the common good', were expected in a discriminating and specialized way by their partners—that is, they were expected most often to exercise control on a specific set of infractors. For example, Partner 20 was often chosen by senior partners to 'talk to' medium-seniority infractors. Partner 5 was often chosen by junior partners to 'talk to' junior partners. In this figure, the three axes help locate the main sanctioners in a way that shows these contrasted specializations by creating a great distance between sanctioners who were rarely chosen together. When a group is close to a sanctioner in that space, it means that respondents in this group chose this sanctioner very often to go and 'talk to' infractors in that same group. This means that, according to the respondents, this important sanctioner was 'specialized' in a specific category of infractors and thus had his or her 'territory' of social control.

This figure is the result of a two-step procedure. First, the 36 individual matrices (called 'slices' by Krackhardt) were stacked vertically to create a single $1,296 \times 36$ matrix. Levers are the variables, because the choices by respondents were choices of levers. The difference between the observed frequencies and the frequencies expected under the model of 'independence' in each cell of the table was computed. The larger the positive deviation, the stronger the link between the target and the lever. Only large *positive* deviations above a specific cut-off, which indicate a very central lever, were retained for graphic representation. This residuals matrix was used, in the second step, to represent the distances between the main levers in a multidimensional space.

To represent respondents, targets, and levers *in the same space*, nine rows of *supplementary* observations were added to the contingency table. They are represented as points in the joint row and column space, but they are not used while determining the locations of the *active* row and column points of the contingency table. This means that supplementary observations were ignored in the computation of eigenvectors. The values in the nine supplementary rows were computed as follows. Respondents and targets were sorted by three levels of seniority: junior, medium, senior. They were assigned to each category based on their place on the letterhead paper and a 'natural' threshold provided by the fact that they were considered within the firm to be different 'generations' of lawyers. Nine categories were thus created: senior respondent/senior target, senior respondent/medium target, and so on, up to junior respondent/junior target. The number of choices of each lever were summed for each of these nine categories—that is, each time a lever was chosen by a respondent of that category to be sent to deal with a target of that category. The values for each category and lever were then added to the table as supplementary observations.

Values in the new 45×36 table were normalized to avoid having groups with a large number of choices brought artificially closer to the centre of the figure. Scores on the three axes were thus computed for rows (targets) and columns (levers) as well as for respondents and targets collapsed into nine groups, as displayed in the figure. For these groups, the points projected on the map are the mean values for all the members of each group. For more precise technical indications about this approach, see Lazega and Vari (1992).

Appendix I. *Who Guards the Guardians? Procedure Used to Build Figure 7.7*

This method uses Euclidean distance as a detector of approximated structural equivalence between partners in the aggregated control network. The matrix aggregating the 36 individual levers by target matrices was used as input to Structure 4.1. Data were treated as direct measures of relations. Equivalence hypotheses were formulated using a hierarchical cluster analysis of the distances between actors' positions based on the Ward error sum of squares method. These hypotheses were tested (to confirm that a set of actors are approximately equivalent) using reliability coefficients based on correlations between distances to an individual with the mean distances to the other actors in the set. Once the positions were defined, the ties between them were determined by building the density table shown in Table I1, where the cell *i, j* is the average relation from someone occupying Position *I* to someone in Position *J*. The average relation between any two people in the network was 23.515. Representation of this table uses this value as a cut-off point.

Position One included Office I partners with low indegree centrality scores. Position Two clustered Office II partners also with low scores; it was the only position in which Office II partners were found. Neither position controlled any other position or themselves. Positions Three, Four, and Five were composed of Office I partners with high scores. Together they controlled Position One. Position Six was composed of two Office I partners; it fulfilled an interesting function: its partners with low centrality scores in the control network guarded partners with high centrality scores. Finally, three partners were not assigned to any position and made a 'residual' category. Two among the most central actors belonged to this category. Partner 5 was lost to the residuals by Position Two, mainly because he was often chosen by Position Two members to control one another. Partner 20 was lost by Position Five because he was more universal, and particularly often chosen to control Office II targets. Partner 4 was lost by Position Four because he was chosen to cover additional and specific targets (Partners 9, 15, and 29). Position Four was composed of the two most senior partners of the firm. Along with Partner 20, they were given—by Office I partners—exclusive lateral responsibility for Position Two (Office II) partners. This position was important, because its members were

Table I1. *Density table for the lateral control network provided by Structure 4.1*

Position	Position						
	One	Two	Three	Four	Five	Six	Residual
One	14.8	7.9	4.1	4.1	7.5	5.9	5.7
Two	2.8	22.5	0.0	5.9	1.4	0.5	10.0
Three	34.7	9.1	230.0	15.0	37.5	167.5	75.0
Four	55.0	54.1	50.0	240.0	68.8	67.5	108.8
Five	41.0	17.0	25.0	23.8	97.5	36.3	32.5
Six	19.7	8.6	85.0	15.0	42.5	20.0	35.0
Residual	51.5	80.2	41.3	80.0	44.4	27.5	48.3

chosen to cut across office boundaries and because it controlled all the other positions without exception. It was watched only by Position Five and Partner 20. In turn, Position Five was controlled by Positions Three, Four, and Six. Note that Positions Three and Five were almost similar in their role; they differed only to the extent that Position Five was chosen to control Position Four, and Position Three was not. Leverage was thus highly concentrated in the hands of the members of three Positions (Three, Four, and Five) and the members of the residual category. It is also important to note that these three positions were chosen to control each other.

Appendix J. *Partners' Influence Network: Density Table for Figure 8.2*

Table J1 shows the density table for the 'listening-at-the-partnership-meeting' network (or influence network): cell i, j is the average relation from someone occupying Position I to someone in Position J. The average relation between any two people in the network was 0.290. Representation of this table uses this value as a cut-off point.

The first and most central position included five among the six oligarchs identified in the text as the most central (in terms of indegree) in this network—i.e. as claiming leadership and framing the debates on policy issues and precarious values (Partners 4, 26, 20, 1, and 14), plus Partner 17, whose presence is explained by his rich informal ties to the oligarchs. All, except 14, were from Office I. The density within the position was high; its members listened to one another. Members of this position said that they listened to members of Position Four, in which all members were from Office I also; and they were cited by members of the three other positions. Thus, they tended not to reciprocate citations by Office II members. The fourth position included eight members (Partners 11, 9, 21, 13, 8, 12, 24, and 22), also all from Office I. These partners included some of the most active in terms of administrative work, especially for the management of associates (9, 13, and 24) and their friends. The density within the position was also high, although less than in Position One, and its members listened to one another. They also listened to members of Positions One and Three. Their profile differs from that of Position One precisely because they tended to listen to Position Three members, who included the three women partners, two of them minders, and the most junior partner. They tended to be cited by members of the positions they cited—One and Three—but not to reciprocate citations by Office II members. The second position included a mix of Office II and Office I partners (Partners 33, 19, 7, 31, 10, 35, 25, 32, 16, 6, and 23), who listened to Positions One and Four members and were the only position to which no other position listened (not even its members among themselves). Some of the latter tended to be considered as eccentric; they were also less interested in management and policy issues. Position Three members were the three women partners in the firm, plus the most junior partner, who had been recently elected. Members of this position listened to members of Positions One and Four, as well as to each other. Figure 8.1 shows that they did not carry exactly the same policy options; three of them backed very moderate changes. They would have been part of

Table J1. *Density table for Figure 8.2*

Position	Position				
	One	Two	Three	Four	Residual
One	0.649	0.099	0.201	0.425	0.349
Two	0.502	0.077	0.207	0.297	0.346
Three	0.617	0.101	0.366	0.377	0.262
Four	0.541	0.072	0.315	0.481	0.260
Residual	0.414	0.120	0.121	0.223	0.326

Position Four if they had been taken more seriously by Position One leaders. The 'residual' category included Partners 2, 3, 5, 15, 18, 28, and 30. These partners included some highly prominent figures in the firm, such as Partners 2 and 5, but also one of the least listened to (Partner 18, who was also among the highest billers/collectors in the firm). Partners 2 and 5 were lost to the 'residual' category by Position One: raw data show that the reason for this was that they were mainly listened to by partners in their own office, not by partners in the other office, which is what characterized Position One. This is confirmed by their relatively low centrality scores.

Notes

Introduction

1. For a review and criticism of this abundant literature on professionals in bureaucracy, see e.g. Davies (1983).
2. See e.g. work by Aharoni (1997); Bosk (1979); Bourrier (1999); Bucher (1970); Crane (1972); Eccles and Crane (1988); Freidson (1975); Freidson and Rhea (1963); Friedberg and Musselin (1989); Frischkopf (1973); Hechter (1987); Heinz and Laumann (1982); Ibarra (1992); Karpik (1995); Kuty (1998); Latour and Woolgar (1988); Laumann and Heinz (1977); McCann (1993); Nelson (1988); Ostrom (1990); Parsons and Platt (1973); Sainsaulieu *et al.* (1983); Sutton and Hargadon (1996); Swidler (1979); Tilley (1981).
3. Remaining at this formal level makes it too easy to dismiss this organizational form as a vague form of 'associational professionalism' (Abbott 1988).
4. They can also be said to be part of a broadly conceived 'corporate social capital' (Leenders and Gabbay 1999), a very general concept encompassing, as in Coleman (1990), any social mechanism characterizing and helping a corporate actor solve problems raised by members' cooperation.
5. Competition and conflict for resources and high level of political activity have long been recognized as characteristic of professional organizations (Bucher and Stelling 1969; Montagna 1968).
6. This notion is borrowed from Portes (1994).
7. In the approach outlined here, however, I do not focus on measuring the relative contribution of such social ties (and their structure) to maximization of individual performance in competitive arenas (Burt 1992). I am instead largely concerned with how members manage their social resources in order to fulfil their commitment to a partnership agreement.
8. This stresses the regulatory and consciously normative dimension of culture, one that is still connected to resource dependencies, as distinguished from the 'autonomous inner logic' and more unconsciously constraining nature of culture (Emirbayer and Goodwin 1994; Mohr and Duquenne 1997). The fact that early and narrow structural approaches to action were promoted in the 1960s and 1970s against the idea of action oriented by socialization, norms, and values should not prevent sociologists from combining these approaches (Hirsch 1997; Kunda 1993; Selznick 1996).
9. This echoes ideas in unorthodox economics, for which conventions are rules that never determine behaviour mechanically, because they have to be interpreted and applied (Favereau 1998). Politicization is thus brought back into economic behaviour, because actors have to have an idea of the collective associated with the correct functioning of the rules—i.e. in which they want to coordinate with others.
10. An abundant literature of interest to my purpose is available on corporate law firms (Brock *et al.* 1999; Dezalay 1992; Flood, 1987; Galanter and Palay 1991; Gallouj 1992;

Gilson and Mnookin 1985; Hazard and Rhode 1988; Heinz and Laumann 1982; Karpik 1995; Maister 1993; Mann 1985; Nelson 1988; Smigel 1969; Starbuck 1993; Wallace 1995; and many others).

11. Privileges that may have something to do with the fact that lawyers, in the USA, have long been the 'shock troops of capitalism' (Sellers 1991).

12. Starbuck relies on sociological literature showing that knowledge-intensive firms downplay formal structures, and try to achieve coordination through social norms and reward systems instead of hierarchical controls (Nelson 1988). He acknowledges work such as that of Bucher and Stelling (1969), suggesting that organizations dominated by professionals had a number of special characteristics, including professionals building their own roles rather than fitting into pre-set roles, spontaneous internal differentiation based on work interests, competition and conflict for resources, and high levels of political activity. He rightly points out that famous consultants such as David Maister (1993) offer an idealized model of knowledge-intensive firms, the model of the 'one-firm firm'. But he himself does the same by overemphasizing the importance of organizational culture in the operation of such firms.

Chapter 1

1. The nature of partnerships is defined by law. Tests are prescribed for determining whether a partnership exists, and what is partnership property. They deal with issues of agency and with the nature of the relations of partners to persons dealing with the partnership. With regard to complexity, Rowley and Rowley (1960: 15) argue that 'there is no other relation known to law which, in its nature, is so complicated as is partnership. A natural person is an entity, and may sue or be sued; may receive, hold, and dispose of, real or personal property. A corporation, or artificial person is in the same position, being endowed with a personality by an act which creates it. The question of the entity of a partnership has been repeatedly raised, and answered in different ways. Is the partnership a unit, having a distinctive personality, a self, or is it merely a convenient mode of expressing the association, and the consequent rights and liabilities of the persons so associated therein? . . . The ordinary mercantile conception of a partnership and the legal conception are largely at variance. For all practical business dealings, the merchant regards a partnership or firm as an entity, up to the time when he must go to court to enforce a liability against it. Creditors charge the firm on their accounts and the books of the partnership are kept as if it had a separate existence.'

2. In fact, this opposition simplifies Weber's approach, whose typology of bureaucracies is neglected in favour of explorations of the monocratic version. This unfairness to Weber characterizes much of what has passed into the received wisdom of organizational studies.

3. This is a clear simplification, because there are other reasons for complying in such organizations, such as losing resources and personal support, as well as commitment to the general value standards of the organization (which Waters attributes to polycratic forms other than the collegial—i.e. mass or direct democracy).

4. Following the socio-technical tradition of the 1950s, these interdependencies can be functional—i.e. related to a formal division of work—or structural—i.e. related to more informal circulation of all sorts of resources through social relationships. In that

respect, structural analysis is compatible with what Crozier (1963; Crozier and Friedberg 1977) calls 'strategic' analysis. Indeed, the former presupposes the latter (Lazega 1994*a*, 1996, 1997; Lazega and Mounier, forthcoming). This is particularly the case because structural analysis offers sophisticated measurements of resource interdependencies, status, and power that are basic concepts of the French school of organizational analysis.

5. This definition of a niche is different from that offered by White (forthcoming), which relies on a theory of monopolistic competition. As will be shown in this chapter, it is defined in network analytical terms as a position that is also a clique. Note that the expression 'niche building' may be slightly misleading, since niches are not built *ex nihilo*, but under pre-existing structural constraints. Thus a dynamic perspective should make a Durkheimian approach to such behaviour (more system oriented) compatible with that of Weber (more actor oriented) thanks to a Simmelian form of manipulation of ties (Blau 1964).

6. In economics, barter is a slow, expensive, and highly restrictive way to do business. The barter economy is inefficient compared to the cash economy. Barter transactions are opaque and approximative. However, in social life, barter is much more widespread than is usually acknowledged (Blau 1964). It is used much more often than cash for many types of exchanges. In effect, pricing many goods or resources is next to impossible for actors involved in transactions connected to production and collective action. This is especially the case for knowledge. Barter's opaque, non explicit, and approximative characters are quite useful to exchange partners. Barter is indeed much more restrictive and it falls under a logic of membership, a symbolic logic of boundary management; it is much more demanding in terms of solidarity with one's reference group—i.e. others minimally considered to be 'one's own people'. Basically, it is identity criteria and particularistic discrimination that drive the barter economy—i.e. principles that are the opposite of those defended by theoreticians of the market mechanism, in which people are supposed to be anonymous and unrelated.

7. On the relationship between identity, appropriateness judgements, and behaviour, see Lazega (1992*a*).

8. This means that exchanges are preceded (analytically speaking) by qualifying rounds. Actors have to show that they qualify as partners for exchanges of resources. The qualification is mainly negotiated based on attributes, values, and past experience. Before qualifying, actors are not yet in business; they are not allowed to barter many resources with the long term in mind. They can be involved only in spot transactions using a currency that opens up exchanges to many others, increasing costs. When exchanges are multiplex, however, there is no general equivalent or currency. Identities are connected to terms of the exchanges defined in the political process.

9. For additional insights into cooperation as politicized versus routine transfers or exchanges of various kinds of resources, see Bearman (1997); Breiger and Ennis (1997); Cook (1987, 1990); Ekeh (1977); Galaskiewicz and Marsden (1978); Gouldner (1960); Han and Breiger (1998); Lazega and Pattison (1999, 2001); Lin (1982, 1995); Levi-Strauss (1949); Raub and Weesie (1990).

10. As shown by Festinger (1954), the comparisons that matter for people are the comparisons with others most like themselves. Combinations of criteria (similarities in terms of office membership, speciality, hierarchical status, etc.) push members to compare themselves to same niche people.

11. These are exogenous identities that are particularistic within the firm—i.e. once members are part of the firm. I do not mean, for instance, that school attended is an 'ascribed' characteristic such as gender.

12. Again, a fundamental aspect of the notion of power is related to the ways in which members politicize their exchanges. In effect, if actors contribute to the construction of the structure that constrains them, some are more active in this structuration than others. In that respect, Friedberg (1993) defines power as the capacity to structure interaction contexts to one's own advantage. From a structural perspective—i.e. centred on transfers and exchanges of resources—this expression has two complementary meanings. 'Having power over someone else' consists, first, in controlling access to resources needed by this person; and, secondly, in defining the terms of exchange with this person and among members of the organization (Reynaud 1989).

13. Contributions by network analysts to the study of 'becoming a player' in organizational politics and social control are useful to mention here. First, becoming a player in the organizational power game requires a trained capacity to perceive who the key players in the system are (i.e. people who can help in getting things done, in getting people to agree, or in getting ahead), what the relationships between them are, what the coalitions and allegiances are, and who the trustworthy people to make deals with are. Analytically, Krackhardt's work (1990, 1992) on perceptions of relations, particularly on three-dimensional data ('perception cubes'), shows that perception of the structure varies according to one's position in it, and that power is also exercised in spite of (or based upon) existing 'blind spots' in members' perception of the structure. Secondly, to be a player in the power game also requires a trained capacity to use interdependence among others. Burt's work (1982, 1992) on manipulation of relations, particularly on co-optation as a defence mechanism, describes members' manipulations of relations in terms of network 'surgery': withdrawal (cutting ties) and expansion (adding new ties to one's network). In this perspective, a strategic player tries to decrease his dependence upon a constraining party (e.g. a powerful supplier of resources) by gaining some leverage over the constrainer ('embedding' the constraining party) and creating a tie over which there is more control. Such co-optation manœuvres can also be indirect (Gargiulo 1993; Lazega and Vari 1992).

14. This argument can also be derived from Heimer (1992).

15. As suggested by Frank (1985), the price of status is high when members interact intensively. This is explained by the assumption that members in a densely connected organization are uniquely isolated from status comparisons with people other than their co-workers. From an individual's perspective, this may also be why an oligarchy of powerful members emerges among peers in the first place. In collegial organizations where networks are relatively dense, many may not be able or prepared to pay such a high price in exchange for status.

16. Blau (1964), for example, thinks that minders cease to compete for superior status and win social acceptance in the group in exchange for the contribution they make to group solidarity. Here, minders are seen as status competitors, just as others are.

17. See Blau (1964) and Fernandez (1991) about the relationship between leadership and 'respect'.

18. See Eccles and Crane (1988) for a slightly comparable situation.

19. Frischkopf (1973), well before network analysis, had the idea that collegial restraint was at the origin of *collegiality as a relational code* among peers.

20. Some exchanges in law partnerships tend to create status equality, as opposed to others that create status differentiation, in particular advice relationships such as that studied by Blau (1964) and Homans (1961), which operate as a mechanism of differentiation of status and status allocation.

21. It should be mentioned that this type of temporary task-force structure, in which partners keep their autonomy in their negotiation of means and ends, makes it difficult for a centre to identify and appropriate real or potential productivity gains. Therefore, governance of these task forces, when work is not defined as a standard process in the Taylorian way, also means that work is evaluated based on other standards—more local, subjective (in partners' minds), or relational ones.

22. For a summary of research on the relationship between social networks and performance, see Flap *et al.* (1998).

23. Indeed, in knowledge-intensive firms, this commitment is even more difficult to measure: the measurement itself is always a politicized issue (Friedberg 1993; Meyer 1994).

24. This is partly at odds with Burt's general statement (1992) about association between low constraint and high performance, and more consistent with Coleman's ideas (1990) on the benefits of closure and embeddedness of ties. Burt's measurement of constraint, however, remains useful regardless (Lazega 1999*a*).

25. This often depends on subtle ways in which members with status influence the salience of some categories in debates about professionalism. Perrow (1986) and many others call this premiss setting. This is consistent with sociological theory, assuming that people are interdependent in terms of affecting each other's categorizations in any given action situation. The influential people in a group are not only those who can sanction and monitor behaviour, but those who can provide information about the relevant stereotypes and categories characterizing a social group (Bourdieu 1980; Lindenberg 1997).

26. This is possible by a relational mechanism that I have called elsewhere 'epistemic alignment' or 'co-orientation' (Lazega 1992*a*), which is based on the interactive dimension of members' 'appropriateness judgements'. Quality control is thus more generally related to epistemic dimensions of collective action.

27. 'A small penalty may be sufficient to remind the infractor of the importance of compliance. Everyone might be in a similar situation in the future and would want some understanding at that time. Everyone will hear about the incident, and the violator's reputation for reliability will depend on complying with the rules in the future' (Ostrom 1990: 97).

28. 'Multiple ties and multiple bases of power provide a stable context for the exertion of influence on a variety of attitudes and behaviors' (Marsden and Friedkin 1993: 131).

29. In this terminology, a lever or a sanctioner fulfils a function similar to that of a broker, especially of a 'coordinator' (as defined by Fernandez and Gould 1994), who remains within the organization and establishes a link between two other members. Analytically, however, members themselves can be considered to be the 'third parties' constraining levers to intervene on behalf of the organization. Such constraints come from the convergent expectations of these members.

30. See e.g. Charles Bosk (1979), who, following Freidson's work (Freidson 1975; Freidson and Rhea 1963), characterizes such collegial settings by their 'atrophy of corporate self-control' and 'hypertrophy of professional self-control' by individual members. The existence of this regime is consistent with Bosk's criticism of organizational studies over-celebrating individual conscience as a source of control in professional services

organizations. A structural approach, while not ignoring the reasons for pointing at the existence of this 'atrophy' also shows that there is among peers at least one informal corporate mechanism for early monitoring and sanctioning. This approach is also consistent with Tannenbaum's theory of control (1968) as a non-zero-sum game. According to Tannenbaum, if one creates a situation where there is solidarity, then everyone has the feeling that they control more than before. In collegial settings, this also means that a partner accepts giving up some control to selected others so that they can be controlled in return. One can thus hopefully focus actors and avoid the dispersion of their actions. This, however, is only part of what happens in collegial settings, because lateral control also tends to concentrate in the hands of a few, who are often forced to accept such a costly shift.

31. By using the word consensus, I do not mean that conformity is obtained by a calm and formal agreement following a politely conducted discussion. Conformity is the result of ongoing negotiation, sometimes including threats and arguments in which this agreement is not necessarily a formal consent but the result of various processes of influence and convergence of expectations. As Bourricaud (1961) puts it, influence includes all the means that members use in their art of having the last word with rival partners who may one day have more status than they. See also, about this issue, network analysts such as Breiger (1990) and White (1992), or social psychologists such as Asch (1951), French and Raven (1959), and Raven (1965).

32. Again, this stresses the regulatory and consciously normative dimension of culture.

33. Parsons (1968; Parsons and Shils, 1951) and other theoreticians (Dingwall 1999; Hughes 1958) have discussed the preservation of precarious values in the larger society by the professions; Selznick pushes the connection between status and values further. This again goes back to the Weberian theme of plurality of legitimacies, or value 'polytheism'.

34. Political participation in general has long been a central process for the study of the interplay of structure and culture. For example, at the macro-sociological level, political scientists such as Putnam (1993), following a well-established Tocquevillian and sociological tradition, argue that dense social networks sustain efficient civic norms. But such studies remain very vague in their structural approach; in particular, they fail to specify how such a political participation takes place—i.e. through which social mechanisms sustaining these norms. Here, I argue that this tradition can be enriched by a broadly conceived structural approach to regulatory processes in collective actors. This means taking into account systematically resource dependencies (Crozier 1963; Pfeffer and Salancik 1978) between actors involved in the regulatory process.

35. Feelings about relative status often govern our decisions about rules (Festinger 1954). Therefore it makes sense to argue that discussions about precarious values are shaped by status heterogeneity in the oligarchy of the organization.

36. Although I do not share some of their assumptions in the study of influence, my understanding of the use of network analysis for the study of this issue is in many ways similar to that of pioneering work by Laumann and Pappi (1976), Laumann *et al.* (1977), Marsden (1981), Marsden and Laumann (1977).

37. In the study of social movements, authors such as McAdam and Paulsen (1993) focus on how social networks matter for processes such as recruitment, mobilization, and collective identity formation. Such approaches to collective action often stress the importance of achieving social cohesion and of concentrating power in the hands of a leadership, or an avant-garde. In my view, however, these studies of political participation

do not sufficiently take into account the diversity of forms of status, and issues of status consistency, in order to explain the mechanism of emergence of specific norms as priorities for a given collective actor.

38. Such a mutual prescription may also be a condition of collective learning (Hatchuel 1995).

Chapter 2

1. With available paralegal and administrative personnel, associates are often able to transfer the 'dirty work' down the hierarchical ladder, thus maintaining a 'collegial' character in their interactions with partners more easily than in other types of professional firms.

2. I did not observe SG&R attorneys carrying out specific tasks from the beginning to the end of a case, mainly because I was not allowed to meet the clients.

3. Putting together transactions means transforming a unilaterally conceived agreement into a consensual one. 'The document's final form is as much a result of the interaction between the two senior lawyers . . . on either side of the transaction as it is a quest for the most profitable and efficient form' (Flood 1987: 237).

4. About litigators' 'agonistic' professional culture, see Starbuck (1992).

5. Several types of partner contributions were recognized at SG&R. For example, Partner 3 was not expected to practise law intensively, but rather—as a former CEO of a large insurance company—to transfer to the firm some of his network of contacts and knowledge of people with clout. Others were involved in large-scale arbitrage.

6. Sometimes they are assigned work which they consider useless. Knowing when and how to correct a partner in a meeting is dangerous for your career and requires tact (if not the associate could be blamed). Fresh associates establish reputations quickly concerning their skills and personalities.

7. Nelson (1988: 91–2) defines traditional management as characterized by '(1) ad hoc and reactive policy-making, with little long-range planning; (2) direct administration by leading lawyers, aided only by a part-time managing partner, with no regular monitoring of internal performance measures or financial information; and (3) informally defined and shifting work groups'. Bureaucratic management is defined as '(1) a specialized policy-making group that actively engages in strategic planning; (2) a developed administrative component consisting of a managing partner and a mechanism for collecting and analyzing data on the financial performance of individual lawyers and work groups; and (3) well-defined work groups (usually taking the form of departments) with recognized heads who supervise the group and report to the central policy-making group'.

8. Advertising was authorized in the legal profession by a 1977 Supreme Court decision.

9. Despite the weak economy, profits were generally said to be going up, but profit rates as a percentage of gross revenue were said to be stagnating (firm-wide, independent of which specialities were considered to be more profitable than others).

10. Partners could not sell or transfer their partnership interest.

11. This agreement could be amended by at least 80% of all partners. For some provisions requiring a specific percentage vote of partners other than a majority, it could be amended only by all the partners. Matters not provided for in the agreement were governed by law (Uniform Partnership Act).

12. Discourse about collegiality does not always reflect rigid positions. Partner 15 left the firm a few years later for a larger and wealthier competitor.
13. Rawls (1971) constructs a rationale for equalizing incomes that is independent of concerns about relative standing. He believes such concerns are not even rational, let alone morally legitimate. See also Frank (1985: 113).
14. The story of former Partner No. 2 who wanted to switch specialities away from a lucrative one is presented in Chapter 7.
15. 'Partner 1 was an interesting exception in the firm, because most of the senior guys except Partner 1 were state patricians with lots of money, married to lots of money, lived a very grand country life, big estates, horses, that kind of thing. Partner 1 was from a working-class family, had gone to Yale College and Yale Law School. It was clear to me from the beginning that he was a truly superb lawyer. He was a big help to me when I was hired there' (No 1 former partner).
16. In this book, this expression refers to the hours worked and collected by the lawyer him or herself; it does not include amounts collected indirectly through work distributed to other partners and associates.
17. 'Partner 4 was the first person who had not gone to Yale. He was from Harvard. Always extremely well organized, very energetic, very good fisherman. They immediately made him a member of some fishing club' (No 1 former partner).

Chapter 3

1. Recall that a multiplex relation is a polyvalent one, in which more than one resource is transferred or exchanged. For members, this polyvalence created new ways for access to resources. A substructure is defined as a configuration of ties linking a small set of network members—e.g. a pair of lawyers joined by mutual co-work ties, or a triplet of lawyers two of whom are linked by mutual advice ties and a third is linked by friendship to one of these two.
2. The description of the multiplex exchange system at work in the firm can only be partial, since it was carried out based on three types of resources only. There were more than three types. However, these resources were central to the production system and to individual 'survival' in this type of firm. I assume that knowledge of an exchange system based on them is sufficient to understand many of the processes at work in this firm.
3. I do not have hard information on who worked with whom in this firm, but I do have information on who relied on whom for strong cooperation for the previous year (for more details, see Lazega 2000*b*).
4. For Goffman (1961), individuals achieve role distance on their own. Surgeons joke and hum during surgery. Here I assume that role distance has a strong relational dimension: members need others to achieve it.
5. Structural equivalence refers to a procedure that represents patterns in complex social networks data in simplified form to reveal subsets of actors who are similarly embedded in these networks of relations, and to describe relationships between these subsets (Wasserman and Faust 1994: 347–93; Degenne and Forsé 1994). Two actors are structurally equivalent if they have identical ties to and from all other actors in the network. Since actors in a real social network are almost never structurally equivalent, the analysis uses a measure of the degree to which pairs or subsets of actors approach

structural equivalence. Analyses described in this book are carried out by available net-work analysis software, particularly Structure 4 (Burt 1991) and Ucinet 4 (Borgatti 1991).

6. Overall densities of the co-workers', advisers', and friends' networks were respectively 0.22, 0.18, and 0.12. For associates among themselves, these densities dropped to 0.13 and 0.16 for the first two networks, and increased to 0.15 for the friendship network.

7. Measurements used here are indegree centrality scores. Indegree centrality represents a measurement of the extent to which members are 'popular' in these networks and therefore accumulate resources circulating in them (Freeman 1979). As summarized by Wasserman and Faust (1994: 169–219), centrality measures identify the 'most important' actors in a social network. Since definitions of importance vary considerably, and a variety of measures has been developed to locate the most central members in a network. I use here one of such measures, called degree centrality, which highlights the difference between the most and the least 'active' members. In the network observed, high indegree centrality scores reflect the most 'popular' members. Network analysts have tried various methodologies to look at the extent to which centrality is an operationalization of power—i.e. the extent to which actors can convert a central position (where they benefit from a high concentration of resources and from competitive advantages) into power (Burt 1982; Cook *et al.* 1983; Markovsky *et al.* 1988; Marsden 1982; Mizruchi 1994). Indegree centrality was chosen (as opposed to other types of measurements of centrality) because it can be considered to be an index of status. For an evaluation of the robustness of this index for measuring status and power in organizations, see Brass (1984) and Brass and Burkhardt (1992).

8. This may be due to the fact that members of the firm did not think of a managing partner's administrative tasks as 'real' legal work.

9. The proportion of dyadic Blau compounds that characterized a member's relational profile decreased as one went down the seniority level; this shows that junior partners either needed more advice or tended to be less 'arrogant' than more senior ones (who did not seek out advice from their advisees). Composition of typical members' pattern of multiplex relationships in this context would be too long to describe here. A summary is presented in Lazega (1999a).

10. In these pages, saying that members of a niche did not rely on each other for a certain type of resource will be considered equivalent to saying that the transfers and exchanges of this resource were not very intense, at least not intense enough to reach the thresholds defined for the density tables presented in Appendix B. Thus a niche characterized by such a weak solidarity was a fragile one.

11. To use Burt's expression (1982) for members whose relational profile is so different from that of others in the networks examined that they are clustered in a common category of members without structurally equivalent colleagues.

12. As mentioned at the beginning of chapter 3, recognizing this distinction more generally, Lévi-Strauss (1949) separates two forms of exchange: direct or restricted exchange (dyadic) and indirect or generalized exchange (structural). However, as seen in the Introduction and in Chapter 1, the micro–macro link is always a matter of politics—of how actors politicize exchanges, control, and especially regulation, for which they support representatives—not a technical issue. Reaching the macro-level and a classi-fication of members based on the description of relational substructures at the dyadic or higher-order level, where the focus is on ties, cannot be done mechanically, as Blau (1964) sometimes thinks. Although the two approaches are complementary, they use

two different units of analysis. Network analysts have often been trained (largely by block-modelling) to think about network structure in terms of identifying (differentiated) social positions (and the relations between them). In this approach, it is the way in which individual nodes in the network are distinguished by patterns of incoming and outgoing ties that is examined. This is a helpful approach, because the interest can focus on how individual outcomes of various sorts differ accross network members. The models fitted below have a different focus, asking what homogeneous local processes might be responsible for the overall structure. They posit local structural constraints (or dependencies) and are explicit in assuming that, once the analysis has taken account of these local structural tendencies, the overall structure is put together 'independently' from these pieces—i.e. there is no global structure beyond the local structural tendencies. This is not to say that global structure cannot be described in block-model-like terms— only that what global structure there is can be explained in terms of local constraints. The models can be seen as akin in theoretical form (but not necessarily substance) to both balance theory and the strong–weak ties argument. Both of the latter accounts are attempts to posit local structural constraints (e.g. tendency for friends of friends to be friends; or strong tie associates of a person to be at least weakly tied) that explain global structural tendencies (a bipartition of the network into friendship cliques in the one case, the global disconnectedness of strong tie networks in the other). This approach is much more tie-based than the block-modelling one and provides a different (and complementary) lens through which to examine network structure. In this section, ties will be the focus, and differences between nodes described indirectly, through their participation in different ties. Of course, it would be useful to take more systematic advantage of the complementarity of the two approaches by lining them up, side by side, but this goes beyond what was needed for the purpose of this chapter (and what is easily done in network analysis).

13. This does not mean that solidarity of another kind did not exist among members sharing this type of characteristic, as will be shown below.

14. 'You scatter when you begin to practise as partners. The bond of friendship may be cut by different practices and lack of opportunity to mix with these people: different floors, different buildings, different specialities' (Partner 24).

15. This is not to say that inter-office ties and cross-speciality ties did not exist. As will also be shown below, friendships spanning boundaries were less frequent than the others, but still important.

16. I am grateful to Marijtje van Duijn, University of Groningen, for help and advice in the data analysis based on the p_2 model. For detailed description of this methodology, especially for the model selection procedure, see Van Duijn and Snijders (1995) and Lazega and Van Duijn (1997).

17. Since the goal of the study is explanation rather than simple description, statistical modelling is relevant even though we have the whole population. The residual terms in the statistical models represent unexplained effects. On model-based and design-based inference, and on non-included influences as a basis for probability models, see Snijders and Bosker (1999).

18. Limiting the analysis of these effects to the dyadic level is not sufficient for a fully-fledged description of niches. But, given the heavy weight of dyadic effects detected above in this specific exchange system (when compared to triadic and higher order substructures), this limited analysis is sufficient to identify broad niche-building constraints under which this exchange system operates.

19. Choices among partners only and among associates only are examined in subsequent chapters.

20. The negative and significant interaction effect between status and speciality similarity shows that these effects are not independent of each other, and that there is a trade-off between them: each absorbs some of the effect of the other. In the p_2 models, there is no need for an independent interpretation of interaction effects, which qualify the separate main effects.

21. Another 'moderator' is the value of ρ: it is quite high, which means that much reciprocity still remains to be explained, but with other effects than those chosen in the model.

22. Partners who created temporary task forces were not allowed to transform them into more permanent ones (see Chapter 6). They could cultivate their autonomy *vis-à-vis* their organization, but only up to a point. They were not allowed to withdraw in a permanent team that could start functioning independently of firm rules, policies, and system.

23. Mobilizing similarities in terms of several attributes could thus be perceived to be a useful mitigating device by advice-seekers of any rank. Other mechanisms that will not be quantified here (and will therefore be included in the 'random' part of the model) operated as well. For instance, with much sought-out and selective advisers, personalized access and multiplex ties could help advice-seekers in stretching advice as much as possible before it became collaboration. But multiplex ties did not exist among all the members of the organization, particularly beyond a certain size. Recall that, in this firm, as in many others, the advice network was less dense than the co-workers' network.

24. Note, for example, that women were not chosen as friends more than men, which contradicts a general idea that, in organizations, role distance or emotional support is provided more by women than by men.

25. Status thus had an effect on members, choices of friends. However, in Office I, associates also tend to choose litigation partners as friends (probably because Partners 13, 24, and 26, all litigators and in charge of the associates committee, were in Office I), much more than Office II associates chose Office II partners as friends. This was probably why the lay-offs of associates, at the end of 1990, came as more of a shock to Office I associates than to Office II associates. To Office I associates, they shed a new light on their friendship ties with partners and on the congenial ambiance in their office. Parameters show that status differences and office membership, but not speciality, did tend to affect socializing with partners.

26. Additional significant effects are rare, but can be strong. They are not interpreted here, since they do not add much to (nor do they contradict) my argument about the creation of niches.

27. Without longitudinal data, it is impossible to show how they emerge from a complex process of self-organization— that is, from mutual adjustments between colleagues who behave according to their short- and long-term interests, gradually leading to these stable patterns of behaviour in the organization.

28. I am grateful to Philippa Pattison, University of Melbourne, for running the p^* models presented in this book and for helping in the data analysis based on them. A more detailed description of this analysis, including model selection procedures and tables reporting the fit statistics for the univariate p^* models, is available in Lazega and Pattison (1999). In all p^* tables below, the negative parameters for each type of tie signify that a tie between two

actors was less likely than no tie (and the relative magnitudes of the parameters confirm, for example, that work ties were the most frequent and friendship ties were the least frequent). Here, too, effects control for one another.

29. In fact, in a separate analysis of symmetric co-work ties, there was additional evidence of a generalized exchange structure. Specifically, the parameter corresponding to a 4-cycle of co-work ties adds substantially to the fit of a model permitting cyclic and joint dyadic exchange, and all three of these parameters are positive. This analysis, together with the one reported in the text, confirms that co-work ties possess a richly overlaid generalized exchange structure.

30. The fact that the Level 6 (and 5) substructures add nothing to the fit of the model indicate that the tendency for 3-cycles to occur is not an artefact of the tendency for higher-order substructures containing them to occur. The 3-cycle parameter estimate is robust across models containing more complex substructures. Some of its occurrences are as constituents of higher-order structures, but only to an extent predicted by the parameters for their other lower-order constituents. Models show a positive tendency for 4-cycles in the network of reciprocated work ties to be fairly compelling with respect to the existence of generalized exchange.

31. Some, however, ended up enjoying the status of permanent associate, with less pressure, weekends, and vacations. This attitude weakened incentives attached to status competition and was not openly encouraged, but increasingly accepted when the associate was strongly specialized.

32. Robins *et al.* p^* models (2000) bring in attributes for substructures beyond the dyadic level.

33. Although I tried, I did not get information on what had gone on in the politics of promotion to partnership for the previous and subsequent years. This would have fleshed out this complex structural position. Partners avoided the issue. There were also not enough (for statistical analysis) cases of associates becoming partners at SG&R in the few years following fieldwork. All of those promoted had strong ties with selected partners who had acted as their champion. Few laterals made it to partnership: they may have lacked the rock-solid support from several sponsors enjoyed by other protégés. Retrospectively, an associate who was passed over told me that, at the end of the day, he still did not know on what basis the decision about him was made. The usual discourse heard in most law firms includes analytical ability, detailed knowledge of two areas of law important to firm clients, the ability to organize work with younger associates, the ability to generate new business from ongoing clients or from new clients, good judgement, and hard work. But serious candidates such as Associate 41, a Yale graduate, close friend to many Office I partners, member of Position Five in Figure 3.1, who participated in big cases and avoided burn-out, did not make it. Cross-your-fingers candidates such as Associate 37, with an atypical career, did; and found themselves well accepted within the firm. Promotion was often as unpredictable as any committee decision, subject to eleventh-hour revisions in a labyrinthine process. Meeting all the tests under broad definitions of economic and professional merit did not mean that one would be promoted. Of course, it was hard for associates not to take their omission personally, feeling that a judgement had been made on them alone on the basis of merit. There still had to be a strong need for new partners, and that need was decided by the partnership meeting. An able specialist in a booming area had a better chance of making it than an able specialist in a depressed area, even if both had the same commitment and relational skills,

not just technical abilities. The only certainty was that the decision, once made, was also made to appear democratic.

Chapter 4

1. This distinction is not simply cosmetic. The idea of distributed knowledge rests upon a different conception of actors' cognitive work. It is driven by what I call 'appropriateness judgements' (Lazega 1992*a*), which involve structural ingredients such as status and authority, two concepts entirely absent from cognitive psychologists' (and sometimes even cognitive sociologists'!) work. In my view, transforming individual knowledge into social and shared knowledge raises issues familiar to economists interested in the production of collective goods. This can be dealt with only by bringing in a different behavioural theory, one that takes into account the existence and competition between various kinds of status and legitimate authority.

2. There were exceptions, of course. For example, in the case of Partner 8, the temptation was strong to do everything by himself, not to seek cooperation with others.

3. Partners were especially well positioned to play on resource dependencies to get associates' commitment to their labour contract (which was not necessarily in the latters' narrow and short-term self-interest).

4. For Burt (1992), network constraint measures 'social capital' as a form of network structure. Specifically, constraint is a function of network size, density, and hierarchy (that measures the extent to which relations are directly or indirectly concentrated in a single contact). A contact in which relations are concentrated is a 'knot' in the network, making it difficult for negotiations to proceed independently in separate relationships. Constrained networks leave little opportunity for individual initiative, little chance to withdraw from difficult relationships. Difficult relations persist because they are interlocked with cooperative relations. The higher the constraint, the fewer opportunities for alternatives offered by one's contacts or contacts' contacts, and the lower the performance.

5. As in Burt's approach (1992), the pattern of relationships in itself constitutes part of members' individual 'social capital'. Here I mainly analyse economic performance understood as the amount of fees brought into the firm at the end of the year. Such amounts depended minimally on the amounts of time worked and on hourly rates. Thus, the more members worked, the more they performed in that sense. Following Coleman (1990), my point is that extracting work from them was easier in a constrained network of work ties. Analysing the determinants of other types of individual performance, such as promotion to partnership, could presumably yield different results and an opposite sign to the association—which would be more in line with Burt's results. About this issue, see also Gabbay (1997) and Lazega (2000*d*).

6. For example, a partner could take an associate with him or her to meet the client. The associate would sit in at the meeting, listening and saying nothing, and the partner would charge the associate's presence time to the client. This is not productivity in the usual sense of the term, and the clients might or might not accept that this time be billed to them.

7. Partners were careful about how their bills were worded. This affected how it was treated by the clients in their books: it could make a difference for tax purposes (whether they put it up as an asset, or as an expense to write off against income that year).

8. However, causal links are difficult to identify with non-longitudinal data; it is impossible to know here whether members were low performers because they established different types of relationships with their colleagues, or whether they established these relationships to try to mitigate the effects of their low performance and carve out a different place for themselves in the group.

9. There were exceptions, of course: Partner 12, for example, had more than ten ties including unreciprocated (by the other party) friendship ties. Seeking role distance from many people nevertheless characterized associates' profiles much more.

10. For some associates, such a combination becomes a handicap. At SG&R, for associates only, centrality in terms of friendship affected collection negatively. This means that associates who were very active socially, and provided on average more moral support to others, played a role that was not recognized by firm accounts. Obviously the link between the two phenomena is very indirect and remains to be explained, but it is nevertheless statistically strong. The more central associates were in terms of their number of co-workers (i.e. the more colleagues they worked with), the more hours they billed. The only associates who significantly collected more hours were those who were also central in the co-workers network, (they tended to be senior associates). On average for associates, seniority was the best predictor of performance in terms of hours collected, but seniority *and* centrality as a co-worker were the best predictors of performance in terms of hours billed.

11. This is not to say that this system, which made the partnership agreement enforceable, disciplined all the members equally. Some paid a higher price to be part of it. For example, as will be shown later in this chapter, some associates were put in a better position to try to build their competitive advantage (in the race to partnership) in the use of these embedded ties.

12. The issue of 'unforgiveable mistakes' will not be dealt with here. Still, Goffman-like gossip or stories, such as the following, did circulate within the firm: 'There is really a distinction between the people who were there from older generations, or because their father was the president of a big utility company, often very decent human beings but sometimes not very smart. One often used to make terrible mistakes; he was not a very good trial lawyer. I realized that at the time, so I would frequently save his ass; I always pushed our clients to settle their case rather than let him screw their case in court' (No 1 former partner).

13. See Burt (1992) and Flap (1999) for the general idea that, in many ways, returns on human capital depend on members' relational capital.

14. This is possible through 'epistemic alignment' or 'co-orientation' (Lazega 1992*a*), which is based on the interactive dimension of members' 'appropriateness judgements'. Quality control is thus more generally related to epistemic dimensions of collective action.

15. Firms recognized that protecting their knowledge was next to impossible, which is why members were encouraged to publish it and use it to be recognized as specialists, in a mix of academic and marketing approach.

16. General density of the advice network was 0.18. Answers varied considerably in quantitative terms. At the two extremes, we have one partner who said that he did not need nor ask anyone for advice, and another partner who declared that he had sought advice from thirty other colleagues.

17. As seen in the univariate p^* models of Table 3.4, the local organization of advice relations shows that the advice network did have positive parameters for transitivity and

reciprocity, but the latter were weaker than for other types of tie, mainly because of status competition. As confirmed by Robins *et al.* (2000), 3-cycles were unlikely. Parameters for 2-in-stars (see τ_{14} in Figure 3.2), 2-out-stars (see τ_{12} in Figure 3.2), and transitive triads are positive (as well as the parameter for reciprocated ties) and the parameter for advice ties of length 2 is negative. The contribution of the advice out-star configuration is to suggest the tendency for an individual to have sought advice from multiple, unrelated others, while the contribution of the advice in-star parameter is to suggest the likelihood that an individual received requests for advice from several unrelated individuals. It is interesting that the parameter for paths of advice ties of length 2 is negative, while the parameter for transitive triads is positive, and it is tempting to hypothesize that paths of advice ties created the potential for new advice ties. Certainly, the collection of important substructures of advice ties is consistent with a relation that exhibits tendencies both to clustering (referring to what Blau (1964) calls 'partnerships of mutual consultation for less competent members') and to hierarchy, but with an emphasis on hierarchical arrangement.

18. Some interpreted this as a form of professional 'arrogance' or complacency. However, recall that this law of seniority also limited their pool of available advisers.

19. For a more detailed analysis of this structure, see Lazega (1995*a*).

20. As shown in Chapter 5, substructures in which advice and friendship were bartered were very likely. Recall as well that dimensions of formal structure had an influence on choice of advisers, and, therefore, indirectly provided some members with more or better resources to deal with strong or diffuse competition (such as access to authoritative advice). For associates, striking a fragile balance between cooperation and competition by playing with the (unspoken) rules paid off for some, but not for others (Lazega 1995*a*).

Chapter 5

1. This term refers to Merton's observation (1957) on status segregation as a mechanism for managing role strain.

2. Corporate lawyers sometimes compared themselves with the highly-compensated corporate executives for whom they worked, but more systematically, and realistically, with other lawyers.

3. This process is similar to the 'subtle give-and-take' identified and analysed by Charles Bosk's classic *Forgive and Remember* (1979: 143) between senior and junior surgeons (in the work of senior members developing the socialization of junior members into the profession). On the one hand, senior members encouraged subordinates to question the grounds of their (the seniors') actions; yet, on the other hand, senior members also tried to limit that questioning so that it would not impair the quick judgements necessary in surgery. This similarity holds, even though ritualized self-criticism seems much more limited in corporate law firms than in surgery wards. Surgeons are socialized into the heroic ideal of grace under pressure (Bosk 1979: 144). Lawyers live in a much more adversarial environment, which both simplifies and complicates the issue of status competition.

4. Note again, for example, that a single unidirectional work tie was very unlikely to come up on its own in this firm. Work ties were mostly embedded in more complex and social substructures.

5. Despite the disjunction of these effects, at the dyadic level, aggregating for all members, after sorting all existing ties between i and j, the most frequent type of tie was the Blau tie (282 occurrences, 5.6% of the total number of possible ties).

6. There may be other plausible interpretations of the relationships between advice and friendship. For instance, one could hypothesize different types of advice relations—those that reflected status differences, and those that were forged through friendship. But the latter option underestimates the pressure of business on members' exchanges of advice. In addition, time-dependent data are especially important for addressing these kinds of issues, since the dynamics of tie generation are critical.

Chapter 6

1. Detection of 'cliques' under strong components in Structure 4.1 (Burt 1991).

2. Cooperation could be imposed, and work was often done, with undesired co-workers: associates and partners had to work with firm colleagues as opposed to lawyers from outside the firm, and often with other partners and associates who would not have been first on *their* list of reliable co-workers. Reluctant cooperation was especially frequent for associates. Firm policies conflicted in particular with lawyers' own personal preferences when they put together a task force to work on a file.

3. I do not have all the detailed information that I would have liked to have to describe how the ATC worked on a daily basis.

4. For example, there were—at the time of the study—few senior associates coming from Ivy League law schools, partly because they were fast-track people and had been moved up as partners already, perhaps to avoid feelings of 'relative deprivation'.

5. For both generalized exchange situations, sources of exploitation were less easily detectable than in dyadic situations: 'Exploitation therein will contribute to social disruption less easily' (Ekeh 1976: 213).

6. Choices of co-workers created a network of strong work ties. The density of this co-workers' network was higher than that of the advice and friendship networks. Recall that overall densities of these networks were respectively 0.22, 0.18, and 0.12. In the co-workers' network, 88% of all possible direct and indirect relations were possible in two steps. The cost of having interaction, or access to cooperation, with most people (except with one isolate) was low in general. Approximation of structural equivalence for this specific network also uses Euclidean distances (Burt 1982, 1991).

7. The office boundary will not be the centre of attention here: the two offices were not large enough to survive individually as a general practice firm, which was why they had merged eight years previously.

8. This definition does not include a small 'boutique' (very specialized firm) that could not survive on its own but that could be bought out by another firm. Given the size of most firms in the region, this case could be assimilated to a more or less individual defection, which is not the topic of this chapter.

9. As in previous chapters, performance is measured by dollars brought in during 1990, the year before fieldwork, and centrality scores are indegree measures in the co-workers' network. Top performers are lawyers who ranked between first and fifteenth in the first measure, and central lawyers are those who received more than twenty citations in the second measure.

10. Associates, the grinders, were represented in Figure 6.2 by Position Three on the litigation side and Position Five on the corporate side. These were two pools of associates for whom it was difficult to distinguish individual clientelistic ties with specific partners. I also included here a position of lateral senior associates on the corporate side (Position Seven), who worked with all the corporate partners in the firm.

11. Members who were not assignable to any position (the 'residual category' in Burt's language) were not, by definition, in a position to create a RED set. I therefore ignored them for this argument. That does not mean that they did not have a role in the integration of the firm, but that this role was stronger in the first integration process described in this chapter, than in the second.

Chapter 7

1. The importance of this influence cannot be underestimated. Very generally, persuasion and influence are essential among peers. Bourricaud (1961, 1964) notes the ambiguity of collegial regimes towards the use of force. If no one is strong enough to impose his or her point of view, the only chance of pushing through one's own preferences is to dilute them, to trim what is too personal and too direct in them, and to create a coalition of members who pursue in this issue their own advantages and interests.

2. The lateral control regime can be seen as supported by a wider micro-political culture (Lazega 1992b; Pfeffer 1992; Van Maanen and Barley 1984). As will be shown below, senior partners could also be chosen as sanctioners, because they had more traditional legitimacy to intervene on behalf of the common good. It is, therefore, difficult to disentangle partners' convergent expectations in their selections of sanctioners from a 'lateral control culture', understood as a set of learned choices that enabled well-socialized partners in a stable organization to match sanctioners and infractors in a way consistent with the 'rule of the collegium'. Such learned ways would make the choice of sanctioners more compatible with face-saving unobtrusiveness (choices of sanctioners might have to signal to infractors that the firm was not going out of its way to remind them of their obligations), would stress a norm of avoidance of conflict escalation, and could also be explained by factors attributed to the subjective make-up of actors. Although the contribution of this chapter is limited to a broadly conceived structural account of choices of sanctioners and its underlying symbolic and strategic logic, some of this material is also consistent with a more cultural account.

3. In this terminology, a lever fulfils a function similar to that of a broker, especially of a 'coordinator' (as defined by Fernandez and Gould 1994). However, reducing leverage in a lateral control regime to a simple form of brokerage ignores the common-good dimension of this process.

4. Another example: 'After I had been in the firm for three years, Mr Spencer called me and told me this: "I am telling you this a year before I would normally tell you. We are going to offer you a partnership a year from now. The reason I am telling you now is that you've been a very close friend of X's. We need help, because there is a real problem with his work." I forget the details of the conversation, but they wanted insight. What did I know that might help them deal with someone who had all the talent in the world, but was obviously not doing first-class work. They didn't want their relationship with X to be a failure. Because of his [elite] social background, they probably cared more than they would have cared about just anybody' (No 1 former partner).

5. This vignette confronted partners with expressive problems that had repercussions on productivity. For example, alcoholism was a problem in the firm, as well as in the profession. Partner 13: 'In the *New York Times* today, an American Bar Association survey gives a statistic I can't believe. 13% of lawyers normally have six drinks a day. Alcoholism due to increasing pressure of the practice of law as a bottom-line oriented practice, and to loss of collegiality within firms. Collegiality disappears among lawyers generally, not only within the firm. Now the lawyers who are older than 50 say, "I am looking forward to getting out of this, it is not as much fun as it used to be."' Partners did not agree to discuss more instrumental, work-related, 'deviant' behaviour. Nevertheless, I assume that this data-set supplemented by thorough organizational analysis, qualitative interviews, and information on partners' individual performance, is sufficient to address the topic of this chapter in a systematic, although limited way.

6. On the conditions under which vignettes can be used to elicit judgements or choices, and the criteria underlying them, see e.g. Rossi (1979). In this situation, the question was based on a reality that was the same for all the respondents, and—given the rotation rule—it left them where they were actually very likely to be. However, it would probably not have been appropriate in a larger and more bureaucratic law firm, where the position of managing partner would carry with it more power and a different status, and where individual performance would not be made as visible to all partners as it was at SG&R (Friedkin 1983).

7. I am grateful to David Krackhardt, Marie-Odile Lebeaux, and Stéphane Vari for help and advice at various stages in the complex statistical analyses of this three-way data. For measurement of each partner's propensity to select a solution with regard to such options, see Lazega and Krackhardt (2000), where Krackhardt's three different indexes (1994) are used: the extent to which members fragmented their control environment (connectivity scores), perceived a hierarchy in it (hierarchy scores), and perceived control to be a task-force effort (graph efficiency scores).

8. In the following calculations, the single Office III partner was counted as an Office I partner. Office III had been set up two years before the study took place, and its members were all originally from Office I.

9. Analyses creating a typology of leverage strategies cross-tabulating cost (expensive or cheap in relational terms—i.e. using one's own personal ties for lateral control) and safety (safe or unsafe from the firm's perspective—i.e. using a multi-target lever or not) in choices of levers reach the same misleading conclusion (with cheap and safe choices representing between 42% and 67% of all choices of levers, depending on the type of tie). This mistake can be avoided by weighting such figures at least by the general density of the observed sociometric network.

10. Again, to avoid a misleading interpretation of Table 7.6, it is useful to know whether or not, in the absolute, respondents and levers had the opportunity to choose personalized paths more or less than they actually did. To proceed with this comparison, distributions of frequencies of impersonal, uniplex, duplex, and triplex ties were reconstituted in the population of partners by examining all the possible paths between any two individuals. To perform this 'frameshift', this distribution was weighted differently for each segment of the influence path (number of paths used by each respondent for the relations between respondent and lever; number of times each partner was chosen as a lever for the relationship between lever and target). For a comparison between observed and weighted (or 'baseline') frequencies, see Lazega and Lebeaux (1995). This confirms the tendency of

respondents to 'spend' the relational capital of the levers more than their own. It was a deliberate strategy of respondents who managed to choose well-connected levers (although one does not know if they would have actually let themselves be used). This framing also confirms that respondents chose most often impersonal influence paths, where there was no privileged relationship between the protagonists.

11. See note 9 for definition of safe/unsafe and expensive/cheap in this situation.

12. 'Lateral' partners are partners who were never associates in the firm. Instead of coming up through the ranks, they had been hired directly as partners, mostly away from another firm.

13. Only the most central levers were included in Figure 7.6, which explains, for example, the absence of members on the negative side of axis 3.

14. For the relationship between this relaxation of a restrictive definition of structural equivalence and influence processes, see Marsden and Friedkin (1993). The latter, however, do not reason in terms of costs of control.

15. A quick look at Appendix G shows that results tend to re-emphasize differences in office membership (Office II partners spread the cost of control less than Office I partners, and tended to shift these costs to specialized MTLs more than Office I levers), and differences in friendship indegree centrality (popular partners in the friendship network also tended to spread less and to shift to specialized, carefully selected levers more than less popular respondents). Targets' dependencies on levers for resources tended to be important additional criteria in partners' choices of levers, as were similarities between lever and target in terms of office location and in terms of level of seniority: the latter criteria were used by partners who tried to 'smooth' the lateral control process by allocating the control costs to targets close to the levers geographically and in terms of experience (but not speciality), while still counting on the levers' use of the target's dependence on such resources.

Chapter 8

1. 'Bestowing benefactions', as Blau (1964) calls it, adding that 'risk is an essential element of responsibility'.

2. Note that switching to a merit-based system would not immediately deprive senior partners of their larger share. The client base changes only gradually, and more senior lawyers were still likely to have greater client responsibility than younger lawyers. In the firm's age-graded pyramid, older lawyers would still control most of the clients and profits.

3. But it was difficult for large law firms to differentiate themselves from other large law firms in the region: 'You know, we all offer the same services; we offer the same turn-around time; we offer equal or better confidence, equal or better substantive coverage—all you can do is simply say, give us a shot and we'll show you what we can do' (A member of the marketing committee).

4. Changes were to be introduced four years later in 1995 under conditions that were not observed systematically.

5. There are no isolates, but there were ten partners to whom almost no one listened.

6. The density of this network (0.33) was high compared to that of other networks observed among the partners.

7. By mobilizing more exogenous identities, the discussion of precarious values shows that the privatization of the firm was an illusion. Members needed and used an 'outside' to create the norms and expectations that helped them think long term. They found that kind of resource in their niche as well as outside it.

8. Fights to impose legitimacy or take it away from each other (Gibson 1999; Vilkas 1996) are not visible in this research.

9. Partner 17 was the partner who would draft the language of a new partnership agreement that was to be institutionalized four years after this study. In this new agreement, merit criteria were introduced in the compensation system and a bonus pool created to reward this merit. Partner 26, who was the 'ringleader' in the changes, was receiving, in 1999, by far the highest percentage of the bonus pool, 'and he seems to deserve it', said the other partners.

10. While all partners were entitled to speak on behalf of the interests of the firm as a whole, members of the oligarchy at the top of the firm could be there only because they also spoke on behalf of a constituency and voiced values supported by this constituency. It was not enough to concentrate social or economic resources to be able to participate influentially in the negotiation of precarious values. Partners 1 and 5 represented senior partners; Partners 4 and 26 represented junior partners; Partners 17 and 20 represented more medium-seniority partners.

11. Simply looking at the correlation between the number of kinds of centrality characterizing each partner with his or her choices of policy provides few, if not misleading, results concerning the relationship between structure and culture (Lazega 2000c). Ethnographic observations did show that some multi-status oligarchs tended to be conservative. When all forms of centrality were conflated without consideration to issues of status consistency between various dimensions, the effects of these dimensions could cancel each other out in undetected ways. This misleading character meant that the analysis had to bring in the notion of compatibility between various dimensions of status.

12. Taken separately, variables reflecting the possible existence of other constituencies, such as speciality and office membership, do not have an effect on policy choices.

13. This, among other things, means that indirect influence of the professional model still has a structural effect on such firms. Whether such influence is strong enough to guarantee ethical conduct is another matter, which I have discussed elsewhere (Lazega 1994b; see also Flood 1993; Hamermesh 1986; Hazard 1987; Powell 1985).

Conclusion

1. In general, an organizational approach has been shown to help understanding trust violations, such as breaking clients' confidence (Reichman 1989; Reiss 1984, 1988; Shapiro 1986; Weisburd et al. 1991; Vaughan 1983, 1998).

2. For more detailed references to the literature about this issue, see Lazega (1994b).

3. It is difficult to study the 'decision to disclose', but there are many incentives not to disclose—just like for the 'decision to prosecute' by inspectors enforcing external regulation (Hawkins and Thomas 1984).

References

Abbott, Andrew (1988), *The System of Professions: An Essay on the Division of Professional Labor*, Chicago: Chicago University Press.

Aharoni, Yair (1997), 'Management Consulting', in Y. Aharoni (ed.), *Changing Role of State Intervention in Services in an Era of Open International Markets*, Albany, NY: SUNY Press.

Alter, Norbert (1993), 'Innovation et organisation: Deux légitimtés en concurrence', *Revue française de sociologie*, 34: 175–97.

Asch, E. E. (1951), 'Effects of Group Pressure upon the Modification and Distorsion of Judgments', in Harold Guetzkow (ed.), *Groups, Leadership, and Men*, Pittsburgh: Carnegie Press.

Baker, Wayne (1992), 'The Network Organization in Theory and Practice' in Nitin Nohria and Robert G. Eccles (ed.) *Networks and Organization: Structure, Form, and Action*, Boston: Harvard Business School Press.

—— (1994), *Networking Smart*, New York: McGraw-Hill.

Barker, James (1993), 'Tightening the Iron Cage: Concertive Control in Self-Managing Teams', *Administrative Science Quarterly*, 38: 408–37.

Bastard, Benoit, Cardia-Vonèche, Laura, Eme, Bernard, and Neyrand, Gérard (1996), *Reconstruire les liens familiaux. Nouvelles pratiques sociales*, Paris: Syros.

Baumol, William J., and Wolff, E. N. (1983), 'Feedback from Productivity Growth to R&D' *Scandinavian Journal of Economics*, 85: 147–57.

Baylis, Thomas A. (1989), *Governing by Committee: Collegial Leadership in Advanced Societies*, Albany, NY: SUNY Press.

Bearman, Peter (1997), 'Generalized Exchange', *American Journal of Sociology*, 102: 1383–415.

Berelson, B., Lazarsfeld, P. F., and McPhee, W. N. (1954), *Voting: A Study of Opinion Formation in a Presidential Campaign*, Chicago: University of Chicago Press.

Bienenstock, Elisa J., and Bonacich, P. (1993), 'Game Theory Models for Exchange Networks: Experimental Results', *Sociological Perspectives*, 36: 117–35.

—— —— (1997), 'Network Exchange as a Cooperative Game', *Rationality and Society*, 9: 37–65.

Black, Donald (1984), 'Social Control as a Dependent Variable', in Donald Black (ed.), *Toward a General Theory of Social Control*, New York: Academic Press.

—— and Baumgartner, M. P. (1983), 'Toward a Theory of the Third Party', in Keith O. Boyum and Lynn Mather (eds.), *Empirical Theories about Courts*, New York: Longman.

Blau, Peter M. (1964), *Exchange and Power in Social Life*, New York: John Wiley.

Blossfeld, Hans-Peter, and Prein, Gerald (1998) (eds.), *Rational Choice Theory and Large Scale Data-Analysis*, Boulder, Colo.: Westview.

Bonacich, Philip, and Bienenstock, E. J. (1997), 'Strategy in Exchange Networks: Exploitation versus Accommodation', in Jacek Szmatka, John Skvoretz, and Joseph Berger (eds.), *Status, Networks and Structure: Theory Development in Group Processes*, Palo Alto, Calif.: Stanford University Press, 1997.

Boorman, Scott, and Levitt Paul, (1980), *The Genetics of Altruism*, New York: Academic Press.

Borgatti, Stephen (1991), *UCINET 4*, Department of Sociology, University of Southern Carolina, Columbia, SC.

—— and Everett, G. Martin (1992), 'Notions of Position in Social Network Analysis', *Sociological Methodology*, 22: 1–35.

Bosk, Charles (1979), *Forgive and Remember*, Chicago: University of Chicago Press.

Boudon, Raymond (1981), *La Logique du social*, Paris: Presses Universitaires de France.

—— (1998), 'Social Mechanisms without Black Boxes', in P. Hedström and R. Swedberg, *Social Mechanisms: An Analytical Approach to Social Theory*, Cambridge: Cambridge University Press.

Bourdieu, Pierre (1980), *Le Sens pratique*, Paris: Seuil.

Bourricaud François (1961), *Esquisse d'une théorie de l'autorité*, Paris: Plon.

—— (1964), 'Sur deux mécanismes de personnalisation du pouvoir', in Léo Hamon and Albert Mabileau (eds.), *La Personnalisation du pouvoir*, Paris: Presses Universitaires de France.

Bourrier, Mathilde (1999), *Le Nucléaire à l'épreuve de l'organisation*, Paris: Presses Universitaires de France.

Bowles, Samuel, and Gintis, H. (1998), 'How Communities Govern: The Structural Basis of Prosocial Norm', in A. Ben Ner and L. Putterman (eds.), *Economics, Values and Organization*, Cambridge: Cambridge University Press.

Bradach, Jeffrey, and Eccles, Robert (1989), 'Price, Authority, and Trust: From Ideal Types to Plural Forms', *Annual Review of Sociology*, 15: 97–118.

Brass, Daniel J. (1984), 'Being in the Right Place: A Structural Analysis of Individual Influence in an Organization', *Administrative Science Quarterly*, 29: 518–39.

—— and Burkhardt, Marlene E. (1992) 'Centrality and Power in Organizations', in Nitin Nohria and Robert G. Eccles (eds.), *Networks and Organizations: Structure, Form, and Action*, Boston: Harvard Business School Press.

Breiger, Ronald L. (1990), 'Social Control and Social Networks: A Model from Georg Simmel', in C. Calhoun, M. W. Meyer, and W. R. Scott (eds.), *Structures of Power and Constraint: Papers in Honour of Peter M. Blau*, Cambridge: Cambridge University Press.

—— and Ennis, J. (1997), 'Generalized Exchange in Social Networks: Statistics and Structure', *L'Année sociologique*, 47: 73–88.

—— and Pattison, Philippa E. (1978), 'The Joint Role Structure in Two Communities' Elites', *Sociological Methods & Research*, 7: 213–26.

Brint, Stephen (1992), 'Hidden Meanings: Cultural Content and Context in Harrison White's Structural Sociology', *Sociological Theory*, 10: 194–208.

Brock, David, Powell M., and Hinings, C. R. (1999) (eds.), *Restructuring the Professional Organization: Accounting, Healthcare and Law*, London: Routledge.

Bucher, Rue (1970), 'Social Process and Power in a Medical School', in Meyer N. Zald (ed.), *Power in Organizations*, Nashville: Vanderbuilt University Press.

—— and Stelling, J. (1969), 'Characteristics of Professional Organizations.' *Journal of Health and Social Behavior*, 10: 3–15.

Burns, Tom, and Stalker, G. M. (1966), *The Management of Innovation*, 2nd edn., London: Tavistock.

Burt, Ronald S. (1982), *Toward a Structural Theory of Action*, New York: Academic Press.

—— (1991), *STRUCTURE 4.1*, Center for the Social Sciences, Columbia University, New York.

—— (1992), *Structural Holes: The Social Structure of Competition*, Cambridge, Mass.: Harvard University Press.

Cartwright, Dorwin (1965), 'Influence, Leadership, Control', in James G. March (ed.), *Handbook of Organizations*, Chicago: Rand McNally.

Chazel, François (1983), 'Pouvoir, structure et domination', *Revue française de sociologie*, 24: 369–93.

Centeno, Miguel A. (1992), *Democracy within Reason*, University Park, Pa.: Pennsylvania University Press.

Coleman, James S. (1990), *Foundations of Social Theory*, Cambridge, Mass.: Harvard University Press.

Cook, Karen S. (1987) (ed.) *Social Exchange Theory*, London: Sage.

——(1990), 'Linking Actors and Structures: An Exchange Network Perspective', in C. Calhoun, M. W. Meyer, and W. R. Scott (eds.), *Structures of Power and Constraint: Papers in Honour of Peter M. Blau*, Cambridge: Cambridge University Press.

—— Emerson, R. M., Gillmore, M. R., and Yamagishi, T. (1983), 'The Distribution of Power in N-Person Exchange Networks: Theory and Experimental Results', *American Journal of Sociology*, 89: 275–305.

Crane, Diane (1972), *Invisible Colleges*, Chicago: University of Chicago Press.

Crozier, Michel (1963), *Le Phénomène bureaucratique*, Paris: Seuil.

—— and Friedberg, Erhard (1977), *L'Acteur et le système*, Paris: Seuil.

Dahl, Robert A. (1985), *A Preface to Economic Democracy*, Berkeley and Los Angeles: University California Press.

Davis, S. M., and Lawrence, P. R. (1977), *Matrix*, Reading, Mass.: Addison-Wesley.

Davies, Celia (1983), 'Professionals in Bureaucracies: The Conflict Thesis Revisited', in R. Dingwall and P. Lewis (eds.), *The Sociology of the Professions*, London: Macmillan.

Degenne, Alain, and Forsé, M. (1994), *Les Réseaux sociaux*, Paris: Colin.

Desroche, Henri (1976), *Le Projet coopératif*, Paris: Editions ouvrières.

Dezalay, Yves (1992), *Marchands de droit: La Restructuration de l'ordre juridique international par les multinationales du droit*, Paris: Fayard.

DiMaggio, Paul (1992), 'Nadel's Paradox Revisited: Relational and Cultural Aspects of Organizational Culture', in Nitin Nohria and Robert G. Eccles (eds.), *Networks and Organization: Structure, Form, and Action*, Boston: Harvard Business School Press.

Dingwall, Robert (1976), 'Accomplishing Profession', *Sociological Review*, 24: 331–49.

—— (1999), 'Professions and Social Order in a Global Society', *International Review of Sociology*, 9: 131–40.

—— and Fenn, Paul (1987), 'A Respectable Profession? Sociological and Economic Perspectives on the Regulation of Professional Services', *International Review of Law and Economics*, 7: 51–64.

—— and Lewis, Philip (1983) (eds.), *The Sociology of the Professions*, London: Macmillan, and New York: St Martin's Press.

Durkheim, Émile (1893), *De la division du travail social*, Paris: Presses Universitaires de France.

Eccles, Robert G., and Crane, Dwight B. (1988), *Doing Deals: Investment Banks at Work*, Boston: Harvard Business School Press.

Eickemeyer, John H. (1988) (ed.), *Law Firms Agreements and Disagreements*, New York: Practising Law Institute.

Ekeh, Peter (1976), *Social Exchange Theory: The Two Traditions*, Cambridge, Mass.: Harvard University Press.

Ellickson, Robert C. (1991), *Order without Law: How Neighbors Settle Disputes*, Cambridge, Mass.: Harvard University Press.

Emirbayer, Mustafa, and Goodwin, Jeff (1994), 'Network Analysis, Culture, and the Problem of Agency', *American Journal of Sociology*, 99: 1411–54.

Esser, Hartmut (1998), 'Why are Bridge Hypotheses Necessary?', in Hans-Peter Blossfeld and Gerald Prein (eds.), *Rational Choice Theory and Large Scale Data-Analysis*, Boulder, Colo.: Westview.

Etzioni, Amitai (1961), *A Comparative Analysis of Complex Organizations*, Glencoe, Ill.: Free Press.

Favereau, Olivier (1994), 'Règles, organisation et apprentissage collectif: Un paradigme non standard pour trois théories hétérodoxes', in A. Orléans (ed.), *Analyse économique des conventions*, Paris: PUF.

—— (1998), 'Décisions, situations, institutions', in Annie Vinokur (ed.), *Décisions économiques*, Paris: Economica.

—— and Lazega, Emmanuel (forthcoming) (eds.), *Conventions and Structures in Economic Organization*, Aldershot: Edward Elgar.

Feld, Scott L. (1981), 'The Focused Organization of Social Ties', *American Journal of Sociology*, 86: 1015–35.

Fernandez, Roberto M. (1991), 'Structural Bases of Leadership in Intraorganizational Networks', *Social Psychology Quarterly*, 54: 36–53.

—— and Gould, Roger V. (1994), 'A Dilemma of State Power: Brokerage and Influence in the National Health Policy Domain', *American Journal of Sociology*, 99: 1455–91.

Ferrand, Alexis (1997), 'La Structure des systèmes de relations', *L'Année sociologique*, 47: 37–54.

Festinger, Leon (1954), 'A Theory of Social Comparison Processes', *Human Relations*, 7: 117–40.

—— Schachter, Stanley, and Back, Kurt (1950), *Social Pressures in Informal Groups: A Study of Human Factors in Housing*, New York: Harper.

Flap, Hendrik D. (1988), *Conflict, Loyalty and Violence. Social Networks in Stateless Societies*, Bern: Peter Lang.

—— (1990), 'Patronage: An Institution in its Own Right', in M. Hechter, K.-D. Opp and R. Wippler (eds.), *Social Institutions: Their Emergence, Maintenance and Effects*, New York: Walter de Gruyter.

—— (1999), 'Creation and Returns of Social Capital: A New Research Program', *Tocqueville Review*, 20: 1–22.

—— and de Graff, Nan D. (1989), 'Social Capital and Attained Occupational Status', *Netherlands Journal of Sociology*, 22: 145–61.

—— Bulder, Bert, and Völker, Beate (1998), 'Intra-Organizational Networks and Performance: A Review', *Computational and Mathematical Organization Theory*, 4: 1–39.

Flood, John A. (1987), 'Anatomy of Lawyering: An Ethnography of a Corporate Law Firm', Ph.D. Dissertation, Department of Sociology, Northwestern University.

—— (1993), 'The Legal and Business Professions of Europe in 1992 and Multidisciplinary Practice', in Y. Dezalay and D. Sugarman (eds.), *Professional Competition and the Social Construction of Markets*, London: Routledge.

Fortado, Bruce (1994), 'Informal Supervisory Control Strategies', *Journal of Management Studies*, 31: 251–74.

Frank, O., and Strauss, D. (1986), 'Markov Graphs', *Journal of the American Statistical Association*, 81: 832–42.

Frank, Robert H. (1985), *Choosing the Right Pond: Human Behaviour and the Quest for Status*, Oxford: Oxford University Press.

Freeman, Linton C. (1979), 'Centrality in Social Networks: Conceptual Clarification', *Social Networks*, 1: 215–39.

—— (1992), 'On the Sociological Concept of "Group": An Empirical Test of Two Models', *American Journal of Sociology*, 98: 152–66.

Freidson, Eliott (1975), *Doctoring Together: A Study of Professional Social Control*, New York: Elsevier.

—— (1986), *Professional Powers*, Chicago: University of Chicago Press.

—— (1999), 'Theory of Professionalism: Method and Substance', *International Review of Sociology*, 9: 117–30.

—— and Buford, Rhea (1963), 'Processes of Control in the Company of Equals', *Social Problems*, 11: 119–31.

French, John R. P., and Raven, Bertram H. (1959), 'The Bases of Social Power', in Dorwin Cartwright (ed.), *Studies in Social Power*, Ann Arbor: University of Michigan Press.

Frey, Bruno S. (1997), *Not Just for the Money: An Economic Theory of Personal Motivation*, Cheltenham: Edward Elgar.

Friedberg, Erhard (1993), *Le Pouvoir et la règle*, Paris: Seuil.

—— and Musselin, Christine (1989), *En quête d'universités*, Paris: L'Harmattan.

Friedkin, Noah E. (1983), 'Horizons of Observability and Limits of Informal Control in Organizations', *Social Forces*, 62: 54–77.

—— (1998), *A Structural Theory of Social Influence*, Cambridge: Cambridge University Press.

Frischkopf, Arthur (1973), 'Modes de gestion facultaires et transformations à l'Université: Fonctions et dysfonctions de la collégialité', Doctoral Thesis, Université Catholique de Louvain.

Gabbay, Shaul M. (1997), *Social Capital in the Creation of Financial Capital: The Case of Network Marketing*, Champaign, Ill.: Stipes Publishing.

Gadrey, Jean (1994), 'La Modernisation des services professionnels: Rationalisation industrielle ou rationalisation professionnelle?' *Revue française de sociologie*, 35: 163–95.

—— (1996), *Services: La productivité en question*, Paris: Desclée de Brouwer.

—— and de Bandt, J. (1994) (eds.), *Relations de service, marchés de services*, Paris: Éditions CNRS.

Galanter, Marc, and Palay, Thomas (1991), *Tournament of Lawyers: The Transformation of the Big Law Firm*, Chicago: University of Chicago Press.

Galaskiewicz, J., and Marsden, P. V. (1978), 'Interorganizational Resource Networks: Formal Patterns of Overlap', *Social Science Research*, 7: 89–107.

Gallouj, Faïz (1992), 'Le Conseil juridique français: d'une logique professionnelle à une logique d'entreprise', in J. Gadrey (ed.), *Manager le conseil*, Paris: Mc-Graw Hill.

—— (forthcoming), 'Knowledge-Intensive Business Services: Processing Knowledge and Producing Innovation', in Faïz Gallouj and Jean Gadrey (eds.), *Performances and Innovation in Services: Economic and Socio-Economic Approaches*, Aldershot: Edward Elgar.

Garfinkel, Harold (1967), *Studies in Ethnomethodology*, Englewood Cliffs, NJ: Prentice-Hall.

Gargiulo, Martin (1993), 'Two-Step Leverage: Managing Constraint in Organizational Politics', *Administrative Science Quarterly*, 38: 1–19.

Gibson, David (1999), 'Taking Turns and Talking Ties: Conversational Sequences in Business Meetings', Ph.D. Dissertation, Department of Sociology, Columbia University.

Gilson, Ronald J., and Mnookin, Robert H. (1985), 'Sharing among Human Capitalists: An Economic Inquiry into the Corporate Law Firm and How Partners Split Profits', *Stanford Law Review*, 37: 313–92.

Glaser, B. and Strauss, A. (1967), *The Discovery of Grounded Theory*, Chicago: Aldine.

Goffman, Erving (1961), *Encounters: Two Studies in the Sociology of Interaction*, Indianapolis: Bobbs-Merrill.

Gouldner, Alvin W. (1954), *Patterns of Industrial Bureaucracy*, New York: Free Press.

—— (1960), 'The Norm of Reciprocity', *American Sociological Review*, 25: 161–78.

Granovetter, Mark S. (1985), 'Economic Action and Social Structure: The Problem of Embeddedness', *American Sociological Review*, 91: 481–510.

Greenwood, R., Hinings, C. R., and Brown, J. L. (1990). ' "P2-Form" Strategic Management: Corporate Practices in Professional Partnerships', *Academy of Management Journal*, 33: 725–55.

Hamermesh, F. W. (1986), 'In Defence of a Double Standard in the Rules of Ethics: A Critical Reevaluation of the Chinese Wall and Vicarious Disqualification', *Journal of Law Reform*, 20: 245–77.

Han, Shin-Kap, and Breiger, Ronald L. (1999), 'Dimensions of Corporate Social Capital: Toward Models and Measures', in Roger Leenders and Shaul Gabbay (eds.), *Corporate Social Capital and Liability*, Boston: Kluwer.

Hatchuel, Armand (1994), 'Modèles de service et activité industrielle: La Place de la prescription' in Jean Gadrey and J. de Bandt (eds.), *Relations de service, marchés de services* Paris: Editions CNRS.

—— (1995), 'Apprentissages collectifs et activité de conception', *Revue française de gestion* (July–Aug.).

Hawkins, Keith O., and Thomas, J. M (1984) (eds.), *Enforcing Regulation*, Boston: Kluwer-Nijhof.

Hazard, Geoffrey C., Jr. (1980), *Ethics in the Practice of Law*, New Haven: Yale University Press.

—— (1987), 'When there are Conflicts over Conflicts', *National Law Journal*, 19 Oct.

—— (1989), 'Teamwork is a Lost Art in Law Firms' *National Law Journal*, 27 Nov.

—— and Rhode, D. L. (1988) (eds.), *The Legal Profession: Responsibility and Regulation*, New York: Foundation Press.

Hechter, Michael (1984), 'When Actors Comply: Monitoring Costs and the Production of Social Order', *Acta Sociologica*, 27: 161–83.

—— (1987), *Principles of Group Solidarity*, Berkeley and Los Angeles: California University Press.

Heckathorn, Douglas (1989), 'Collective Action and the Second-Order Free-Rider Problem', *Rationality and Society*, 1: 78–100.

—— (1990), 'Collective Sanctions and Compliance Norms: A Formal Theory of Group-Mediated Social Control', *American Sociological Review*, 55: 366–84.

Hedström, Peter, and Swedberg, Richard (1998*a*), *Social Mechanisms*, Cambridge: Cambridge University Press.

———— (1998*b*) 'Rational Choice, Situational Analysis, and Empirical Research', in Hans-Peter Blossfeld and Gerald Prein (eds.), *Rational Choice Theory and Large Scale Data-Analysis*, Boulder, Colo.: Westview.

Heimer, Carol A. (1992), 'Doing your Job *and* Helping your Friends: Universalistic Norms about Obligations to Particular Others in Networks', in Nitin Nohria and Robert G. Eccles (eds.), *Networks and Organizations: Structure, Form, and Action*, Boston: Harvard Business School Press.

Heinz, J. P., and Laumann, E. O. (1982), *Chicago Lawyers: The Social Structure of the Bar*, New York: Russell Sage Foundation and American Bar Foundation.

Hinings, C. R., Brown, J. L., and Greenwood, R. (1991). 'Change in an Autonomous Professional Organization', *Journal of Management Studies*, 28: 375–93.

Hirsch, Paul M. (1997), 'Sociology without Social Structure: Neoinstitutional Theory Meets Brave New World', *American Journal of Sociology*, 102: 1702–23.

Hodson, Randy, Welsh, Sandy, Rieble, Sabine, Sorenson Jamison, Cheryl, and Creighton, Sean (1993), 'Is Worker Solidarity Undermined by Autonomy and Participation? Patterns from the Ethnographic Literature', *American Sociological Review*, 58: 398–416.

Homans, George (1961), *Social Behavior: Its Elementary Forms*, New York, Harcourt.

Hughes, Everett C. (1945), 'Dilemmas and Contradictions of Status', *American Journal of Sociology*, 50: 353–9.

—— (1958), *Men and their Work*, Glencoe, Ill.: Free Press.

Ibarra, Herminia (1992), 'Homophily Returns: Sex Differences in Network Structure and Access in an Advertising Firm', *Administrative Science Quarterly*, 37: 422–47.

Kandel, Eugene, and Lazear, Edward (1992), 'Peer Pressure and Partnerships', *Journal of Political Economy*, 100: 801–17.

Karpik, Lucien (1995), *Les Avocats*, Paris: Gallimard.

Katz, Jack (1977), 'Concerted Ignorance: The Social Construction of Cover-up', *Urban Life*, 8: 295–316.

Kellerhals, Jean, Coenen-Huther, Josette, and Modak, Marianne (1988), *Figures de l'équité: La Construction des normes de justice dans les groupes*, Paris: Presses Universitaires de France.

Krackhardt, David (1987), 'Cognitive Social Structures', *Social Networks*, 9: 109–34.

—— (1988), 'Predicting with Networks: Nonparametric Multiple Regression Analysis of Dyadic Data', *Social Networks*, 10: 359–81.

—— (1990), 'Assessing the Political Landscape: Structure, Cognition, and Power in Organizations', *Administrative Science Quarterly*, 35: 342–69.

—— (1992), 'The Strength of Strong Ties: The Importance of Philos in Organizations', in Nitin Nohria and Robert G. Eccles (eds.), *Networks and Organizations: Structure, Form, and Action*, Boston: Harvard Business School Press.

—— (1994), 'Graph Theoretical Dimensions of Informal Organizations', in Kathleen Carley and Michael Prietula (eds.), *Computational Organizational Theory*, Hillsdale, NJ: Lawrence Erlbaum Associates.

—— and Kilduff, Martin (1990), 'Friendship Patterns and Culture: The Control of Organizational Diversity', *American Anthropologist*, 92: 142–54.

Kunda, Gideon (1993), *Engineering Culture: Control and Commitment in a High-Tech Corporation*, Philadelphia: Temple University Press.

Kuty, Olgierd (1998), *La Négociation des valeurs: Introduction à la sociologie*, Brussels: De Boeck & Larcier.

Latour, Bruno, and Woolgar, S. (1988), *La Vie de laboratoire*, Paris: La Découverte.

Laumann, Edward O., and Heinz, John P. (1977), 'Specialization and Prestige in the Legal Profession: The Structure of Deference', *American Bar Foundation Research Journal*, 1: 155–216.

—— and Pappi, Franz U. (1976), *Networks of Collective Action: A Perspective on Community Influence Systems*, New York: Academic Press.

Laumann, Edward O., Marsden, Peter V., and Galaskiewicz, Joseph (1977), 'Community Elites Influence Structures: Extensions of a Network Approach', *American Journal of Sociology*, 83: 594–631.

Lazega, Emmanuel (1992*a*), *The Micro-Politics of Knowledge: Communication and Indirect Control in Workgroups*, New York: Aldine-de Gruyter.

—— (1992*b*), 'Analyse de réseaux d'une organisation collégiale: Les Avocats d'affaires', *Revue française de sociologie*, 33: 559–89.

—— (1993), 'Bureaucratie et collégialité dans les firmes américaines d'avocats d'affaires', *Droit et société*, 23–4: 15–40.

—— (1994*a*), 'Analyse de réseaux et sociologie des organisations', *Revue française de sociologie*, 35: 293–320.

—— (1994*b*), 'Les Conflits d'intérêts dans les cabinets américains d'avocats d'affaires: Concurrence et auto-régulation', *Sociologie du travail*, 35: 315–36.

—— (1995*a*), 'Concurrence, coopération et flux de conseils dans un cabinet américain d'avocats d'affaires: Les Échanges d'idées entre collègues', *Revue suisse de sociologie*, 21: 61–84.

—— (1995*b*), 'Protecting the Common Good among Equals: A Lateral Control Regime of Partners in a Law Firm', LASMAS Preprint no. 96/1.

—— (1996), 'Arrangements contractuels et structures relationnelles', *Revue française de sociologie*, 37: 439–56.

—— (1997), 'Network Analysis and Qualitative Research: A Method of Contextualization', in Gale Miller and Robert Dingwall (eds.), *Context and Method in Qualitative Research*, London: Sage.

—— (1999*a*), 'Generalized Exchange and Economic Performance: Social Embeddedness of Labor Contracts in a Corporate Law Firm', in Roger Leenders and Shaul Gabbay (eds.), *Corporate Social Capital and Liabilities*, Boston: Kluwer.

—— (1999*b*), 'Le Phénomène collégial: Une théorie structurale de l'action collective entre pairs', *Revue française de sociologie*, 40: 639–70.

—— (2000*a*), 'Enforcing Rules among Peers: A Lateral Control Regime', *Organization Studies*, 21: 193–214.

—— (2000*b*), 'Teaming Up and Out? Cooperation and Solidarity in a Collegial Organization', *European Sociological Review*, 16: 245–66.

—— (2000*c*), 'Structure and Culture in the Constitutional Process: Multi-Status Oligarchs and the Negotiation of Precarious Values', paper presented at the American Sociological Association Annual Meeting, Washington, DC.

—— (forthcoming), 'Networks, Distributed Knowledge and Economic Performance: Evidence from Corporate Legal Services', in Faïz Gallouj and Jean Gadrey (eds.), *Performances and Innovation in Services: Economic and Socio-Economic Approaches*, Aldershot: Edward Elgar.

—— and Krackhardt, David (2000), 'Spreading and Shifting Costs of Lateral Control in a Law Partnership: A Structural Analysis at the Individual Level', *Quality and Quantity*, 34: 153–75.

—— and Lebeaux, Marie-Odile (1995), 'Capital social et contrainte latérale', *Revue française de sociologie*, 36: 759–77.

—— and Mounier, Lise (forthcoming), 'Structural Economic Sociology in a Society of Organizations', in O. Favereau and E. Lazega (eds.), *Conventions and Structures in Economic Organization*, Aldershot: Edward Elgar.

—— and Pattison, Philippa E. (1999), 'Multiplexity, Generalized Exchange and Cooperation in Organizations: A Case Study', *Social Networks*, 21: 67–90.

—— —— (forthcoming), 'Social Mechanisms as Social Capital: Status Auctions among Peers', in Nan Lin, Karen Cook, and Ronald Burt (eds.), *Social Capital: Theory and Research*, New York: Aldine-de Gruyter.

—— and Van Duijn, Marijtje (1997), 'Position in Formal Structure, Personal Characteristics and Choices of Advisors in a Law Firm: A Logistic Regression Model for Dyadic Network Data', *Social Networks*, 19: 375–97.

—— and Vari, Stéphane (1992), 'Acteurs, cibles et leviers: Analyse factorielle de réseaux de contrôle dans une firme américaine d'avocats d'affaires', *Bulletin de méthodologie socio-logique*, 37: 41–51.

Leenders, Roger, and Gabbay, Shaul (1999) (eds.), *Corporate Social Capital and Liabilities*, Boston: Kluwer.

Lenski, G. E. (1954), 'Status Crystallization: A Non-Vertical Dimension of Social Status', *American Sociological Review*, 19: 405–13.

Levi, Margaret (1988), *Of Rule and Revenue*, Berkeley and Los Angeles: University of California Press.

Lévi-Strauss, C. (1949), *Les Formes élémentaires de la parenté*, Paris: Plon.

Lewin, K. (1952), 'Group Decision and Social Change', in G. E. Swanson, T. M. Newcomb, and E. L. Hartley (eds.), *Readings in Social Psychology*, New York: Holt.

Lin, Nan (1982), 'Social Resources and Instrumental Action', in Peter V. Marsden and Nan Lin (eds.), *Social Structure and Network Analysis*, London: Sage.

—— (1995), 'Les Ressources sociales: Une théorie du capital social', *Revue française de sociologie*, 36: 685–704.

—— and Dumin, Mary (1986), 'Access to Occupations through Social ties', *Social Networks*, 8: 365–85.

Lincoln, J. R., and Miller, J. (1979), 'Work and Friendship Ties in Organizations: A Comparative Analysis of Relational Networks', *Administrative Science Quarterly*, 24: 181–99.

Lindenberg, Siegwart (1990), 'Homo Socio-Economicus: The Emergence of a General Model of Man in the Social Sciences', *Journal of Institutional and Theoretical Economics*, 146: 727–48.

—— (1993), 'Club Hierarchy, Social Metering, and Context Instruction: Governance Structures in Response to Varying Self-Command Capital', in S. Lindenberg and H. Schreuder (eds.), *Interdisciplinary Perspectives on Organization Studies*, London: Pergamon Press.

—— (1995), 'Complex Constraint Modeling (CCM): A Bridge between Rational Choice and Structuralism', *Journal of Institutional and Theoretical Economics*, 151: 80–8.

—— (1996), 'Multiple-Tie Networks, Structural Dependence, and Path-Dependency: Another Look at Hybrid Forms of Governance', *Journal of Institutional and Theoretical Economics*, 152: 188–96.

—— (1997), 'Grounding Groups in Theory: Functional, Cognitive, and Structural Inter-dependencies', in B. Markovsky, M. Lovaglia, and L. Troyer (eds.), *Advances in Group Processes*, vol. 14, Greenwich, Conn.: JAI Press.

—— (1998), 'Solidarity: Its Microfoundations and Macro Dependence: A Framing Approach', in Patrick Doreian and Thomas J. Fararo (eds.), *The Problem of Solidarity: Theories and Models*, Amsterdam: Gordon & Breach.

Linton, R. (1958), *Cultural Background of Personality*, London: Routledge & Kegan Paul.

Lipset, Seymour M., Trow, Martin, and Coleman, James (1956), *Union Democracy: The Inside Politics of the International Typographical Union*, New York: Free Press.

Lomnitz, Larissa (1988), 'Informal Exchange Networks in Formal Systems', *American Anthropologist*, 90: 42–55.

McAdam, Doug, and Paulsen, Ronelle (1993), 'Specifying the Relationship between Social Ties and Activism', *American Journal of Sociology*, 99: 640–67.

Macaulay, S. (1963), 'Non-Contractual Relations in Business', *American Sociological Review*, 28: 55–66.

McCann, J. F. (1993), *Church and Organization*, London: Associated University Press.

McPherson, J. Miller, and Smith-Lovin, Linda (1987). 'Homophily in Voluntary Organizations: Status Distance and the Composition of Face to Face Groups', *American Sociological Review*, 52: 370–9.

Maister, David H. (1993), *Managing the Professional Service Firm*, New York: Free Press.

Mann, Kenneth (1985), *Defending White-Collar Crime: A Portrait of Attorneys at Work*, New Haven: Yale University Press.

Markovsky, B., Willer, D., and Patton, T. (1988), 'Power Relations in Exchange Networks', *American Sociological Review*, 53: 220–36.

Marsden, Peter V. (1981), 'Introducing Influence Processes into a System of Collective Decisions', *American Journal of Sociology*, 86: 1203–35.

—— (1982) 'Brokerage Behavior in Restricted Exchange Networks', in P. V. Marsden and Nan Lin (eds.), *Social Stracture and Network Analysis*, Beverly Hills, Calif.: Sage.

—— and Friedkin, Noah E. (1993), 'Network Studies of Social Influence', *Sociological Methods and Research*, 22: 127–51.

—— and Laumann, Edward O. (1977), 'Collective Action in a Community Elite: Exchange, Influence Resources and Issue Resolution', in Roland J. Liebert and Allen Imershein (eds.), *Power, Paradigms, and Community Research*, London: Sage.

Mauss, Marcel (1923), *Essai sur le don: Forme et raison de l'échange dans les sociétés archaïques*, *L'Année sociologique*, vol. 1, reprinted in *Sociologie et anthropologie*, Paris: Presses Universitaires de France, 1973.

Meister, Albert (1972), *La Participation dans les associations*, Paris: Les Éditions Ouvrières.

Merton, R. K. (1957), *Social Theory and Social Structure*, 2nd edn., Glencoe, Ill.: Free Press.

Meyer, Marshall (1994), 'Measuring Performance in Economic Organizations', in Neil Smelser and Richard Swedberg (eds.), *Handbook of Economic Sociology*, Princeton: Russell Sage Foundation.

Michels, R. (1962 edn.), *Political Parties: A Sociological Study of the Oligarchical Tendencies of Modern Democracy*, New York: Free Press; 1st edn., 1911.

Mintzberg, Henry (1979), *The Structuring of Organizations*, Englewood Cliffs, NJ: Prentice-Hall.

Mizruchi, M. S. (1994), 'Social Network Analysis: Recent Achievements and Current Controversies', *Acta Sociologica*, 37: 329–43.

Mohr, John, and Duquenne, Vincent (1997), 'The Duality of Culture and Practice: Poverty Relief in New York City, 1888–1917', *Theory and Society*, 26: 305–56.

Montagna, P. D. (1968), 'Professionalization and Bureaucratization in Large Professional Organizations', *American Journal of Sociology*, 73: 138–45.

Morrill, Calvin (1995), *The Executive Way: Conflict Management in Corporations*, Chicago: Chicago University Press.

Moss Kanter, Rosabeth (1988), 'When a Thousand Flowers Bloom: Structural, Collective, and Social Conditions for Innovation in Organizations', *Research in Organizational Behavior*, 10: 169–211.

Musselin, Christine (1990), 'Structures formelles et Capacités d'intégration dans les universités françaises et allemandes', *Revue française de sociologie*, 31: 439–61.

Myers, Paul S. (1996) (ed.), *Knowledge Management and Organizational Design*, Newton, Mass.: Butterworth-Heinemann.

Nadel, Sigfried F. (1957), *The Theory of Social Structure*, London: Cohen & West.

Nelson, Robert L. (1988), *Partners with Power: The Social Transformation of the Large Law Firm*, Berkeley and Los Angeles: University of California Press.

—— Trubek, David M., and Solomon, Rayman L. (1992) (eds.), *Lawyers' Ideals/Lawyers' Practices: Transformations in the American Legal Profession*, Ithaca, NY: Cornell University Press.

Oliver, Pamela (1980), 'Rewards and Punishments as Selective Incentives for Collective Action: Theoretical Investigations', *American Journal of Sociology*, 85: 356–75.

Olson, Mancur (1965), *The Logic of Collective Action*, Cambridge, Mass.: Harvard University Press.

Ostrom, Elinor (1990), *Governing the Commons: The Evolution of Institutions for Collective Action*, Cambridge: Cambridge University Press.

Parsons, Talcott (1951), *The Social System*, Glencoe, Ill.: Free Press.

—— (1956a), 'A Sociological Approach to the Theory of Organizations, I', *Administrative Science Quarterly*, 1: 63–85.

—— (1956b), 'Some Ingredients of a General Theory of Formal Organizations', *Administrative Science Quarterly*, 1: 225–39.

—— (1968), 'Professions', in *International Encyclopaedia of the Social Science*, New York: Macmillan and Free Press.

—— and Platt, G. M. (1973), *The American University*, Cambridge, Mass.: Harvard University Press.

—— and Shils, Edward (1951), *Toward a General Theory of Action*, Cambridge, Mass.: Harvard University Press.

Pattison, Philippa E. (1993), *Algebraic Models for Social Networks*, Cambridge: Cambridge University Press.

—— and Wasserman, Stanley (1999), 'Logit Models and Logistic Regressions for Social Networks, II: Multivariate Relations', *British Journal of Mathematical and Statistical Psychology*, 52: 169–93.

Pfeffer, Jeffrey, (1992), *Managing with Power*, Boston: Harvard Business School Press.

—— and Salancik, G. R. (1978), *The External Control of Organizations: A Resource Dependence Perspective*, New York: Harper & Row.

Perrow, Charles (1986), *Complex Organizations: A Critical Essay*, New York: Random House.

—— (1991), 'A Society of Organizations', *Theory and Society*, 20: 725–62.

Portes, Alejandro (1994), 'The Informal Economy and its Paradoxes', in N. Smelser and R. Swedberg (eds.), *Handbook of Economic Sociology*, Princeton: Russell Sage Foundation.

Powell, M. J. (1985) 'Developments in the Regulation of Lawyers', *Social Forces*, 64: 281–305.

Putnam, Robert D. (1993), *Making Democracy Work*, Princeton: Princeton University Press.

Raub, Werner, and Weesie, Jeroen (1990) 'Reputation and Efficiency in Social Interactions: An Example of Network Effects', *American Journal of Sociology*, 96: 626–54.

Rawls, John (1971), *A Theory of Justice*, Cambridge, Mass.: Harvard University Press.

Raven, Bertram H. (1965), 'Social Influence and Power', in Ivan D. Steiner and Martin Fishbein (eds.), *Current Studies in Social Psychology*, New York: Holt, Rinehart & Winston.

Reichman, Nancy (1989), 'Breaking Confidences: Organizational Influences on Insider Trading', *Sociological Quarterly*, 30: 185–204.

Reiss, A. J., Jr. (1984), 'Selecting Strategies of Social Control over Organizational Life', in K. O. Hawkins and J. M. Thomas (eds.), *Enforcing Regulation*, Boston: Kluwer-Nijhof.

—— (1988), 'The Control of Organizational Life', in *Conflict and Integration: Comparative Law in the World Today*, Institute of Comparative Law in Japan, Chuo University.

Reynaud, Jean-Daniel (1989), *La Règle du jeu: L'Action collective et la régulation sociale*, Paris: Armand Colin.

—— and Reynaud, E. (1996), 'La Régulation des marchés internes du travail', *Revue française de sociologie*, 37: 337–68.

Robins, Garry, Elliott, Peter, and Pattison, Philippa (2000), 'Network Models for Social Selection Process', manuscript.

—— Pattison, Philippa, and Wasserman, Stanley (forthcoming), 'Logit Models and Logistic Regressions for Social Networks, III. Valued Relations', *Psychometrika*.

Rossi, Peter (1979), 'Vignette Analysis: Uncovering the Normative Structure of Complex Judgments', in Robert Merton, James Coleman, and Peter Rossi (eds.), *Qualitative and Quantitative Social Research. Papers in Honor of Paul Lazarsfeld*, New York: Macmillan.

Rothschild, Joyce, and Whitt, J. Allen (1986), *The Cooperative Workplace*, Cambridge: Cambridge University Press.

Rowley, Scott, and Rowley, Reed (1960), *Rowley on Partnership*, New York: Bobbs-Merrill; 1st edn., 1916.

Sainsaulieu, Renaud (1977), *L'Identité au travail*, Paris: Presses de la FNSP.

—— Tixier, P.-E., Marty, M.-O. (1983), *La Démocratie en organisation*, Paris: Méridiens.

Scaff, Lawrence A. (1981), 'Max Weber and Robert Michels', *American Journal of Sociology*, 86: 1269–86.

Schon, Donald A. (1983), *The Reflective Practitioner: How Professionals Think in Action*, New York: Basic Books.

Sciulli, David (1986), *Theory of Societal Constitutionalism*, Cambridge: Cambridge University Press.

Sellers, Charles (1991), *The Market Revolution: Jacksonian America 1815–1846*, New York: Cambridge University Press.

Selznick, Philip (1957), *Leadership in Administration*, Evanston, Ill.: Row, Peterson & Co.

—— (1996), 'Institutionalism "Old" and "New"', *Adminstrative Science Quarterly*, 41: 270–7.

Seron, Carol (1992), 'Managing Entrepreneurial Legal Services: The Transformation of Small-Firm Practice', in R. L. Nelson, D. M. Trubek, and R. L. Solomon (eds.), *Lawyers' Ideals/ Lawyers' Practices: Transformations in the American Legal Profession*, Ithaca, NY: Cornell University Press.

Shapiro, Susan (1986), 'The Social Control of Impersonal Trust', *American Journal of Sociology*, 93: 623–58.

Shils, Edward, and Janowitz, Morris (1948), 'Cohesion and Disintegration in the Wehrmacht in World War II', *Public Opinion Quarterly*, 12: 300–15.

Simpson, Richard L. (1971), 'Imperative Control, Associationalism, and the Moral Order', in Herman Turk and Richard L. Simpson (eds.), *Institutions and Social Exchange*, New York: Bobbs-Merrill.

Smelser, Neil, and Swedberg, Richard (1994) (eds.), *Handbook of Economic Sociology*, Princeton: Russell Sage Foundation.

Smigel, E. (1969), *The Wall Street Lawyer: Professional Organizational Man?*, Bloomington, Ind.: Indiana University Press.

Smithson, M. (1985), 'Toward a Social Theory of Ignorance', *Journal for the Theory of Social Behavior*, 15: 151–72.

Snijders, Tom A. B., and Bosker, Roel (1999), *Multilevel Analysis*, London: Sage.

—— and Van Duijn, M. A. J. (1997), 'Simulation for Statistical Inference in Dynamic Network Models', in R. Conte, R. Hegselmann, and P. Terna (eds.), *Simulating Social Phenomena*, Berlin: Springer.

Starbuck, William H. (1992), 'Learning by Knowledge-Intensive Firms' *Journal of Management Studies*, 29: 713–40.

—— (1993), 'Keeping a Butterfly and an Elephant in a House of Cards: The Elements of Exceptional Success', *Journal of Management Studies*, 30: 885–921.

Stevenson, William B. (1990), 'Formal Structure and Networks of Interaction within Organizations', *Social Science Research*, 19: 113–31.

Stinchcombe, Arthur L. (1959), 'Bureaucratic and Craft Administration of Production', *Administrative Science Quarterly*, 4: 168–87.

—— (1991), 'The Conditions of Fruitfulness in Theorizing about Mechanisms in the Social Sciences', *Philosophy of the Social Sciences*, 21: 367–88.

—— (1997), 'On the Virtues of the Old Institutionalism', *Annual Review of Sociology*, 23: 1–18.

Strauss, D., and Ikeda, M. (1990), 'Pseudolikelihood Estimation for Social Networks', *Journal of the American Statistical Association*, 85: 204–12.

Strong, P. M., and Dingwall, R. (1985), 'The Interactional Study of Organizations: A Critique and Reformulation', *Urban Life*, 14: 205–31.

Sutton, Robert I., and Hargadon, Andrew (1996), 'Brainstorming Groups in Context: Effectiveness in a Product Design Firm', *Administrative Science Quarterly*, 41: 685–718.

Swidler, Ann (1979), *Organization without Authority: Dilemmas of Social Control of Free Schools*, Cambridge, Mass.: Harvard University Press.

Tannenbaum, Arnold S. (1968), *Control in Organizations*, New York: McGraw Hill.

Taylor, Michael (1987), *The Possibility of Cooperation*, Cambridge: Cambridge University Press.

Tilley, N. (1981), 'The Logic of Laboratory Life', *Sociology*, 15: 117–26.

Tolbert, Pamela S. (1988), 'Institutional Sources of Culture in Major Law Firms' in Lynn Zucker (ed.), *Institutional Patterns in Organizations: Culture and Environment*, Cambridge, Mass.: Ballinger.

Useem, Michael (1986 edn.), *The Inner Circle: Large Corporations and the Rise of Business Political Activity in the US and UK*, Oxford: Oxford University Press.

Uzzi, Brian (1997), 'Social Structure and Competition in Interfirm Networks: The Paradox of Embeddedness', *Administrative Science Quarterly*, 42: 35–67.

Van Duijn, M. (1995), 'Estimation of a Random Effects Model for Directed Graphs', in *Toeval zit Overall, Programmatuur voor Random-Coëfficiënt Modellen*, Zevende Symposium Statistische Software, Groningen: ProGAMMA.

Van Duijn, M. and Snijders, T. A. B. (1995), 'The P2 Model', internal publication, VSM, University of Groningen.

Van Maanen, John, and Barley, Stephen R. (1984), 'Occupational Communities: Culture and Control in Organizations', in B. M. Staw and L. L. Cummings (eds.), *Research in Organizational Behavior*, Greenwich, Conn.: JAI Press, 6: 287–365.

Vaughan, Diane (1983), *Controlling Unlawful Organizational Behavior: Social Structure and Corporate Misconduct*, Chicago: University of Chicago Press.

Vaughan, Diane (1998), 'Rational Choice, Situated Action, and the Social Control of Organizations', *Law & Society Review*, 32: 23–61.

Vilkas Catherine (1996), 'Évaluations scientifiques et décisions collectives: Le Comité national de la recherche scientifique, *Sociologie du Travail*, 3/96: 331–48.

Wallace, Jean E. (1995), 'Corporatist Control and Organizational Commitment among Professionals', *Social Forces*, 73: 811–39.

Walzer, Michael (1965), *The Revolution of the Saints*, Princeton: Princeton University Press.

Wasserman, Stanley, and Faust, Katherine (1994), *Social Network Analysis: Methods and Applications*, Cambridge: Cambridge University Press.

—— and Pattison Philippa E. (1996), 'Logit Models and Logistic Regressions for Social Networks, I. An Introduction to Markov Graphs and p^*', *Psychometrika*, 61: 401–25.

—— —— (forthcoming), *Multivariate Random Graph Distributions*, Berlin: Springer Verlag.

Waters, Malcolm (1989), 'Collegiality, Bureaucratization, and Professionalization: A Weberian Analysis', *American Journal of Sociology*, 94: 945–72.

—— (1993), 'Alternative Organizational Formations: A Neo-Weberian Typology of Polycratic Administrative Systems', *Sociological Review*, 55–81.

Weber, Max (1978 edn.), *Economy and Society*, (ed.) Guenther Roth and Claus Wittich, Berkeley and Los Angeles: University of California Press; 1st edn., 1920.

Weesie, Jeroen and Raub, Werner (2000) (eds.), *The Management of Durable Relations*, Amsterdam: Thela Thesis.

Wheare, K. C. (1955), *Government by Committee*, Oxford: Oxford University Press.

Weisburd, D., Wheeler, S., Waring, E., and Bode, N. (1991), *Crimes of the Middle-Classes*, New Haven: Yale University Press.

White, Harrison C. (1981), 'Where do Markets Come from?' *American Journal of Sociology*, 87: 517–47.

—— (1985), 'Agency as Control', in J. W. Pratt and R. Zeckhauser (eds.), *Principals and Agents: The Structure of Business*, Boston: Harvard Business School Press.

—— (1992), 'Agency as Control in Formal Networks', in Nitin Nohria and Robert G. Eccles (eds.), *Networks and Organizations: Structure, Form, and Action*, Boston: Harvard Business School Press.

—— (forthcoming), *Markets in Networks*, Princeton: Princeton University Press.

—— Boorman, Scott A. and Breiger, Ronald L. (1976), 'Social Structure from Multiple Networks, I. Blockmodels of Roles and Positions', *American Journal of Sociology* 81: 730–80.

Wilensky, Harold L. (1967), *Organizational Intelligence*, New York: Basic Books.

Willer, David (1999) (ed.), *Network Exchange Theory*, New York: Praeger.

Wippler, Reinhardt, and Lindenberg, S. (1987), 'Collective Phenomena and Rational Choice' in J. Alexander *et al.* (eds.), *The Micro-Macro Link*, Berkeley and Los Angeles: University of California Press.

Wittek, Rafael (1999), 'Interdependence and Informal Control in Organizations', Doctoral Thesis, ICS, University of Groningen.

—— and Wielers, Rudi (1998), 'Gossip in Organizations', *Computational and Mathematical Organization Theory*, 4: 189–204.

Woodward, Joan (1965), *Industrial Organization: Theory and Practice*, London: Oxford University Press.

Yamagishi, Toshio (1986), 'The Provision of a Sanctioning System as a Public Good', *Journal of Personality and Social Psychology*, 51: 110–16.

Name Index

Subject Index